# Blue Mafia

## Police Brutality & Consent Decrees in Ohio

## Tim Tolka

## Dedication

This work is dedicated to those that stand up for victims of crime, including the cops who investigate crimes, the attorneys and advocates who defend their rights and the officials who prosecute offenders.

# Table of Contents

1. 2003: Warren's police brutality goes viral...................11
2. 1992: Leaked letter causes feud with police chief..........19
3. 1992: Two drug arrests challenged in court..................31
4. 1994: Hython takes the city to the Sixth Circuit............44
5. 1995: Justice comes to Steubenville..........................53
6. 2000: Innocent inmate appeals to Justice....................66
7. June 2003: The Kimble case begins..........................81
8. September 2003: Beaten for running stop sign.............97
9. September 2003: Routine strip searches....................107
10. Fall 2003: Local judges retaliate.............................123
11. October 2003: The case of the stolen four wheelers......128
12. January 2004: Kimble case begins..........................138
13. March 2004: "You're black now"............................147
14. January 2005: The chief & his enemies testify............160
15. April 2005: McNally brings the hammer down...........171
16. January 2005: Steubenville decree lifted...................185
17. August 2005: No-knock raid finds nothing................199
18. 2007: Scipio and the city ....................................207
19. 2006: Ohio Supreme Court investigates Olivito.........212
20. 2007: Suspended but not disbarred.........................225
21. 2009: Mando steps down.....................................235
22. 2011: Whistleblower detective alleges cover-up........242
23. 2011: Olivito gets a taste of brutality......................252
24. 2012: DOJ puts Warren under consent decree...........256
25. 2013: The Steubenville rape case...........................263
26. 2017: Pistol-packing judge survives shootout............278
27. 2017: Trump DOJ lifts Warren consent decree..........290

## Characters

Richard Olivito, former attorney at law
Jerry McCartney, former Steubenville Chief of Police
William McCafferty, Steubenville Chief of Police
James Bernard, president of Fort Steuben Fraternal Order of Police
Lloyd King Sr., former secret service agent, Federal Drug Task Force
Jack Palkovic, late sergeant, Steubenville Police Department
Stephen Stern, former Jefferson County Prosecutor
John Mandopoulos, late Warren Chief of Police
Eric Merkel, current Warren Chief of Police
Greg Hoso, current captain, Warren Police Department
Jeff Hoolihan, retired detective, Warren Police Department
Fred Harris, former Safety Services Director, Warren
Robert Galanis, retired judge, Ohio Federal District Court of the Northern District
Hilary Taylor, senior partner, Weston Hurd

## Civil Rights Plaintiffs

| | |
|---|---|
| Andrew Hython | Steubenville |
| Daniel Walker Jr. | Steubenville |
| Sean Scipio | Steubenville |
| Dawn Kelley | Steubenville |
| Lyndal Kimble | Warren |
| Clarence Clay | Warren |
| John Rogers, II | Warren |
| Lea Dotson | Warren |

## Acronyms

| | |
|---|---|
| American Civil Liberties Union | ACLU |
| Bureau of Criminal Investigation | BCI |
| Civil Rights Division | CRD |
| Civil Service Commission | CSC |
| Department of Justice | DOJ |
| Drug Enforcement Agency | DEA |
| Federal Bureau of Investigation | FBI |
| Fraternal Order of Police | FOP |
| U.S. Department of Housing and Urban Development | HUD |
| Internal Affairs | IA |
| Law Enforcement Automated Data System | LEADS |
| Ku Klux Klan | KKK |
| National Association for the Advancement of Colored People | NAACP |
| Office of the Inspector General | OIG |
| Ohio Revised Code | ORC |
| Parents Against Police Abuse | PAPA |
| Police Officers for Equal Rights | POER |
| Steubenville Police Department | SPD |
| Warren Police Department | WPD |

## Author's Note

This is a work of nonfiction. The events are described as people re-member and as the public record reflects them. The names of various officials and informants have been changed or omitted to protect sources and methods, as well as victims and the family members of those who abused their power.

# Litigation Timeline

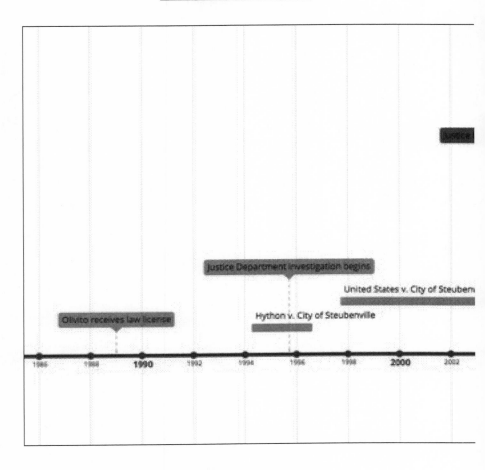

■ Steubenville  ■ Warren

7

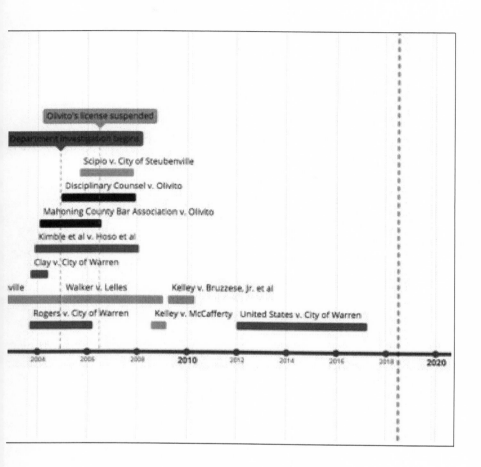

Olivito's license suspended

Department Investigation begins

Scipio v. City of Steubenville

Disciplinary Counsel v. Olivito

Mahoning County Bar Association v. Olivito

Kimble et al v. Hoso et al

Clay v. City of Warren

ville

Walker v. Lelles

Kelley v. Bruzzese, Jr. et al

Rogers v. City of Warren

Kelley v. McCafferty

United States v. City of Warren

2004   2006   2008   **2010**   2012   2014   2016   2018   **2020**

■ Attorney discipline cases

# Federal Police Misconduct Investigations

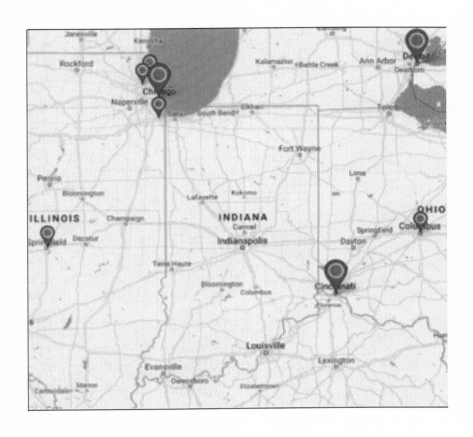

📍 Civil rights investigation*
(*probable cause of a pattern or practice of police misconduct)

## & "Pattern or Practice" Lawsuits

 Court-enforced consent decree or
other settlement agreement**
(**Mediated settlement, as in Cincinnati or memorandum
of agreement, as in Columbus)

## 1

Warren has never been a good place to be caught breaking the law. Particularly, if you're poor or if you've been in trouble before. If you've ever been caught with drugs? Pray.

- Anonymous[1]

Warren, Ohio is like ten thousand other rural American communities: unchanging, parochial and proud of itself. In Warren, people drive under the speed limit out of fear of the local police. Previously the main rival of Youngstown, Warren is now but a depressed shadow of its halcyon days of steel and segregation. However, a street dealer can still make a million dollars in Warren because the children of Youngstown's white middle-class line up their cars to buy drugs on Warren's dead-end streets. As a result, Warren has more than its share of violent crime and gang activity, and that's why the local police ruled "with an iron fist and rubber gloves," according to one journalist.[2] The police were frustrated with the community, with city hall, and with each other as the streets they spent their careers patrolling steadily deteriorated and locals, especially the town's African American residents, became more desperate and more hostile.

Attorney Richard Olivito was an advocate of due process in an era marked by crime control. He was a small-time solo civil rights lawyer from Steubenville. When he learned about injustice, he took it personally, and so it was one sunny afternoon in 2003 when he happened to see the headline, "Police beat drug dealer bloody, kids watch" above a picture of the beaten black man with his arm in a sling. After reading the article, Olivito felt a responsibility to check out the case.

According to Warren's chief of police, John Mandopoulos, the officers did nothing wrong and to hell with the public outcry. For Mando, as he was locally known, Kimble's arrest was "ugly but necessary." Mando identified with officers, and he always defended them without

---

[1] Aina Hunter. "Blue Mob: Pity those caught by the Warren police, who rule with iron fists and rubber gloves." *Cleveland Scene*, 25 February 2004.

[2] Ibid.

question. He worked long hours, and he was dedicated to rooting out crime and protecting his own. Never a husband or father, he was a brother and a devoted son. For Mando, no other occupation, role, hobby or identity came before that of police officer, and he was like a father to a lot of guys on the force. Unfortunately, this made him reluctant to discipline them, and the WPD had been locally known for brutality for decades before Mando became chief in 2000.

Mando had round jowls, a greying mustache and a bulbous nose echoing the shape of his belly. The chief was balding, with hair like steel wool that cropped out on the sides as if he were wearing a swimming cap. When he smiled, his face softened and lit up. However, Mandopoulos was courting death with his lifestyle of high pressure eighteen-hour days and nothing but fast food. Before becoming chief, he had open heart surgery during which he had to be revived on the operating table.[3] After his surgery, he wasn't supposed to let himself get upset, yet he rarely passed up an opportunity to raise his voice or get physical. A year after becoming chief, Mando allegedly shouted at an eighteen-year-old driver, "I'm the chief of fucking police, I don't care who you are and if you don't show me some ID, I'll drag you out of the car," after which he grabbed the young man by the throat.[4] His health problems only got worse as he guided the WPD deeper into infamy.

After twenty-seven years on the force, Mando's first few years as chief created a public relations crisis and a battle among Warren's public servants. Former Assistant Fire Chief James Nutt described the situation in his autobiography, "The mayor was trying to straighten out the police department, and the chief wanted to be autonomous from any authority and would do anything in the scope of his power to keep it that way."[5]

Kimble's beating would have been a local affair but for the video, which provided the nation another glimpse of the problem most Americans overlooked. The video featured Kimble, a slender twenty-eight-year-old drug dealer, getting body-slammed, beaten, and pepper-sprayed by three police officers. With a prior criminal record and no apparent job to support his wife and five kids, Lyndal "Dimebag" Kimble was an unlikely candidate to build a civil rights campaign around, but the video gave him leverage and his indignation would keep him going through years of litigation, public scrutiny, and police harass-

---

[3] Ed Runyan. "Mandopoulos cared about officers first." *The Vindicator*, January 24, 2012.

[4] *Dye v. City of Warren*. 367 F. Supp. 2d 1175. N. D. Ohio. 2005.

[5] James L. Nutt. Confessions of a Bipolar Firefighter. AuthorHouse, 26 March 2012.

ment.

When Richard Olivito got wind of the incident, he high-tailed it immediately from Youngstown to the address listed in the article as Kimble's residence. Years before, Olivito had turned Steubenville upside down by setting in motion an investigation that unseated the police chief and put the whole department under a federal monitor. Amid civil rights lawsuits that drove up his blood pressure, Warren's Chief of Police John Mandopoulos remained defiant that his officers had done nothing wrong. For Mandopoulos, the media narrative was the problem, and so he publicly threatened a reporter and claimed that he would organize a boycott against the newspaper.

The day of his arrest, Lyndal Kimble intended to wash his uncle's Cadillac. After pulling onto the lawn, he was sitting in the front seat when Officer Greg Hoso suddenly poked his head in the driver's side window and asked for Kimble's driver's license and registration. According to the lawsuit, as Kimble "turned to hand the insurance card to the officer, Officer Hoso allegedly reached into the car and grabbed him by the throat." Speaking to a reporter, Hoso claimed he was trying to dislodge an object Kimble had put into his mouth, "to protect him from choking."[6]

Lionel Hughley was sitting on his front porch that sunny Saturday afternoon. He later testified that he had his camcorder at his side expressly for the purpose of documenting police misconduct.[7] Witnessing police misconduct from your front porch was a pastime in Warren. City Councilwoman Helen Rucker remembers watching cops conduct illegal searches on fellow black residents while relaxing outside in her rocking chair. When Hughley saw Officer Hoso put his hands around Kimble's neck, he knew it was the moment he had been waiting for.[8] In a flash, the camera was rolling.

In the complaint Olivito filed in the Northern District Court, the plaintiff described feeling as if "his windpipe was being crushed by Officer Hoso's muscular hold on his neck."[9] Melanise Kimble stated that "the car was rocking back and forth while he was choking him."[10]

---

[6] Anonymous. "Action 19 News digs deeper into violent videotaped arrest." *Action 19 News*. No date.

[7] Peggy Sinkovich. Warren: Video camera kept close by to record police harassment, beaten man says. *The Vindicator*, 5 July 2003.

[8] *Kimble v. Hoso et al.* 439 F. 3d 331. Sixth Cir. 2006. P. 641.

[9] Ibid. p. 4.

[10] Ibid. p. 620.

Karen Bryant, Jamell Warfield, and Melanise Kimble confirmed they had seen Hoso choke Kimble in sworn testimony.[11]

Officer Frank Tempesta was walking towards the car, and Melanise testified in the trial that she began "screaming and hollering." She said Tempesta told her to shut up and go inside,[12] but she remained outside to watch what unfolded. Her kids came out and watched, too. Tempesta and Hoso pulled Kimble out of the car. According to the plaintiffs, Hoso punched him three times in the face. In court, Hoso denied striking the plaintiff.

With more people gathering, and an amateur cameraman zooming too fast for the camera to focus, Tempesta hauled Kimble onto the hood of the police cruiser. Officer Michael Stabile arrived on the scene and joined the melee. Officer Tempesta continued to restrain Kimble while Hoso walked away. After a search of the vicinity, Officer Hoso "held a small plastic bag in his right hand, which he had just retrieved from near the front of the plaintiff's parked vehicle."[13]

All three cops competed for a good grip on the man, and then, Tempesta edged behind with an arm around his neck, which Tempesta later denied. In the video, Tempesta can be seen on the driver's side with his arm around Kimble's neck. Stabile grabbed at his throat, which Stabile later admitted. Then, Tempesta picked him up like a sack of potatoes and slammed him on the ground. He later denied this, although Hughley testified to the contrary.[14] The officers piled onto Kimble's prone body, taking turns spraying and striking him. Hoso shoved his knee into Kimble's head with all of his weight and then pepper-sprayed his face. Hoso later admitted to striking Kimble's right shoulder twice with his knee, to "break his resistance."[15] Kimble was huddled on the ground, attempting to cover his eyes with his hands. He felt dizzy and was feeling dizzy from the blows.

According to the court's summary of the incident, Kimble was maced at least seven separate times. Hoso later confirmed that Kimble was maced, but he denied that it was "repeatedly." Officer Stabile jammed his baton into Kimble's back and ribs a dozen times "with little effect," according to their account. Stabile looked like he was bored and trying to stay busy. By then, his heart didn't seem to be in it, but

---

[11] Ibid. p. 596.

[12] *Kimble v. Hoso et al.* 439 F. 3d 331. Sixth Cir. 2006. 621.

[13] Ibid. p. 5.

[14] Ibid. p. 1109.

[15] Ibid. p. 211.

Hoso and Tempesta kept going until they were exhausted.[16] Out of concern for Kimble's injuries, a neighbor called an ambulance, hoping that would stop the beating. Amy Price, a white nurse who lived nearby, was yelling, "Stop! Stop! You're going to kill him!"[17] Before a packed courtroom with many local journalists present, she later testified that Kimble was telling the officers, "Quit, you got me!" over and over.[18] The officers didn't say anything, much less official statements like "You're under arrest."[19] They stopped beating Kimble shortly after the arrival of Terrence Eddington, one of the town's few black police officers. When the ambulance arrived, police did not allow the paramedics to treat Kimble.[20]

Melanise testified that during the beating, "I seen Lyndal's arms out like this talking about 'What did I do?'" Hughley testified that Kimble was motioning "like he was giving up like."[21] Jamell Warfield testified, "He laid down, took it better than what I would have took it."[22] Kimble's counsel argued, "The plaintiff stretched out his arms in a self-effacing, vulnerable type of gesture, facing Hoso."[23] Kimble raised his hands defensively, pleading with the officers that he had had enough. He attempted to minimize the damage of the blows by assuming a fetal position on the ground.[24]

The video of Kimble's violent arrest, disseminated by the media and viewed across the nation, gave African American residents irrefutable evidence of the brutality they had been complaining of for decades. However, many locals said Kimble was resisting arrest. This was the argument made by the police. Former chief of the NYPD Internal Affairs Bureau Charles Campisi explains:

> ...Most of the time, if a suspect is resisting arrest, it winds up in a flat-out brawl, with one or two or three cops rolling

---

[16] Ibid. p. 9.

[17] Ibid. p. 908.

[18] Ibid. p. 906.

[19] Ibid. p. 913.

[20] Ibid. p. 911.

[21] Ibid. p. 1109.

[22] Ibid. p. 600.

[23] Ibid. p. 5.

[24] Ibid. p. 596, 906.

around with a flailing suspect on a sidewalk or in a filthy stairwell in a high-rise. Later, from the perspective of a nice, clean, air-conditioned courtroom, with the "victim" all spiffed up in a new suit with his attorney at his side, it may be easy for civilians who've never been in a fight before to decide that, yes, the cops used too much force, that they gave the guy one too many baton strokes after he stopped resisting. But it's not so easy when you're in the stairwell or on that sidewalk.[25]

Regardless of Kimble's guilt or innocence, the video harnessed anger long pent up and unleashed it into the streets, in the media, and in the courts. Kimble's civil rights lawsuit would drag on for four years, during which time it divided the community and attracted attorneys even more troublesome than Olivito from the Justice Department.

Three years earlier, in 2000, Richard Olivito set up shop in Youngstown. His father was a Steubenville judge, and he was a fervent believer in the rule of law. At the turn of the twenty-first century, Youngstown was a city "mired in fear and corruption,"[26] with an ailing economy marked by bombed out brownfields formerly home to blast furnaces that had churned for generations. During the previous two hundred years, Italians, Greeks, Poles, and Irish had come in search of work. Slavs and Syrians made their way. Formerly enslaved Africans came sneaking along the Underground Railroad. All of the newcomers inspired the prejudice of white Protestants, but the black community bore the brunt of the abuse. Around the turn of the century, the public torture and murder of black people by lynch mobs in Ohio prompted embarrassing comparisons to the south.[27]

In the 1920s, the legacy of mob action and impunity in the Youngstown region made it a convenient regional headquarters for the Ku Klux Klan (KKK). Six towns within thirty miles were reputed "sundown" towns, which didn't allow blacks until the 1970s, including Poland, Austintown, Newton Falls, Niles, Columbiana, and Canfield. Youngstown would have become a sundown city, one historian noted,

[25] Charles Campisi. *Blue on Blue*. Scribner, 2017.

[26] Michael D. Sallah. "Youngstown: a city mired in fear and corruption." *The Toledo Blade*, 29 July 2001.

[27] Marilyn Howard. "Black Lynching in the Promised Land: Mob Violence in Ohio, 1877-1916." Ohio Academy of History.

except that the mobs were prevented by the scale of the undertaking.[28] Nevertheless, after the trade unions integrated, many black families in the area were able to put their kids through college with their wages at the steel mill. But then, all of the high-wage, unionized jobs in the steel industry began to migrate elsewhere, depriving Steel Valley of its lifeblood.

Despite the collapse of the steel industry, there was still plenty of work for an enterprising attorney. For the first few years in Youngstown, Olivito built relationships in the local courts. He was just getting back on his feet, after his early work in police misconduct cases wrecked his life. His practice was having a second wind, and he didn't want to spoil it. That changed after he met Kimble and began to learn about Warren.

The Warren police' account of the altercation emerged in the press and later in the response of the defense counsel to the federal complaint. They said Kimble refused to cooperate while seated in the car and that he attempted to exit the passenger side door, disobeying an order to show what he had in his mouth. According to the police, there were fewer blows struck to subdue Kimble, which happened after a few minutes.

When caught by police, people in Warren would ingest potentially fatal amounts of drugs, out of fear for the consequences. This presented a pickle for the WPD. They could try to stop the person and be accused of police brutality or let them die and be sued for wrongful death. According to the police, Kimble then spat the object out and tried to grab Hoso by the throat during the struggle outside the car. In the aftermath of a use-of-force incident, citizens could file a complaint, but in Warren, filing a complaint typically resulted in a visit by the officer specified in the complaint. Kimble didn't bother to file a complaint. By that time, no one trusted the WPD to investigate itself.

Richard Olivito relied on his gut to evaluate people. He trusted his intuition, and he was a keen observer of subtext, suggestion, and body language. Having grown up in Steubenville, he was suspicious of authority. Once he started digging, he was relentless. However, Olivito was trying to put the days of war and nights of terror in Steubenville behind him. He was tired of praying as he walked down the street and every time he turned the key in the ignition. He was tired of the feeling of being watched. But Lyndal Kimble was Warren's Rodney King. The video of Kimble's beating by three WPD officers caused the floodgates of community grievance to burst open. Warren residents had complained about the police for decades, but that summer they took to the streets.

---

[28] Dan Carter. "Forgotten story of America's whites-only towns." UU World, 21 January 2008.

The Ohio Supreme Court later began building a case against Olivito for attorney misconduct and eventually questioned his sanity. Olivito contested the charges and tried to expose underhanded machinations used by the disciplinary counsel to discredit him. Olivito had evidence of corruption at the highest levels of the supreme court, so the supreme court put his career on ice. The DOJ would later open an investigation and impose a consent decree on the WPD as it had done eight years before in Steubenville, largely as a result of his efforts. Olivito's civil rights career reflects two decades of federal reform efforts by the DOJ under four pendular presidential administrations that saw the massive expansion of the penal and surveillance state, as well as co-optations and social movements against it.

To understand how he came to represent victims of police brutality in Warren, it is necessary to go back to Steubenville in 1992, the year Los Angeles residents rioted in response to the acquittal of the officers who beat Rodney King. This is the story of two police departments, their turbulent relationship with the local community, and how a "crazy" lawyer risked everything to bring in a higher authority.

## 2

The police should not be condemned. There is nothing wrong with the police.

-Councilman Gorman in 1946[29]

Steubenville, Ohio, only an hour's drive south of Youngstown, is a town known for steel and football, while its police and local officials are better known for corruption. It isn't from the moral failings of any particular person, although one or two well-placed individuals can do a lot of damage. There is a culture of corruption, another legacy of the steel industry. Jefferson County has a distinctive political character shaped by the interplay between steel companies and unions, between racketeers and the state. If you're not from there, you wouldn't understand. In Jefferson County today, few residents seem to remember, and only a handful of officials remain from the days when the DOJ sued the police department for civil rights violations. Few people want to revisit that history. Locals are more proud of the Rat Pack legend Dean Martin, whose painted guise still benevolently looks down on all those who enter Kroger.

The town grew out of the banks of the Ohio River in a valley between foothills, just a stone's throw from West Virginia. On one side of the river, there was a granite cliff with a view of the hill over which Steubenville expanded from a lonely frontier fort to a bustling steel town with subdivisions of cookie-cutter houses reaching out like filigree. In those rugged hills, there used to be enough hard work and personal liberty to satisfy anyone. Closer to the river, there also used to be a red light district spotted with dingy bars where they ran the numbers. When the town was "open," people would come from miles around to blow their paychecks on their favorite vice.

Before being eclipsed by Las Vegas, Steubenville was a national gambling hub. After that, young men from Steubenville streamed into Vegas to work in the casinos. "Back in the 60s and 70s, when you graduated high school," remembers David Hindman, "You could get off a plane [in Vegas], tell them you're from Steubenville and you had a job before you put your bags on the ground." Steubenville boys worked

---

[29] Norman E. Nygarrd. 12 Against The Underworld. The Hobson Book Press, 1947, Page 53.

as pit bosses and managers in Vegas casinos for decades because gambling was as much a part of their culture as steel and football.

Beyond the vice dens, the forges of the steel mills drove commerce downtown on Fourth Street for a century. A local lawyer, Adam Scurti, told *The New York Times* in 2006, "Certainly, thirty years ago, that was a prevailing sense here in the valley that if there's dirt on the air, there's food on the table." In the days when soot filled the air, the dregs of local society concentrated close to the river, either in the slums or the local jail. Sometimes, they ended up floating in the river, and in Steubenville, criminal investigations often went cold when the involvement of certain perpetrators emerged. Steubenville was awash in illicit wealth, and the mob wanted cooperation from the local authorities. Only the county prosecutor can file charges, making the prosecutor the most powerful official in the county. Because of this, officers of the court and law enforcement tended to be targets of bribes, threats, and blackmail. It made public service a messy business. Luckily, local authorities didn't suffer much interference from an independent press, and things were handled either amiably behind closed doors or violently in a back alley.

In 1989, Richard Olivito passed the bar exam and received his law license, a rite of passage in his family. He was the youngest son of longtime Common Pleas Judge Dominick Olivito, and he felt he would never be able to fill his father's shoes. One of his older brothers, as well as his uncle, were lawyers, yet Richard had suffered two crushing defeats on the bar exam. When he called the Ohio Supreme Court to find out that he'd passed on his third attempt, the news of his success left him stunned and incredulous. He didn't expect to be offered a job at the family firm, and they did not surprise him. When asked by his wife to call a contact in D.C. to help Richard get a foot in the door of Senator John Glenn's office, Judge Olivito demurred without a word of explanation. Richard later attributed it to the judge's disapproval of nepotism, saying, "He always kept his cards close to his chest, and he wanted us to work for our own achievements."

Judge Olivito grew up in the West Virginia coal country as one of seven in a house with dirt floors and oil lamps. On June 6, 1944, he stormed Omaha Beach in Normandy, France with the 29th Division. Despite being wounded, he rejoined his regiment which fought in the Battle of the Bulge and pressed to within sixty miles of Berlin. After returning from war with a Purple Heart, he got his law degree and opened up a private practice in Steubenville in 1949. He married Theresa Kalinowski, a Polish Catholic. Their son Richard deviated from the family's denomination, becoming a "born again" Protestant. In high school in Wheeling, West Virginia, he handed out tracts with information about Jesus. Then, his faith led him to choose Oral Roberts University in Tulsa, Oklahoma, where he played football, majored in international relations and attended spirit-filled churches. During his second year of law school at Ohio Northern University, Olivito was the student campus minister. He didn't often speak about his faith after college, but he felt close to God.

Before he became a lawyer, Olivito worked at the Ohio Labor Department for three years, and he intended to return to Columbus with the hope of working for the attorney general. When that opportunity didn't materialize, Olivito set up shop as a general practice attorney on the fifth floor of the Sinclair Building, the most imposing building in the downtown area, named after a man with a vision for the city, Dohrman Sinclair. When Olivito rented his office in 1990, no one talked any more about Sinclair or his vision, except when bemoaning the lack of his abilities and leadership to drive economic development. Many locals didn't know why the building carried Sinclair's name. Later, in deserted storefronts down the street, posters of the Sinclair Building reminisced that Steubenville was "Founded in Business."

Olivito met and fell in love with to Joyce Iott, a quick-witted, beautiful, and well-read Lebanese American union organizer from Virginia. She was passionate about her convictions and spoke with a southern accent that entranced Olivito. They got married, and Joyce became director of the Hutton House, a local homeless shelter in downtown Steubenville, while Olivito launched his law practice. Olivito benefitted from Joyce's advice and her instincts about people. As a criminal defense attorney, Olivito viewed the multi-million dollar drug market from the front row. It didn't initially change his practice or his life, but it changed the way he saw his hometown. Together, he and Joyce became acquainted with the underworld of Little Chicago.

For New Yorkers, Steubenville is a backwater, and Ohio is a flyover state, yet the steel and iron that went into the girders of skyscrapers up and down the East Coast came from towns just like Steubenville. The steel industry brought thousands into this rough river city at the turn of the century and caused other businesses like the sex trade, casinos and drug-trafficking to thrive. In the mid-1980s, when Olivito was in his late twenties, Steubenville rebranded itself as the City of Murals, focusing on the hopes and dreams people brought to Steubenville, rather than the criminality and vice they tolerated while trying to realize them. Behind the majestic mural scenes, the Black Hand was battling a new generation of criminal entrepreneurs for control of the drug trade, and the Steubenville police were playing an outsized role.

<><><>

In the fall of 1992, Olivito decided to represent a young man named Leroy Slappy in a low-level felony case. Slappy pled guilty, but before sentencing, he requested a continuance. The judge ROR-ed him, or released him on his own recognizance, with the obligation to report to the Eastern Ohio Correction Center (EOCC) two weeks later to serve a short prison sentence. When he left the courthouse, the police allegedly followed him and beat him down. Then, the man's mother came to Olivito's office, crying, "The police beat my son!" She wanted Olivito to write a letter to the National Association for the Advancement of Colored People (NAACP) to ask for a review of what happened.

Olivito went to the local minimum security facility where Slappy was being held to get a look at his injuries. Leroy Slappy, a young man barely out of his teens, had been dragged over uneven pavement, which rubbed his face raw on one side. Some of his teeth were damaged, and his left eye was bleeding. He was African American, but the left side of his face was pink where the skin had been scraped off by the pavement. Slappy looked down in shame as the white lawyer gaped at his appearance. Olivito later wrote, "I couldn't believe they did this to a kid that had already pled guilty. They took advantage of this vulnerable kid who was soon to report to the EOCC."

For Olivito, it was his first moment of radicalization. He called the experience his "Lundy moment," a reference to the first exposure of Benjamin Lundy, a nineteenth-century abolitionist, to the brutality of the slave trade a hundred miles downriver in Wheeling, West Virginia. Previously, Olivito envisioned his future as a thoughtful bureaucrat, but he began to play the role of the detective, the reformist, the traitor.

In October, Olivito wrote a letter describing the SPD's racial bias and frequent use of excessive force. He suggested that the local police may need extra training, counseling, time off or some other form of sanction. However, months before writing this letter, Olivito had taken the issue up with the Ohio Attorney General's Office. He told the AG's chief of staff, Kent Markus, with whom he had worked as campaign manager, "I've got a problem in my hometown. The police are out of control." The AG at the time, Lee Fisher, was aware of the conversation, but he remained noncommittal. Then, shortly after the Slappy incident occurred, Olivito delivered his letter to the vice president of the NAACP at a Friday dinner in the local Baptist Church. The letter was intended for official eyes only, specifically the president of the local chapter, Alberta Dixon.

Olivito then left town and drove to Virginia for a long weekend with his wife. The following Tuesday, as he was getting off the elevator on the fifth floor of the Sinclair Building, he was confronted by Skip Mixon, Steubenville's lone African American city councilman. Skip was an outspoken critic of the local police and a close friend of James McNamara, the Columbus civil rights lawyer who had sued the local police dozens of times with the councilman's assistance.

"What are you going to do?" asked Mixon, his eyes wide with expectation.

"About what?" Olivito responded, regretting that his vacation was too short.

"You haven't heard? The NAACP leaked your letter to the police. Chief McCartney is livid. He wants an apology." Mixon thrust the latest issue of *The Herald-Star* into Olivito's hand. On October 16, four area police chiefs had responded to the leaked letter, calling it "reckless, slanderous and false."[30] Olivito didn't think his letter was controversial, but he never expected the NAACP to leak it to the press. He expected their collaboration. It was his first hard lesson in the politics of civil rights. "These issues will cause even those who are supposedly devoted and publicly dedicated to the cause of civil rights, even in the black community itself, to turn against someone who has stood up," Olivito later wrote. For him, the knowledge of the SPD's brutality was certain and easily deduced. He had seen it firsthand with Slappy after hearing of it for years. However, Olivito underestimated the sensitivity of police and their defenders who immediately challenged him to produce evidence of his claims. Skip Mixon was the only local city official who didn't openly condemn Olivito in the press.[31]

Olivito read the bawdy denunciation of the chiefs over again, savoring it. McCartney told *The Herald-Star*, "He did not just say the Steubenville Police Department. He involved all of us."[32] The chiefs responded with their own letter to Prosecutor Stern and AG Fisher, demanding that Olivito be called before a Jefferson County grand jury to substantiate his allegations.

"What are you gonna do?" repeated Mixon.

"Well, I'm not going to apologize," said Olivito, handing the newspaper back to Mixon. He later admitted that, after working for the AG and other high officials and attorneys, he was a bit arrogant and didn't take the local police chiefs' criticism seriously. A week later, local authorities called in the AG's Bureau of Criminal Investigation (BCI) to conduct a probe.

After Olivito didn't back down and didn't apologize, Prosecutor Stern sensed an opportunity. Olivito's father, Judge Olivito, had recently defeated Stern in what would be his last local judicial election. The media openly endorsed Judge Olivito against Stern, as did the

---

[30] Paul Giannamore. "Four police chiefs respond to Olivito's racial bias comments." *The Herald-Star,* 16 October 1992.

[31] Paul Giannamore. "City backs investigation." *The Herald-Star*, 21 October 1992.

[32] Ibid.

23

county bar association. But now, Stern could convene a grand jury and get revenge on the judge's youngest son, in his stead. In response, Richard pointed out Stern's conflict of interest in any criminal investigation of local police misconduct.

"Stern would be carrying out a prosecution of the people he represents," Olivito told reporters.[33]

"Olivito has no standing to seek a special prosecutor in the probe," Stern retorted. Chief McCartney criticized Olivito for not reporting his allegations to the proper authorities and refused Olivito's request for documents of lawsuits and settlements from the past five years.[34] At the same time, Chief McCartney affirmed, "If it is determined that my men are guilty, I will take disciplinary action." However, James McNamara, who sported a ponytail and sandals in court, but who was responsible for forty-four civil rights settlements against the SPD, cast doubt on the chief's statements. "He is treating this as a public relations problem, not a problem with poor citizens being beaten up by police officers. What would happen in a real city with a real police department is that they would fix the problem."

Olivito called McNamara to thank him, and McNamara remarked, "I'm surprised that you're taking this up in your hometown with your family there. I can always get in my car and drive back to Columbus."

McCartney publicly repeated that he was open to the investigation of police misconduct, but the SPD had been quietly settling police brutality lawsuits for years without investigation or punishment. McCartney voiced his wish to fight civil rights lawsuits in court, all the while lamenting that he was prodded to settle by the city's insurance company. This gave McCartney the convenient excuse, often heard up to the current day, that settlements do not prove an officer is guilty.[35]

As the public relations battle between Olivito and the police and prosecutor intensified, Olivito started getting tips from lawyers in the region on other cases of SPD brutality. Residents were also streaming into his office quietly but consistently to report police abuse. A white British woman, Carol Jones, the wife of an African American guy, came forward with her story.

---

[33] Paul Giannamore. "Probe begins Tuesday." *The Herald-Star*, 23 October 1992.

[34] Paul Giannamore. "Request upsets McCartney." *The Herald-Star*, 22 October 1992.

[35] Paul Giannamore. "Probe begins Tuesday." *The Herald-Star*, 23 October 1992.

In 1986, Carol and her husband, Joseph, were at Steubenville's Bob Evans restaurant when Joseph's firearm fell out of his pocket and onto the floor. Jerry McCartney happened to be there and saw it. Although Ohio is an open-carry state, and Joseph had a license to carry a firearm, seeing an interracial couple caused McCartney to lose his temper. So, McCartney, then-president of the Fort Steuben Lodge of the Fraternal Order of Police (FOP), handcuffed both Carol and Joseph. Then, in front of everyone in the restaurant, he rained his fists down on Carol, shouting, "Niggerlover!"

Joseph Jones was then charged with carrying a concealed weapon, and his wife was charged with disorderly conduct. Carol provided Olivito with photos showing the bruises on her chest, face and arms from the beating. Councilman Skip Mixon described the incident to *The Pittsburgh Courier*, which noted that McCartney had demanded Mixon's resignation only a few months prior because Mixon suggested Steubenville had a serious police brutality problem.[36]

As the testimonies of victims and witnesses mounted, Olivito intensified the pressure on the authorities by reporting to the press that he was aware of eight or nine substantial cases of police brutality, which suggested that Leroy Slappy's experience was not an isolated incident. Olivito concluded, "I see a problem that I think needs to be addressed."[37] When Stern fired back that Olivito had overstepped by not reporting directly to local authorities, Olivito declared that he already had gone to the Ohio AG's office several months prior.

This put Attorney General Fisher in an uncomfortable position because Olivito had been Fisher's campaign manager over nineteen Southeastern Ohio counties, delivering a pivotal advantage of Democratic turnout. He could hardly betray his own former political operative. Fisher not only acknowledged the meeting but called upon the authorities to provide his office with evidence of police misconduct, which was left many in Jefferson County stunned and flabbergasted. The tension grew as Olivito marshaled evidence from several cases other lawyers and residents provided, forwarding the documentation on to Kent Markus, the AG's chief of staff. States are not uniform in the authority invested in the AG to regulate police forces. Even if they have the authority, which most don't, state AGs have stayed the hell out of such endeavors with the notable exception of California.

It was Olivito's first experience of grappling with the question of how to prove a pattern of police misconduct in a court of law, and

---

[36] Marty Willis. "Steubenville FOP Head Accused of Police Brutality." *Pittsburgh Courier*, 29 March 1986.

[37] Paul Giannamore. "Olivito had discussion before sending letter." *The Herald-Star*, 22 October 1992.

there were few sources of guidance in the legal community or in precedent cases. The process of gathering evidence, done in secret over several months, put pressure on Olivito's fledgling law practice. Whereas he had relied on testimony, court settlements and the empirical evidence he'd seen, the system demanded all this and much more. The courts wanted it in writing, preferably by the chief's own hand, while police refused to release records and frequently sought to destroy them. They challenged the notion that a pattern could exist, silencing anybody who argued the contrary. Olivito wanted to prove them wrong.

In late December, the AG's Office suddenly announced that the evidence Olivito presented was insufficient to prove a pattern of police misconduct. A reporter blindsided Olivito with a question about the announcement as he was coming out of a courtroom. He was furious at the AG's Office for denying the validity of his clients' claims, and so he called Fisher's office to respond directly. During the call, AG Lee Fisher announced that several of his administrative heads were listening to the call on speaker, and they all took turns introducing themselves. After the introductions, Olivito told the group, "I'm happy to meet you all, and I'm glad to have you on the line to hear this. You've pissed on my work here, leaving my poor clients exposed to a madman." Olivito went on, "You've undermined everything you told the public about the kind of official you were going to be!"

Attorney General Fisher tried to make an accommodation, stating that, if any other issues arose, his office would be available to investigate. Olivito cut him off, "You've covered up clear police abuse, and you made a public announcement without consulting me!" Fisher went silent. "Fuck you, Lee!" Olivito shouted as he hung up the phone.

Stern responded to the statement of the AG with a kind of public threat to Olivito, "If he can't produce this evidence, I'll consider indicting him for making false allegations." Stern then convened a grand jury to consider the indictment, but he publicized the normally confidential process in the press, telling local residents that Olivito's supposed victims of police brutality had more than a hundred years of criminal history between them. Those who testified to the grand jury were faced with a phalanx of Steubenville police as they came off the stand and potential criminal charges for trying to provide their stories.

It was risky to speak out against police abuse not only because local and state officials would greet these kinds of claims with indifference or outright hostility. Police power was so fearsome that even the leaders of the Steubenville NAACP denied that there was a police brutality problem. NAACP President Alberta Dixon stated that the NAACP had never received complaints of police misconduct. When Sheriff Abdalla and his jailer George Johnson went on trial for accepting bribes to protect local organized crime, Alberta Dixon agreed to monitor the trial in case their civil rights were violated.[38] Olivito was later told by a relative of the local NAACP president that Dixon's family was protected as long as she supported them publicly. He said, "Everybody knew the police were rough. We were all fearful of them, but the white people didn't have to deal with it and the black leaders kept silent in return for protection."

However, people beyond Steubenville noticed what was happening. Olivito received an anonymous call from someone in New York City.

"You are in very dangerous territory, my friend," the caller warned. "My advice is to get a bishop. In New York, having a church leader present was one way we kept our whistleblowers alive." He also received calls from anonymous Ohio police officers. One caller claiming to be an officer said, "Keep it up for those of us who want our fellow officers to do their jobs better!"

After the AG's denial of the pattern and Stern's farcical grand jury, Joyce and Olivito continued to collect citizen complaints against the SPD. They gathered over three hundred complaints through the fall and into the dark winter months. However, the Steubenville NAACP didn't want anything to do with the complaints. Later, after Joyce made inquiries elsewhere, the Dayton chapter of the NAACP agreed to examine and investigate them, so Olivito sent a package containing all of the complaints by express mail from the Steubenville Post Office. It never arrived.

By the end of the year, a pall of denial had settled on the city like the fine soot particles from the steel plant that infused the scent of burnt metal into the breeze. Meanwhile, Olivito continued to experience backlash. "You've embarrassed your entire family. You've embarrassed your father," sneered an older man Olivito encountered in the restroom of a local restaurant. He began to have doubts about the efforts he had made for Leroy Slappy. Much of his young life, Olivito had worked in and around government and held dreams of becoming a senior public official. It did not seem that working in his hometown would lead him to the heights his father had achieved, but in contrast to so many others, he could not avert his eyes from the corruption and abuse of power in Little Chicago.

◇◇◇

After working for the family law firm, Stern, Stern & Stern, Co., Stephen Stern had strode into the prosecutor's office in 1980 with the intention to change the way law enforcement did business. He put

---

[38] Staff. "Local NAACP branch will monitor trials." *The Herald-Star*, 4 December 1990.

racketeering and drug enforcement at the top of his campaign, dubbed "Operation Stern Message." On paper, Stern was a Democrat. In his heart, he was only interested in public office for the sake of power, but one couldn't say that and get elected. Stern had wavy hair and brown glasses. Clad in impeccable suits and flashy ties, he developed influence that reached the state supreme court and the AG's office. "[Stern] had a lot of people in this town very intimidated," remembered one official who spoke on condition of anonymity. Stern was not a people person. He was a power broker.

In 1986, County Prosecutor Stern had set his sights on the top judicial position in the state of Ohio. He campaigned on the Democratic ticket for the supreme court against the Democratic incumbent, Chief Justice Frank Celebrezze, a pro-labor progressive who was upsetting the all-powerful insurance companies with his favor towards plaintiffs and unions. Subsequently, Stern found himself the target of an attorney misconduct investigation by the disciplinary counsel of Ohio Supreme Court. The disciplinary counsel was a handy tool for unscrupulous individuals to stymie their enemies if they happened to be lawyers, because they investigated every allegation forwarded to them by the local Bar Associations. The process would tie up any attorney who wasn't a senior partner in a big firm with years of paperwork and many thousands of dollars in legal fees. A local judge and supreme court candidate John Corrigan later admitted that there were "political overtones" in the disciplinary counsel's investigation of Stephen Stern.[39] After the investigation was dropped, Stern campaigned against "in-fighting" in the Ohio Supreme Court.

However, Stern realized he was beaten before the election, and he decided to back the Republican challenger, an Irish jurist, Thomas Moyer, who then defeated Celebrezze. Moyer was a partner at a major Columbus corporate law firm and a Franklin County judge. He was young, but he had been fast-tracked up the political ladder in Franklin County's conservative circles. His victory over Celebrezze was a sign of the growing power of insurance companies and the waning of the union movement in Ohio. As chief justice, Moyer "brought calm to a troubled court after a partisan era,"[40] according to the former chairman of the Ohio Republican Party, Kevin DeWine. In fact, political in-fighting among Ohio's attorneys continued with the supreme court used as a cudgel, except now it was in the hands of the other side.

---

[39] Linda Shambarger. "Stern tackles tough foe in political arena." *The Bryan Times*, 8 April 1986.

[40] Jim Provance. "Ohio's Chief Justice Moyer dies at age 70; led top bench since 87." *Toledo Blade*, 4 April 2010.

Over the next quarter century, the business community, led by the insurance companies, transformed the Ohio Supreme Court into an institution wholly supportive of their interests, pouring millions of dollars into the campaign coffers of any Republican who ran for a seat on the bench. In 2002, the last Democrat was replaced.[41] Moyer would rule the supreme court for decades as a strong-armed politician who understood the power of big donor money just then beginning to impact America's state supreme courts. Ohio's supreme court led the nation, and the state's Republican party became known as the party that Moyer built.

In 1987, Moyer intervened in a criminal gambling case in Steubenville. Prosecutor Stern was trying to convict two bookies that have a gambling business in downtown Steubenville, the Spot Bar, still in operation today. The prosecution of the case hit a snag when Jefferson County Common Pleas Judge Mascio would not recognize the law against gambling. Mascio was a long-time Italian common pleas judge who later co-founded a law firm in 2003 with his son, Mascio & Mascio Law Services. A decade later, it would emerge that Mascio's partners in a liquor business were distributors of the poker machines then found in Steubenville's taverns and private clubs.[42] The case went before the supreme court with Stern representing the state and Frank Bruzzese representing the racketeers. Chief Justice Moyer wrote the decision for the majority, affirming the constitutionality of the Ohio Revised Code (ORC) regarding the prohibition of gambling. The supreme court granted Stern's writ against the judge and voided Macio's contempt charge against Stern.[43] Despite Stern's victory, gambling laws are still not enforced in Steubenville up to the present day.

With punishment for gambling unofficially forsworn, law enforcement maintained a steady flow of kickbacks from the rackets. In 1991, a federal grand jury in Columbus acquitted Jefferson County Sheriff Fred Abdalla of five counts of extortion for allegedly taking an $11,000-bribe from undercover FBI agents posing as racketeers.[44] Although Abdalla was undoubtedly guilty, jurors refused to convict. Knowing this, law enforcement officers started their own rackets. Over two decades later, in 2013, *The Atlantic Wire* reported that Sheriff Ab-

---

[41] Jim Provance. "Chief justice's defeat in '86 marked turning point." *The Toledo Blade*, 28 March 2010.

[42] *State Stern v. Mascio*. Supreme Court of Ohio. 6 March 1998. Print.

[43] Ibid.

[44] Staff. "Jury finds sheriff innocent of gambling protection." *The Vindicator*, 16 July 1991.

dalla was running a gambling racket.[45] Many in the community didn't mind. It was easy to like Sheriff Abdalla, and most people did. McCartney and Stern were easier to dislike, but people in the area were scared of them, even in city hall. However, local residents were trying to make a living and had little to gain by speaking out.

In their acerbic, mid-century way, the people of Steubenville acknowledged the suborning of the justice system. Former local bookie Joseph Koniski confirmed that there were "at least" eight gambling establishments operating in the city in 2015. He concluded, "Somebody isn't doing their job. Somebody is getting paid." Regardless of which political party was in office, the political establishment was handed down through prominent families in bed with the racketeers. Everybody around town knew this to be true. One resident wrote, "Don't be surprised if the people who ran the illegal gambling joints and make millions in unreported income escape charges. There is no one around that isn't in bed with them, including judges, local prosecutors, federal prosecutors and the attorney general."[46]

On the local level, organized crime cannot operate under the noses of police, city government, and residents without their consent, but at the end of the day, apathy is pervasive. *The Herald-Star* continues to make it easier by pretending everything is peachy in Little Chicago, which is not surprising when one considers that crusading newspaper editors have been murdered in the past.[47] More than a decade later, Stern's unscrupulousness set in motion a chain of events which drew the attention of federal attorneys in Washington, D.C.

---

[45] Alexander Abad-Santos. "Inside the Search for the Truth about Steubenville- 1,000 Tips at a Time." *The Atlantic Wire*, 8 January 2013.

[46] Anonymous comment posted in response to article from newspaper re-posted in blog with local following: "Herald Star: Illegal gambling alleged." *Radionewz.net*, 17 May 2014.

[47] Norman E. Nygarrd. 12 Against The Underworld. *The Hobson Book Press*, 1947.

Police officer perjury to justify illegal dope searches is commonplace. One of the dirty little not-so-secret secrets of the criminal justice system that strikes directly at the rule of law. Yet, it is the routine way of doing business in courtrooms everywhere in America.

-Former San Francisco Police Commissioner Peter Keane[48]

What led to the BCI investigation of the SPD started earlier, in March of 1992. Olivito was thirty-three years old. He had four days of stubble, shoulder-length hair and a strong sense of personal integrity. In the Jefferson County jail, he sat before Andre Hython discussing his arrest for drug trafficking. Andre was a twenty-eight-year-old African American, born and raised in Steubenville. He had three brothers, Clint, Brawson, and Andrew, who the police later mistook for Andre, his younger brother. Andrew will be referred to as Hython to reduce confusion. In contrast to his law-abiding siblings, Andre sold drugs for a living, and it was no secret. For that reason, he was on the radar of local law enforcement. "I do bad things," Andre told Olivito, "but I didn't throw a bag of crack down in front of a bunch of cops."

Andre and his friend maintained that officers on the Federal Drug Task Force planted the drugs. However, because seven police officers accused Hython of drug possession, the odds of avoiding a decade or more in prison were bleak. Still, the spark in Andre's eyes persuaded Olivito that his account of the arrest was true. At *The Herald-Star*, there was no crime reporter, but there was a crime blotter around which local gossip swirled. The newspaper focused on the fact that Andre, a guy accused of drug trafficking, had the nickname "Pink."

Andre's trial was set for April 8. Three days before the trial, the task force performed a sting on him in hopes of shoring up their case with additional charges. Sergeant Andriano, a tough Italian American cop, had led the SPD contingent of the task force for fifteen years. Most of the other cops on the scene were also veteran officers. Lloyd King, an African American secret service officer, had worked for the task force for more than a decade and was its leader. Officer James Bernard was a white, second-generation cop and bodybuilder who sported a crew cut and a barbed wire tattoo. Bernard was new to the

---

[48] Peter Keane. "Why cops lie." *SFGate.com*, 15 March 2011.

task force, but he had nine years of law enforcement experience between Steubenville and neighboring Wintersville. He was the son of a respected Wintersville police officer with the path into law enforcement laid out for him.

John Myers of the Mingo PD accompanied Andriano, King, and Bernard that day. Myers would be engulfed in scandal a month later because of his unofficial status working under the command of the mayor of Mingo Junction, John Corrigan, rather than any local police chief. When residents noticed him stalking them and snapping photos without an official uniform, they started asking questions, which caused police chiefs in the area to forbid him from operating in their jurisdictions. Mingo Mayor Corrigan stated, many years later, "They were trying to muzzle me. I said 'no' to firing him. Mingo paid him, and I authorized him to go outside of his jurisdiction." Many in the area were indifferent to the tactics used by the task force, but some public officials and police chiefs were wary because of the potential for lawsuits and bad press.

Prosecutor Stern called the task force "Federal" because he wanted it to have the same guise of official authority as the Federal Bureau of Investigation (FBI). Stern defended Myers' failure to notify the police chief of Toronto, Ohio, saying that the FBI would do the same.[49] Not everyone was convinced. Sheriff Abdalla had attacked Myers' credibility in 1991, saying that one investigation was carried out "unethically and illegally."[50] Stern didn't care about lawsuits or the public perception of drug enforcement; he wanted dealers off the streets.

On August 5, the task force sent an informant to do a "controlled buy" from Andre. Next, they combed the streets looking for him. In the process, they spotted his brother, Hython, while he was driving around with his older brother, Brawson, and two friends, Lamont Whatley and Gary Thomas. According to the police, the car stopped at a liquor store where Hython bought a 40 oz. When Hython pulled out of the parking lot, there were two unmarked police cars on his tail. After going through a series of stop signs and arriving next to an abandoned factory lot, the second unmarked car pulled around the first and stopped in front of Hython's vehicle. Then, the officers jumped out with guns drawn. The officers ordered the guys out of the car and searched the vehicle without permission. Officer Bernard testified that he recognized Lamont Whatley from "being on the street and being in

---

[49] Jeff Dixon and Edward R. Sunkin. "Toronto police 'on alert' for Mingo officer." *The Herald-Star*, 17 September 1992.

[50] Mark Law and Edward R. Sunkin. "Defamation suit filed." *The Herald-Star*, 22 September 1992.

several high drug areas within the city."[51] He claimed that he observed Whatley throwing a white baggie from the rear passenger window. Bernard claimed that he got out of Myers' car and retrieved the baggie. Then, Andriano stopped, and he got into Andriano's car.

The police arrested Hython as well as Whatley allegedly because they found bills they claimed were connected to the earlier controlled-buy wrapped around Hython's license. They suggested that Hython had been trying to evade the unmarked cars, leading them on a chase. Hython claimed he wasn't aware the police were chasing him. According to his account, he didn't break any laws, traffic or otherwise, but he was charged with paraphernalia, complicity in drug trafficking, as well as fleeing and eluding.

While Andre was out on bail awaiting his trial, Hython was in jail for three days awaiting his probable cause hearing. This was new territory for him. *The Herald-Star* ran a one-paragraph blurb under the headline, "Drug force arrests man due in court."[52] The paper not only dragged the brothers' last name through the mud but also erroneously reported that Andre, not his brother Andrew, was caught just days before his court date.

This was advantageous to the prosecution because Olivito would have to explain to an all-white jury how the August 5 arrest wasn't Andre "Pink" Hython, the drug-pushing black man they had already read about in the papers; it was his older brother, Andrew. Olivito feared that the bad light cast on the defendant might remain in the juror's minds because they might get the impression that the brothers were both criminals. Many years later, Olivito explained, "This is how Stern and King worked. The public and the media usually just followed blindly."

<><><>

Olivito met Hython for the first time in jail as his attorney. Unlike his younger brother Andre, Hython had never been in trouble before. He was in jail until the day of his little brother Andre's trial. Hython was set to be railroaded into the same fate, but he told Olivito, "I didn't do nothing. I don't know what the fuck these cops talking about." His eyes met Olivito's then sunk to the floor. He saw his future in jeopardy, and he was alternately outraged, dejected and terrified.

---

[51] *State of Ohio v Hython*. Steubenville Municipal Court. 25 April 1994. p. 7. Print.

[52] Staff. "Drug force arrests man due in court." *The Herald-Star*, 8 April 1992.

"Your brother must be involved," Olivito said, "I know he is, even though I believe him about this other case."

"Listen," said Hython, cutting him off with a weary gesture, "I went in and bought a forty ounce. I had two dollars and some change. That's it." He shot a hard glance at the lawyer.

"They didn't find any drugs on you? Are you sure they didn't find any residue on the bills or something?"

"There wasn't nothing for them to find," Hython responded.

Olivito began to suspect that Hython's arrest was a ploy by Stern to solidify the case against his brother. Perhaps, they had arrested Hython by accident. Again, the man on the scene making the arrest was Lloyd King. Olivito assumed that King would be the prime witness against both Hythons.

James McNamara summarized the SPD's approach to law enforcement, "If they thought you were doing something, they were gonna grab you, search you and take you in. If you said something they didn't like, you might get hit for it."[53] These types of arrests were happening bi-weekly in Steubenville, but there was another layer in Andre's case, Lloyd King's signature move: "flaked" or planted evidence.

When he asked for a jury trial, Andre knew that Prosecutor Stern would likely seek the maximum penalty, twenty years in prison. Stern's jogging partner, Judge Mascio Sr. presided over the trial at the Jefferson County Court of Common Pleas, an imposing stone building with Corinthian columns and a golden, unblindfolded effigy of lady justice on top. The former statue had a blindfold, but it had to be replaced when it fell through the ceiling after a storm. The defense was facing almost insurmountable odds. For one, Andre had drug-related felonies on his record. Six police officers and Lloyd King claimed they witnessed him drop the drugs in the parking lot. Then, there was Prosecutor Stern putting the full weight of his office against it.

Daunted by his estimation of the odds and pressed by conscience upon consideration of the punishment, Olivito asked his client if he wanted to make a plea deal. Andre glared at his lawyer and replied, "You gotta believe me!" Then, with a steely firmness that stuck with his attorney for years, he asserted, "I'm not taking no plea." His eyes burned with resolve. Olivito knew it would be tricky to try to convince a jury of his client's innocence against the testimony of seven narcotics officers that they caught him red-handed. Then, Olivito considered how he came to believe Andre's story and decided on a strategy most attorneys would never attempt. Olivito instructed him to admit that he sold drugs for a living to the all-white, all-female jury.

---

[53] Pierre Thomas. "Police misconduct allegations not confined to big cities." *CNN.com*, 10 November 1999.

As his client was called to the stand, Olivito felt emboldened but still anxious. He held his breath as Andre walked through the courtroom. He wasted no time getting to the point, "Andre, I want you to look at the jury and answer this question. What you do for a living?"

"I sell drugs," Andre stated.

"Andre, did you drop these thirty-four pieces of crack at your feet when the officers approached you?"

"I did not. I did not have these drugs on me. I was just walking home when they approached me."

"Where did these drugs come from, Andre?"

"Lloyd King dropped them at my feet. I had never seen them before," he said, looking squarely at the jurors. Complete silence reigned in the courtroom.

"So you deny the allegations against you, correct?"

"That's right. I had nothing on me that night."

The problem with the arrest, Olivito argued, was that there was no probable cause. Olivito then called Brawson Hython, Andre's oldest brother, to testify. Brawson attested to seeing Lloyd King draw his gun on others repeatedly. Then, he described an incident where he was with Lloyd King Jr. in the basement of the King house. He and the other kids pried open a door and discovered "dozens and dozens" bags of white powder. The kids knew the bags of powder were kilos of cocaine. According to Brawson's testimony, after Lloyd King Sr. found out, he allegedly beat his son.

The officers were then called to the stand, and Olivito questioned each one on what he was doing when the drugs appeared, establishing that only Lloyd King had allegedly seen the crack fall from Andre's hand. Stern's chief agent, Lloyd King was the last one called to the stand.

"So you are the head of the federal drug task force?" Olivito began.

"Yes, for the past seven years."

"Who do you work for exactly?"

"For the drug task force," King replied, a little uncomfortable.

"Are you a police officer certified by the state of Ohio?"

"I have taught many police," said King, growing defensive.

"Do you hold a peace officer's status in Ohio?"

King had never faced this line of questioning. He brought up his military service in Vietnam, but Olivito hammered the point.

"Under the law, you do not have the power to make arrests as if you were a police officer, do you?"

"I have enough credits to be one." His eyes flashed with anger which he smothered. "I have a special status. I am a secret service agent." King recovered himself.

"What is that?"

"I have a special appointment from the Jefferson County Prosecutor's Office. I am a special agent working under their authority. I work directly for the prosecutor."

There was statutory legitimacy to his claim. King's salary was paid by a grant for each local prosecutor to appoint a highly qualified peace officer to serve as a special agent, so Olivito chipped away at King's qualifications. Now, he was going for the jugular.

"How many drug arrest have you made over the years?"

"Thousands," said King swelling with pride.

"Were many of these what is called 'controlled buys'?"

"Yes. Many of them were."

Olivito approached him, walking past the jurors. Then, standing only a few feet away, Olivito asked:

"Tell me this, Mr. King, why do you have hundreds of bags of powder cocaine inside a room in the basement of your house?"

King froze. Audible gasps came from the jury box, but no one in the courtroom said a word. Assistant Prosecutor Puskarich was too dumbstruck to utter an objection. Olivito looked at the judge and noticed Judge Mascio was looking away from Mr. King. Olivito sensed an opening to proceed.

"Answer the question, Mr. King."

King glared at the defense attorney, eyes smoldering, but he didn't say a word. Olivito waited for a long minute, expecting the judge or prosecutor to intervene. Then, he looked at the stunned and riveted jurors.

"I have no more questions of this witness, your honor," Olivito added before sitting down. King's family's activities were "well-known among officials and dealers alike," according to *The Cleveland Scene*, "but no one had ever raised the issue publicly."[54] Years later, Olivito mused that Assistant Prosecutor Puskarich, "should have objected, but he was too surprised, I guess. He came off as...not credible." King and Prosecutor Puskarich's stunned silence was fatal for the case against Andre.

The jurors went into deliberate on a verdict. Within twenty minutes, they agreed unanimously that Andre was innocent, but they were all so scared to deliver a "not guilty" verdict that they delayed, pretending to deliberate. There was no confession, but King's guilty silence which established doubt in the jury that the defendant was guilty. Finally, the jurors marched back into the courtroom and announced the acquittal of a drug dealer against the word of seven police officers, making local history. Andre stood up against seven cops, a

---

[54] Aina Hunter. "Blue Mob: Pity those caught by the Warren police, who rule with iron fists and rubber gloves." *Cleveland Scene*, 25 February 2004.

hostile judge, and prosecutor, and he won by destroying the credibility of the veteran commander of the task force. King allegedly warned each member of the Hythons family in the courtroom, including their 70-year-old mother, "You're dead." King said the same to Olivito. Nevertheless, Hython interpreted the dismissal of the cases against his little brother Andre as a ray of hope. Prosecutor Stern was not giving up.

<><><>

Andrew Hython's trial took place on April 22, 1994, almost two years after Andre's, in the first venue of every criminal trial, the Steubenville Municipal Court House.[55] If it were a serious charge and did not fail after a preliminary investigation by the court, it would be bound over to the Jefferson County Court of Common Pleas, the domain of Stern and Mascio. Although Lloyd King was again the arresting officer on the scene, now his credibility was in question. Therefore, Prosecutor Stern selected the least senior officer, James Bernard, to testify against Hython.

Judge Richard Powell heard the case. Powell was a longtime trustee on the board of the public library, a veteran officer of the Steubenville City Schools Foundation, a professor at Steubenville's Franciscan University and a booster of the celebrated Big Red football team. City Prosecutor Michael Bednar, who is now a judge, initiated the questioning of Bernard.

"On April 5, you charged Andrew Hython with complicity. Why did you do that?"[56] Prosecutor Bednar asked.

"We talked the case over with Prosecutor Stern, and he directed us to file the charge," Bernard responded.

Olivito was shocked to hear this answer. The revelation suggested that Stern was calling the shots and potentially compromised the state's case against the defendant. Communication between the officers of the court and law enforcement when the accused is absent is called *ex parte* communication. It can be the cause of a mistrial if the communication influences the proceedings in a way unfair to the defendant, but courts enforce the rules unevenly. There was no reaction from the audience. Prosecutor Bednar ignored the can of worms opened by Bernard's response and continued his examination.

"How did Andrew Hython aid or abet?" he asked.

---

[55] There was a pretrial hearing before the criminal trial, but the testimony of both is being combined for simplicity's sake.

[56] *State of Ohio v Hython*. Steubenville Municipal Court. 25 April 1994. p. 5-23. Print.

"We conducted a plain view search of the vehicle after—after pursuing him. We found a driver's license which had two dollar bills wrapped around it, which was buy money which we purchased crack cocaine earlier in the day with."

"Whose driver's license was it?"

"Mr. Hython's," Bernard responded.

"How did you identify that as being buy money?"

"Through the serial numbers."

Olivito gritted his teeth. Hython tried not to betray emotion. Not long after, Prosecutor Bednar finished, and Frank LaRue, Lamont Whatley's attorney, took over. He asked further questions about the moment when Bernard stated that he saw Whatley throw the baggie from the vehicle. At length, LaRue recreated the circumstances of the arrest. Mr. LaRue asked Bernard, "And they could see you following them. Do you see them look back at you?"

"Yes, sir," Bernard answered.

"As you observed them?"

"As he threw the bag of cocaine out the window, he looked back," Bernard clarified.

"He looked back while he was throwing it out the window? I'm not going to ask you to speculate why he would drop something in full—in your full view out of the car..." LaRue raised a compelling issue and dropped it just as quickly, making Olivito's blood boil. Afterward, Olivito glared at Officer Bernard and walked silently along the gate in front of the jury before he began his cross-examination. He could tell that Bernard was not sure of himself on the stand, and he sensed the officer's story would unravel if he could pull the right string.

"Now, how far did you travel from the first time you turned around until you stopped the defendant?"

"At least four blocks."

"And did they stop for any stop signs during that time?"

"Not to my knowledge."

"You're directly behind them?"

"After I jumped out, no."

"No. I'm saying when you were driving behind them, you're directly behind the car, right?"

"Yes."

"Weren't there stop signs somewhere in these four blocks?"

"I would imagine."

"Your testimony is they drove through the stop signs."

"No, it's not."

"So, you're saying possibly they stopped. You're saying they stopped at a stop sign and kept going and you followed them through the stop sign."

"I don't recall." Bernard was growing uncomfortable, Olivito remembered, many years later. Olivito was perspiring. His pulse quickened. He was having a good time.

"Were there any cars between you and them?"

"No."

"So, you stopped at the stop signs, didn't you?"

"Oh, yes, sir."

"Why was that [fleeing and eluding] citation issued?" Olivito asked.

"As we were behind him with lights and sirens on, he failed to pull over."

"Is that car equipped with lights on it?"

"Yes."

"An unmarked car," Olivito stated rather than asked. Painstakingly, they established that Officer Myer's car, in which Bernard was a passenger, was a blue Pontiac.

"Is it one of those hand sort of lights or is it a mounted light?"

"It's a hand light."

"Okay. Now, is there a hand siren put up there, too?"

Olivito remembered hearing suppressed laughter in the court. He could tell that he was scoring points. Just a few minutes before, Bernard was engaged in a dramatization played out hundreds of thousands of times every year in courtrooms across the country. He was mischaracterizing the defendant's actions to make them seem criminal. His narrative had sounded like a hot pursuit, but now Bernard was backpedaling.

"Where's the siren at?" Olivito continued.

"It was in Sgt. Andriano's car... which was directly behind ours."

"So, the siren is on the second car?" Olivito qualified.

"Yes."

"Is that an unmarked car?"

"Yes."

More awkward exchanges followed. Since both cars were unmarked, it was debatable whether Hython should have been at fault for failing to pull over. Similar plainclothes units in major cities like D.C. and L.A. have been known to shake down or even abduct motorists and pedestrians, at random. All over the country, narcotics squads were running roughshod over citizens' rights. In the case of the SPD, it was highly targeted, and Olivito was determined to expose the unconstitutional operating logic. However, Judge Powell intervened.

"Who has the complicity charge here?" the judge demanded.

"My client," Olivito answered.

"Well, what's the basis for that charge? That he was driving the car?" the judge asked.

Bernard was silent.

"Okay," Judge Powell concluded, "The two $1 bills. Couldn't his brother have given him that for any reason, loaned it to him, given it to him? If he has the marked money that someone else used, is that a crime?"

Bernard remained silent. Olivito's comments went unrecorded. And the judge's impatience grew.

"I want to know what's the connection between the two bills and the— I mean, is there— is there going to be any testimony that he was in on the drug buy?"

At this point, City Prosecutor Bednar spoke up, but again the court reporter failed to record the answer. The judge implored someone to prompt Bernard to explain the logic behind the charge, resolving, "Let Mr. Bednar ask him!"

"Officer, why was Andrew Hython charged with complicity in this case?" asked Prosecutor Bednar, obediently.

"It was referred to Prosecutor Stern and he advised us to charge him with complicity due to the fact that he had the two $1 bills..." Bernard reiterated, washing his hands of responsibility.

"I mean, does anyone know how he got the—do you know how he got the bills?" The judge all but threw up his hands.

"No, I don't."

"Does anyone that you know of?"

"Not to my knowledge," replied Bernard, pinned.

"I don't think we need to go forward," the judge declared. "That charge is dismissed. Now, the other case against him is a misdemeanor one, right?"

Olivito confirmed that this was true, after thanking the judge. Hython looked at the faces of the city prosecutor, his attorney and the judge in quick succession. Prosecutor Bednar looked shocked and dejected. Olivito was standing with his chest forward and his arms back, ready to take on the state. Then, Judge Powell uttered, "He's discharged at this time. That $2 could have come from anyplace. There's no connection between him and the buy and the $2 as I can see." Olivito was able to recall the order of Bernard's testimony almost verbatim twenty years later. In the contest in the courts between crime control and due process, it was a victory for due process during an era dominated by crime control.

Judge Powell dispensed with Hython's charges within minutes, once the dubious circumstances of the arrest were clear. The dismissal of the charges was an embarrassment for Bernard and the SPD as well as Prosecutor Stern and the task force because it showed that this arrest lacked probable cause, violating the Fourth Amendment against improper searches and seizures. Bernard said in the course of his testimony that he felt they had probable cause to arrest Andrew Hython "under suspicion" of his criminal activities, although Hython had a clean record. Reasonable suspicion is less than probable cause, but it is more than a hunch in the courts. The distinction can be significant when a person's freedom depends on it, but police are trained to concoct rationales for probable cause to manage the risks inherent in the job. A former Los Angeles police officer, Brian S. Bentley, explained:

> Police officers are trained to circumvent civil rights with the precision of brain surgeons. I was taught that every good police officer could find probable cause or reasonable suspicion to detain anyone, especially a black man. In roll call, I was provided with crime statistics and enough general suspect descriptions to stop any black man I chose.[57]

Bernard did not share Judge Powell's concern with the grounds of the arrest because his priority was to get the Hythons and Whatley off the streets. He felt Hython's presence in "high drug areas" of Steubenville was grounds for arrest. It was reasoning heard in courtrooms around the country, but in Steubenville, it was part of Operation Stern Message, which led to a pattern of Fourth Amendment violations and court settlements that city officials knew about but tolerated.

After Bernard's testimony, Brawson Hython was again called to the stand, this time as a witness for Lamont Whatley. Shortly after the start of his testimony, the judge again interrupted to conduct the questioning personally.

"I only want to hear what may have some relationship with this arrest. I don't care about if he went to church," Judge Powell grumbled.

On the stand, Brawson explained that the task force stopped and released Lamont Whatley. Then, five minutes later, they stopped him again and arrested him.

"They was not in uniform," Brawson told the court.

"And as a result of the second stop, he was charged with a crime?" the judge repeated, incredulously. Why would Whatley throw a bag of crack out the window if he had just been searched? Judge Powell turned it over in his head.

In the course of his testimony, Brawson Hython reported, "King just come back from the car saying, 'I know Richard Olivito's your attorney,' and then he started saying that, and then he said, 'yeah, cause I just talked to [Judge] Mascio.'"

Olivito was curious about the call between the task force and

[57] Anthony Stanford. Copping Out: The Consequences of Police Corruption and Misconduct. *Praeger*, 2015.

County Prosecutor Stern, so he ordered Lloyd King's phone records from the phone company. The company was oddly obliging, and the records came within a few days. It turned out that King had called the number listed for Judge Mascio's house. *The Pittsburgh Gazette* reported in 1998 that Stern and Mascio were neighbors and jogging partners.[58] According to Olivito, this relationship made local criminal defense lawyers nervous because they knew that many nights the prosecutor was carrying on *ex parte* with the county judge.

Judge Powell released all the defendants, but the case's collapse pulled the curtain back on the machinations of the justice system. In 2011, former San Francisco Police Commissioner Peter Keane published an op-ed entitled "Why cops lie."[59] Keane describes an oddly familiar courtroom scene:

> Often in search hearings, it is embarrassingly clear to everyone—judge, prosecutor, defense attorney, even spectators—that the officer is lying under oath. Yet nothing is done about it. There are rare cases in which the nature of the testimony and the physical evidence make it absolutely impossible to credit an officer's version, and the judge must rule the search illegal. When this happens, the judge rules hesitatingly and grudgingly for the defense. Indeed, judges sometimes apologize to the officer for tossing out illegally seized evidence where the cop has just committed felony perjury in the judge's presence.

Judge Powell didn't apologize or hesitate, to his credit, but he also didn't pressure the prosecutor's office to investigate King's activities. In his court, as in many others, criminal charges were out of the question when police committed crimes. Judge Powell had once left the courtroom while an officer beat a handcuffed woman with a chair. Prosecutor Stern was almost always behind the police. The prosecutor works directly with law enforcement every day, and especially in small towns like Steubenville, prosecutors have every incentive not to work against their law enforcement colleagues for the sake of their own careers in public office as well as the efficient administration of justice.

After the defendants were released, Olivito recalled City Prosecutor Bednar fuming, "That's the last case I take from Lloyd King!"

Lloyd King wasn't the ultimate decision-maker. It was County Prosecutor Stern who put City Prosecutor Bednar in that awkward position. The relationship between the judge and the county prosecutor was unseemly, then King calls them at home, discussing which lawyer rep-

---

[58] Johnna A. Pro. "Chief Justice settles judge-prosecutor dispute." *Pittsburgh Post-Gazette*, 1 April 1998.

[59] Peter Keane. "Why cops lie." *SFGate.com*, 15 March 2011.

resents the guys his task force is arresting. Regardless, the Hython case was not highly publicized in the local community, not by *The Herald-Star*, not much beyond the local gossip. It was a relief for the Hython family, which had been demoralized by the fear of having two sons imprisoned. Instead, both were freed as if by the hand of god. For the SPD, it was deeply embarrassing because it suggested the force was unprofessional, if not unconstitutional. But many residents couldn't have cared less. For those who did, it fed the rumor mill, spreading bitterness and distrust. The DOJ would hear about it, largely because of what followed. For Lloyd King, it was the beginning of the end of his career. For Olivito, it was an opening that would change the course his life.

**4**

The good name of the city of Steubenville has been besmirched for long years in the headlines of the nation's press and over microphones of national radio hookups.

-Harry Cochran in 1946[60]

After both Hythons were exonerated, there were, documented in the public record, two felony drug cases in which the Federal Drug Task Force was implicated in planting evidence and false arrest. However, by itself, the failure of the charges wasn't enough to change anything. It was but a moment missed by the media where the authorities violated the rights of one of Steubenville's minority residents. So, Olivito and Hython decided to file a Section 1983 civil rights complaint against the city. Section 1983 is an old law, enacted back in 1871, to address the deprivation of rights by the Ku Klux Klan (KKK). Today, it is used most often to hold government officials accountable for civil rights violations. Hython's counsel filed the lawsuit just one day before the statute of limitations expired on April 4, 1994, and three weeks before his criminal trial.

Olivito told an attorney who helped him with the brief, "If we fuck this up, we might as well throw our law licenses in the river." By then, his work on the Hython case had acquired a whole new meaning, and there was a corresponding length he would now go to defend his client. It began to consume him in idle moments, while waiting in line at the supermarket, eating dinner with Joyce and during sleepless nights.

Meanwhile, they dealt with the backlash. Olivito made enemies by bringing up King's family's activities in court and causing the case against Andre to fall apart. The jurors were right to worry about the consequences of a "not guilty" verdict. The Hython and Olivito families began to receive death threats. There would be late night phone calls to Judge Olivito. "This doesn't come from me, but tell your boy to back off or else." One night, a caller told his father that Richard had been killed and his body dumped in an alley. The judge spent the evening searching the alleys of downtown Steubenville, while Richard

---

[60] Norman E. Nygarrd. 12 Against The Underworld. *The Hobson Book Press*, 1947.

was in a settlement conference that lasted until after nightfall. Richard didn't know about the call his father received, but he noticed his father's curious sigh of relief when he later answered the phone back at his apartment, twenty minutes outside of town. Richard didn't find out about his father searching for his corpse until a decade later when the judge volunteered the story to a journalist. Like many veterans of his generation who fought in the Second World War, the judge never spoke with anyone about his deepest fears.

Olivito and Joyce occasionally came home to find their place ransacked. The stalker left half-smoked cigarettes, urine stains and Joyce's underwear displayed prominently on the lawn. Joyce felt embarrassed and violated by the thought of malicious strangers handling her intimate garments. The sight of their display on the lawn made her shudder, but more than anything it made her angry. These episodes cemented her desire to hold the police accountable.

This went on for a few months. Richard Olivito sometimes received a police escort from sympathetic officers on his way home. A sheriff's deputy from out of town would sometimes come by and demand Richard take a ride on his Harley. Another set of deputies checked under his car before he started it. Still, flares were lit by their bedroom window during the night. They began to feel hunted. Eventually, Olivito's enemy didn't stop at threatening murder and breaking into their home.

One night, about eight months after the charges against Andre were dismissed, Joyce was in the bedroom, lying on the bed when a little red dot caught her eye as it played on the ceiling. She went downstairs to tell Richard what she had seen, but before she did, their neighbor, Dale Lackey, suddenly pounded his fists on the outside wall of their duplex, shouting, "Get down! Get down now!"

Lackey had been on his way home after he was out late shooting his bow when he and his relative saw the laser light flicker against the upper bedroom window. The large windows of the duplex offered unobstructed visibility from the front lawn into the living room and up the stairs into the second floor. Lackey put it together instantly when he then saw a crouched figure across the street. When he heard Lackey's warning, terror seized hold of Richard, and he immediately grabbed Joyce and forced her to the floor. They crawled up against the dividing wall between the kitchen and living room, one of the only places where someone out front would not be able to see them. Lackey ran after the gunman, who he fled into the wilderness and was never caught.

After this incident, Joyce and Olivito went to Virginia to stay at a friend's place for a month. They did not take calls and rarely spoke to his family. No one except his father and one Virginia friend knew of their whereabouts. Reluctantly, the couple came back to begin life again as if everything were normal. Olivito took up collecting the best counter-surveillance equipment on the market as a hobby. Concerned friends brought weapons and stood guard at Olivito's house.

It was during these years that Olivito strongly felt God's presence. He prayed while starting his car in the morning and slept with a loaded Glock under his pillow at night. Meanwhile, the perpetrator walked free, and the city litigated on his behalf. No investigation was opened into the assassination attempt. Olivito found out that having this veteran narcotics agent and the local prosecutor as enemies was a heavy cross to bear, but he wasn't going to be intimidated into submission.

The *Hython v. City of Steubenville* case went to the Sixth Circuit Court of Appeals with Chief Circuit Judge Merritt and his fellow fifteen justices in 1996. The Honorable Judge Merritt, a Democratic Carter appointee, was a brilliant, swaggering attorney from Nashville who liked the limelight and had friends in high places. Merritt stood up for his principles, but he was able to remain solidly part of the establishment. He was known for having a drink on the rocks while court was in session. Under Merritt's stewardship, the Sixth Circuit gained renown as the circuit court most often reversed by the U.S. Supreme Court.[61] For Olivito, the Sixth Circuit became an invaluable venue to escape the politics of the lower courts.

Before an elevated bank of judges and a backdrop of wood-paneling, Hython's defense disputed the allegations of the police officers that he broke any laws while they pursued him, contending that there was no probable cause for the officers to draw their guns and search his car, which violated his Fourth Amendment rights. Olivito accused the city of poor accounting because they did not retain the bag of crack allegedly thrown by Lamont Whatley.

Furthermore, the plaintiff contended that Prosecutor Stern had deprived him of his constitutional rights by advising the officers to arrest and charge him without probable cause. Olivito accused Prosecutor Stern of having a "custom" of bad probable cause determinations[62], thereby attempting to tie his client's claims to a policy of the City of Steubenville. Most attorneys would not pursue policy or *Monell* claims because of the prolonged litigation, the higher burdens of evidence and the unlikelihood of victory. Still, Law Director Gary Repella had become worried over the years because as the settlements mounted, the

[61] Mark Walsh. "A Sixth Sense: Sixth Circuit has surpassed the 9th as the most reversed appeals court. *ABA Journal*, 1 December 2012.

[62] *Hython v. City of Steubenville*. 94 F.3d 644. U.S. Court of Appeals, Sixth Circuit. 12 August 1996.

probability increased of a *Monell* claim citing a pattern of indifference and abuse. Repella explained, many years later:

> All cities fear it. Cities have to guard against it. First, you go to court over the event, then once that's decided you move to the ballbuster, a pattern of indifference and abuse, that's what you gotta be scared of; if a plaintiff can prove what happened is part of a pattern, it can bring a big judgment against you.

The plaintiff has to prove that the local public authorities approved of the policy responsible for the violation. Absolute immunity from suit would shield Stern from liability or criminal charges, but the city was on the hook and the language of the lawsuit sought to hold the municipality responsible for Stern's misdeeds. After delineating the inconsistencies in the defendant's account of the arrest, Olivito had concluded: "The defendants...have vainly attempted to construct an after-the-fact defense based upon the rule of 'totality of the circumstances.'"[63] However, to prove a policy claim accusing the city of a policy of false arrests, Olivito needed a dozen cases with the same pattern rather than one case where everything was crooked. Therefore, Chief Judge Merritt found no evidence of any such custom in the Jefferson County Prosecutor's Office.

The judge rebuked Olivito for his "overlong, poorly argued, and nearly incomprehensible appellate brief."[64] Olivito's writing was always overlong. When McNamara filed a Section 1983 civil rights complaint, it was two or three pages. Olivito's complaints were twenty to thirty pages. His strategy was to pack the brief with so many detailed facts as to overwhelm the defense in the motion to dismiss, the first hurdle for any civil rights case. Merritt was having none of it, but that didn't prejudice the prospects for Hython's case.

The institutional arm-wrestling ended with Judge Merritt and Judge Jones ruling in Hython's favor, citing that there were "genuine issues of material fact" whether or not King violated Hython's Fourth Amendment rights, implying that the county court needed to establish whose account was consistent with the facts. Stern received summary judgment because he relied on Lloyd King's description of events, but Chief Judge Merritt remanded the case back to the Southern District Court in Columbus to determine whether King had the same entitlement. In effect, the Sixth Circuit Court ordered the Southern District to find out who was lying. Based on this ruling, the Southern District later denied King summary judgment, an acknowledgment that the defendant's actions were not reasonable and usually a step towards a settle-

---

[63] Ibid. "Plaintiff's Memorandum in Opposition to Defendants' Motion for Summary Judgment." page. 19. Print.

[64] Ibid.

ment. The the county settled for $20,000, with Mingo kicking in $5,000. The next year, after the Southern District ruled against Terry, the county coughed up another $22,000. Stern was reportedly furious. For Olivito, after it was divvied up, the settlement worked out to an hourly rate of around $10. Joyce joked, "We're legal aid, without the aid."

According to local sources, King often wore a vest with "FBI Agent" on the back, although he was not an agent of the FBI. It turned out that King was not even a licensed peace officer in the State of Ohio. When he wasn't acting under the direct orders of Stern, Lloyd King was not authorized to arrest anyone. Stern was acting outside of the remit of his legal authority by deputizing agents who were not already experienced law enforcement officers. In doing so, he circumvented the obligations of the SPD regarding training, oversight, and accountability for peace officers.

Law Director Repella asked Stern to appoint King as a secret service officer in 1992 after people started asking questions that Stern didn't want to answer. King was hired by Sheriff Abdalla in 1985, but somewhere down the line, he came under Stern's command. Stern claimed King wasn't being paid and refused to say whether or not King was a secret service officer because of his policy of not commenting on secret service officers.[65]

Similar issues came up fifty years beforehand with a proposal to deputize a group of ministers and veterans of WWII as "special policemen." In 1946, a coalition of twelve Steubenville ministers suggested that the special policemen would be able to stamp out the rackets and political graft, if only they could be granted the legal powers to carry out a program of "rat extermination."[66] The ministers' proposal faced a divided city council where the Republicans were in favor, and the Democrats were against it. Stern merely bypassed city council. For those in the know, it was a big deal for this supposedly unpaid secret service officer to be outed in open court for planting drugs on defendants personally selected by the prosecutor.

However, the unconstitutional enforcement of vice laws was an old political maneuver that seemed never to lose its shine in Ohio because it riled up the white Protestant base. The KKK had used this strategy in the Mahoning Valley in the 1920s to exploit ethnic and religious animosities against Jews, Catholics, and African Americans, to

---

[65] Ibid.

[66] Norman E. Nygarrd. 12 Against The Underworld. *The Hobson Book Press*, 1947, Page 26.

swell their membership and build regional political influence.[67] The Methodists and the Anti-Saloon League used this passion of locals during Prohibition to push their agenda.[68] The famed "pistol-packing parsons" of 1946 had used religious piety and characterizations of racketeers as "rats" and "a cancer" to justify destroying their machines and, if they retaliated, burning down their places of business.[69]

Stephen Stern wasn't the type to greet elderly ladies on the street, but he understood the mentality of his constituents. Nothing excited locals like the prospect of imposing their values on others, which could enable Stern to go outside of the law to clean up the mean streets of Steubenville. He would need to subvert the provisions of the U.S. Constitution, but with absolute immunity, Prosecutor Stern could cover for the police and influence juries to suspect whoever the police set up on his orders.

A former official who wished to remain anonymous heard Stern declare, "If I can't indict you, I'll cost you money." Stern's original cause was noble. He believed he could succeed where prior public officials, law enforcement, religious reformers, and activists had failed. However, Stern had become corrupt. Like McCartney, he began conniving ways to seize cash or assets he felt entitled to. Following Stern's lead, King began stockpiling cocaine stolen from dealers who competed against his son. Olivito's ideological commitment combined with the city's vulnerability to civil rights claims created a problem for "Operation Stern Message." Olivito was committed to bringing about a moral transformation in Steubenville. He was like the pistol-packing parsons, an anachronism, incompatible with the times.

<><><>

One night, in early 1995, Olivito and his wife awoke, choking and gasping for air. Joyce immediately reached for a cigarette, but Olivito stopped her just before she lit it. The apartment was full of gas, which one spark would ignite. Olivito later discovered a tiny rubber

---

[67] William D. Jenkins. Steel Valley Klan: The Ku Klux Klan in Ohio's Mahoning Valley. *Kent State University Press*, 1990, page 156: "Heffernan also echoed the reformers in his struggle to enforce the vice laws. Limited by a police force that was understaffed, underpaid, and corruptible... He also created vice squads because he could exert greater control over their pay, evaluations, and firing."

[68] Ibid. page 25.

[69] Norman E. Nygarrd. 12 Against The Underworld. *The Hobson Book Press*, 1947, Page 145.

filament that snaked through his yard and covertly entered his house. He and Joyce never filed a police report. The assassination attempt only hardened their will. They lived by passion, and each outrage only stoked their shared determination. After this, however, even the feel of the Glock under his pillow no longer offered comfort.

Months later, in early 1995, Olivito called the DOJ in D.C. because he and Joyce wanted to follow up on a civil rights case Olivito had filed against the Roanoke, Virginia jail where Joyce's brother was serving time. By chance, Olivito was able to get his call routed to the Attorney General Janet Reno's office. An official answered the phone and was not at all pleased to receive a request for information that should have been handled by a subordinate. Nevertheless, after discussing the issue of the Virginia inmate, she asked, "Is there anything else I can help you with?" Olivito took this as a polite gesture to get off the phone.

"We have a problem," he confided, "but I can call back another time." To his surprise, the official asked, "Where are you calling from?"

"A small town called Steubenville in Ohio."

"I used to go to school in Bethany, West Virginia," she exclaimed. This was pivotal. "Talk to me," she half-invited, half-ordered.

"Well, my wife and I are being harassed by local law enforcement because I helped expose a pattern of planted evidence and false arrests by our police. Now, I've filed a civil rights lawsuit against the city, and we're being stalked. Someone tried to kill us."

"Can you come to D.C. this week?"

Olivito sensed God's hand in this, and he prayed after the call. Joyce and Olivito left the next day for D.C. Joyce felt like someone was outside the window of the hotel room where they stayed in Maryland. They had an appointment the next day with attorneys at the Justice Department. Olivito later wrote, *When the gates closed behind us the next day, Joyce and I felt as if we were coming in from the cold, like a couple on the run from a mafia hit team. For the first time in years, we could breathe and not look behind us. The release brought tears to our eyes.*

They met with attorneys from the Civil Rights Division (CRD) and told them about the stalking, death threats and assassination attempts. They told them about Prosecutor Stern and the task force, about Chief McCartney and the resistance of the community to acknowledge the abuses. They described the retaliation and terror that kept residents quiet and the corrupting influence of the mob. Just in time, too, because starting in 1994, the DOJ started shining a light into the darkest corners of the nation's police departments.[70]

Six months after Joyce and Olivito visited D.C., one of the DOJ attorneys, Mark Masling, called Olivito to announce that the DOJ had found probable cause to investigate. It vindicated his and Joyce's work and held the promise of putting a stop to the abuse of residents, not only in Jefferson County but in many other little towns that would hear about what happened in Steubenville.

Today, Ohio is as its state motto proclaims, "in the heart of it all." Ohio served as a historical pathway for the police union movement as it reverberated out from Pittsburgh during the early 20th century, which would be echoed by the DOJ as it began probing police departments. Today, Ohio is one of the only three states where seven or more DOJ investigations have been undertaken over patterns of police misconduct as of 2016. Not only have Columbus, Cincinnati, Steubenville, Warren, and Lorain been investigated, but Cleveland has hosted investigations twice. As of this writing, only California has hosted more investigations, and New York has an equal number, both of which have metropolitan areas with many more inhabitants than the total population of the State of Ohio.[71] As such, only Maryland and Louisiana have more investigations per capita than Ohio, primarily because they have much smaller populations. Ohio is easily in the top five states with the most federal attention for police misconduct. No state in the nation has had more consent decrees than Ohio,[72] reserved for the worst 3% of cases, yet no state has fought harder against DOJ enforcement.

As an example of what happened before the DOJ was given this enforcement authority, back in the spring of 1920, a scandal emerged in Cleveland when a chief municipal judge was found to have many "underworld connections" and implicated in a murder. In response, a seven-hundred-page report was written about the Cleveland

---

[70] Congress gave the DOJ the power to investigate and prosecute local police misconduct in 1994 with the Violent Crime Control and Law Enforcement Act. Thereafter, the Civil Rights Division could investigate and the Special Litigation Section could file suit against cities for violating citizens' rights.

[71] Sarah Childress. "Fixing the Force." *Frontline PBS and Washington Post*, 14 December 2015.

[72] Police Executive Research Forum. "Civil Rights Investigations of Local Police: Lessons Learned." 2013.

criminal justice system.[73] In 1922, all the problems still festering today were revealed, but little was done. When such a pattern emerges, it is typical for every case handled by the corrupt officers or officials to be reviewed and potentially overturned.

In Jefferson County, on top of a mafia history that has inspired writers for a century, a few informed public records searches could turn up transcripts of the prosecutor plotting to kill a guy, an officer planting drugs, and the sheriff accepting bribes. If one went further back, there were murders, lynchings. One death well-known among older African Americans involved Michael Jarrett, age 19, for dating a white girl in 1981. Police traced the gun used to blow Jarrett's brains out to a white youth, who was arrested and then released, although 500 people marched to protest police inaction in the case.[74] Nevertheless, in Steubenville, no review of questionable convictions was made and no commission would be appointed to issue a report enumerating problems well known since the 1920s. It was the DOJ's turn to implement a superior solution.

---

[73] Roscoe Pound et al. *Criminal Justice in Cleveland*. The Cleveland Foundation, 1922.

[74] Manning Marable. *How Capitalism Undeveloped Black America, Problems in Race, Political Economy, and Society*. Haymarket Books, 2015.

## 5

Our city has a bad reputation. They know about the lawlessness of this city all over our nation.

-Councilman Andrew Matigan in 1946[75]

In 1995, the DOJ sent two attorneys, Margo Schlanger and Mark Masling, to investigate. They later came to meet Olivito in his office in the Sinclair Building. After taking their seats, one of them remarked that they noticed two men in plainclothes walking behind them through an alley from the parking lot around the block.

"Do you think we've been followed?"

"Welcome to Steubenville! This is my hometown!" Olivito declared with a flourish. The investigators didn't laugh; they called the DOJ for backup. Olivito had already told them about the Hython case, but he got out his case files and began to recount the stories of other malcontents in Steubenville. The investigation seemed to grow out of the investigation of the Pittsburgh police. James McNamara had sent the DOJ court documents illustrating the SPD's problems, but so had many other lawyers and civil rights groups around the country. When Olivito and Joyce showed up in the DOJ's Washington office, terrified and telling stories of death threats and assassination attempts, there was an impact that court documents couldn't match.

Schlanger joined the DOJ after graduating from Yale Law School and clerking for Supreme Court Justice Ruth Bader Ginsburg. Schlanger would later serve as the chief civil rights official in the Department of Homeland Security and teach at Harvard, Washington University, and the University of Michigan. Masling would go on to become a senior attorney in the Office of Professional Responsibility and the Office of the Inspector General. In 2006, he would be tapped to lead the investigation into the "politicized hiring" by a Bush administration official in the CRD. When they came to Steubenville, Schlanger was a promising attorney at the beginning of her career, and Masling was a senior trial lawyer at the CRD.

Olivito remembers that he and Joyce met with Schlanger and Masling one night in a local restaurant. Olivito told them of a young man in his early twenties he briefly represented who had made enough

---

[75] Norman E. Nygarrd. 12 Against The Underworld. *The Hobson Book Press*, 1947, Page 51.

money selling drugs to live in penthouses and have a limo driver. Olivito recounted that Lloyd King Jr. invited him to go to another town under the pretense of playing cards. On the way, an unknown vehicle drove up and shot the guy in the back of the head. The crime was never solved, and no one was indicted. However, the boy's girlfriend alleged that King Jr. was the perpetrator. Upon hearing this story, one of the attorneys asked Olivito if they could speak to the victim's girlfriend.

"She won't come within the city limits anymore," replied Olivito with a piercing glare.

"Why?" asked one of the attorneys.

"What do you think we're talking about here?" Olivito asked coldly. The place was nearly empty, only one other patron was seated nearby. The server remarked, "That man over there seems very interested in your conversation." She noted that the man hadn't ordered anything to eat, but he remained a few tables away as the conversation wore on.

Subsequently, the investigators were able to visit the girl outside of Steubenville, but nothing ever came of it. Christy Lopez, a former consent decree monitor and DOJ official who worked on various pattern or practice investigations, noted:

> Usually [serious criminal investigations] are handled by the criminal division...We have to be careful when we find out about these kinds of crimes. If we tell a police supervisor without knowing about relationships, we could put a whistle-blower in danger. There have been conversations with local prosecutors where we said, 'This is what we're hearing. You need to look into this,' but we have to know who is trustworthy locally. We could just be telling a bad cop's friend.

Olivito also told the federal attorneys of the deaths of women alleged to be sex workers, some of whom were found hanging in abandoned buildings. Their deaths were rumored to serve as a message to others who thought about exposing the sexual misconduct and extortion of Steubenville police. Joseph Koniski remembered hearing about dead prostitutes and that their deaths faded away, unsolved, as they had half a century before. Sometimes, when a prostitute was found dead in Steubenville, locals suspected she knew too much. Although the guy on the street might conclude that prostitutes don't commit suicide, their deaths often were classified as suicides or went unsolved.[76]

Olivito had already heard an allegation of sexual misconduct concerning an SPD officer. One day, he received a phone call at the office. An anonymous voice spoke of being forced at gunpoint to perform oral sex on a Steubenville police officer, but the victim was too

---

[76] Norman E. Nygarrd. 12 Against The Underworld. *The Hobson Book Press*, 1947, Page 56.

afraid to come forward publicly. This information and more was given to the attorneys from the DOJ, which included "sexually coercive practices,"[77] as well as racial profiling, among themes of the investigation, although no evidence was ever found to substantiate them.

Finally, they asked Olivito if they could use Olivito's office as a covert meeting place and staging point for their investigation. Olivito agreed. A former attorney who worked in the DOJ during the Steubenville investigation confirmed that the DOJ looks at local civil rights lawyers as sources of information. Margo Schlanger heard the name of Rosalind Watson as a potential source because of her son's frequent interactions with the courts. Rosalind said she kept missing Margo's calls, but when they finally talked, Rosalind remembered a woman told her, "We're from the Justice Department. Your name was given to us. We would like to come in and talk to some people." She agreed to host the attorneys and a few local people, who according to Rosalind, "didn't have anything to do with the police but had problems with them."

Rosalind and her husband later hosted five young African American guys and two attorneys, "a woman and a man." The meeting lasted about five hours, which surprised Rosalind, who tried to leave them alone so they could speak more freely. She did overhear the guys tell the attorneys that the police had stolen money and dope from them. Rosalind confirmed, "It was a lawyer who had called her. Olivito. He had called them...I found out whose office they were in. Olivito's office. That's whose office they were in." She noted that Ms. Schlanger had said, "We're in town," reasoning, "I don't know what hotel they were staying at, but it was too late to go back to D.C." Rosalind recalled, "That's when the consent decree came out, after that."

DOJ attorneys requested documents pertaining to over one hundred civil rights complaints, according to *The Columbus Dispatch*.[78] In contrast to the refusals previously given to Olivito, the city responded to the DOJ by giving them enough paperwork and court documents to fill a pickup truck. Many years later, Law Director Repella confirmed, "They sent us a letter. They started talking to community people. They did a record's request and took a truckload of documents. Six months later, they threatened to sue us."

<><><>

---

[77] Joe Lawlor. "Steubenville, Justice reach agreement." *The Herald-Star*, 24 August 1997.

[78] Bruce Cadwallader. "Auditor watches over police Steubenville changes its ways to meet consent decree criteria." *The Columbus Dispatch*, 23 April 2000.

In August of 1997, the DOJ filed a federal complaint against the City of Steubenville. Rather than contest the charges, the SPD, the city, and the city manager signed a consent decree the same day. The agreement between the DOJ and the city was one of the first of its kind, and the model implemented in Steubenville would be applied in Section 14141 "pattern or practice" investigations and agreements afterward. Four months before Steubenville, Pittsburgh was the first city in America to sign a consent decree in April of 1997, against the advice of the local FOP. Many reforms were instituted against the union's active resistance, as would later happen in other cities, including Steubenville. Law Director Repella confirmed, "We sat down and negotiated. We decided to implement the changes."

Professor James J. Fyfe, the former NYPD lieutenant, turned celebrity police researcher, took the stand as an expert witness.[79] He explained the value of some provisions of the consent decree, including revisions of the SPD guidelines on the use of force, field interrogation, searches, seizures, arrests and record keeping. Interestingly, Fyfe commented on the phenomenon of "contempt of cop" charges, such as resisting arrest or assaulting a police officer, as indicative of problem officers because, for them, it becomes more about policing perceived disrespect, rather than "any legitimate law enforcement purpose."[80]

The decree cited "[The SPD]'s management systems for police training, misconduct investigations, supervision and discipline," in a detailed list of failures.[81] The DOJ accused the SPD of retaliating against those who complained of or witnessed misconduct, which may have been based on vivid descriptions by Olivito and Joyce of being

---

[79] *United States v. City of Steubenville.* S. D. Ohio. 4 March 2005. Print.

[80] "Reasonable police administrators and other public officials have come to recognize the existence of a category of so-called 'contempt of cop' arrests which typically involve charges in which officers are the only complainants. Such charges include assaults on officers; resisting arrest; and such public order offenses as disorderly conduct; public intoxication; and obstruction of justice. Review of such charges… indicates that some small percentage of officers repeatedly are involved in such cases, while others rarely or never make such arrests. This research also shows that such charges often are filed because officers were offended by citizens' demeanor rather than to accomplish any legitimate law enforcement purpose."

[81] *United States of America v. City of Steubenville.* S. D. Ohio Eastern Division, 4 March 2005.

stalked and terrorized for years. McNamara might have told them how cops in plain clothes sat in the bar of his hotel and followed him around. The DOJ further charged the SPD with engaging in a pattern of false arrests and charges against known critics of the police, persons disliked by police and those who behaved disrespectfully to police. One resident reported that an officer followed them for two years after a smart remark during a traffic stop.

Chief McCartney was reluctant to admit there was a problem, as he had been for two decades, and he found the newly granted powers of federal civil rights enforcement hostile and disconcerting. So, he counterattacked those he saw as his enemies, indirectly vilifying the DOJ in a comment to CNN: "I think it was railroaded. I think it was very sneaky. I think it was intimidation and I don't appreciate that."[82]

In the twilight of his career, however, McCartney decided to open a dialogue with Richard Olivito. They met various times in his office, and they came to an understanding. Olivito came to see Jerry McCartney as an officer who had come up through the ranks. McCartney believed in what he was doing no less than Olivito. The chief began to respect Olivito's motives for doing what he did and told him so. They discussed who was responsible for what happened with the Hython case. Olivito later wrote, *We also came to agree on one major thing, that it wasn't the police department... alone... that was the problem in Jefferson County.*

The DOJ wanted Chief McCartney replaced with someone from outside of Steubenville. Fort Steuben's FOP Lodge #1 moved the local district court to allow the union to intervene in the litigation, arguing that the provisions of the consent decree violated the collective bargaining agreement between the FOP and the city. According to the FOP's motion, every officer deserved a chance at becoming chief, so the chief should come from the internal ranks. The FOP was unable to beat the DOJ, but it wasn't just the FOP that opposed having an outsider replace the chief; the city fathers were prepared to fight for years against it, even if the outsider candidate was more qualified.

Olivito wanted to start a citizen review board for complaints against the SPD, which has long been the dream of reformers across the nation. He was ready to put together such an organization and doubtlessly ready to lead it, encouraging others to participate. According to Olivito, the young investigators told him that the DOJ would hand down indictments on those implicated in their investigation. That never happened. Olivito maintained that Schlanger told him to go "three thousand miles away." Years later, she denied advising Olivito to leave Steubenville and declined requests for an interview. Schlanger

---

[82] Pierre Thomas. "Police misconduct allegations not confined to big cities." *CNN.com*, 10 November 1999.

told *PBS Frontline* and *The Washington Post* that McNamara's civil rights cases caught the DOJ's attention. Schlanger did give Olivito an oblique shout-out on the website of the Civil Rights Litigation Clearinghouse, an organization she founded. On the webpage devoted to the Steubenville consent decree, she listed Olivito's name alongside James McNamara, Bill Hinnant, as well as others from Ohio and D.C. On occasion, she gave his contact information to reporters interested in the Steubenville consent decree.

For Olivito, the chief's respect did not restrain the retaliation of Steubenville's cops, or whoever was acting on their behalf. *The Cleveland Scene* magazine reported in 2004, "Even after the DOJ took over the SPD, the stalking and death threats multiplied."[83] Olivito later confided that he and Joyce were in a state of total exhaustion. His brother told him, "You did the work of the FBI." They didn't care about taking any credit for any role in the consent decree. However, they were both annoyed when the local NAACP claimed credit when they had done so little for the local black community. Delores Wiggins, the cantankerous African American woman who became NAACP president in January of 1997, may not have known how her predecessor had turned a blind eye to police abuse.

Olivito and Joyce fled to North Carolina. It was only because of Joyce that he was able to sustain the legal battle against the city. He benefited from her instincts, encouragement, and strength. Eventually, after laying low on North Carolina beaches, he couldn't stay away from Ohio, but Joyce couldn't go back, so they agreed to separate. She told Richard, "I know why we met and married. Our purpose was the consent decree." Many years later, Olivito reflected, "When I lost Joyce, I lost a shield." Olivito didn't show his face in Steubenville for almost eight years. Then, just before the consent decree was lifted, he came out of the woodwork, filing a slew of police misconduct lawsuits.

Steubenville City Council was not enthusiastic about federal enforcement of police reform. Councilman Craig Petrella was quoted on August 29, 1997, saying that the consent decree was going to "tweak...current policies" of the SPD, which was "one of the best police departments in the Tri-State Area."[84] For Petrella, the purpose of

---

[83] Aina Hunter. "Blue Mob: Pity those caught by the Warren police, who rule with iron fists and rubber gloves." *Cleveland Scene*, 25 February 2004.

[84] Joe Lawlor. Steubenville, Justice reach agreement. *The Herald-Star*, 24 August 1997.

the consent decree was "to get rid of frivolous lawsuits." *The Herald-Star* chided Petrella for these "bold" comments, reporting, "To his credit, Petrella has since backpedaled and said there have been problems."[85] City Manager Gary DeFour was also the target of *The Herald-Star*'s condemnation of his assertion that federal scrutiny of the SPD arose due to "events that happened twenty-five years ago." *The Herald-Star* trumpeted its approval of the decree in an editorial entitled, "Justice report takes away chance for police denial."[86] In a show of moral courage not seen in decades, the newspaper requested the city leaders "for some sign...that their heads aren't permanently buried in the sand."[87]

On September 2, Edward "Skip" Mixon walked out of a city council meeting because of his frustration with the attitude of his fellow council members. Mixon vented to *The Herald-Star*, "It's like they're saying, 'Oh this justice department thing is done with now. This isn't our problem anymore.'"[88] Council was discussing the issue of who would be contracted for the work of rewriting the SPD's policies. Mixon was not sure that the consent decree was going to change anything because the city was still in denial. The chief would rather have died than acknowledge any merit to the allegations, possibly because the DOJ's findings indicated that the pattern of civil rights abuses was squarely his fault. McCartney blamed the city for not providing the money for training, sidestepping the issue of inadequate supervision and discipline. He also fell back on the 1992-BCI investigation of Olivito's letter to the NAACP, arguing that "the department was exonerated because the grand jury didn't indict any police officers."[89] He was grasping at straws, but he wasn't going to allow those he saw as his enemies the satisfaction.

Law Director Repella, a former police prosecutor, understood that history was in the making. He told *The Herald-Star*, "This is a historic and monumental change because there's a federal judge sitting in Columbus overseeing all of this. If we're ever going to get out of this

---

[85] Editorial Board. "Our opinion: Justice report takes away chance for police denial." *The Herald-Star*, 29 August 1997.

[86] Ibid.

[87] Ibid.

[88] Joe Lawlor. "Mixon not happy with council reasons." *The Herald-Star*, 3 September 1997.

[89] Joe Lawlor. "Police used excessive force, Justice reports." *The Herald-Star*, 23 August 1997.

consent decree, we're going to have to be in full compliance."[90] Chief McCartney got hung up on with the language of the decree, "I didn't see any 'mays' in there. All I saw were 'shalls.' If I didn't uphold the decree, I would be in contempt of court."[91] Though he ferociously opposed being commanded to respect people's rights, the chief promised to fulfill the demands of the decree, and once an expert was procured, the difficult work of police reform would begin in earnest, for the first time in U.S. history.

Former longtime Police Chief Charlie Reynolds was selected to serve as the auditor to keep tabs on the SPD's progress as a condition of the decree. From 2000 to 2013, only nine out of 325 police departments were saddled with an auditor.[92] *The Herald-Star* drew attention to the fact that Steubenville was only the second police department in the entire nation to be sued by the U.S. DOJ for a pattern of civil rights violations.[93]

Charlie Reynolds had been a police chief for twenty-six years and later consulted in eighteen states and internationally on police organizational and management issues.[94] He also worked as an auditor or deputy monitor with four other police departments, but Steubenville was the first. For Reynolds, police brutality was an administrative issue he knew how to weed out with robust management systems. He told *The Columbus Dispatch*, "I understand the inner workings of a police department and understand their management systems. From my perspective, everybody started off with a clean slate here."[95] He was frank with members of the media, and he later met with the victims of the SPD at the behest of Skip Mixon.

Chief McCartney was expecting Reynolds to come down on the city like a sledgehammer, but Reynolds was more of a police chief

---

[90] Joe Lawlor. "Judge OKs Steubenville consent decree." *The Herald-Star*, 4 September 1997.

[91] Joe Lawlor. "Here are details of agreement." *The Herald-Star*, 1 September 1997.

[92] Stephen Rushin. "Federal Enforcement of Police Reform." *Fordham Law Review* Vol. 82, Issue 6, page. 3226.

[93] Editorial board. "Our opinion: Justice report takes away chance for police denial." *The Herald-Star,* 29 August 1997.

[94] "Charles Reynolds." *AELE Law Enforcement.*

[95] Bruce Cadwallader. "Auditor watches over police Steubenville changes its ways to meet consent decree criteria." *The Columbus Dispatch*, 23 April 2000.

mentor than a police reformer, which may be why he was chosen. Roy Austin, who worked in the Criminal Section of the CRD and later served as Deputy Assistant Attorney General for Civil Rights, explained, "A monitor's job is not to replace a police chief in any way shape or form. A monitor's job is to be able to be on the outside observing, not just the chief, but how the entire operation runs." Reynolds tried to allay the SPD's misgivings, saying, "You shouldn't be afraid of me...I don't see or feel from [the DOJ] a desire to have the police department do anything more than what is generally expected of a police department."[96]

However, McCartney's annoyance with the idea of oversight was contagious. Reynolds stated in an interview that the SPD officers and command staff were "uncertain, inquisitive and misinformed about the decree."[97] During one meeting with senior staff, a sergeant complained of the requirement of the decree that they fully investigate every citizen complaint. After listening to the sergeant describe "with some contempt" the type of people who filed complaints against the police, Reynolds asked him, "When a citizen believes he or she has a complaint, where should he or she go?"[98] Then he rattled off several potential officials that could handle complaints, including the sheriff, the county prosecutor, state patrol, BCI, the AG, the U.S. attorney, the FBI and the media. The sergeant realized the correct answer and replied, "They should come right here."

The contempt Reynolds noticed in the statements by the sergeant ultimately emanated from Chief McCartney who told CNN, "A lot of people that we have arrested here I consider...to be undesirables."[99] Although Reynolds handled the misgivings of the SPD frankly and transparently, he admitted that, "There are those still resisting the decree for reasons even they cannot explain..." Reynolds did not say that the chief was one of them, but according to Reynolds' reports on the SPD's progress, McCartney failed to attend the training required of all officers. This type of "check-the-box" requirement was typical of early consent decrees. Now, police chiefs are given more latitude on how to achieve the goals set by the DOJ. Regardless, Chief McCartney was not on board, and it showed.

---

[96] Ibid.

[97] Police Assessment Resource Center. "Interview with Charlie Reynolds." November 2002.

[98] Ibid.

[99] Pierre Thomas. "Police misconduct allegations not confined to big cities." *CNN.com*, 10 November 1999.

Reynolds' quarterly reports were at least fifty pages long, and he made detailed notes on areas where the SPD failed to deliver on the requirements of the decree. In general, Reynolds was understanding, but it was his job to point the problems out and the city's responsibility to remedy them. He painstakingly made the chief aware that, if he disagreed with anything in his quarterly report, the chief could come and talk to him about it.[100] Nevertheless, according to Reynolds' reports, the chief began to leave a captain in charge while he took time off.

In the sixth quarterly report, Reynolds observed that the city had developed the relevant policies and procedures during the first year of the decree and worked to familiarize officers with the new policies through training.[101] Implementation began during the last quarter of 1998, but in the first quarter of 1999, operational compliance proved to be a challenge and "progress was minimal." During the sixth quarter, the city backslid, decreasing compliance. Command staff was in short supply because the chief was absent, and one captain was wearing three hats: training officer, systems administrator and operations commander. Meanwhile, the rank and file drained away as veteran officers left the department. In an interview, Reynolds mentioned that the "necessary talent and experience was not available internally and funds were not readily available to hire outside technical assistance." Still, Reynolds was always optimistic and constantly praised the efforts of the SPD.

"The establishment and ongoing effectiveness of the Internal Affairs (IA) Division is a significant accomplishment for the city and SPD," Reynolds wrote in June 1999. The city was required to rent a separate office space for IA as a condition of the decree, and two officers—a captain and a sergeant, would work full time investigating their fellow officers.

CNN quoted Law Director Gary Repella in November of 1999 saying, "Since the decree has been put in, we're working on our third year of no lawsuits."[102] Repella must have forgotten that he told *The Wheeling Intelligencer* in February that two lawsuits had recently been dismissed, noting that it had been twenty-three years since the city had

---

[100] Police Assessment Resource Center. "Interview with Charlie Reynolds." November 2002.

[101] Charles D. Reynolds. "Auditor's Quarterly Report: Compliance Audit for the Steubenville, Ohio Police Department." April 1- June 30, 1999. Print.

[102] Pierre Thomas. "Police misconduct allegations not confined to big cities." *CNN.com*, 10 November 1999.

enjoyed a moment in which there was no pending litigation.[103] Perhaps, he meant settlements rather than lawsuits. In any case, city officials were eager to tout the improvements and with good reason. The city had lost its insurance coverage twice and was required to pay a rate $360,000 a year just for coverage because of court settlements over civil rights violations.[104] Since then, the city's insurance company lowered its premium by two-thirds because of the increased training.

Chief McCartney was quoted in *The Herald-Star* stating, "No one likes change, but we have to change."[105] Citizen complaints could be made anonymously, an important condition of the decree because of the alleged retaliation against those who filed complaints in the past. However, the local FOP managed to remove that provision from later SPD union contracts. Despite Reynolds' praise for the IA program, he described the city's approach to officer discipline as "inconsistent," saying that it "continues to be reluctant to embrace the concept of preventative discipline."[106] Instead of counseling an officer immediately after the first instance of misconduct, the SPD brass would wait until an officer became involved in more serious incidents. The decree required the city to conduct a multiple complaint review when an officer was the subject of three complaints in three years, but Reynolds reported that the thoroughness of the reviews during the second quarter of 2000 was inconsistent in the cases of seven officers.[107]

Reynolds admitted that he had the most difficulty measuring compliance with the decree's requirements on supervision and discipline because, "This entails more than developing policies, completing forms and checking the correct boxes."[108] He stated that supervision and discipline must be "internalized and practiced not only by the chief

---

[103] Eric Ayres. "Repella: No litigation against police for first time in 23 years." *The Wheeling Intelligencer,* 3 February 1999.

[104] Ibid.

[105] Joe Lawlor. "Police want to move 2 to new department." *The Herald-Star*, 27 August 1997.

[106] Charles D. Reynolds. "Auditor's Quarterly Report: Compliance Audit for the Steubenville, Ohio Police Department." April 1- June 30, 1999, Page 23. Print.

[107] Charles D. Reynolds. "Auditor's Quarterly Report: Compliance Audit for the Steubenville, Ohio Police Department." April 1- June 30, 2000, Page xi. Print.

[108] Police Assessment Resource Center. "Interview with Charlie Reynolds." November 2002.

but by middle managers, first line supervisors and ultimately by the officers on the street." McNamara described this pattern for years, and Chief McCartney always denied it. The decree rebuked every line of argument the chief had relied on to shield the SPD from criticism, including the excuse that civil lawsuits didn't prove anything. According to the decree, civil suits were to be used by the city as "supervisory tools to alert management of potential misconduct," rather than as annoyances to be denied and passed off to the law department for settlement.

All the same, the chief continued to protect his officers against discipline when they were the subject of complaints. Reynolds noted that one IA investigation lingered unresolved because the chief refused to use a polygraph to discover if two officers accused of theft were lying.[109] Most of the cases decided by superior courts involving polygraphs concerned whether and when chiefs could discipline officers for refusing to submit to the tests. The case law differs by state, but it appears to be novel that a chief would refuse to use polygraphs in IA investigations *on behalf* of officers. As chief of police, McCartney's attitude remained essentially unchanged from his former role as president of the FOP; he always came out in defense of officers, instead of concerning himself with the institutional integrity of the department or its reputation in the public domain.

Stern, at first, denied the DOJ's allegations of civil rights abuse, but he later acquiesced as if it were his idea. Stern's role with the drug task force and his abuse of his office indicting victims of police misconduct with 'cover' charges evaded scrutiny. When asked if this problem was something that the DOJ was watching in the 1990s, former DOJ attorney and monitor Christy Lopez acknowledged, "This is something the DOJ is not doing so well. There wasn't as much innovation in the 90s. Consent decrees were in such a nascent stage then...Now that the DOJ has been doing this for a while, we've developed methods to apply this to courts, as in Ferguson."

Stern ran for the judgeship of the Jefferson County Court of Common Pleas in '97, but he lost to Mascio, his erstwhile jogging partner. Judge Olivito retired from the bench that same year.[110] Joseph J. Bruzzese, Jr., Frank Bruzzese's brother, took his seat on the bench of the Common Pleas Court. One era ended, and another commenced, but it would be years until the changing of the guard was complete. .Stern stayed on as prosecutor, but he eventually clashed with Judge Mascio when his crusade against gambling ran up against the investments of

---

[109] Ibid. Page xii.

[110] Staff. "Judge Dominick E. Olivito." *Weirton Daily Times*, 5 July 2009.

Mascio's associates, which Stern then used as a means to disqualify the judge. Then, the deterioration of the alliance between Stern and Mascio became part of the public record in *Stern v. Mascio*, a bare-knuckle legal battle, which the Olivitos watched with a mixture of amusement and annoyance.

What few people knew is that Stern had filed for bankruptcy around the time he became prosecutor. Rumors between insiders said that Stern allegedly took a loan from Dr. Frank L. Petrola, a mobbed-up doctor who was on all sorts of boards and commissions, out on the country club golf course, meeting with decision-makers and doing them favors. Afterward, Petrola and his allies could manipulate their man Stern, the prosecutor who wanted to get his hands on power, but who became a mid-level bagman in a pre-established power structure with the mafia on top.

## 6

U.S. Department of Justice
Civil Rights Section
10th St. & Constitution Ave. NW
Wash. D.C.   20530                                    July 17, 2000

To Whom it May Concern,

        I am writing to you at the suggestion of Special Agent Philip
W. Lucas of the Ohio Bureau of Criminal Investigation.  Mr. Lucas came
to visit me at MCCI in regards to the allegations I've made against
Prosecutor Steve Stern (Jefferson County, Ohio) and the Steubenville,
Ohio  Police Dept. which I have listed on the Internet at www.vhfsys.
com/norris, see Joe Koniski.

        Although Mr. Lucas deemed these allegations to be true, he in-
formed me that his department could not get involved unless recommended
by a prosecuting attorney or another law enforcement agency.  Being as
the allegations concerned both of the aforementioned parties it was
improbable that they would recommend investigating themselves.

        Therefore Mr. Lucas suggested I pursue my quest for justice by
contacting you in hopes that you would peruse the material of Joe Koniski
on the Internet which might lead to your recommending the OBCI to investigate both Prosecutor Stern and the Steubenville Police Dept. which will
hopefully lead to exonerating me.

        I realize that I have made some serious allegations such as
prosecutorial misconduct by ordering his vice squad to frame people,
to rob people and to MURDER people, but I am prepared to substantiate
and prove each and every allegation.

        You may better understand the scope of this conspiracy which
led to my incarceration by viewing the material at www.vhfsys.com/norris.

        Thank you for your consideration and I am anxiously awaiting
your reply.

                                        *Joe Koniski*

                                        Joe Koniski 218-518
                                        POB 1812
                                        Marion, Ohio

When Koniski wrote the DOJ, he had spent a decade in prison. By 2000, the Steubenville police were already under a consent decree, and Prosecutor Stern had retired. There was public recognition that the police had engaged a pattern of false arrests and retaliation, but the authorities stopped short of demanding an investigation and overturning of all tainted criminal cases. Local officials were making a good faith effort, as far as the DOJ knew, and that was enough. So, Koniski remained in prison.

Joseph K. Koniski spent twenty-five years of his life as a bookie in Steubenville. His business was one of a conspicuous number of illegal gambling houses posing as cigar stores in the 1970s. He knew why Steubenville was known as Little Chicago. One night, a narcotics officer from the Federal Drug Task Force knocked on his door. At the time, Koniski was addicted to cocaine and was financing deals. However, instead of busting him, the officer warned that Koniski's life was in danger. Koniski didn't believe him, but the man came again the next night with tape recordings of Jefferson County Prosecutor Stephen Stern and a member of his Federal Drug Task Force, "conspiring to set people up, rob people, and even murder."[111]

In his living room, Koniski and his wife recognized the voice of Prosecutor Stern talking to his special agent, Earl George.[112]

"If you can figure out a pattern where he is making his drop I got a guy who will look him up. I got a guy that will strong arm him," George muttered.

Prosecutor Stern responded with a leading question, "Take Ratsy out right on the spot?"

"Okay, yeah," said George. "No problem."

As he heard this, Koniski sat back in his chair and felt his stomach turn. His nickname was Ratsy. His heart began to race, as he asked himself when the killer might come. The eyes of the officer narrowed. If Koniski was scared, he might pay up for the tapes.

"Okay, if you can't get him that way before I leave with Lloyd, I don't want to blow it."

Lloyd King was a secret service agent of the Jefferson County Prosecutor's Office, an African American "as underhanded as they come," according to Koniski. Next, Stern instructed George:

"Just leave right after that happens. I mean just be gone."

"I got somebody to strong arm him. I'm not worried about that," George replied.

---

[111] Ibid.

[112] Joseph J. Koniski. "Transcript of Stephen Stern Tape Recording." *Innocent Inmates of Ohio Association.*

"You're not supposed to come alone. I didn't know you were talking $30,000 as a witness chair or I wouldn't," George went on, "Yeah. When his nephew was arrested, he had $37,000. They gave the money back to Ratsy."

"Is that right? I don't understand it," said Stern. "What's wrong with all of you? Can't we get someone on a major bust that you bought your way out of him already? We need to set someone up, have him arrested, have him busted, and go to a certain attorney and buy their way out."

"Oh, that can't be me. I don't think...because he would suspect me too much with stuff like that going on."

"Okay, if you get a call from that [District Attorney] down there..." said Stern, insinuating that he could arrange special treatment. The officer stopped the tape with a wry grin and eyes like drills. He wanted cash for tapes, but Koniski compelled him to produce copies of the tapes and a notarized affidavit swearing that Stern had instructed one of his men to plant drugs in the house of Ed Cunningham, a local guy, while Lloyd King waited outside to make the arrest. Koniski declined to reveal how he compelled the officer to do his bidding. He only remarked, looking straight ahead with a mischievous smile, "It's too late to charge me for anything I've done." Then, he shuffled away.

When the affidavit detailing Stern's conduct was presented in court, the narcotics officer recanted his statement and admitted the drugs were planted.[113] He testified that he and his partner had been working undercover for prosecutors in three states, sending dozens of people to prison. Much to Stern's chagrin and Cunningham's tearful elation, Judge Dominick Olivito threw out the case. Koniski remembered that Judge Olivito tore up the paper listing the charges. After word leaked out that Koniski was responsible for his humiliation, Stern indicted Koniski for his past involvement in drug-trafficking and sent him to prison for longer than any of his accomplices.

When Koniski was hawking newspapers on the corners downtown, men from out of town would ask him to point out which houses were brothels. Though only five years old, he knew where love was for sale, and he charged 25 cents for that information. In these subtle ways, locals could not resist the profits to be reaped from vice, like the crime families from Cleveland and Pittsburgh. Eventually, mothers defended prostitution, fearing their daughters would fall prey to lecherous men from out-of-town who brought commerce to the area. Money and fear

---

[113] Joseph J. Koniski. "Statement of Events: Chapter 1." *Innocent Inmates of Ohio Association*, p. 4-5.

undermined their Christian values, though they knew vice was a cancer. Courageous ministers harangued against it, but they were bought and sold, replaced by silent traitors of the good.

Koniski had a prominent nose and an easy smile, but like many young Ohioans, he didn't like the rules and set about breaking them. In high school, Koniski and his friend Jerry McCartney got caught shoplifting and were taken downtown to the police station. Luckily for them, McCartney's dad was the police chief, so they were not charged, and the papers never got ahold of the story. It was their first taste of the perversion of justice. Koniski later went into organized crime, and McCartney went into law enforcement. In the city of Steubenville, this meant they would be seeing a lot of each other.

After serving in the U.S. Air Force, Koniski went to work for a metallurgical company where he assisted the company's bookie. Then, he started his own book. Koniski later wrote, "A bookie not only made money but was protected under the aegis of the local law enforcement agencies. The reason he was protected is because he paid off the cops."[114] According to him, Officer McCartney and Officer Leon Stinson were "two officers who never hesitated to pick up their graft money."[115] A local source who wished to remain anonymous indicated that the chief continued to collect weekly pay-offs even after the DOJ sued his police department.

After getting out of prison in the late 1980s, Koniski partnered with two card sharks in another gambling business, this time according to the letter of the law. Pete Demos, a retired captain from the sheriff's office and George Fisher, a guy from out of town, had assured Koniski that their business plan was above board. So, when the police showed up expecting an envelope of cash, Koniski refused to pay, confident that he was in the right. The police began harassing him, so Koniski complained in writing to city hall and the FBI.[116] In effect, Koniski bit the Black Hand.

Days later, Chief McCartney showed up in Koniski's shop with Captain Stinson and two patrolmen. According to Koniski, McCartney shouted, "What the hell do you think you're doing?" When Koniski coolly replied that he was just trying to get along, the chief

---

[114] Joseph J. Koniski. "Joe has been released on parole!" *Innocent Inmates of Ohio Association*, 2002-2004.

[115] Joseph J. Koniski. "Statement of Events: Chapter 1." *Innocent Inmates of Ohio Association*.

[116] Joseph J. Koniski. "Complaint Filed with the FBI." *Innocent Inmates of Ohio Association*.

warned, "Not in my town! You're never going to operate here. I'm either going to run you out of town or send you back to prison!"[117]

The stout, stiff-lipped second-generation Chief of Police was devoted to maintaining the *status quo*. It had always been the same deal for criminal entrepreneurs: an envelope of cash was like a temporary operating license. The next day, he and his business partners convened at the office of Fisher's attorney. Koniski's business partners admonished him, and Fisher's attorney advised them to pay the bribe or cease operations. Koniski later claimed that he was against it, but he agreed. Accordingly, Fisher gave his attorney a thousand dollars in an envelope to deliver to the police station. The attorney reportedly gave it to Captain Burchfield, who said he would see that the chief received it.

The police knew all the operators of the underworld. They had been walking in and out of gambling joints for a century without making arrests, and the reason why was well known to everyone. In 1946, a local minister told the city council: "[The Steubenville police] themselves are either paid not to see what is happening or have been ordered to do nothing about it."[118] The cops knew where racketeers worked. They knew where they slept. Law enforcement could be counted on to turn a blind eye when they needed it, but this required investment. A former FBI agent described Jefferson County law enforcement in the 1940s, "The sheriff did occasionally stage a raid upon places where slot machines were displayed, but it was almost always against a spot which had been recently established and where the proper 'connections' had not been made."

<><><>

A few days after McCartney's threat, on October 6, 1989, Koniski was still waiting for a sign of resolution. Between poker, pinochle, and television, he whiled away the day. As afternoon turned to evening with no sign of the cops, he breathed easier. When the game was over, Koniski pocketed more than a thousand dollars, and his adrenaline was flowing. He went out to his Datsun and turned on the radio. The leaves were burning up in vivid colors that distracted attention from the onset of winter. That night, Big Red was playing Weir High at Harding Stadium, right on his way home. Still, twenty-four hours of cards had taken its toll. If the game were close, he would be

---

[117] Joseph J. Koniski. "Statement of Events: Chapter 1." *Innocent Inmates of Ohio Association*, p. 4-5.

[118] Norman E. Nygarrd. 12 Against The Underworld. *The Hobson Book Press*, 1947, p. 53.

obliged to stop and watch the rest of it. For guys like Joe, Big Red might as well have been the NFL.

Koniski headed north on Fourth Street, more involved in the football game than driving. Big Red was leading by four. When he reached Adams Street, he pulled into the left turn lane and stopped at a red light. At the other side of the intersection, directly facing him there was a Steubenville police cruiser. Koniski felt dread, although he was doing nothing illegal. When the light turned green, Koniski waited for the officer to advance southward, but he didn't move. Instead, the officer gestured for Koniski to go ahead. Then, the officer turned right and followed him. Koniski eyed his mirrors without moving his head. With the cruiser bearing down on him, Koniski adhered to the traffic laws as if his driver's ed teacher were in the car. He hit a green light at Fifth Street but caught a red light at Seventh. When the light turned green, Koniski counted to himself, "one-thousand-one, one-thousand-two," before rolling through the intersection.

Koniski and his tail traveled in tandem westward, then uphill onto the ramp from Washington Street to 43, which becomes a freeway for a half a mile. Koniski was careful to stay within the speed limit, although his Datsun 280Z would get up and go. Just then, blue lights splashed across the intermittently lit landscape. Koniski pulled onto the shoulder with an eerie feeling in the pit of his stomach. There were no houses, no buildings, no lights, and no people on this stretch of road, although it's in the middle of Steubenville, between downtown and the high school.

Officer Jack Palkovic walked up to the car with a casual gait. Koniski rolled down the window, swallowing hard. "License and registration," he commanded. Koniski grabbed the registration card from the visor and handed it to Palkovic, apologizing that he didn't have his license. "You can verify my license with my Social Security number." He recited it to Palkovic, who echoed it into his radio. The reply came back, "Yes, valid driver's license to Joe Koniski, 221 Cunningham Lane."

Stroking his mustache and looking away, Palkovic asked Koniski to exit the vehicle and to walk to the rear of the cruiser, where he told him to put his hands on the trunk and spread his legs. After frisking him, the officer ordered him into the back seat of the cruiser and proceeded to search his car. Koniski watched with a grin, knowing that his car was clean as a whistle. Next, the officer came back and ordered to the rear of the cruiser to search him again. This time, Palkovic put Koniski in cuffs. "What's the problem?" Koniski asked, but the officer neglected to answer. He stashed Koniski in the back of the cruiser again.

Standing with his back to the vehicle, Palkovic withdrew a screwdriver from his coat. Next, he stabbed his hand a few times, scratching the skin but drawing no blood. Koniski heard the officer grunt. Then, another cruiser pulled up with lights ablaze, and Chief McCartney was on the scene. The way Palkovic told the story, Koniski was shouting obscenities when he came up to the car, and Koniski viciously stabbed Palkovic's hand with a screwdriver when he rested it on the car door. Palkovic told the chief, "He was choking me; he stabbed me; he tried to kill me." Hearing this, Koniski started yelling to his old friend, "Jerry! Jerry! Jerry!" Koniski later claimed the police had framed him in retaliation for his complaints of harassment and his initial refusal to pay a bribe. In his detailed account of the incident, he wrote:

> Now I know the question arises as to why Palkovic would frame me after the bribe was paid and accepted, and it's a question that I, myself, have pondered. Maybe, the attorney didn't give the money to Burchfield like he said he did. Maybe, Burchfield didn't give the money to McCartney. Maybe, McCartney got the money, but was still hostile over my actions and decided to frame me anyway. Maybe, Palkovic had not gotten the word to lay off me and was still following instructions formerly issued by the chief. All of these are only conjectures on my part, but there are too many weak links in the chain for the truth not to emerge eventually.

While he was getting booked at the sheriff's office, the deputy asked jocularly, "So, you're the infamous police slasher?" Koniski asked what he meant, and the deputy remarked, "We just got a call that they were bringing in a guy who just slashed up a cop. Man, we thought that you would have bumps and bruises all over your head. We thought they would really fuck you up." Koniski tried to reason with the deputies, "I'm not drunk. I'm not stoned. I am perfectly calm and totally rational. What's more is, I don't have any bumps. I don't have any bruises, and I'm not all fucked up, and all of us know what the Steubenville Police [standard operating procedure] is, especially if a cop gets hurt." Though the deputies believed him, they weren't going to push back against the SPD.

<><><>

The trial took place at the Jefferson County Court of Common Pleas. During testimony, the police gave contradictory accounts of the arrest, but Prosecutor Stern portrayed Koniski as a crime boss before the jury[119] which he rigged with only people of the opinion that the Steubenville police were "among the finest in the land," according to

---

[119] *State of Ohio v. Koniski.* Jefferson County Court of Common Pleas. 31 January 1990. Print.

Koniski.[120] Five out of twelve jurors were colleagues and childhood friends of the police and the prosecutor.[121] One of the jurors was a police dispatcher. Koniski knew full well who they would believe. A decade later, Koniski listed the names and the connections of each juror to officers of the court or the police on the website of the Innocent Inmates Association of Ohio.

Judge Mascio took the stabbing story at face value, but he later found inconsistency in police testimony that the officer continued to rest his value on the window, allowing Koniski to stab him no less than three times. While the jury deliberated, Stern offered Koniski a deal, plead guilty to a misdemeanor and the state will drop the felony charge. Koniski rejected the deal because it would violate his probation, with the same result.

After the jury found Koniski guilty of felonious assault of a police officer, he watched in disbelief as the bars closed on the first of 4,445 days he spent in prison. No higher authority came to Koniski's aid because they all supported the police protection racket. They were part of it. The mob had infiltrated the city government as well as the FBI office in Steubenville, which the U.S. Attorney's Office in Columbus quietly removed in 1995.

Though Koniski tried to alert people to the machinations behind his trial, people were disinclined to believe him. At the time, Americans championed harsh punishments for lawbreakers at the ballot box, selecting prosecutors like Stern who would do what was necessary to keep criminals off the streets. Stern had selected someone from every dominant ethnic group in Steubenville to work in the Jefferson County Prosecutor's Office, and his friendship with Judge Mascio enabled him to use the county court as his kangaroo court. Stern trusted his instincts when examining a criminal case, and he believed he was dispensing justice. Sometimes, he was right, but even as Jefferson County put away murderers, rapists, and assorted lesser criminals, there was a stream of lives ruined for nefarious purposes. They rationalized that those wrongly convicted would have, sooner or later, be found guilty of some crime. In the eyes of locals, "Operation Stern Message" enhanced Stern's appearance of being tough on crime. In reality, Stern and his cronies crossed over from upholding to undermining the rule of law.

By going around the chief and creating his own squad of drug war commandos, Stern was innovative. He wanted to exercise direct

---

[120] Joseph J. Koniski. "Statement of Events: Chapter 2." *Innocent Inmates Association of Ohio*, 2000.

[121] *State of Ohio v. Joseph J. Koniski*. Jefferson County Court of Common Pleas. 31 January 1990. Print.

on-the-ground control of police powers. Local mayors, sheriffs and police chiefs in the surrounding hamlets were uneasy, but Stern used his office to target anyone who dared to cross him with intense scrutiny by local law enforcement agencies. In 2018, Assistant County Prosecutor Lamatrice stated, "Stern was a self-aggrandizing piece of shit. He used his office for personal vendettas. He had a hit list." Stern's leverage with the press and his reputation discouraged his political opponents from opposing him publicly and deterred defense lawyers from taking their cases to jury trials. Meanwhile, Stern bragged about his perfect conviction rate.

Nevertheless, in the city of Steubenville, the facts recorded by the city's own investigators brought Stern under political pressure. His excesses had created a whistleblower, but luckily for Stern, all he wanted was a payoff. Around the same time, a Steubenville policeman was caught with a car full of stolen tires, raising questions whether officers of the SPD had been operating a stolen tire racket. In the end, it was almost always as an off-duty Steubenville cop drunkenly yelled at a football game in another town: "In Steubenville, cops don't arrest other cops!"[122]

In 1996, Prosecutor Stern indicted Chief McCartney, an SPD sergeant and a local attorney for using the Law Enforcement Automated Data System (LEADS) to get information about the criminal histories of jurors thought to be biased for indicting Captain Stinson and Captain Gary Burchfield on theft charges.[123] Stern convened a grand jury and then recused himself to serve as a witness before the jurors.[124] McCartney's defense counsel found it "shocking" how Stern manipulated the grand jury process, releasing detailed information to the press and using hearsay as evidence, but Stern had done the same thing in other cases, like Koniski's, without a peep from anybody.[125] It was different when Stern railroaded someone with power.

Koniski was later set free after imploring every official in Steubenville, as well as the FBI, BCI, and the DOJ, to give an opportu-

[122] Staff. "Steubenville police officer arrested at Tiger freshman game." *IndeOnline*, 21 September 2009.

[123] Ibid.

[124] *State of Ohio v. Jerry McCartney*. Jefferson County Court of Common Pleas. 29 Mar. 1996. p. 3. Print.

[125] Ibid. p. 14. Print.

nity for him to prove his innocence. Chief McCafferty finally granted his petition, under pressure from Charlie Reynolds, among others. After three polygraph tests, Koniski recalled the day a guard shouted, "Koniski, get your shit, you're out of here!" It took three years after the original *writ of habeas corpus* in 2000. During his thirteen years behind bars, he had taken charge of the commissary, which meant that he controlled much of the prison economy, and he ran a book. As he walked through the halls toward freedom, he wondered if there was going to be someone waiting for him on the outside. The next thing he knew he was, "out front of the joint, no buses, no taxis." He had to bang on the door and ask them for a phone call. When his brother answered the phone, he said, "I'm out!"

"What? Did you escape?" His brother responded. When asked how he celebrated the night of his release, Koniski said he had a cheeseburger and a big bowl of ice cream. For Chief McCafferty, Koniski's release was his most satisfying accomplishment.[126] When Koniski heard this, he said, "God bless him for saying that." Chief McCafferty later confirmed in an interview that many were convinced Koniski was innocent. From time to time, people would come up to Koniski around town, apologizing because they didn't realize the police were so corrupt. Koniski blamed then-city manager, Gary Repella, because he failed to stand up to former Chief McCartney, who was technically his subordinate in the hierarchy of the city government. When Koniski complained of police harassment, he could see that Repella was intimidated by McCartney while the two were on the phone discussing the situation.

The court settlements for complaints against Palkovic alone amounted to hundreds of thousands of dollars. In one of the cases, Lloyd King tried unsuccessfully to stop Palkovic from arresting a guy on the street who complained of racial profiling. In another incident, Palkovic repeatedly struck a handcuffed suspect in the head with a flashlight in '91. Then, he drunkenly pulled a gun, assaulted, and arrested a guy while off-duty in a local restaurant in '92. That didn't stop him from becoming patrolman of the year in '93 and later being promoted to sergeant, which is suggestive of the type of officers McCartney valued.

Palkovic was fired in 2000 after he lied to IA about pepper-spraying a security guard while off-duty at a Pearl Jam concert. Still, he managed to keep his job for another four years before pleading guilty to multiple charges of illegally processing drug documents, drug possession and drug trafficking in 2004. Instead of prosecuting him and sending him to prison, all the court did was strip him of his badge, meaning

---

[126] "Interview with Police Chief McCafferty." *Police Assessment Resource Center*, April 2005, Page 6.

that he would be able to keep his pension. Koniski sent a letter to the editor of *The Herald-Star* to complain. He wrote, "[Palkovic] was among the most despicable and atrocious people to ever put on a law enforcement uniform in what once was one of the most horrific police departments in the U.S. of A." In 2009, Palkovic passed away in his house at age forty-eight. No cause of death was given.

<><><>

Before he retired in September 2000, Chief McCartney conceded that the consent decree was the best thing ever to happen to the SPD. Then, in February 2001, after stalling for three years and operating without a chief for six months, the city contracted the search for a new chief to the Ohio Association of Police Chiefs (OAPC), stymied by conflicts between city hall, the SPD, and the DOJ. In turn, the OAPC selected and recommended two candidates, both of whom were outsiders, to City Manager Gary DuFour.

At the end of March, the city announced that the new chief would be from outside the SPD. In response, Captain Mark Sweeney, who had participated in the test by the OAPC but was not selected, cried foul and sued the city with counsel from Bruzzese & Calabria. Frank Bruzzese co-founded the firm. His brother Joseph, Jr. is the county common pleas judge, and the younger brother Jeff is an assistant prosecutor. The Bruzzeses call the shots in Jefferson County, and anybody who speaks out could lose their jobs and wind up with warrants for their arrest, facing a judge and prosecutor whose careers were made by Frank Bruzzese.

Judge Edmund Sargus dismissed the lawsuit, noting that the city had already spent $15,000 in the selection process while operating without a chief for a year. The judge sharply criticized Sweeney for attempting to "overturn the extensive and carefully crafted agreement reached by the parties in the prior litigation," by which he meant the consent decree.[127] Sweeney argued that he was not privy to the decree when it was signed, which the court disputed, concluding, "Sweeney's attempt is without merit."

In spite of the selection of the OAPC and the decision of the Southern District Court, the city confounded everybody and chose Sweeney to serve as the new chief. With the law firm as a mouthpiece, the city resisted this clause of the consent decree, and the DOJ eventually buckled and gave in to the will of the new city fathers. Then, within a year and without explanation, William McCafferty replaced Sweeney. McCafferty was an Irish captain who had been on the force

---

[127] *Sweeney v. City of Steubenville.* 202 514 0212, p. 3/25 S.D. Ohio. 15 November 2001.

since 1989. He understood the intentions of the DOJ and was on board with the reform initiative, according to Reynolds, who was convinced by McCafferty's willingness to fire James Bernard, then-president of the FOP. Bernard had assaulted and pointed a gun at his stepson, Judge Powell's grandson. Bernard committed perjury during sworn testimony early in his career and has a reputation for bullying community members over perceived slights.

Bernard is not well-liked or trusted by some in the community, not even by Delores Wiggins, the woman who saved his career by testifying in his favor at his arbitration hearing. Later, she referred to Bernard as "a damn racist," adding, "Oh yeah, I said it." Wiggins and Skip Mixon publicly asked Bernard to remove a sticker of the Confederate flag from his car's back window, and he refused. There is no doubt that Bernard has gone through a lot, being a police officer, then an administrator and public figure in the FOP, while facing difficulties at home. Bernard did not respond to a request for comment.

McCafferty fired Bernard, but Bernard appealed the decision and won his job back through arbitration. This was a defeat and a lesson for the new chief, who had not risen to the top rank after serving as FOP president, like his predecessor. Initially, the new chief did not depart from the talking points of McCartney. Perhaps for the sake of local pride, Chief McCafferty told *The Herald-Star*, "The DOJ allegations have not been proven in court and they wouldn't have withstood a court challenge."[128] He may have been right; the burden of evidence to prove a pattern or practice of police misconduct is heavy, but he also knew the DOJ had a truckload of court documents, on top of their own interviews with residents. In an interview with Police Assessment Resource Center (PARC), the chief gave a more candid portrayal of what gave rise to the consent decree, acknowledging deficiencies cited by the DOJ:

> In the late 1970s through the early 1990s, there were a lot of civil lawsuits brought against the city for excessive force and unlawful arrests. To make matters worse, there really wasn't an internal affairs division in the police department to manage the cases. The operations captain, second to the chief, handled most of the cases, and they weren't handled very well, leaving us open to even more lawsuits. Also, if you were a party to a lawsuit as an officer, there was no counseling, no type of discipline, no training. The police department never changed with the times; it stayed the way it had been in the 1960s. It just continued to maintain the status quo.[129]

---

[128] Ibid.

[129] Ibid.

McCafferty rallied support internally for compliance with the feds by informing his subordinates that the changes were meant to get the SPD up to date like other PD's nationwide.[130] Chief McCafferty remembered the past victims of the SPD. He knew the names of those who had come forward publicly with the harshest accounts of brutality, and he tried to make it right. However, with Bernard as president, the Fort Steuben FOP was able to prohibit anonymous complaints. Although the SPD was notorious for terrorizing those who complained, the union argued that it would bog down the investigative resources of the department with false complaints. This argument contrasts with the assessment of the former first deputy commissioner of the NYPD, "Every seasoned police officer knows...a sizable minority [of anonymous complaints] contain information that is of critical value and unobtainable in any other way."[131]

Though the chief didn't acknowledge it directly, Bernard's success implementing his political agenda effectively undermined his ability to weed out corrupt and brutal officers. McCafferty struggled to win arbitrations against officers found guilty of misconduct by IA because, the chief said, "It comes down to who has the best lawyer." Nevertheless, the consent decree caused attrition among the rank and file. Half the veteran officers left the force during the first two years of the decree because, according to McCafferty, "They didn't want somebody else running their department."[132] McCafferty maintained that while he was chief, the SPD was not going to go back to the way it had been.

While reassuring, there was still the lack of restorative justice for victims in Steubenville. There were other victims of the pattern of collusion between County Prosecutor Stern and the SPD. Lloyd King was a police officer in Steubenville for almost two decades before he eventually lost his badge. A future client of Olivito's would state in an interview with IA, "there were and are people in jail for serious crimes they have not committed...The police department is still full of corruption and lies."[133] Though this may have been true, the problem wasn't in the SPD alone.

McNamara's string of civil rights settlements was the "on-the-

[130] "Interview." *Police Assessment Resource Center*, April 2005.

[131] International Association of Chiefs of Police. "National Symposium on Police Labor Relations." 9-12 June 1974.

[132] Ibid.

[133] Steubenville Police Department, Internal Affairs Division. "Case Investigation - Final Report." September 2004, Page 25.

record" reason why the DOJ came to Steubenville.[134] However, Olivito's visit to D.C., his play-by-play account of the Hython case, and his collaboration in the investigation—giving them access to witnesses so that they could go beyond the evidence contained in the public record —were influential in the background of the consent decree. He was a local activist stakeholder with whom it was naturally convenient for the federal attorneys to collaborate, but this collaboration would not be reported in *The Herald-Star* until 2017. When *The Washington Post* and *PBS Frontline* came to town in 2015, they used Olivito as a source but only published a four-hundred word summary of the consent decree, in line with their project's purpose to provide a bird's eye view of police reform across the nation.[135]

The broad outlines of the causes and consequences of Steubenville's federal investigation were, according to the official narrative, McNamara's lawsuits attracted federal attention to problems of excessive force and a lack of administrative oversight, after which a new chief took over, vowing never to let it happen again. The murkier narrative beneath the official version, which was beyond the scope of prior journalistic endeavor and federal mandate, involved a drug cartel operating within the county narcotics squad. At best, the county prosecutor was officially responsible as the direct supervisor of the kingpin of the cartel. At worst, the prosecutor was acting as the attorney of a *narco*.

Four years after Olivito raised the issue of the King family's involvement in drug trafficking in the Hython trial, and one year after he and Joyce left, Lloyd King's son got busted. *The Cleveland Scene* reported, "In 1998, Lloyd King Jr. was charged with possession of a hundred grams of cocaine, fifty grams of crack, a hundred grams of meth, and five pounds of pot, which resulted in a sentence of fifteen years in federal prison."[136]

Sheriff Abdalla wanted nothing to do with King after King testified against him when Abdalla was on trial for bribery. King even lied about his military record in federal court.[137] Abdalla later stated that he remembered the King family well, "Lloyd King's son was one of the biggest dealers in this area. And the thing about Lloyd Sr. was,

---

[134] Sarah Childress et al. "Steubenville Police Department." *PBS Frontline*.

[135] Ibid.

[136] Ibid.

[137] Mark Law. "Questions surround King's position." *The Herald-Star*, 17 July 1991.

officers would search a vehicle and find nothing, then along comes King and there [were the drugs] . . . If his lips were moving, he was lying."[138] When asked about King, Abdalla said only, "Lowest of the low" and "Liar!" Yet King remained an officer or agent or whatever he was for nearly two decades.

The federal government's ultimate aim is to preserve the integrity of the justice system, and federal attorneys must weigh the value of public investment in accountability against the decrease in efficiency in processing cases at the local level. Overturning and reprocessing the criminal cases of a longtime undercover narcotics officer could overwhelm the local justice system's capacity to process its caseload. The consideration overturning Lloyd King's arrests or Stephen Stern's prosecutions was likewise politically unattractive. In that sense, Steubenville may have gotten off easy with a consent decree.

---

[138] Aina Hunter. "Blue Mob: Pity those caught by the Warren police, who rule with iron fists and rubber gloves." *Cleveland Scene*, 25 February 2004.

## 7

Don't judge unless you see first hand what a Warren Police officer goes through on a daily basis. Got a suggestion for all of you, do a ride along program then you can see for yourselves.

- "Michelle"[139]

Beneath the stately facades, Warren is a rough town. It was once removed from Youngstown by Niles, another town known for underground gambling and KKK organizing. Fred Harris said, "In the Warren where I grew up, a police officer could do anything he wanted to do to you, and you had no recourse. There was no one you could go to." Fear had kept victims quiet in Warren, but the codes of silence started to break down a few years before Olivito came to town.

In 2000, Olivito rented an office and an apartment in Boardman, a lily-white suburb on the southern side of Youngstown. He had been out of the game for three years, hiding out in North Carolina after he and Joyce fled Steubenville, leaving food on the table. He didn't need others to acknowledge his role in the consent decree. That was in the past; or so he told himself and his new love, Rosa. His legal practice was entering a new phase, and he was forging relationships and coloring inside the lines.

A local judge he did not know, Judge Robert Milich "seconded" his membership to the Mahoning County Bar Association. The judge was pleasant in conversation and reputedly a stand-up guy. Olivito got to know Milich and his staff. Being on the list for case assignments in a few local courts enabled Olivito to become familiar with the judges and their bailiffs. Case assignments kept the lights on in his small office. He also had occasion to meet many attorneys. Olivito later stated that the members of the Mahoning County Bar Association he had come to know in criminal cases, "were a collegial bunch...not just cutthroat competitors."

Meanwhile, Olivito was in search of the origins the federal law he had come to utilize in his hometown. He knew the law was a leftover from the post-Civil War era when the Fourteenth Amendment

---

[139] Michelle. Warren Police. *The Vindicator: Talk of the Valley*, 16 January 2007.

was added. So, he sought out a mentor in the head of the history department at Youngstown State University and started a master's program, focusing on abolitionism and Fourteenth Amendment law. Rosa moved in with him in 2001, and the next year she got pregnant.

In the Summer of 2003, when Olivito learned of the beating of Lyndal Kimble while reading the newspaper, he had one-year-old Joshua at his side. He had turned down police brutality claims because he knew too well how damaging this area of the law practice can be to any sense of normalcy for a solo lawyer in Eastern Ohio. Nevertheless, he felt obliged to check into the case and drove to the address listed for the alleged drug dealer, Lyndal Kimble, in Warren. That was the end of his attempt at a normal life.

There were fifty people assembled at the Kimble household on the sweltering afternoon of Olivito's arrival in Warren. Lyndal Kimble was still in jail over the weekend. According to Olivito, when he drove up with Joshua in tow, everyone stopped talking for a moment. They later told him, "We were ready to tell you to get the fuck away." At first, nobody trusted Olivito or understood what he was mumbling about.[140] Olivito recalled, many years later, that he made it to Melanise Kimble and her inner circle after being screened by Kimble's brother, Antwon. Olivito didn't know yet that there was a video. He just knew that there was controversy over the arrest.

Olivito wasn't able to meet Kimble until the following Monday, June 30, two days after his arrest. Five men watched him carefully after he was allowed into Kimble's living room. Kimble was bruised and had one arm in a sling. He could not eat and had difficulty remembering the event clearly. He did not smile and cared about only one thing: "Are you from this area?" "No," Richard answered. Kimble relaxed, and Olivito felt the pressure of the room dissipate. "Okay. We don't trust anyone from this area." Then, Lyndal invited Richard to a game of pool in his basement, where he was able to hear Kimble's account of the arrest for the first time. Olivito focused on Kimble's case due to the publicity, but he quickly realized that Kimble's was not the worst beating; it was just the first one caught on video.

Police experts later told Olivito that his client could have been killed or seriously injured, especially by the impact on concrete, yet the officers saw to it that Kimble went to jail before being treated for his injuries at the local hospital. Kimble's wife Melanise testified that when she visited him in the hospital he had a black eye, could barely talk and

---

[140] Aina Hunter. "Blue Mob: Pity those caught by the Warren police, who rule with iron fists and rubber gloves." Cleveland Scene, 25 February 2004.

vomited up black fluid on her.[141] Cleveland doctors who examined Kimble began to question whether or not he might have permanent injuries after his post-attack car accident and moving violations.

The way the police saw it, they were the victims. The public just believed the media, which would lionize any criminal with a police brutality allegation in order to sell papers. Nobody had the patience to wait for the police to carry out an investigation. Instead, the public relished the media's crucifixion of good cops. Warren's mean streets necessitated force. Their job was as hard as the steelworkers' and even more dangerous, but their starting hourly wage was less. They had to show up and tell area men to stop beating their wives and girlfriends. They had to examine the scenes of grisly murders and barge into unknown dwellings where they could be shot. The police had to be tougher than Warren's toughest criminals and prepared to have all their decisions publicly questioned. It was hardly an enviable position, but the collapse of the steel industry made it one of the best opportunities left to put food on the table and your kids through college.

The attitudes of the officers of the WPD were old-fashioned. They were used to autonomy. They didn't like being challenged, and usually, city officials stood behind them. The WPD was regarded by some as Warren's most dangerous gang, but the officers saw themselves as cowboys. When they gave a beating, it was deserved. Nightsticks were their weapon of choice. Excessive force was frequent because it had never been punished by Chief Galgozy, who ran the WPD throughout the '80s, or Chief Hutson, who took over from 1991 to 1996. As far as the safety services director knew in 2016, no Warren officer has ever been fired for excessive force. They were quick on the draw, but they were a tight-knit group; they loved to give each other shit. A few of them had been known to pursue women in the course of their duties. Although they would squabble amongst themselves, Mando always stood up for them.

Warren cops demanded respect, and they used brute force and their political power to break even the strongest defendants and plaintiffs, but that didn't stop people from trying. There were fifty lawsuits filed against the city of Warren from 1980 to 1996 over police abuse, but they were quietly settled for a few thousand dollars a pop. No records were kept, and no one was disciplined. The WPD was exactly as many police union leaders wish all police departments could be: unaccountable.

In response to the charges in *Kimble v. Hoso et al.*, the officers counter-charged Kimble for "broken bones, scratches, soft tissue physical injuries and great emotional distress after having been attacked by plaintiff Lyndal Kimble." The defendants went on in the counterclaim

---

[141] Ibid. p. 628.

to say they "have suffered the physical injuries, lost wages, payment for the medical treatment they received, apprehension for the fear of the offensive/harmful touching and suffered the harmful touching upon them by plaintiff Lyndal Kimble." Then, they claimed entitlement to damages of "in excess" of $25,000 each for assault, defamation, and negligence. This was how the WPD silenced their victims or anybody else who opposed them. The plaintiff responded to the counter-charges with categorical denials and the assertion that "truth is a defense against [these claims]."

On or just before July 4, Kimble told his side of the story to Diane Sawyer on *Good Morning America*. Kimble recalled that during the brutal arrest he thought, "They going to kill me if somebody don't stop this." Bush had prematurely declared victory in Iraq, and Olivito drew a parallel between the two, saying, "We have to learn to connect the dots between downtown Baghdad and downtown Warren. If this country is going to get democracy right, we can't go fight a war in downtown Baghdad if we can't seem to control our cops in downtown Warren." Afterward, the producer asked if it was their first national interview. When they both said yes, she assured that they did well and "It won't be your last. Others will come knocking."

After the *Good Morning America* appearance, other networks picked up the story. The vans of various media outlets were parked up and down the streets of Warren for weeks. News teams with all their gear and cameras set up shop right out front of Lyndal's house. So, Lyndal and Olivito held a press conference and fielded questions from the reporters. He did so well that media outlets began to realize that Lyndal could articulate things in a way that resonated across the color barrier. He had instincts instilled from the streets as well as speech that belied intelligence. He seemed slightly humbled by the spotlight, but he was still indignant and refused to settle. All this made him an attractive if unlikely spokesperson for many who had taken beatings silently in Warren for decades.

Reporters were loitering on the Kimble's lawn when a representative of the NAACP came and tried to start a conversation with him. In front of the cameras, he told the person, "Get off my fucking property! Y'all never helped us!" CNN did a segment a few days later, followed by interviews on MSNBC and Fox. About a month later, Kimble and his counsel were invited on *The O'Reilly Factor*. Olivito declined to appear, but Kimble went on with Olivito's co-counsel, Sarah Kovoor, a former Trumbull County assistant prosecutor who worked on the case. O'Reilly asked questions about the videotaped assault and then needled Kimble about what he did for a living, causing Kimble to fall silent. Then, before the interview concluded, O'Reilly declared, "No American should be treated that way." Olivito watched the interview while enjoying a coke at a pub not far from the Rayburn

Building in D.C. He was stunned by the statement in defense of his client's rights.

People in Warren weren't so sure if Kimble should be the people's representative. Many also opined that nobody should challenge the police. One Warren resident put the dilemma this way, "Every vote against the police is a vote for crackheads."[142] However, going all out on crackheads and drug dealers was leading to a situation where, according to another resident, "The police run around like Gestapo, setting up checkpoints and harassing non-criminals."[143]

The town was deeply divided, but one thing was certain: The tactics of the WPD were becoming costly for taxpayers. The city's insurance deductible had risen from $25,000 to $250,000 in four years because of misconduct-related lawsuits. The insurer also reduced the maximum they would cover from three million dollars to one million.[144] Meanwhile, as Olivito later wrote, "many citizens of Warren face a suffocating darkness which approaches something of a spiritual nature, a literal nightmare on South Street, going forward rapidly into the past."[145]

Karen Bryant was fed up with the violence of the WPD. She immediately recognized Officer Hoso when she saw him choking Kimble in his car. *The Cleveland Scene* reported that, in 2002, "Hoso was one of four officers who beat her son so severely that he ended up in the hospital."[146] Her son had no criminal record. His sole infraction was not appearing in court for a traffic violation. After the Kimble event, Bryant reportedly told Hughley, the owner of the video camera, "I said run with that motherfucker, and don't stop until I figure out what to do!"[147]

---

[142] Aina Hunter. "Blue Mob: Pity those caught by the Warren police, who rule with iron fists and rubber gloves." *Cleveland Scene*, 25 February 2004.

[143] Ibid.

[144] Ibid.

[145] *Kimble v. Hoso et al.* 439 F. 3d 331. Sixth Cir. 2006. p. 19.

[146] Aina Hunter. "Blue Mob: Beware the Warren cops, the city's most violent gang. The second of a two-part series." *Cleveland Scene*, March 3, 2004.

[147] Ibid.

According to Olivito, the video was given to Michelle Nicks, who worked for local outlet WFMJ, the day after it happened. After being aired by the local media, it quickly went national. Mediapolis, another local outlet, later traced it back to Nicks. During a press conference a few days later, Chief Mandopoulos was excited to talk about the WPD's recent seizure of drugs, guns and more than $200,000 in collaboration with the DEA. When Nicks asked about Kimble, Mando became irate and threatened to give drug dealers Nicks' address so that they "could move in next to her." A year and a half later, when she was called to testify in court about the threat in the Kimble's criminal trial, Nicks still felt like her life was in danger and only testified after being prodded by subpoena. She declined to comment for this book. She remains a journalist in the area. WFMJ, Nicks' employer, sent a sworn statement to the mayor's office, explaining that Mandopoulos didn't just threaten Mrs. Nicks, but all of WFMJ's staff. He also said that he would organize labor unions to boycott the outlet.

Mando was a bully, and others like him rose up the ranks in his shadow. Violence was a common language in Steel Valley, and police had to be able to hold their own. Warren G. Harding High School, previously a football rival of Steubenville's Big Red, was so beset with racially motivated violence that friends had to guard each other while using the bathroom, like America's prisoners, and police had to guard the school for thirteen days after Martin Luther King's assassination. In one incident, a white guy, who would go on to become mayor, was thrown through the trophy case because of the color of his skin. And that was during a decade when the economy was good.

The children of that generation inherited the decline of steel. The economic losses from the collapse were more severe in the south and west parts of town. African American participation in the labor force dropped by half. These losses manifested in the form of prolonged unemployment, depression, drug addiction, alcoholism, and violence. Growing up in Warren, you always had to be on your guard. James Nutt wrote of Warren in the '60s, "If you didn't live in this vicinity at the time, you wouldn't understand how prevalent the tension and violence was. Union versus non-union, black versus white, blue collar versus white collar, old versus young, rich versus poor, and so on."[148]

In such an environment, police were as violent as they needed to be, and nobody had much sympathy for those who whined about it. "Who was you gonna go to?" asked Fred Harris, former safety services director, "The law director [Greg Hicks]? He's a former cop. The chief? He's the worst one!" When Fred Harris became the first African American safety services director in Warren's history, he decided to use the power of his office to challenge the chief.

---

[148] Ibid.

On January 30, 2002, *The Tribune Chronicle* published an article about the brewing conflict between the police chief and his boss, Harris, who had been showing up at crime scenes to make sure officers were following departmental policy. The paper expressed approval of the director's surveillance, calling the officers' complaints, "immature."[149] Harris had recently issued an order that the officers wear their Stetson hats at all times. The issue arose after Officer Jeff Miller mistakenly shot another officer, thinking he was a criminal. The move was for the purpose of officer safety because the hats made them easily recognizable. It was also a signal by Harris that was gearing up to exert the statutory power of his office over the chief. The police did not take it well, not only because they hated the hats.

With this public brouhaha heating up, Officer Brian Crites addressed Harris' appearance on service calls as well as a statement by Harris that he could "require the officers to wear pink gun belts if he so desired." Crites commented on *The Tribune*'s website:

> Yo... For yo info. homey - Harris is an office [sic] worker, not some street cop and shouldn't be showing up on police calls. Police work should be left to professionals, not some arrogant political hack trying to do a Martin Luther King Jr. imitation. As for wearing pink hats, how about WPD start wearing white sheet instead.[150]

Crites' response was posted by his full name and his email address. His reference to the KKK was intended as a threat not only to Director Harris but to all people of color in Warren. If Harris persisted in exerting the power of his office over the police department, the WPD would retaliate.

Harris was nonchalant about these kinds of threats. He recalled receiving a Christmas card signed "the KKK." He came home one night and noticed a bullet hole in the kitchen window. Harris didn't flinch because he was accustomed to it. WPD officers used to hit his friends with clubs rolled up in issues of *The Saturday Evening Post*, although they had done nothing illegal. Warren police enforced informal segregation in public spaces when he was growing up. While working as a teenager at a catered event on Country Club Road, Harris was retrieving extra silverware when a cop stopped his car and insisted on talking to the white owner of the house to make sure he had a reason to be in a white part of town. When his dad asked what happened and Fred told him, he remembered how his dad lowered his head with a helpless look on his face. These memories hardened his heart and

---

[149] Editorial Board. "Police force heads need to think first." *The Warren Tribune Chronicle*, 26 January 2002.

[150] Ibid.

steeled his will to fight back. After his tires were slashed, Fred took Mando's car.

Mando was the one wearing a helpless look in Harris' office a few days after Crites' threat. Harris called the police department and told Mando's secretary to send him over as soon as he arrived. When Mando arrived, Fred told him to wait outside. Then, he left and spent more than an hour doing other things while Mando waited, walking around in a circle outside his office. Fred made him wait for another hour after he came back, and finally, he told Mando to get out of his office. The safety services director also ordered the chief to toss his new stationery, which featured the chief's name at the top. Fred forced Mando to put the mayor's name at the top, with Fred Harris below, and his own name in the margin. The symbolism and the demonstrations of Fred's authority angered the chief, but he would fight until his dying day for the autonomy of his department.

Mandopoulos never reprimanded officers for using racial slurs and he referred to Harris, as well as Councilman Doc Pugh and Councilwoman Helen Rucker as "the head niggers" around the station. When one of the few black officers complained, he was reprimanded. The black officers were outraged, but they smothered their indignation until they were forced out of the department. "If [the WPD] behaved with so much disrespect towards their chief's boss," Fred Harris often remarked, "imagine how they treated the African American residents of Warren." When Mayor Angelo put Harris in charge of safety services, all of those experiences factored into Harris' approach to the WPD. "I wasn't gonna put up with their shenanigans," he said, shaking his head, "Uh-uh." but he was also a joker. Sometimes, people didn't know which Mando was talking. He threatened people, but then he would say it was only a joke. His jokes occasionally deflected annoying requests. When a few community leaders asked for the officers involved in Kimble's assault to be placed on paid leave, Mandopoulos replied, "If they are willing to pay, I'd be happy to do it."[151] This statement subtly shifted blame to Safety Services Director Fred Harris and the mayor, as well as the auditor and others he had disagreed with over budgetary issues.

Mando wouldn't budge on the budget, but he was wasteful. He hated accounting for costs and maintaining records of the time clock, which was installed over his vehement resistance and later removed. Fred Harris joked, "No officer had been late in the WPD for ten years." Still, Mando was a master of deflecting blame. For him, nothing was ever proven or settled unless it made the department look good.

Mando brought the community to a boil with his harsh tactics and his evident disregard for the safety of certain residents. All the local media outlets were spewing out stories of police abuse residents had

---

[151] "Arrest." *Warren Tribune Chronicle*, 7 July 2003.

suffered. Hundreds marched to city hall demanding transparency and justice. Kimble contrasted the treatment he was dealt by the police against those who lived on the other end of Kenilworth. It wouldn't happen to them, Kimble told reporters. He said, "This didn't happen because of racism, it's because I'm poor."

Olivito's first thought was the Justice Department, but he knew that one case was not necessarily going to bring the DOJ. President George W. Bush was in the White House, and his administration scaled back federal civil rights enforcement. In Warren, with Mando as chief and Republicans in charge of DOJ, Olivito would have to pursue a more aggressive strategy. In the weeks that followed, Olivito gathered narratives of police abuse, searching for the right configuration of events, facts, and witnesses, which had to be less than two years old because of the statute of limitations. He would need various cases of arrests entirely lacking in probable cause, or beatings backed up by extensive medical records and video evidence. Kimble's arrest was a double whammy because there was video and medical evidence of the assault. The Sixth Circuit had already chided him for trying to argue a policy claim based on one singularly impressive instance of police misconduct. Therefore, Olivito set about building the policy claim first. Kimble's lawsuit was the last he would file.

At night, Olivito walked along the cemetery at the end of Kenilworth and through the humble streets with his mind absorbed in the composition of upcoming lawsuits. He was in the process of deciding which victims would make the best plaintiffs. Then, he would level multiple complaints in quick succession. Olivito's goal was to pack the same amount of potency into four or five civil rights lawsuits that James McNamara achieved with his forty-four legal victories over the SPD. Olivito reckoned that the DOJ would not be able to ignore Warren.

<><><>

One local media outlet reported the account of the police in an article entitled, "Action 19 News digs deeper into violent videotaped arrest."[152] *Action 19 News* wrote that Kimble had prior arrests, had done time for drugs and that police had recovered .65 grams of cocaine and $2,200 from him in the course of the arrest. Although airing an indictment against his credibility, the article didn't include any statement from Kimble. Instead, it gave a voice to the police chief, who denied that the officers had used excessive force. *Action 19 News* reported that Officer Greg Hoso "has been the subject of a number of complaints filed by known drug dealers to stop loitering."

---

[152] Anonymous. "Action 19 News digs deeper into violent videotaped arrest." *Action 19 News*, No date.

*Action 19 News* was taking the chief's word for it because there was no way to verify; the WPD always fought anybody that tried to get public records, especially of internal investigations. At the same time, the article noted, "The chief added that Hoso is perhaps the most religious officer on the force." Tempesta had been disciplined for writing too few tickets. Stabile had no prior record of misconduct. This only meant that he had not been disciplined for two years because the union contract allowed for disciplinary records to be expunged every two years, if the WPD kept any records, at all.

In response to Kimble's claim that the cops had dislocated his shoulder, the police said they were unsure and that they would subpoena medical records. The outlet reminded readers, "Police are asking folks to not jump to conclusions. They're conducting an internal probe and will call in the feds if necessary." This was unbelievable. Even public officials in Warren didn't take these kinds of statements from the chief seriously. In September of 2001, Councilman Doc Pugh delivered an official letter to the chief via the DOJ Criminal Division, stating, "We believe that the WPD is incapable of doing an unbiased investigation." *Action 19 News* later interviewed Kimble and published an associated article about Alphonse Hogan, who, after being beaten by police, filed a lawsuit with Olivito as counsel.

What *Action 19 News* got right was that Hoso had a good reputation in the WPD, where he is currently a lieutenant. Hoso had a bachelor's degree from Youngstown State University, which was out of the ordinary among the officers on the force. He was from a large, important Warren family and was the great-nephew of an influential Catholic monsignor. His sister became a victim's advocate in the prosecutor's office. His brother also later became a cop. His other brother, who later died of a drug overdose, was refused employment at the WPD, despite attempts by his great uncle, the monsignor, to pressure the mayor and safety services director.

Hoso's wife is the daughter of a local former football coach and reputed crime boss Anthony Napolet. His best friend since high school, Enzo Cantalamessa was once Warren public defender and would later become safety services director, giving him the final say on IA investigations of citizen complaints about Hoso and his longtime associates. In 2013, Hoso and two other officers, as well as a few witnesses, were heralded as heroes for helping lift a Ford Explorer off of a motorcyclist trapped underneath it.[153] One commenter expressed his wish that "all officers were like that."

However, Hoso wasn't uniformly regarded as a hero in Warren. He had a bad reputation not only among "known drug dealers," but

---

[153] Peggy Gallek. "Officers Heavy Lifting Save Man's Life." *Fox8.com*, 1 November 2013.

also among the people of Kimble's neighborhood and beyond. Then-Safety Services Director Harris acknowledged, "He has a certain reputation among the African American communities. People are scared to death of Hoso!"[154] At the beginning of the Kimble video, angry voices can be heard shouting Hoso's name. When asked about Hoso's reputation, many years later, former Mayor Angelo said, "I got the same feedback on several cops and Mando." Hoso was known to terrorize black families together with Rob Massucci, currently a captain in the WPD, with the support of the prosecutor's office and local courts. Both officers continued to be the cause of citizen complaints in 2012, although IA investigations invariably exonerated them.

Olivito began spending his evenings on Kenilworth Avenue, to the annoyance of the mother of his child. The Kimbles have five children and were quick to offer one of their tricycles to Joshua, which kept him entertained while the adults discussed police brutality. The fact that Olivito had Joshua with him during this time endeared him to the black community. He wanted his son to know about Warren's inequality, racism and police brutality. Olivito commuted at first, but then Karen Bryant invited him to sleep on the couch at her house, just a few houses down from the Kimbles. Bryant was a boisterous, articulate and determined African American woman who had been praying for what she called an "Armani lawyer." For her, that meant a polished and powerful attorney who would bring his influence to bear on Warren's police. Olivito, who would often drop by asking to use her bathroom, was a far cry from what she had envisioned, but he was willing to take on the police. Nobody knew what that would look like, but Olivito assured them that he knew what to do. Over the next few weeks, he composed a civil rights symphony with the alleged grievances of Warren's oppressed.

After the afternoon heat subsided, he would sit on the porch of the Kimbles' house next to Karen Bryant and others. People would gather round until the crowd stretched into the yards of the houses on either side. Children played on the sidewalks and into the street. Someone would volunteer what happened to them at the hands of the WPD. Then another. And another. Residents re-lived their experiences of beatings, of strip searches, of false charges and citizen complaints ignored. The police were aware of the situation on Kenilworth. Cruisers crept by as bystanders made space in the street.

Warren's police ruled with an iron fist over the black community, but people fought back by telling their stories. The black community was the only place where these stories previously had any validity,

---

[154] Aina Hunter. "Blue Mob: Beware the Warren cops, the city's most violent gang. The second of a two-part series." *Cleveland Scene*, 3 March 2004.

but now an out-of-town attorney wanted to hear them. Olivito was the sole white person in attendance. A few kids watched him from a distance. Night after night, as he began to get more acquainted with members of the community, he noticed that one little girl watched him more steadily than the other kids, but the outpouring of residents' painful memories dominated his attention. The two years leading up to that summer were riddled with public controversy in Warren over police tactics. Olivito felt he was taking part in something meaningful and unique. It was an informal truth commission on the drug war and an oral history of Midwestern racial oppression. He knew there had to be many other towns just like Warren.

The girl who had been attentively observing him sent an older friend tell him to come to her house and meet her family. Olivito was later introduced to her older brother, Darnell Warfield. When Olivito met Warfield, he was taken aback because of the boy's forehead. His face had to be reconstructed after being pounded in by Warren police officers. Titanium rods supporting his eye sockets stuck out on both sides of his forehead. The public defender had assured Warfield that a complaint would be filed on his behalf. When Olivito checked into the case with the public defender's office, an administrative complaint had been filed, but the statute of limitations had run out, so it was too late to file a federal civil rights complaint.

Olivito heard about the beating of another young man named Lamont Murray. In 2001, he had a good job in Indianapolis and was in town on Christmas break visiting his family. He was in the car with his mother, his aunt and another young man his age, Kevin Parks, when Sergeant Rob Massucci pulled him over. Murray reacted when the officers accosted his mother in the front passenger side. Witnesses said that was when the police came after him. Massucci hit Murray with his baton, putting a gash on his head later sewn up with thirty staples.

In a deposition, Chief Mandopoulos could not remember whether Sgt. Massucci had used his baton to split open Murray's head "or if he bumped his head." Karen Bryant later told Olivito that witnesses claimed that an officer or officers had urinated on Murray. The police maintained that they had offered him water to wash the mace out of his eyes. Fred Harris stated, "I never did get that right." All the chief remembered was that Murray was found guilty. When Olivito pressed the chief about what charge he was found guilty of, asking sarcastically, if it was, "writing a bad check?" The chief could not recall, concluding "I just remember guilty."[155] After BCI returned the case to the city,

---

[155] *Kimble v. Hoso et al.* 439 F. 3d 331. Sixth Cir. 2006. Page 720-721.

there was no follow-up with the family, no investigation, no media statement and, most importantly, no change.[156]

The WPD began harassing Murray and filing spurious charges against him. It eventually drove him indoors, into his parent's basement, where he lived for some time as a traumatized recluse. Olivito had little to offer the family in the way of solace or remedy because the statute of limitations had run out. This was infuriating because Olivito suspected that lawyers and judges in the area knew only too well that these types of abuses were happening. He believed that the local authorities were not taking adequate measures, but nobody had seen how Olivito handled allegations of police brutality.

Warren attorneys Gilbert Rucker and Sarah Kovoor filed and litigated federal civil rights lawsuits against the WPD. Fred Harris exerted administrative pressure on Chief Mandopoulos and criticized the police in the press. Harris leaked damaging information to journalists and encouraged others to file lawsuits. Olivito would paper the city with lawsuits, criticize the chief in the press and try to bring in federal officials to investigate the department.

Olivito became, "a sort of de facto civil rights complaint clearinghouse,"[157] and the local papers announced his arrival as if he might save the city. Sitting in a lawn chair on Kenilworth Avenue, he listened to hour after hour of horror stories. He told *The Vindicator* that he had received many calls from residents complaining of the city's police.[158] Most of the complaints were not actionable in court because of the statute of limitations had expired or because of a dearth of witnesses. *The Vindicator* reported that Olivito was reviewing the complaints.

Prior to Olivito's arrival in Warren, the string of racially-charged incidents in the spring and summer of 2003 caused the tension to develop into unrest. Racial tension was nothing new in Warren; it had built up over decades of frustrated aspirations towards racial equity. However, outside of 77 Soul, a Warren nightclub, a racially charged altercation between police and black residents was videotaped and published by the local media.

---

[156] Ibid. Page 33.

[157] Aina Hunter. "Blue Mob: Pity those caught by the Warren police, who rule with iron fists and rubber gloves." *Cleveland Scene*, 25 February 2004.

[158] Peggy Sinkovich. "Attorney studies police reports." *The Vindicator*, 6 July 2003.

The owner of the club, LaShawn Zeigler, had beef with the police, who had been harassing him in their customary way, but it wasn't just the police. The city government was hell-bent on closing the club after becoming aware of various code violations. Zeigler suspected they had other motivations. He knew that the other residents and businesses on the block weren't exactly pleased about 77 Soul, and he was right. They cheered when Zeigler's business was shuttered in 2008, and WKBN trumpeted their glee when the building was finally bulldozed in 2015.

Around midnight on May 24, 2003, Chief Mandopoulos and Officer Manny Nites walked up to a crowd of club-goers standing in line outside 77 Soul. The cameraman appointed by Zeigler started recording even before the police had a chance to offend the crowd. The film shows Chief Mandopoulos saying "They're heeeere!" as he peered into the camera. Officer Nites held his arm aloft like a Nazi while Mandopoulos proceeded to make faces at the camera, asking, "Is anybody in there?"

Then, two African American guys believed by police to be drug dealers walked up. They asked Charlie Adams, the man with the camera, what he was doing. Nites loudly announced, "He's snitching on you!" The men became angry, and one of them replied, "Charlie wouldn't do that. A snitch is a bitch. A snitch is a nigger!" Then, Officer Nites commented in a loud voice to the cameraman, "Did you hear that? He called you a snitch." He added, "He called you a bitch," and finally, "He called you a nigger."

Nites manipulated the situation of being recorded with complete confidence, knowing that anybody called a snitch could end up dead. It was Charlie's punishment for filming the police. Nites was standing within an arm's length of the chief, but Mandopoulos said nothing in response to the offensive language of his subordinate. He later said he didn't hear it.[159] The meaning of the comments and the greater significance of the incident were not lost on residents, but according to Fred Harris, several within the WPD needed explanations as to why Nites' choice of words was problematic.

For Mando, Nites didn't deserve any more than a reprimand, but he wasn't going to have his hand forced by the public. When faced with criticism, Mando would sidestep it and complain about how hard he worked. Addressing criticism that he had failed to move an internal investigation along, he complained that he hadn't found time while working sixteen to eighteen hours a day. It was not the first time the WPD had been criticized, but it was the first time there was video evidence the police could not dismiss or bury internally. Eventually, the

---

[159] Sinkovich, Peggy. "Warren police chief to fight suspension." *The Vindicator*, 21 November 2003.

policies of Chief Mandopoulos, approved by the courts and Warren's law department, led to a string of explosive lawsuits against the city, about which their insurance company was not pleased.[160] As the summer of 2003 drew to a close, the WPD had what was termed a "perception problem,"[161] focused on the chief.

The local media fixated on allegations of excessive force, as well as Mandopoulos' belligerent and disrespectful behavior. At the end of the summer of 2003, Thomas Conley of the Greater Warren Youngstown Urban League and City Councilor James "Doc" Pugh called for the DOJ to intervene. *The Vindicator* reported that DOJ officials declined to comment, according to DOJ policy, but Warren was now on the radar of federal civil rights officials.

On August 1, 2003, after almost a month in Warren, Olivito filed two civil rights lawsuits against the WPD. Ten days later, he filed a third. A month after that, he filed a fourth. The first two went to Judge Gwin and Judge Adams. The third went to Judge Nugent. The fourth to Judge Galanis. Safety Services Director Fred Harris asserted, "None of the judges in the area liked what he was doing." Olivito later wrote, "Then, all of [the local judges] instantly turned against my economic interests. It had to be a bar decision. It was organized. It was uniform." Suddenly, Olivito's steady stream of case assignments from local judges dried up. By the end of 2003, the decision-makers at the Mahoning County Bar Association probably rued the day they admitted Richard Olivito.

By December of that year, Judge Robert Galanis, who sat on the bench of the Ohio Northern District Court, referred to Olivito's "series" of lawsuits, including a list of seven. Judge Galanis, a Democrat appointed by Clinton, was well-respected because he remained untainted by corruption during an era when many of his colleagues went down in infamy. Galanis seemed to defer to local custom with civil rights claims against police, but not if it was obvious that a defendant was lying. Every one of Olivito's lawsuits alleged a "pattern or practice" of misconduct, for which the chief, his city bosses and the city itself were liable. "I filed multiple cases like movements in a symphony," Olivito explained many years later, "to build the policy claim." Each of the cases illuminated particular aspects of the WPD's culture, but together they pointed to a pattern of excessive force, discrimination, illegal searches, poor training, and a failure to discipline.

---

[160] "Warren police chief reopens strip searches investigation." *Action 19 News*, No date.

[161] Connie Mabin. "Warren police face perception problem." *Cincinnati Enquirer*, 9 August 2003.

Few attorneys in Ohio were filing policy claims against PDs at the time. Fewer were spending days and nights in black neighborhoods to gather complaints. These opening salvos were a declaration of war against the police chief, the law director, the prosecutors and the judges. Later, burning crosses appeared in West Warren, and someone ransacked Sarah Kovoor's law office. The burglars took one computer and left a note calling Kovoor "nigger-lover." Olivito knew he had a fight on his hands, and he began to take steps to protect himself.

## 8

To all you idiots who keep complaining about our police officers, if you don't like our city, why in the hell do you still live here? Not that anyone's asking, but my opinion is this: Whatever the police have to do to keep a crack dealer out of my neighborhood is okay by me.

-Anonymous, Summer of 2003

Although it was the Kimble incident that lured Olivito to Warren, the Clay case was the first Olivito filed on August 1. Clarence Clay had been a crane operator for thirty years at a local steel mill, Warren's equivalent of a working stiff, but at fifty-two, he had long since turned to repair work after a back injury stopped him from returning to the mill. He's a family man, father of two. The eldest was attending Ohio State on a full scholarship for engineering. Clarence Clay Jr. was at home during his father's experience with the WPD.

Clay's initial infraction was running a stop sign around the corner from his house. First, Clay pulled into his driveway, and Officers Joseph Kistler and Edward Hunt pulled in behind him. Then, they ordered him out of the car. The police's version of events has Clay getting out of the car without their permission, which could have been excused, considering the man was in his own driveway. The officers said they ordered him to get back in the car, but then they ordered him back to the rear of the car, after which confusion ensued. According to the police report, "The suspect immediately attempted to return to the vehicle but was prevented by officers. The suspect was ordered to place his hands on the vehicle but again attempted to return to the vehicle."

In the complaint to the Northern District Court, Clay maintained that the officers placed him in handcuffs without giving any reason why.[162] While the officers searched his car, Clay sat in the cruiser with his hands bound in front. The officers did not mention searching the vehicle in the police report or their version of the arrest in affidavits.[163] At this point, Clay said that one of the officers returned and shined a flashlight on him from behind the car. Then, an officer ordered Clay out of the car, but as he stood up, the officers claimed that Clay

---

[162] *Clay v. City of Warren*. Ohio N. D. Court. 2004. Print.

[163] Ibid. 182 and 244.

reached into his left, front pocket. [164] The officers stated that they became fearful he had a weapon and therefore attempted to take him into custody.

Kistler and Hunt claimed that neither of them could manage to get ahold of his hands because "Mr. Clay was pulling them to his person."[165] Clay's action of pulling his arms to his sides was enough to "actively prevent" them from grasping his limbs. The officers reacted by taking Clay to the ground. The officers did not include any count of how many blows they visited on Clay's body, but they specified two. They claimed that they had "struck [the plaintiff] in the upper arms, in an attempt to halt his progress, which seemed to have no effect."[166] After he was in handcuffs, while being patted down, Clay reportedly tried to "push away from the vehicle," necessitating a closed-fist blow to Clay's left shoulder by Hunt.[167] According to the police, having failed to lay hold of the suspect's arms, the police hit him in the arm.

The officers' portrayal of Clay's behavior raises questions because Clay had no reason to be reaching into his pocket. However, it does conveniently establish a rationale for the obstructing charge and their use of force as well as a basis for their counterclaim of negligence against Clay for his infliction of "severe emotional distress upon Kistler and Hunt as they were in genuine fear of physical consequences to their person."[168] The police report noted, "The suspect sustained abrasions to the face, believed to be the result of his being taken to the ground." The police thought Clay might have hidden drugs in his mouth, but the white substance on his lip turned out to be the pieces of a molar crown broken by the impact of undisclosed blows to his jaw.[169] However, both *The Tribune Chronicle* and *The Vindicator* reported only that police saw a substance they believed was crack on his lip.[170]

---

[164] Ibid. 243.

[165] Ibid.

[166] Ibid. 182.

[167] Ibid. 244.

[168] Ibid. 28.

[169] Ibid.

[170] Peggy Sinkovich. "Strip Search Case: Warren will pay to settle with man." *The Vindicator*, 22 July 2004.

Clay had a drug charge on his record, which according to Olivito, meant "a license to brutalize," for the Warren police.[171] According to the police report, the officers observed Clay's car "exiting the driveway of a residence known to participate in the distribution of illegal narcotics," although the jury was later instructed by Prosecutor Susan Shipley to disregard this pretext.

The video recorded by the cruiser's dashcam debunked the arm-punching story. The video showed the officers rush up to Clay and wrench his arms behind his back before they dragged and slammed him against the hood of the police car. Clay disappeared from view, while hollow thuds are heard as the officers pounded Clay with their fists and stomped on him with their feet. In the complaint, Olivito described, "The officers began to grip his head and...began to bang his head against the pavement of his driveway and curb areas repeatedly."[172] Clay asked the officers why he was under arrest, but he received no answer as they kicked him in the ribs. After they were finished, one of them shouted, "Shut the fuck up! Get in the fucking car!"[173] Eventually, they answered his question. His crime was "obstructing official business," which Clay repeated in disbelief.

After the beating, Clay's ordeal was not over until he could be strip-searched at the station. Hunt put his fingers in Clay's rectum after ordering him to "spread himself." Hunt and Kistler both maintained under oath, "I did not, at any time, strip search Clarence Clay; I do not have any reason to believe Clarence Clay was strip-searched by anyone at the Warren Police Department."[174] The police charged him with resisting arrest and obstruction of official business. Then, the county judge, Thomas Hager, in his wisdom, added the charges of running a stop sign and failure to comply with an order. When Clay was finally released that night, he had to walk home with a bruised rib, a missing tooth, a swollen face, and no glasses.

Three days later, Clay was obliged to get a pacemaker after visiting the hospital because of chest pains. A medical expert later confirmed Clay suffered a heart attack as a direct result of the beating. He reportedly has difficulty talking at length without shortness of breath

---

[171] Ibid.

[172] *Clay v. City of Warren.* 4:03 CV 01636. 3. Ohio N. D. Court. 2004. Print. Page 3.

[173] Aina Hunter. "Blue Mob: Pity those caught by the Warren police, who rule with iron fists and rubber gloves." *Cleveland Scene*, 25 February 2004.

[174] Ibid.

and a fragment of a broken rib permanently jutting out of his back.[175] His indignity can be fathomed by the lengths to which he and his wife went for justice.

◇◇◇

In early August 2003, Olivito decided to go personally to the DOJ's office in Washington, D.C., only a week after filing the *Clay v. City of Warren* lawsuit. He was sitting in his office in Boardman on the other side of Youngstown when an older African American woman came in with both hands grasping her purse. Olivito invited her to sit down, though she said nothing. Slowly, gravely, she opened her purse and took out a slim manila folder.

"These are the records of my son's death. You look at this, and you tell me: Did the police kill my boy?"

Olivito stared at the woman and then at the manila folder as he opened it. In 2003, the case was already ten or fifteen years old. The police report said that officers were responding to a call about a domestic dispute. Her son had broken up the dispute, but after being alone with the cops for two minutes, he ended up dead. The coroner, Joseph Sudimack, had said the cause of death was undetermined, but an independent autopsy found that the cause of death was a crushed larynx. Every case Sudimack handled during his career as coroner had to be reviewed by BCI in 1996, but none of the police shootings or deaths in police custody were revisited, although half a dozen deserving cases were dug up by *The Tribune Chronicle*.[176] Olivito apologized to the woman and admitted that there was nothing he could do. The statute of limitations was two years, and the authorities saw no reason why it should be longer. On the contrary, they saw every reason to make it more difficult to pursue justice, as the U.S. Supreme Court demonstrated with every new decision. As he saw it, Olivito had only one option.

A few days after the visit by the bereaved mother, Olivito was with Rosa and Joshua at a wedding. Afterward, Olivito told Rosa he had something important to take care of, and he drove to Washington, D.C. On the way, he called a contact and set up a meeting with officials at the DOJ. A representative from the CRD met with him at a café nearby and then escorted him to the new DOJ offices. Once seated at a table in front of federal attorneys and investigators, he remembered, many years later, he was asked, "Is it as bad as Steubenville?"

"I think it's worse," Olivito replied.

---

[175] Ibid.

[176] Edgar Simpson and Alyssa Lenhoff. "Disorderly Conduct." *Warren Tribune Chronicle*, 14 April 1996.

"Are you serious?" exclaimed one official. Olivito noticed a container on a shelf against the wall labeled "Steubenville, Ohio."

"It's every bit as bad, but it's laced with racism. I wouldn't be here if it was just a few cases..." said Olivito.

He then recounted some of what he had learned during his month as the de facto civil rights clearinghouse in Warren. He spoke of gangland-style beatings with batons, the routine strip searches, and the harassment that followed those who complained. He recounted the stories of two women who had been stripped naked, strapped into chairs, sprayed with cold water and left for hours. Olivito told them that people were getting killed and their relatives couldn't get answers. He didn't have the specific dates and names of all the victims, but he was right that people were being quietly exterminated in Warren, and the police were either doing the killing, covering it up or too incompetent to register the crimes. James Hill Groves was murdered because he allegedly took an incriminating picture, but it was made to look like a suicide.[177] Others ingested or were forced to ingest or were said to have ingested drugs, like Matthew Perhacs, whose murder was made to look like a drug overdose.

Many died in custody of the WPD, and the coroner recorded them essentially without much examination of the corpse. A 1996 special investigation by *The Tribune Chronicle* listed the names of various mysterious deaths, exhuming the ghosts of Warren's past, "Daisey Gilmore, Orin Waddell, James Osmon, Harold Freeman, David Charles Daniels, John Edmondson."[178] There were many others. Stanley Karey was run over with a bulldozer and shot, but his death was ruled a suicide. An inmate died "hung" yet on his knees with toilet paper in his mouth. Tom Conley remembered a guy who allegedly died from an overdose before he was shot in the back of the head by a Warren police officer. Conley saw the chief afterward and felt obliged by custom to shake his hand like nothing happened, but he had already resolved to stand up publicly against them.

The deaths of area residents, black and white, men and women, passed without autopsy and without inquiry, especially if they were in state custody. One resident exclaimed, "They killed my husband and beat my baby boy." She wished to remain anonymous out of fear of the WPD. Those left without their loved ones were powerless. The same anonymous resident exclaimed, "The papers were full of unsolved murders, but the WPD shut it down!" Disturbing allegations of inmate deaths bubbled up in the community discussion forums of

---

[177] Ibid.

[178] Ibid.

local media websites for more than a decade after the special investigation by *The Tribune Chronicle*.[179]

In December of 1995, Marvin Lane, an inmate at Trumbull Correctional Institute (TCI) in Leavittsburg, died from a beating while he was hogtied,[180] which caused the state prison officials to wonder who had given the officers the idea that hogtying inmates was the standard operating procedure. It didn't seem to occur to prison officials or the AG's Office that the corrections officers (COs) weren't concerned with policy because they knew there would be no punishment. Three agencies investigated the homicide, and Ohio prisons changed their practices, but no one was punished. Twelve years later, there were COs coming forward to admit that the truth had been hidden, but the Lane family had disappeared without a trace, and nobody around had an incentive to file charges or a civil lawsuit.[181]

The newspapers rarely looked into nearly a dozen inmate deaths that occurred over the years, even though COs, or somebody doing a damn good job of impersonating them, bragged about their abuses in the community forums. A person claiming to work at TCI felt comfortable enough to add this comment to the thread below a post criticizing the WPD in a forum on the website of *The Vindicator*:

> That's what we do at TCI, since we have opened we have killed approximately ten inmates, we're known throughout the ODR&C as the real death row. Why waste all the taxpayers' money in meaningless courtroom battles, we stomp them and tell the county coroner he the dead inmate had a bad heart, hang them, tell the county he committed suicide. We once put a flaming homosexual in a cell with a serious white supremacist, no more gay inmate, then we tell the county coroner it was a bad fight, last year we put a blood and a crip in the same cell you guessed no more blood or was it no more crip,

Warren Youngstown just keep sending them boys to TCI.[182]
Unanswered questions haunted the surviving relatives as Warren police stonewalled inquiry. The police chief didn't worry about keeping

---

[179] "Warren city police should investigate the Lane death." *The Vindicator. Discussion Group: Talk of the valley*, 9 May 2007.

[180] Ed Runyan. "TCI death: 12 years and still no answer Case sparked statewide reform in use of force against prison inmates." *The Vindicator,* 29 April 2007.

[181] Ibid.

[182] Nate. "Warren Police." *The Vindicator: Talk of the Valley*, 8 February 2007.

records of internal investigations, or their resolutions, while hundreds of citizen complaints remained, including beatings and rapes, left to "linger and die," in the words of Chief Hutson,[183] unfounded or ignored by those officers' supervisors. If they persisted asking questions, the family members of victims were threatened.[184]

Tales of the WPD's strip search policy, the pattern of excessive force, and the cover-ups were percolating up the chain of command in the CRD. James "Doc" Pugh was in communication with the DOJ. Olivito visited and sat down with attorneys. Local journalists called for comment. The DOJ wanted to focus its enforcement efforts on large metro PDs, but according to Tom Conley, who was in contact with DOJ officials, one or two attorneys fervently argued to their superiors that the CRD should open an investigation in Warren. However, the Bush administration had been adding onerous documentation requirements to the process and replacing career attorneys in the CRD. Plus, the presidential election was on the horizon, a politically sensitive period before which DOJ activity often ebbs. No team of investigators would show up for another sixteen months after Olivito's visit. Instead, DOJ officials told Olivito, "We're watching. We're watching."

On August 10, only days after meeting with DOJ officials in D.C., Olivito filed a third civil rights lawsuit at the Northern District Court. The complaint concerned an incident that crystallized the frustrations of Warren's African American residents. It named as plaintiffs several young men and women, later referred to as the "Lynnwood Five," who were arrested at a bachelorette party on August 11, 2001. According to *The Vindicator*, former Officer Jeff Miller, former Officer Gerald Roth and Officer Manny Nites, now a lieutenant, allegedly used excessive force along with a generous smattering of racial slurs. Judging by the version of events agreed upon by the plaintiffs, the officers decided to beat some ass after discovering that one of the party-goers was packing a firearm. It didn't matter that it was legal, or that Ohio is an open carry state; after the officers knew there was a gun, they marauded around the property indiscriminately striking and shouting at the young African American partygoers.

Willie Owens was on crutches at the party, and the lawsuit stated, "Officers Roth and Miller knocked Owens' crutches out from under him and commenced to beat and use excessive force against him,

---

[183] Edgar Simpson and Alyssa Lenhoff. "Disorderly Conduct." *Warren Tribune Chronicle*, 14 April 1996.

[184] Ibid.

punching, kicking and kneeing him in the back."[185] Then, Roth angrily smashed Owen's legs in the door, according to the complaint. Lea Dotson remembered that she was in the basement with her friends when word spread that the police had arrived. They hurried outside just in time to witness the beating of Owens. Dotson saw Officer Nites checking if any cars were unlocked, presumably to search them. "You can't go through cars like that!" she yelled. Nites asked her name, and she refused to give it. Nites warned her, "You need to go into the house."

Her friends were pulling her back, and she relented, throwing up her hands in frustration. Nites saw this and jeered, "That's right, girlfriend, talk to the hand!" Dotson turned around, unwilling to let Nites' disrespect go unanswered. "I don't talk like that," she protested. "Look, girl," Nites continued, "I suggest you go back inside." Dotson obeyed, muttering as she walked away, "You fuckin' pigs." At that point, she heard Nites yell, "Get her ass!" Then, she felt a blow to her back. Nites grabbed her by the neck, flinging her to the ground. As he was pulling her arm behind her back with one hand, she bit his other hand. After she bit him, Nites punched Dotson in the mouth, splitting open her lip, and proceeded to drag her to the squad car in handcuffs. While in the cruiser, she got no answers as to why the police came to the party or why she was arrested. The prosecutor charged her with assaulting a police officer. The felony charge would trash her life plans, not to mention her civil and political rights. She pled to a reduced charge of disorderly conduct and spent ten days in the Trumbull County jail in Warren.

In a police cruiser on the way to the station, the officers allegedly called two of the partygoers, one of whom was a black officer's son, "stupid niggers." According to the officer, they "needed to be beat." The officer went on, "We know your mother, we fuck her all the time."[186] Five of those beaten later filed a lawsuit composed by Olivito, calling for a DOJ investigation. The opposing counsel undermined the case by raising the issue that Olivito was not licensed to practice before the Northern District Court.[187] The reputedly progressive Judge Oliver sustained the opposing counsel's objection and threw out the case although it was within his discretion to waive the requirement.

Dotson says cops harassed her after she filed a complaint. James "Doc" Pugh was guiding her efforts, like Councilor Skip Mixon

---

[185] Peggy Sinkovich. "Warren cops' son 4 others file a suit allege force." *The Vindicator*, 15 August 2003.

[186] Ibid.

[187] Peggy Sinkovich. "Warren: Lawyer's status puts cases at risk." *The Vindicator*. 10 September 2003.

in Steubenville. Pugh knew how the WPD worked, and he sent a statement to the chief, demanding an investigation by the DOJ Criminal Division because of the inability of the WPD to investigate their own. When Dotson called back repeatedly to track the progress of her complaint, it was obvious nobody had lifted a finger to investigate. Instead, one of the cops who came to the party pulled her over three times with dubious pretexts. In one instance, the officer put Dotson in handcuffs while he went to run her license in his car. He left all the doors open, as Dotson's daughter sat alone in the backseat on a chilly, autumn day.

"They were horrible cops," she stated many years later, "Mando was their safeguard. After he left, they all came up on crazy charges." This was true of Jeff Miller and Manny Nites. Miller shot one of his fellow officers by mistake and was arrested for drunk driving and domestic violence before he was fired in 2012.[188] Manny Nites was fired and rehired the same year. He remains on the force today, now a sergeant, despite his volatile temper, which resulted in nine complaints of excessive force between '91 and '93 alone, and his past fraud and dishonesty, for which he was repeatedly disciplined later in his career.

Not even Mandopoulos could protect his godson Gerald Roth's career because Roth wasn't just a horrible cop. He was a violent drunk, and by the time the authorities finally took away his badge, he had been accused of rape and convicted of manslaughter. In 1996, Albert Shipley had just become chief when Roth led another Warren police officer, Wayne Mackey, on a high-speed chase. After pulling Roth over, Mackey avoided saying Roth's name on the radio by substituting his badge number. Roth was charged with running a red light and reckless driving, but Mackey conveniently neglected to give Roth a breathalyzer, although he had a well-known drinking problem and owned a bar, the Paris Cafe. Shipley had promised a new era of accountability, after Hutson, under whose tenure 45% of complaints were never resolved, including one by a Warren woman who alleged Roth and another officer had raped her.[189] The lack of punishment informed residents what they could expect from Chief Shipley.

There were eleven citizen complaints against Roth between '91 and '93, and he failed two lie detector tests on complaints that were investigated. In one incident, Roth broke into the house of a woman who he had briefly dated and terrorized her, her child, and her new boyfriend. Nevertheless, Law Director Greg Hicks blamed the victim, saying she was a "little girl" with "two boyfriends," tacitly excusing

---

[188] Ed Runyan. "Warren cop fired after incidents with alcohol abuse." *The Vindicator*, 6 December 2012.

[189] Edgar Simpson and Alyssa Lenhoff. "Disorderly Conduct." *Warren Tribune Chronicle*. 14 April 1996,

Roth's felony breaking and entering. The investigation was dropped without charges, and Roth kept his badge for another decade. Then, in 2003, six years before Mandopoulos' departure, Roth pled guilty to vehicular manslaughter after he killed somebody while drinking and driving off-duty. Fred Harris remembers he was at a football game when officers came to notify him that Roth had killed somebody. Harris remembered one of the officers said, "I'm not surprised." The parents of his victim complained that Roth's one-year prison sentence was not enough.[190]

The Lynwood Five voiced opposition to the overreactions of the WPD against the children of Warren's African American residents. The lawsuit had added significance because one of the plaintiffs was a black officer's son. Officer Terrence Edington attended a protest against his employer because of his son's experience, which caused him to get flack from his white coworkers. Another plaintiff didn't trust white people and didn't like lawyers, but he signed on because he wanted to stand up for his friends.

Olivito had high hopes for the case, and he was bitter, as were the plaintiffs, over its dismissal. There wasn't even a hearing held on the issue that the judge raised before the judge dismissed the case with prejudice. For Olivito, a sense of foreboding immediately set in. If a black liberal judge from Cleveland found a reason to dismiss a volatile police misconduct lawsuit against the WPD over a technicality, Olivito and his other clients on the civil rights campaign train were in for a rough ride.

All eyes were on Lea Dotson as she held court at city council meetings that year. Although just twenty-two, she organized protests that drew several hundred people, a good turnout even in neighboring Cleveland. After one particularly tense meeting at city hall, Dotson remembered that Mandopoulos came up and asked her, "You think you can get the DOJ to come here? They're not going to come here."

---

[190] Peggy Sinkovich. "Warren: Ex-cop to spend year in prison for death." *The Vindicator*, 17 May 2003.

## 9

Shame on the Warren Police Department for not ever realizing it is illegal to do this.

- Attorney Kenneth Myers[191]

After filing a federal lawsuit under U.S. Code Section 1983 on August 1, 2003, with Olivito's help, Clarence Clay was due in the Trumbull County Court on the twenty-first for his plea hearing. Olivito wasn't there immediately, so Clay talked to the public defender, Melissa Dinsio, who had represented him at the arraignment on March 27, before he met Olivito. Dinsio advised him to take a plea rather than face jail time with a jury trial. After all, he had resisted the police for a moment, thinking the cops were going to take him somewhere and kill him.

The way the public defender framed it, copping a plea seemed like a good idea, but just after Clay began making his plea to resisting arrest, Olivito sprinted in, causing a bit of commotion, as usual. Olivito interrupted the proceedings and reasoned with Clay, "If you said these guys violated your rights, why are you pleading?"[192] Judge Hager granted a recess for Clay to make up his mind, after which he took Olivito's advice. *The Vindicator* reported on August 23:

> Leaving the courtroom, Clay appeared to be confused about the choice he had made and asked Olivito if prosecutors would still recommend no jail time at his trial. When informed that would not happen, Clay abruptly left the building.[193]

The article was written in such a way that people could get the idea that Olivito was pressuring Clay. "He's just upset because he has a bad health condition," Olivito told *The Vindicator*. "This court proceeding is a lot of stress on him, and they wanted to make him take a plea." The pressure by Olivito on Clay to persist was in Clay's interests if he

---

[191] Peggy Sinkovich and Stephen Siff. "Warren Probe: Cops strip-search against the law." *The Vindicator*, 23 July 2003.

[192] Peggy Sinkovich. "City man chooses jury trial in traffic-stop case." *The Vindicator*, 25 August 2003.

[193] Ibid.

wanted justice and any hope of a settlement to cover his medical costs. The article ended with a line that cleared up some of the ambiguity: "[Clay] did, however, say to Olivito in the courtroom that he 'remembers what the police did to him.'"[194]

Some Warren residents criticized public defenders like Dinsio, who later married a Warren police officer, because of their tendency to go along with the prosecutor rather than defending their indigent clients. The public defenders would urge clients to plead guilty or no contest to "contempt of cop" charges such as resisting arrest, disorderly conduct or assaulting a police officer. After that, according to former City Councilman Ron White, "It's virtually impossible to win a civil rights suit for police brutality."[195] By advising their clients to take a plea, the "less-than-scrupulous public defenders," according to the *Cleveland Scene*, "did their part to keep the city from being sued," because of their desire "to stay on the good side of the judges and prosecutors who run the show."[196]

Rather than getting into a contentious lawsuit and jury trial, Clay's wife Joanne wanted her husband to take a plea and be done with it. Although Clay knew he had a viable claim against the city's police— one that could temporarily lift financial burdens off his shoulders—he couldn't make up his mind.

◇◇◇

In the Warren Municipal Court, Judge Thomas Hager would hear the case. Before becoming a judge in 1995, Judge Hager was assistant city prosecutor. He has been a part-time professor at Kent State for almost three decades, and he is a member of the ACLU, as well as a volunteer for the American Legion, Board President of Free In Deed Prison Ministry and board member of the Warren Urban Minority Drug and Alcohol Outreach program, in addition to the former centennial president of the Warren Rotary Club. In addition to these civic activities, as of 2010, Judge Hager had been in four plays at TNT Playhouse.[197]

---

[194] Ibid.

[195] Aina Hunter. "Blue Mob: Pity those caught by the Warren police, who rule with iron fists and rubber gloves." *Cleveland Scene*, 25 February 2004.

[196] Ibid.

[197] Nicholas Verina. "Club Spotlight - Thomas Hager." *Warren Rotary Club*, 5 December 2010.

Before the trial, Olivito's father attended a status hearing. During the hearing, Judge Hager's behavior so angered the former judge that he declared, "I'm going to come out of retirement to sit at the defendant's counsel table!"

"You won't have time, the trial's this week," Judge Hager replied, dismissively.

"Well, I'm going to be in the courtroom every day," Olivito Sr. countered.

Olivito Sr. made the drive from Steubenville and sat quietly but conspicuously on the defendant's side of the courtroom during the two days of Clay's trial.

When Judge Hager called the court to order on September 15, the city's side had all seats nearly filled with police officers as well as various city officials, including the law director, Greg Hicks, the mayor, Hank Angelo and Chief Mandopoulos. Behind Olivito and Clarence Clay, there was only Joanne Clay and Judge Olivito. Richard concluded, "police took so much interest because the trial represented a milestone. Even if they are strip searched or beat up, working-class people in Warren rarely request jury trials."[198]

The jurors described the atmosphere in the courtroom as "unbearably tense."[199] According to Olivito and his client, the city's side of the courtroom became unruly at times. At one point, Officer Greg Hoso stood up and began to taunt Olivito. Clay confirmed that Hoso heckled him while he was testifying about his experience on the stand.[200] The *Cleveland Scene* described a moment when, "After a particularly obnoxious guffaw from Hoso, Olivito complained to Judge Hager. To the spectators' glee, Hager announced that Hoso was welcome to tell jokes."[201] Chief Mandopoulos claimed that he had not heard any heckling. When asked if he told his officers to attend the trial, Mandopoulos responded as he had when Urban League President Conley asked if the officers who beat up Kimble would be put on paid leave, "I would have to pay them overtime!"[202]

After Olivito filed the civil suit on August 1, Judge Hager became outraged by the mention of that lawsuit or its language during the

---

[198] Aina Hunter. "Blue Mob: Pity those caught by the Warren police, who rule with iron fists and rubber gloves." *Cleveland Scene*, 25 February 2004.

[199] Ibid.

[200] Ibid.

[201] Ibid.

[202] Ibid.

proceedings because he thought it could influence the jury. However, when both Assistant Prosecutor Susan Shipley and Olivito violated this prohibition, Hager finally lost his temper, threatening to hold Olivito in contempt, after which he ordered both attorneys into his chambers and slammed the door.[203]

The courtroom was silent while the jurors watched the video, giving the sounds of Clay's beating cringe-worthy emphasis. Hunt and Kistler suggested to the jury that Clay had white residue near his mouth to create the impression that the defendant's arrest had something to do with drugs, but Olivito made sure the record reflected that no substances were taken, tested, or examined from Clay's arrest. During her closing statements, Assistant Prosecutor Shipley additionally clarified that the jury should disregard the statement by the officers that Clay had come from a suspected drug house.[204]

On September 17, after eight hours of deliberation, the jury cleared Clay of the resisting arrest and failure to obey an order charges, but they found him guilty of obstructing official business and running a stop sign. Despite the guilty charge for obstruction, it was a major victory because Clay's civil rights case couldn't go forward without the dismissal of the resisting charge. *The Vindicator* reported that Clay did not cease to smile after hearing "not guilty" twice.

The jurors did not want to speak to the media, but they did speak to Assistant Prosecutor Shipley and Olivito after the verdict was announced. Olivito stated many years later that one of the jurors inquired about the "distinguished man" sitting in the back of the courtroom. Olivito responded that it was his father, feeling proud that the eighty-year-old retired judge's presence may have had an impact on the outcome. Watching the trial had an impact on Judge Olivito. Olivito remembers later when seated back at Karen Bryant's house's front porch, that his father told him, "Son, you are not just a good attorney, you are an excellent attorney." He added, seeing the neighbors looking upon his youngest son with smiles and congratulations, "and I'm beginning to understand you and why you do what you do a lot more now." Richard turned away, looking at the black children playing down the street with tears in his eyes.

Shipley relayed to *The Tribune Chronicle* the jurors' feeling that both the police and Clay had made mistakes on the evening of the arrest. Olivito explained that the jurors found fault that, "the officers didn't state their purpose for stopping him and placing him under arrest

---

[203] John Grant Emeigh. "Jury deliberates resisting arrest case." *Warren Tribune Chronicle*, 27 September 2003.

[204] *State of Ohio v. Clarence Clay*. 03-TR-134. The Eleventh Court of Appeals. 30 September 2003. Print.

soon enough." It was clear to the jurors that Clay did not know why he was being arrested. However, because he delayed getting in the patrol car for a moment, they decided he was guilty of obstruction. Clay was candid to a fault; he testified that he *had* resisted for a moment because he was afraid for his life. If he were a police officer, his fear would mean he was legally sanctioned to kill, but for Clay, it meant that he got beaten, strip and cavity searched, and two misdemeanors on his record.

After repeating only the discredited account of the police, and leaving out the beating and the strip search, *The Vindicator* quoted Conley's statement that the verdict was good news and that Karen Bryant wiped tears from her eyes, saying she was happy that people were recognizing what many had long known to be true. Assistant Prosecutor Shipley, an attractive blond so passionate in defending law enforcement that she was said to have cried over the verdict, recommended two years probation and no jail time.[205] However, "To everyone's surprise," Judge Hager rejected the recommendation, calling Clay a "dangerous and repeat offender" and "a threat to the community."[206] Although the jury had come back with a split verdict, Judge Hager sentenced Clay to the maximum thirty days in jail and declared that Clay "has not led a law-abiding life in recent years."[207] Hager was referring to a 1998 misdemeanor drug charge, but he seemed to incorporate the false charges dismissed by the jury when describing Clay's "pattern of repetitive, compulsive and aggressive behavior with heedless indifference to the consequences."[208]

On September 25, Olivito filed for temporary injunctive relief to stay the prosecution of Mr. Clay in the lower court because of what he alleged were irregularities of the trial in Judge Hager's court. According to Olivito's appeal, Clay had been ordered to participate in a "linkage order" that included six drug tests, although the charges had nothing to do with drugs. Assistant Prosecutor Shipley had originally offered the treatment program as a condition of his guilty plea, as she confirmed in an affidavit.[209] The linkage order was "commonly used

[205] Aina Hunter. "Blue Mob: Pity those caught by the Warren police, who rule with iron fists and rubber gloves." *Cleveland Scene*, 25 February 2004.

[206] Idib.

[207] *City of Warren v. Clay*. 2003 CR B 00766. Warren Municipal Court. September 25, 2003. Print.

[208] Ibid.

[209] *Clay v. City of Warren*. 4:03 CV 01636. 4. N. D. Court of Ohio. 2004. Print. p. 90.

for issues of alcohol and/or substance abuse, mental health issues and/or anger management." From Shipley's assessment of the situation in the affidavit, Olivito interrupted the orderly proceedings, which would likely have resulted in Clay undergoing treatment for being afraid of two officers who had just beaten him within an inch of his life.

Although he was officially presumed innocent, Clay could only contest the charges by allowing the additional variable of jail time to be added into his gamble with justice, as if to punish him for lying about his innocence.[210] Clay proved six times that he was drug-free, but Judge Hager prohibited the negative test results from being entered into the municipal court's record. The judge was clearly on the side of the prosecution, even though three of the four charges, as well as the linkage order, had no basis in law. Clay "may" have run a stop sign; the other charges were to cover for the brutality and sexual assault by Kistler and Hunt. Olivito further argued to the appellate court that Hager had no legal grounds to declare Clay a dangerous and repeat offender, which was language reserved for felony charges and acts of violence.[211] Hager even admitted as much in his ruling, but he reverted to Clay's 1998 drug conviction and 1999 trespassing violation in an attempt to trump up Clay's "aggression" and "lack of remorse."[212] He even referred to Hunt and Kistler as victims of the 53-year old non-violent defendant.

*The Tribune Chronicle* reported that, when she heard the sentence, Clay's wife screamed, "What an idiot!" Then, to Hager, she cried, "I hate you! I hate you! How could you do this?"[213] After Joanne Clay was removed from the courtroom, she could still be heard yelling in the hall. Few, if any, of the white officials, had any understanding or awareness of how this family was being victimized. When the jury rejected most of the false charges, Assistant Prosecutor Shipley took it as a personal defeat because of the way it reflected on her office. Her job was to uphold the arrests of law enforcement, and it meant everything to her. That was her family.

---

[210] Warren PD included a similar threat in their citizen complaint form, resisting calls to remove it three years earlier although they had signed a memorandum of understanding concerning it and many other issues with the NAACP and the DOJ.

[211] *State of Ohio v. Clay.* 03 T 134. 10. 11th District Court of Appeals.

[212] *City of Warren v. Clay.* 2003 CR B 00766. Warren Municipal Court. September 25, 2003. Print.

[213] John Grant Emeigh. "Jury deliberates resisting arrest case." *Warren Tribune Chronicle,* 27 September 2003.

The paper reported that members of Parents Against Police Abuse (PAPA) were outraged by the judge's decision.[214] Ron White, a former councilman and vice president of PAPA, concurred, "This is another way injustice is happening in this town." Olivito believed the sentence was, "retribution—payback for refusing to plead, payback for hiring a noisy outsider lawyer who thought he could shake the status quo." As if to underline the point, Chief Mandopoulos told *The Tribune Chronicle* "Clay would have been better off taking a plea bargain the prosecutor originally proposed."[215] It was a warning to others who might get ideas about justice and rights supposedly granted by the Constitution. Mando was having none of it. Olivito knew that they had won a significant legal victory, but he also knew that the payback was about to begin.

<><><>

In the complaint filed at the Ohio Northern District Court, Olivito described the deprivations Clay suffered in soaring prose armored with the language of the law. The officers' use of excessive force was in a manner "which evinces malice and ill-will...wantonly and recklessly with deliberate indifference to the civil rights of Mr. Clay on the evening in question."[216] The officers, "while they had the plaintiff in protective custody, assaulted and seriously beat and slammed him and his head areas repeatedly to the pavement while he was on his own property after an alleged minor traffic stop." The next outrage in store was the "infamous holding cell" in which they ordered him to strip, bend over and spread himself so an officer could stick his finger in Clay's rectum "to their satisfaction."[217] According to Olivito:

> The strip search policy was maintained, utilized and routinely performed by a number of Warren Police Officers on a regular basis for routine minor traffic violations according to internal police department records and findings made public within the past month.[218]

To bolster the *Monell* claim of municipal liability, Olivito needed to show that the policy or custom of the government agency responsible

---

[214] Ibid.

[215] "Verdict." *Warren Tribune Chronicle*. 28 September 2003.

[216] *Clay v. City of Warren*. 4:03 CV 01636. 4. U.S. N. D. Court of Ohio. 2004. Print.

[217] Ibid. P. 5.

[218] Ibid. 5.

for depriving his client of rights was a "moving force" behind the alleged violation of federal law. To that end, Olivito singled out Chief Mandopoulos as the final decision-maker on policy in the department, for which he bore responsibility: "Chief Mandopoulos never repudiated such a policy or practice within his department and has not done so, to the present. The chief either knew of the policy and/or should have known."[219] After assigning liability to the chief, the suit targeted the city of Warren, which is the first public entity named in the suit. Then, Olivito held forth:

> Because the city of Warren has allowed, through its most recent police chief, certain officers to operate in a manner more like an occupational army than a civilized police force, the city should be made to pay monetary reparations for all those who may have any impact from this unconstitutional modern day terror-like municipal custom, practice and/or policy which is a remnant and akin to the very Ku Klux Klan's historical terrorism upon American citizens for which Section 1983 litigation was specifically and expressly designed, in 1871, to legally redress.[220]

Drawing this parallel was controversial in the extreme. Although his strategy was to pack the complaints with so much specific, factual and damning information that the courts would be loath to dismiss the suit without concern for the political repercussions, he drummed up sympathy for the chief and the WPD by vilifying them. Local journalists would focus on the most controversial passages, asking the chief and Olivito's erstwhile allies about the brash rhetoric in the lawsuits, which enabled Mando to play the victim and caused Sarah Kovoor to all but publicly disavow him. Olivito grew up during the Cold War in Little Chicago. He was battle-hardened and willfully reductive of his enemies.

Olivito couldn't resist polishing literary pretensions, and he was just getting warmed up on why the city of Warren was liable. Olivito went on to describe, "a nightmarish existence of political and personal repression on a scale almost unimaginable in America."[221] The section of the citizenry suffering under this regime was "a unique class of victims" experiencing, "disparate and seriously unequal enforcement and application and system of the laws, based on class, ethnicity, and often race." This led to a "historical and constitutionally deprived population within the city of Warren, from being afforded fundamental per-

---

[219] Ibid. 6.

[220] Ibid. 7.

[221] Ibid. 8.

sonal liberties and constitutional protections which other neighbor-hoods and citizens...enjoy and fully exercise, every day."[222] For this reason, Warren's white residents were almost incapable of understanding their black neighbors' complaints. A Warren city councilman repeated in 2016 what white residents had argued for years, "The police protect us," which was true, but that protection was disparately applied.

People of color will tell anybody who drives up that Warren is unequal and segregated and corrupt, but calling out the police chief in court is another matter entirely. Safety Services Director Harris, as well as a few journalists and community leaders, would express their convictions publicly, but their comments were usually civil in tone.[223] Olivito went on:

> Many citizens in the affected areas have come to live in fear of routine, customary, overly aggressive police tactics, which include various brutal gang-like beatings by rogue cops, harassment, and all too common, strip searches, and other constitutional deprivations which shock and awe the American imagination.[224]

This language goes beyond what is normally stated in a Section 1983 complaint. Olivito intended to appeal to the wording of Section 14141, the "pattern or practice" clause, with the purpose of triggering a DOJ inquiry. Olivito explained, many years later, that he wanted to be the first lawyer in the U.S. to merge a 1983 complaint and a 14141 pattern or practice charge. Although the words used to describe how the violations arise in each law are similar, as is the spirit in which each originated, they are distinctly different in purpose and jurisdiction. Section 1983 was meant to provide a remedy for victims and their families against the unconstitutional actions of one or more individuals, while Section 14141 was passed as a means to obtain injunctive relief for the DOJ against a pattern of constitutional violations by one of its subdivisions.[225] However, private attorneys can file a pattern or practice suit, and the DOJ can refer to individual 1983 cases to support one.

Olivito reckoned that the constitutional deprivations in Clay's

---

[222] Ibid.

[223] One notable exception was a Vindicator editorial published the next year, entitled: "Warren police problems won't end with gag order." *The Vindicator,* 17 June 2004.

[224] *Clay v. City of Warren.* 4:03 CV 01636. 4. N. D. Court of Ohio. 2004. Print. Page 8

[225] *United States v. City of Columbus.* C2-99-1097. 10. S. D. Court of Ohio.

case were sufficient for a settlement in the hundreds of thousands. He had litigated medical malpractice cases, and he knew the ballpark liability figures when serious damage to a plaintiff's health verified by expert medical witnesses was tied to the actions of a defendant. For this reason, Olivito counseled Clay to stay the course, despite the pressure. Clay's ultimate hope of avoiding jail time rested with the Ohio Northern District Court in Akron with presiding Judge Adams, whom his counsel had beseeched for injunctive relief from the sentence of Judge Hager. Clay was terrified to go to jail with his new pacemaker because he feared being denied medical care if something went wrong. He told Olivito, "I think they gonna kill me in that jail. You don't know this town, Richard. This is a wicked, wicked town!"

<><><>

When Olivito, his statuesque paralegal, Brooke, and Clay met with Judge Adams in chambers to discuss the case, the judge inquired about the injuries and health problems mentioned in the complaint.

"You've alleged that Mr. Clay had a serious medical issue? What is the evidence? I understand he was beaten, and he was strip-searched, but there were no broken bones." Then, he turned to Mr. Clay. "Please tell me in your own words what happened to you."
Clay responded, "Well, I'm okay judge, I got hurt, they broke my glasses. I stumbled home, but I was humiliated, I was strip-searched."

"What about your medical injuries?"

"Well, I went to the doctor, later on, they treated me for heart failure." Then, the judge spoke to Olivito, "How are you going to prove this didn't preexist the beating?"

"I can do it, judge," Olivito responded.

"No, I'm not saying that…" Clay interjected, but he abruptly stopped speaking because Olivito's paralegal, Brooke, jammed the heel of her shoe into his foot.

"Yeah, I can do it," Olivito added hastily, to distract the judge from Clay's modesty regarding his injuries.

Olivito believed the heart attack was correlated with the beating, and he told the judge that the damages would amount to $400,000 to $500,000. Olivito then contacted board-certified heart doctors and had one of them examine Clay. Then, the doctor signed a letter stating his belief based on the examination that Clay's heart attack stemmed from the beating by the officers. Nevertheless, the defendants' counsel foisted the blame on Clay, stating, "Plaintiff was negligent and/or contributorily negligent as he assumed the risk of injury, said risk was open and obvious to him."[226] This puzzling statement is accurate insofar as Clay perceived that there was a risk when the officers approached him and a threat when they began to cajole him to get in the car. When he stood for an instant, paralyzed with fear and expecting to die as the officers ordered him into the cruiser, he was insubordinate, assuming in that act of negligence the blame and liability for what befell him thereafter. The opposing counsel, Hilary Taylor, who often defended cops and corrections officers, was an old hand at blaming the victim.

Officers Hunt and Kistler created headlines and another lawsuit two months after assaulting Clay with another assault on a young man, Alphonse Hogan. The two used their police cruiser to knock the teenager off his bike. Then, they followed him to his girlfriend's house where they beat him up with batons, although he had no record and had broken no laws.[227] In the last days of December, the same two officers sparked yet another lawsuit for grabbing a guy's crotch and illegally searching his car after he ran a red light. Kistler and Hunt were put on desk duty and later suspended for five days without pay.[228] In the course of the illegal search and seizure in that incident, Kistler switched off the cruiser's mobile video recorder, suggesting his consciousness of guilt.

Kistler was in the process of appealing suspension for three charges associated with that illegal search, seizure, and concealment when another internal investigation was triggered by a complaint from a woman whose license Kistler confiscated and kept in his cruiser after giving her a traffic citation. It turned out Officer Kistler had kept hold of the licenses of fourteen different motorists from December 2002 to November 2003. According to Chief Mandopoulos, when a captain investigating the complaint asked Kistler to return the licenses in the spring of 2004, Kistler instead entered them into evidence, for which he was charged with insubordination. He got a deal where the insubordination charge would be held in abeyance for two years if he would cooperate. In this episode, the WPD had to pacify an officer who had re-

---

[226] *Clay v. City of Warren.* 4:03 CV 01636. 3.   N. D. Court of Ohio. 2004. Print. Page 77.

[227] Hunter, Aina. "Blue Mob: Pity those caught by the Warren police, who rule with iron fists and rubber gloves." *Cleveland Scene*, 25 February 2004.

[228] Peggy Sinkovich. "Search suit settled for cash." *The Vindicator*, 23 June 2004.

peatedly disrespected residents, broken the law, flouted the authority of his bosses and then become grievously offended that his superiors had a problem with it. It would not be the last time community outrage, media condemnation and numerous sustained charges of misconduct would suffer an ignominious face-plant at the feet of a single defiant officer. Despite all, Kistler is now a sergeant. He did not respond to a request for comment.

It was overwhelmingly clear from Chief Mandopoulos' leniency and willingness to pacify his officers when they were insubordinate or refused to treat residents with respect: Mandopoulos cared about nothing so much as his officers. He would publicly attack the mayor and his boss before allowing himself to see his employees' misdeeds, like a father who spoils his children and refuses to hear accounts of their misbehavior. Edward Hunt signed on as the lead plaintiff among four suing the city of Warren in 2015 after a coveted lieutenant position was eliminated as the result of a budget shortfall. With his history of militant advocacy against budget cuts and his typical promotion of the most forceful officers, Mandopoulos would have been proud.

<><><>

Clarence Clay suffered the humiliation of being stripped naked and digitally sodomized by Hunt only three days after the WPD received the first citizen complaint of many regarding the illegal strip and cavity searches. Dominic Gambone was pulled over by Officers Timothy Parana and Robert Trimble in February of 2002 because he had blocked traffic at a stop light by the Trumbull Municipal Housing Authority (TMHA), which was not an area of town where traffic violations went unpunished. Gambone alleged that he had been subjected to a strip search after the officers ran his social security number and discovered that his license was suspended. On the day of Clay's arrest, March 27, 2003, Lieutenant Joe Kavanagh recorded the two officer's statements regarding the strip search of Gambone. Officer Parana challenged a few details of Gambone's account, such as his contention that Parana and Tremble conducted the cavity search with flashlights and gloves. Parana countered that he had not worn gloves.

Although neither officer included the cavity search in their report of Gambone's detention, Parana stated that he strip searched everyone he arrested. When asked to clarify, he replied, "I don't do females or juveniles," to everyone's great relief. Safety Services Director Harris was present for the conversation between Parana and Kavanagh, and he demanded to know, "Who told you that you can strip search?" Officer Parana demurred, but Harris threatened to fire him on the spot if he didn't fess up. Harris was expecting to hear that it was

Mandopoulos, but Parana surprised him. The officer said the Law Director Greg Hicks, three county prosecutors, and Judge Hager told him that it was legal to do strip searches routinely on anyone brought to the police station.

On March 28, Lt. Kavanagh talked with a WPD captain, as well as with local attorneys, Law Director Hicks and three Trumbull County prosecutors. When Lt. Kavanagh asked the prosecutors if they told officers they could do strip searches, they all denied it.[229] Hicks was under the impression that officers could do strip searches until Lt. Kavanagh showed him the section of the ORC on strip searches. Lt. When Kavanagh went to Judge Hager with Officer Parana and another officer seeking his interpretation of the law in question, Judge Hager told the men that the law said officers could "conduct a full search of a person's body incident to arrest."[230] Lt. Kavanagh asked the judge about the restrictions of the statute, and Hager replied that he didn't know. Kavanagh later stated that he believed the judge had taken the part about searching a person's body out of context.

Assistant Prosecutor Shipley came by Lt. Kavanagh's office later that afternoon, and they spoke about strip searches. Shipley thought, like Judge Hager and Law Director Hicks, that it was proper for officers to do strip searches, but after reading the section of the ORC Kavanagh had dug up, she changed her mind. Afterward, Kavanagh spoke again with Officer Parana, and Kavanagh stated that Parana "was adamant that it was okay to do strip searches and he does them on everyone." At that point, Lt. Kavanagh asked Parana if he wanted to talk about the Gambone incident in his office, but Parana declined, telling his superior that he was too aggressive about the strip searches.[231]

On April 1, Lt. Kavanagh spoke again with Assistant Prosecutor Shipley to clarify how certain officers got the idea that strip searches were routine. She maintained that she had spoken to officers about specific cases but that she never told them that every person arrested could be strip searched. Instead, she had explained to the officers that there had to be "probable cause, exigent circumstances or it could be done at a detention facility." Both Kavanagh and Shipley agreed that the holding cell at the police station could not legally be considered a detention facility, although the WPD had been using it as such for decades. Upon consideration of the unsettling potential consequences

---

[229] Confirmed by Safety Service Director Fred Harris in Affidavit.

[230] *Kimble v. Hoso et al.* N. D. Court of Ohio. 2008. p. 844. Print.

[231] Ibid.

of their previous support, officials were naturally trying to distance themselves from the decades-old WPD strip-search policy.

The next year, in February of 2004, Aina Hunter covered the Gambone strip-search case in her article in the *Cleveland Scene* magazine. She wrote that Kavanagh found that "most officers believed they could conduct cavity searches on anyone for any reason." Sgt. Rob Massucci, now a captain, who led the officers patrolling the TMHA, had allegedly ordered all officers to strip search every suspect. Hunter reasoned, "Massucci's abuses could not have continued without the complicity of police lawyers, the prosecutor's office, and at least one municipal judge—Thomas Hager." When Hager was questioned by Lt. Kavanagh about the strip searches, "Hager seemed confused and argued that the police were in the right. It wasn't the first time Hager was confused about the law."[232][233]

Lt. Kavanagh delivered his completed IA investigation to the police chief on April 7, 2003. Upon receipt of the investigation, Chief Mandopoulos not only declined to discipline the officers, he refused to accept that routine strip searches without probable cause were unconstitutional. Fred Harris was in Mandopoulos' office when Lt. Kavanagh supplied him with the disputed passages of the ORC. According to Harris, when Lt. Kavanagh broke it to Mandopoulos that he doubted strip searches were legal, Mandopoulos shouted, "Yes we can!" In his mind, strip searches were just another part of smart police work. Nobody, not even the ORC, was going to tell him what to do. Mando was a law unto himself, but he maintained the culture and procedures of his forbears, Shipley and Galgozy. In 1988, a black man was strip-searched on the direct order of Chief Galgozy after being cited for a "wandering

---

[232] Aina Hunter. "Blue Mob: Pity those caught by the Warren police, who rule with iron fists and rubber gloves." *Cleveland Scene*, 25 February 2004.

[233] Hunter may have been alluding to a case in November of 2003 in which Hager charged a man with 'importuning,' a crime that was no longer on the books in the state of Ohio. Keith E. Phillips, age 21, was charged under a law that made it illegal to ask someone of the same sex to have sexual intercourse if it might offend them, but the law had been repealed a month beforehand. Hager first responded, "It's not my job to look up this stuff," then commented to *The Warren Tribune Chronicle*, "[Phillips] has a habit of pulling down his pants around young boys, and as far as I'm concerned, that's still illegal in the state of Ohio." Phillips filed a $10 million suit against the City, the municipal court, and a few former employees. From Eric Resnick. "Judge who jailed man for nonexistent crime is sued." *Gay People's Chronicle*, 23 November 2003.

dog."[234]

On July 23, 2003, *The Vindicator* reported on the strip and cavity searches and the chief's decision not to discipline the officers. Although the WPD, the law director, and the judge were left looking incompetent, the article noted that "a new departmental policy, with strict guidelines on strip searches, has been created. The new guidelines...require [sic] doctors to be present during the most invasive searches."[235] Mayor Angelo declined to comment. The article ended quoting Harris, who exclaimed that he would recommend a punishment "180 degrees different" than Mandopoulos.

When the chief made his decision regarding the outcome of an internal investigation, he would send it to the Safety Services Director for approval. Director Harris took the opportunity when the Gambone investigation landed on his desk to send it right back to the chief and demand Mando reopen the investigation. Mandopoulos later reopened the investigation, but it wasn't at the behest of his boss. Instead, Action 19 News reported that an independent investigation by a Cleveland attorney concluded that the officers broke the law and should have faced misdemeanor charges.[236] Mandopoulos was quoted saying they would take a second look because, "We want to make sure we're doing the right thing."

The DOJ report, which came later, announced that the WPD had waited until the statute of limitations ran out to refer its investigation of strip searches to a special prosecutor. The DOJ "recommended" that the WPD should add language to its policy on citizen complaints and internal investigations regarding when a case should be referred to a local or federal prosecutor for a criminal investigation.[237] Mando was just following in a long line of chiefs who had intentionally buried citizen complaints of serious criminal conduct, like sexual assault and other high-level felonies, in compromised internal investigations. He wasn't about to break with tradition.

[234] Alyssa Lenhoff and Edgar Simpson. "Disorderly Conduct." *Warren Tribune Chronicle.* 14 April 1996.

[235] Peggy Sinkovich. "Report: Cops' strip-searches illegal." *The Vindicator*, 23 July 2003.

[236] Action 19 News. "Warren police chief reopens strip searches investigation." No date.

[237] Shanetta Y. Cutlar. "Re: Warren Police Department." *U.S. Department of Justice, Civil Rights Division*, 2 March 2006.

In August of 2003, two other Warren residents filed complaints about illegal strip searches conducted in June of 2002 by Sgt. Rob Massucci after he discovered that one of the men, LaShawn Ziegler, owner of 77 Soul and public enemy of the WPD, was driving with a suspended license. Massucci inexplicably charged both men for driving on a suspended license and strip-searched them. The city settled the lawsuit two months later.[238] Fred Harris told Ziegler that if he resisted a quick settlement, he would be able to obtain a higher sum, but he needed the money, so he took 25K for each strip search. The city may have been lucky that Ziegler walked away from a protracted legal battle because Zeigler stated, many years later, that the search he sued for was just one of four in which the same two officers "kidnapped" him but wrote no citation and filed no charges. These strip searches were treated like King stops and given the old Cleveland treatment of "no-papering."[239]

Zeigler's business was controversial. After 77 Soul went out of business, he says he was told that he would "never work in this town again." When asked if he still has problems with the WPD, he responded with a smile, "I don't get harassed if I'm not in business." There was a movement of local political and economic interests gathering momentum to find out who was enabling organized crime to flourish in that neighborhood. A private investigator was hired by a local power-broker who was looking to remove whoever was responsible for the corruption. It later came to light that the law director had real estate interests in the area. Hicks refused to shut down the bars even as liquor violations, gang activity, and shootings took place. Zeigler was managing the bars. Bob Cregar, a bail bondsman who was a former business partner and continuing landlord of Hicks, owned one of the bars.[240] Questions arose whether Hicks could discharge his duties without bias while being so closely connected to bail bondsmen who were involved in racketeering and employed violent felons, but the investigation was called off. It wouldn't be the last time questions emerged about Hicks' investments, but he remains slippery and impregnable.

---

[238] Peggy Sinkovich. "Strip-search lawsuit costs city $52,000." *The Vindicator*, 5 February 2004.

[239] Roscoe Pound and Felix Frankfurter. "Criminal Justice in Cleveland." *The Cleveland Foundation*, 1922.

[240] Tribune Chronicle. "Hicks: There is no conflict of interest." 16 December 2012.

## 10

Politics in the valley are often euphemistically described as "rough and tumble," but it can be downright life-changing and dangerous. We seem to punish those who do not "go along" with the powerful status-quo players.

-Anonymous[241]

On September 23, 2003, Olivito missed a post-sentencing status hearing for a minor case at the Youngstown Municipal Court so that he could be present at the Trumbull County Court of Common Pleas Court for a grand jury meeting.[242] On that day, Olivito was scheduled to present witnesses for Lyndal Kimble. The case was the primary focus of Olivito's thoughts because a lot of area residents were watching it. When he tried to explain the situation over the phone, Olivito stated that he was told by the prosecutor, "Don't worry, I'll find someone to stand in, but Judge Milich is very upset with you."

Judge Milich was a retired caucasian U.S. Air Force lieutenant with wire-framed glasses, and a bouffant of brown hair brushed back. When Olivito's criminal cases brought him before Judge Milich, they maintained amicable terms and had cordial, arm's-length conversations. Thinking of the friendly relations he and Judge Milich maintained, Olivito responded, "I think he will understand if you tell him where I am. I'll call back to make sure that you've found someone."

When he did so, he noticed that the prosecutor sounded worried, "Judge Milich won't allow someone to fill in." Olivito was baffled. Having another attorney stand-in was common practice when there were scheduling conflicts. Besides, everybody knew that the Kimble incident was unprecedented in the town's history; no African American defendant from Warren had ever dared assert innocence on national media outlets. Olivito assumed that the issue with Judge Milich was just a misunderstanding.

---

[241] David Skolnick. "Ex-judge faces fraud charges." *The Vindicator*, 4 December 2009.

[242] Patricia Meade. "Judge finds Boardman attorney in contempt of court." *The Vindicator*, 6 October 2003,

Then, another impediment came up to delay Olivito's arrival in the Youngstown Municipal Court. Clarence Clay was scheduled to be incarcerated at the Trumbull County jail that afternoon, and he was scared to death because of the jail's reputation in the black community. Warren's history was tainted with suspicious deaths in custody, and Clay believed he was a prime target. Olivito did the dutiful thing and accompanied his client while he was processed at the jail. Clay held Olivito's hand tightly throughout, using Olivito's white privilege like a life preserver.

Afterward, Olivito went to the Youngstown Municipal Court to mollify Judge Milich. He remembered Milich red with anger, unlike he had ever seen him. Ironically, Olivito's client had also missed the hearing but was not held in contempt. Even if Olivito had appeared at the appointed time, there would have been no hearing. Normally, in response to such conduct from defendants and attorneys, Judge Milich would order the defendant to show cause, which obliges the offender to appear and grovel before the judge. This time, however, Judge Milich immediately initiated the contempt process for the first time ever in his court.[243] The judge later generated headlines after he jailed a lawyer for contempt because she refused to remove a Black Lives Matter pin. Olivito was obliged to meet with a probation officer, who allegedly told him, "I don't know what this is all about. We don't get it ourselves." Milich would not rule on the contempt charge until February. Until then, Olivito had the charge hanging over his head. He was surprised that the police cases were causing such a heated response, but he wasn't overly concerned.

<><><>

"This attorney has created a vision in everybody's mind that he's some kind of civil rights leader," Chief Mandopoulos later said of Olivito.[244] Seven months after the first lawsuit was filed, Mandopoulos was still trying to cast doubt on Olivito's qualifications asking, "Is this guy even a lawyer?"[245] The next month, Mandopoulos himself would

---

[243] Patricia Meade. "Judge finds Boardman attorney in contempt of court." *The Vindicator*, 6 October 2003.

[244] John Grant Emeigh. "Warren chief expects more brutality claims." *Warren Tribune Chronicle*, 8 July 2003.

[245] Aina Hunter. "Blue Mob: Beware the Warren cops, the city's most violent gang. The second of a two-part series." *Cleveland Scene*, 3 March 2004.

be denied summary judgment in a lawsuit filed by Olivito, though it was not reported in the press. In the lawsuits, the chief followed the instructions of his attorneys. In one affidavit filed in the Clay case, Mandopoulos used the words of his attorney, stating that he worked "with a number of community organizations in a continuing effort to assure that the law enforcement efforts…meet the needs of the community."

On September 25, 2003, the mayor's office sent a letter to Chief Mandopoulos listing the actions for which he was requested to appear for a pre-disciplinary hearing. The infractions included failing to discipline Officer Manny Nites for his use of racial slurs in front of 77 Soul, as well as the threat Mandopoulos made to Michelle Nicks on August 1, which had people calling for his dismissal.

In November, *The Vindicator* ran a front page headline, "Police department torn by internal strife," which detailed an atmosphere of division and disorder within the WPD.[246] Some officers were not on speaking terms with their fellow officers. Harris stated many years later that a few officers had come into his office complaining about misconduct they witnessed. "They were upset, but they wouldn't speak out against the bad officers." The lack of discipline flowed from the chief, so he was charged with "acting in a manner that brings disrespect to the police department, failing to control the actions of a lower ranking officer and threatening a television reporter."[247] On December 8, Mayor Angelo recommended a ten-day suspension for Chief Mandopoulos.

The next day, *The Tribune Chronicle* reported that the chief had not bothered to open the letter. Defiantly, Chief Mandopoulos stated, "I'll open it when I get around to it. [Mayor Angelo] is not important to me."[248] The article went on to describe the 77 Soul incident, omitting the racial slurs used by Officer Nites. As usual, the paper glossed over the most provocative details of any controversy. The charges against Mandopoulos were presented before the CSC, which adjudicates all matters involving the city's personnel, but the chief could appeal the decision by the CSC at the common pleas court, which according to Harris, "gives the chief a lot of power."

The charges seemed serious enough, but there were other allegations against Mandopoulos in the media and among community resi-

---

[246] Peggy Sinkovich and Stephen Siff. "Warren: Police department torn by internal strife. *Warren Tribune Chronicle,* 17 November 2003.

[247] Raymond L. Smith. "Police Chief may be suspended." *Warren Tribune Chronicle*, 18 November 2003.

[248] John Grant Emeigh. "Letter from mayor left unopened." *Warren Tribune Chronicle*, 26 September 2003.

dents. Tom Conley referred to the strip searches, the brutality, and the failure to discipline. *The Tribune Chronicle* quoted Conley as saying, "You take all these incidents as a whole, and it's clear that a change of leadership must take place."[249] This call was echoed by people within the city government who alleged that Mandopoulos interfered with the investigation of the 77 Soul incident. Critics pointed to a discrepancy that arose in a hearing. Mandopoulos claimed the investigation of the 77 Soul incident was ongoing while Lt. Kavanagh said it had been concluded and turned over to the chief.

Mandopoulos was not about to let the public take its anger out on him alone. He countered that the assistant law director had told him to "stop investigations about racial incidents and strip searches." When asked by journalists, Mayor Angelo declined to comment on the issue, but he stood his ground against the chief in the hearing of the CSC. The paper included an unusually forceful statement by Mayor Angelo:

> I further find that your claims that [Assistant Law Director] Mr. Sanders counseled you not to conclude any investigations surrounding Officer Nites and your claim that the investigation of Officer Nites was not concluded, when in fact you knew it was concluded, to be a disturbing pattern of dishonesty.[250]

This was not enough for many residents, but PAPA Vice President Ron White said it was "a start." The chief was not one to take discipline lying down. On November 21, 2003, *The Vindicator* reported Mandopoulos' resistance under the headline, "Police Chief to fight suspension."[251] The charge for threatening a journalist seemed to falter because no witness came forward to corroborate Nicks' complaint. However, according to a transcript of the disciplinary hearing, the mayor ordered Mando to stop making threats in the course of the hearing. He appealed his ten-day suspension and pointedly told Fred Harris, "I'll be here when you're gone!" Although Mando may have been wrong about many things, among them public relations, discipline, citizen complaints, cost accounting and record-keeping, he was right that he would outlast Harris and Mayor Angelo.

As a boy in the TMHA, Harris said that he had grown up dealing with the deprivations and outrages of the WPD, and no one was going to stop him from exerting the power of his position for the sake of the next generation. He considered asking an organization such as

[249] Raymond L. Smith. "Police Chief may be suspended." *Warren Tribune Chronicle*, 18 November 2003.

[250] Ibid.

[251] Peggy Sinkovich. "Police Chief to fight suspension." *The Vindicator,* 21 November 2003.

the NAACP or the Greater Warren Youngstown Urban League to file a complaint about the strip searches. The Warren NAACP would require the approval of the state and the national office. Their attorneys could try to interfere, and NAACP leaders often showcased their involvement in such cases in the press. Harris was not looking for more publicity with uncertain results, so he called Tom Conley. Harris told Conley, "Look, I don't have any other organization that can do this. I need you to do this."

Conley wanted to avoid the animosity between Mando's many supporters and those who wanted him held accountable, but despite initial reservations, Conley agreed. City officials worried that settlements for strip searches could bankrupt Warren. Fred Harris wasn't worried about the city; he was worried the police would get away with it.

## 11

As far as Warren PD goes, sometimes you just have to kick ass to let certain people in your community know that THEY DON'T RUN THE CITY. In Warren, the thugs fear the cops.

-"Toad"[252]

Olivito's visits to Kimble in the Trumbull County jail caused the word to spread among the inmates that someone filed a lawsuit against the WPD for excessive force. These rumors attracted the attention of one particular inmate, John Rogers II, who had been locked up for two months. He had a broken tooth developing into an abscess due to being pummeled by an officer, but he was denied medical attention. Rogers was a white guy in his early twenties, still a kid at heart, excited by breaking the rules. He was not popular or privileged, but he was well-liked, and despite his size, he was not a bully. Most importantly for Olivito, Rogers was honest. *Rogers v. City of Warren* was the third of four lawsuits filed by Olivito against the Warren police at the Ohio Northern District Court.

On the morning of April 29, 2003, Charles Berry let his dog out and observed the door to his barn standing open. Upon entering the barn, he noticed his hunting clothes littering the floor and his green Kawasaki four-wheeler conspicuously absent. He called the Champion police department, which sent out the report to other local law enforcement agencies, including the WPD. Several days later, on May 4, two other Champion residents reported missing four-wheelers. Later that day, Warren police officers spotted three guys apparently joyriding on ATVs out by the WCI Steel Company, one of the largest steelmakers in Warren. Later that year, WCI filed for Chapter 11 bankruptcy and was sold off to Russian investors.[253] According to the complaint filed by Rogers, the guys on their way to return the four-wheelers when they noticed Warren police were following them.

According to the police report of the incident, Officer Eric Merkel, who is now the chief, drove his cruiser into the path of the

---

[252] Toad. "Re: Warren Police." The Vindicator: Discussion Groups: Talk of the Valley, 10 February 2006.

[253] Larry Ringler. "WCI files Chapter 11: Steelmaker to arrange financing to stay open." Warren Tribune Chronicle, 17 September 2003.

ATVs and stopped. As Merkel was getting out of the cruiser, the four-wheelers slid to a stop, crunching rocks and gravel under tread. Then, suddenly they took off again, and one of them struck the cruiser's door, which slammed into Merkel's nose, opening up a bloody gash. Merkel fell to the ground, confident his nose was broken, but he soon recovered himself and apprehended one of the men, Raymond Dickey, who was riding Berry's green Kawasaki. At 5:05, the officer radioed, "Send a unit to Atlas, think I broke my nose." Merkel's statements in the police report reflect that he believed it was the red Yamaha that struck his cruiser's door.

Officer Richard Kovach showed up in response to Merkel's call and described the scene in the police report: "As I arrived, I saw Arrestee #1 [Raymond Dickey] lying on the ground in handcuffs with Merkel standing over top of him bleeding profusely from his face." Kovach gave Merkel a towel, noting that his nose looked broken. Then Kovach, who would later be fired for tasering a female seven times,[254] was called back to the station. He drove Dickey to the station for booking while Merkel got stitches in his nose.

Police located the other two ATVs within two hours. Officers pursued the red Yamaha on foot and in their cruiser, trading their locations and the movements of the suspect over the radio. They worked quickly to establish whether the suspects were at loved ones and family members' houses. At 5:40, Officers Doug Holmes, Brian Crites, and Jeff Miller apprehended John Rogers II at his cousin's house, where he was living temporarily. Upon emerging from a shower, Rogers was taken into custody still "dripping wet."

Many years later, Rogers recounted that he answered the door to Officer Holmes, who immediately asked Rogers to lift his shirt. Holmes used Rogers' lock tattoo to verify Rogers' identity. Next, he ordered Rogers to turn around and handcuffed his hands behind his back. The officers found the red Yamaha and noted that the engine was warm. Then, they radioed the vehicle identification number so that WPD staff at headquarters could run it through the LEADS system. The WPD coordinated efficiently to reclaim the allegedly stolen four-wheelers, but, as usual, there had to be some violence. In his account of the arrest, Officer Holmes stated that he ended up dragging Rogers into the infamous holding cell, allegedly because Rogers had become "physically aggressive."

At 7:30 in the evening, Officer Kovach, and Dewey received information that Wayne Mitchell, who had the white Polaris, was at his girlfriend's house. Once there, they discovered Mitchell hiding in the attic. The officers said Mitchell was shouting at them before his arrest.

---

[254] Ed Runyan. "Tasered woman settles lawsuit for $300,000." The Vindicator, 20 August 2010.

Around 8:15, they took him into custody and confiscated two firearms at the premises, but the girlfriend was unaware or unwilling to say whose they were. Officers reported that Mitchell continued to be belligerent and knocked over a bench in the lobby of the police station, resulting in the use of pepper spray to subdue him.

So far, it was a normal day, just a little force and pepper spray to smooth out the rough edges. According to the police account of the arrest, the only uses of force were pepper spray on Mitchell and the dragging of Rogers. However, Rogers told another story in his civil rights complaint and in the affidavits and depositions that followed, as well as a decade later in conversations on Facebook. The events of May 4, 2003 were burned in his memory.

According to his recollection, the officer we'll call Officer Holmes pushed him into the cruiser so that during the ride to the police station he was on his stomach with his hands cuffed behind his back. This was irregular and inconsiderate, but Rogers kept quiet. Once there, Holmes opened the door by Rogers' head and when Rogers looked up, Holmes promptly punched him just above his left eye. Then, Holmes walked around the car to the other door and yanked him out of the car by his ankles. Rogers' body landed hard face first on the blacktop because his hands were cuffed behind his back and couldn't break his fall. Next, Holmes dragged him along the ground, pulled him up and slammed him into a desk and bench. At first, Rogers had been indignant, but now he was terrified. The officer seemed to be losing it.

Holmes allegedly punched him, smashed his face against a concrete wall, and slammed him up against a garbage can. Next, Rogers recalled that he was shoved over a couple of benches and up against a glass pane by a Coke machine. In the process, Rogers lost two toenails, because his sandals left his feet vulnerable as the officer dragged and tossed him around. During this assault, Holmes allegedly repeated that Officer Merkel was "a fellow officer," alluding to Merkel's injury. Holmes was showing the same priority instilled by Chief Mandopoulos, officers' safety over that of Warren residents. Rogers protested that Merkel's injury wasn't his doing, which was true. Merkel attested to the mistake in the initial police report in a note dated June 20; it was the white Polaris, not the red Yamaha, which struck the police cruiser's door. Still, Holmes was going to get the answer he wanted.

Finally, Holmes transported Rogers to the jail and threw him into a cell. Thinking it was over, Rogers asked if he could make a phone call, which inspired Holmes to lay into him again with his fists. Rogers thought the officer was trying to knock him out, but the repeated blows failed to make him lose consciousness. Rogers wrote, "He just kept hitting me and hitting me and hitting me with my hands behind my back till finally he turned and walked away and left the area. That's when I started yelling I needed to see a doctor or go to the hospital." After Rogers screamed for ten minutes about his need for medical attention, Officer Holmes came back and threw the sandal Rogers' had lost through the bars. Rogers remembers that his sandal hit him in the chest and fell to the ground. With nothing else to do, he slid his foot into the sandal and sat on the bench, feeling incredible pain.

At that moment on May 5, Holmes was under the mistaken impression that Rogers was responsible for Merkel's injury, and Holmes was trying to "beat a confession out of him," according to Olivito's account in the complaint. Holmes' counsel wrote in the motion for summary judgment in December of that year, "Plaintiff was resisting arrest, acting aggressively and Defendant Holmes was cautious due to the fact that plaintiff had already seriously injured another police officer during the pursuit."[255]

The internal documents provided by the WPD to the court reflect that Rogers was taken a few blocks away to the jail after being in the station for approximately twenty-five minutes. During that time, the record of the police radio supports Rogers' account of events. At 5:40, officers radioed that they had John Rogers in custody. At 5:43, one officer asked, "will he fess up where the white one is?" The response was, "He don't know what we are talking about." Then, five minutes later, officers mentioned the hospital before saying, "started to fight on HQ will need double unit to transport." At 7:20 pm, Rogers stood before a camera for his mug shot, which was included in the police report provided to the court. In the photo, Rogers' face has dark areas, referred to in the course of the lawsuit by his attorney as evidence of the beating omitted from the arrest report.

Officer Holmes was later awarded a medal for bravery by President Obama for charging into a burning house to save three disabled women. One of the women later died from her injuries, and Holmes later sued the city over the case. The *Tribune Chronicle* ran an article enumerating all of his positive attributes, such as his exploits as a crisis negotiator, his exemplary attendance, his diversity training and nearly a dozen commendation letters in his personnel file.[256] The WPD would not have informed the media of his disciplinary record, which the union contract allows to be erased every two years. Officer Holmes was less prominent in the media for his brutality, and his record shows that he will risk his own life for others. Merkel's injury seemed to be the most likely rationale for Holmes' treatment of Rogers. This should

---

[255] *Rogers v. City of Warren.* JU 4.15 N. D. Ohio. March 20, 2006. Page 167. Print.

[256] Darcie Loreno. "Officer, women hospitalized." *Warren Tribune Chronicle*, 29 April 2009.

have been the subject of routine internal investigation and discipline, but it wasn't.

In court documents, Holmes stated that Rogers "was repeatedly commanded to comply with the instruction standard of the holding cell, as well as to exit the vehicle and enter the building." In the statement of the facts by the defense, the officers alleged that Rogers "resisted arrest and was physically aggressive towards the officers," which Rogers denied. In the original report, Holmes described his treatment of Rogers as "placing physical control," and didn't include WPD's official use of force form, but then two hours later he added a few lines describing the use of pepper spray on Mitchell as well as the use of force form. These kinds of discrepancies might raise red flags in a normal police department, but in the WPD, the attitude towards the use-of-force was as casual as the use of racial slurs, and it came directly from the chief.

Officer Crites, who once suggested the WPD wear "white hoods," employed Roger's nickname, 'Porky,' in his report of the incident, perhaps because Rogers' cousin referred to him using his nickname and the officers thought it was funny. His mug shot lists his height at 5'11" and his weight at 245 lbs., earning him his nickname. For the officers to continue to use this name in signed affidavits during the trial was a form of overt disrespect. In his affidavit, Officer Holmes confirmed that he was "familiar with the facts in the arrest of Rogers, whose street name is 'Porky...'" Holmes then repeated Rogers' nickname five times throughout the affidavit, sometimes followed by "a.k.a. Rogers." As in the case of Andre Hython, the nickname became a "street name" in the hands of the state's attorney. It was used to imply a criminal background or deficient character rather than a sign of endearment. The lawyer for the police, Hilary Taylor, later advised the attendees of a police conference that he preferred to use "plaintiff,"[257] perhaps to avoid the appearance of disrespect, which doesn't score points with juries. The police counted on never having to appear before a jury for their brutality. The city would settle the cases before that ever happened.

Between Rogers, Mitchell, and Dickey, thirteen charges and two victims arose from the incident. Mitchell was charged with receiving stolen property, failure to comply, obstructing official business and criminal trespass. Police arrested his girlfriend for obstructing justice with the guns. John Rogers II was booked on resisting arrest, failure to comply with an order, receiving stolen property, felonious assault against a police officer and criminal trespass. Rogers sat in jail for three months, during which he was refused medical treatment, although Holmes had broken one of his teeth. He was finally given aspirin after

---

[257] Hilary Taylor. "Defense of Monell Claims." *Defense Research Institute*, Course Materials 2013.

three months, and when it had been four months, they provided him with a dentist who discovered that Rogers had an abscessed tooth. Olivito described Rogers' detention, "Such a summary punishment delivered by the state actor defendant, prior to conviction, constitutes a cruel and unusual form of punishment, which is in derogation of the plaintiff's fundamental liberties and due process rights and equal protection of the law." *The Vindicator* reported that a guy was suing the city and the chief for two million dollars.[258] Law Director Greg Hicks was used to nickel and diming plaintiffs throughout the '90s, five thousand for a case of excessive force, two thousand for a false arrest, with settlements reaching similar heights as Steubenville in McCartney's heyday. Now, the sums involved were larger and a policy claim hung in the balance.

Officer Holmes denied striking Rogers under oath, and no video or audio evidence was available to verify the truth of the matter. Holmes was equipped with a microphone and camera, but there was an alleged battery failure, a common occurrence when officers use force. The battery failure became the subject of an investigation by the WPD. There was a bank of cameras in the entrance to the jail, but according to Mando, none of them were working at the time. There was a camera above the garbage area where Holmes interrogated him, but Rogers noted that the camera was facing away from the scene he remembered so well. Olivito tried and failed to obtain documentation to verify what happened, so he let Mando's excuses and obfuscations speak for themselves. Although hundreds of thousands of dollars were set aside to repair and upgrade such equipment, the chief was not in a hurry to fix it. The case proceeded on the merits of Rogers' testimony, the health problems he developed while in jail without medical care and because of the divergence between Rogers' account and that of the police.

It later emerged that Roger's suffered from mental illness, and his mother and little brother were both battling hemophilia. They didn't have a stable living situation. For Olivito, Rogers' case was a sign that the tendency of excessive force was not only about race. Olivito declared under Count III of the *Rogers v. City of Warren* complaint, "The city should be made to pay reparation to those affected poorer classes, white and black, who have suffered such constitutional deprivations on a scale unseen or undisclosed, anywhere in the present American experience." Under Count IV against the chief, that the deprivations and losses for Rogers resulted "from the Police Chief's personal and official attitude and policy of denial and cover-up as to his subordinate officers' routine, customary and typical...use of excessive force."

Olivito didn't stop there. He wanted to set up a truth commission for the city of Warren, where residents could tell their stories with-

---

[258] Staff. "Man sues Warren police chief, officer." *The Vindicator*, 13 September 2003.

out fear of retaliation, monitored by the likes of the DOJ or Human Rights Watch. Olivito knew from his experience in Steubenville that corrupt cops tend to prey on those who have witnessed misconduct, and he had by September become aware of the well-known tendency of certain officers, even the chief himself, to stalk those who complained. John Rogers II would be their next target.

◇◇◇

On October 17, 2003, the parties named in the *Rogers V. City of Warren* complaint convened for the first meeting on the case. In the judge's chambers, Olivito, his paralegal, and Rogers sat on one side. On the other, Hilary Taylor, a senior partner at Weston Hurd, and three of his colleagues accompanied Officer Holmes, as well as Chief Mandopoulos and Law Director Greg Hicks. Judge Robert C. Galanis was in charge of two of the cases Olivito had filed, both of which named the police chief and the city as defendants.

By Ohio standards, Weston Hurd is an old white-shoe firm with staying power gained through more than ninety years of complex litigation experience. Weston Hurd's clients in the judge's chambers were cowboys from hardscrabble families who got jobs in municipal government. Hicks was a former cop and bail bondsman. Mando was a Greek policeman who moved up through the ranks. The city's defense counsel, Hilary Taylor, later remarked, "Mandopoulos was a dinosaur."

Like the ancestors of Galanis and Mandopoulos, many Greek families emigrated to Steel Valley during the 1910s and 1920s to work in the steel mills. Many in Warren were from the island of Rhodes and Chios in the Aegean Sea. They pressured their children to go to college, and a large majority of them did.[259] Then, they went into medicine, law, and business. The courthouse where Galanis sat on the bench carried the name of a Greek federal judge. Galanis himself came from a family of Greek lawyers.

After Olivito and his client and paralegal took their seats, Judge Galanis and Hilary Taylor continued the conversation they were having. Olivito took out a file and busied himself for a moment getting organized. Many years later, Olivito recalled that Taylor and Judge Galanis were reminiscing about a baseball game they had attended together, which Olivito immediately took as an ominous sign for his client. Then, the conversation turned to the lunch Judge Galanis and Taylor had attended and who had addressed the group that day. From there, it went to the rule-making committee that Taylor was on. Every

---

[259] Dr. James Kiriazis. "Ethnic Groups of Youngstown: Personal Experience." *Youngstown State University Oral History Program*, 5 August 1988.

turn in the conversation compounded Olivito's foreboding. He looked over and noticed Rogers was beginning to feel uncomfortable.

Suddenly, Judge Galanis looked up and exclaimed, "Mr. Olivito, you're not dressed appropriately to be in this room!"

"Judge, I'm sorry I didn't know the dress code," said Olivito, fumbling.

"You don't have a tie on." Many years later, Taylor explained that some judges are not so concerned with the dress code, but wearing a tie was something he never took a chance on. Taylor is a veteran of Vietnam from a military family. His father's father's father was in the military, and one of his ancestors was a black Confederate soldier. His first impression of Olivito was that he was disheveled and disorganized. Taylor stated, "With these federal judges, you gotta be ready to go."

Nevertheless, once he was ready and the conversation between the judge and Taylor didn't stop, Olivito snapped, "Judge, it's not baseball, but we should start talking about the case."

Olivito knew he was not making a good impression on the judge, who he remembers as a thin, diminutive guy with glasses and parted hair. Judge Robert Galanis, whose father got his GED from a YMCA program and whose grandfather was a shepherd, did not take kindly to hubris or disrespect in his court. Galanis could be severe. No lawyer was going to come into his chambers late, without proper attire, and disrespect the court. Olivito wasn't going to grovel before any judge, so he and Galanis butted heads from the beginning.

"I don't know if you know what you're doing, Mr. Olivito. Have you ever tried a case like this? What do you know about civil rights cases?" Judge Galanis asked, probing the upstart sitting before him.

"You may not know that in '99, I was asked by the Ohio State Bar Association to do the outline for a CLE [Continuing Legal Education] course on how to litigate Section 1983 cases."

Hilary Taylor looked at Olivito for the first time with curiosity. After the tie issue and the civil rights hazing, the judge turned the conversation to the case. Olivito still recalls the faint smile of Taylor, who he once referred to as "the smiling black Buddha." As a result of the meeting in chambers, Judge Galanis delayed discovery until the issue of qualified immunity was resolved, as is standard in civil rights cases. The judge also called upon the plaintiff to file an amended complaint by the end of the next week and set the schedule for the next two months of litigation.

Olivito was struck by the fact that Warren had hired Hilary Taylor. To Olivito, the move suggested that the city was sparing no expense. Taylor is an authority on the defense of government against liability claims. His mentor was Frank "Bud" Hurd, one of the founding partners of the firm, Weston, Hurd, Fallon, Paisley & Howley. Weston Hurd was wielded like a club by St. Paul Travelers Companies, a $25 billion company that contributed millions over the years to state and national politicians. Taylor was voted best in government liability and insurance defense by the firm in 2013, defending the likes of Dow Chemical, Toyota Motor Corporation as well as a coterie of municipal entities who carried insurance with St. Paul Travelers Companies. Taylor is also a law professor at Western Reserve University Law School, president of the Bedford School Foundation and previously a captain in the Vietnam War. He never lost his cool and he got along with everyone, even plaintiffs' attorneys, which is something his mentor instilled in him.

Taylor later said that Olivito was difficult to deal with, although he was not aware of any personal animosity between them. Olivito vaguely knew of Hilary Taylor and wondered what tricks he had in store. With experience in excessive force cases, drug raids, chases, jail suicides, jail conditions, and liability claims related to streets and roadways,[260] Taylor was in the business of defending officers accused of crimes. After he defended the city of Warren, he started billing himself as a specialist in how to avoid consent decrees. Taylor is a member of the International Association of Chiefs of Police (IACP) and teaches courses on *Monell* claims, which accuse government entities of a policy of deliberate indifference to citizens' rights, at IACP conferences. Olivito sensed Hilary's influence behind the words exchanged during the meeting in chambers, but he was only dimly aware of the strategy already at work between the lines, undermining the plaintiff's prospects of victory. Pitted in a contest against Taylor, the only thing the plaintiff had going for him was the facts of the case, if his attorney could manage to shape the narrative in court.

The legal community in Ohio is insular. As Taylor and Judge Galanis obsequiously demonstrated in chambers, the members of Ohio's legal elite run in the same circles and have interlocking official relationships. Cops, bailiffs, law clerks, and other private and public employees encountered each other in the hallways of the local courts. Galanis would have known Hicks from his days as a WPD sergeant and bail bondsman. Now, Hicks could exert pressure from his position as law director on investigations or ignore them and later deny knowing about them. For those on the outside, legal cliques gave the impression of collusion.

As a solo lawyer without a partnership at a big firm, and without connections in the high courts, Olivito didn't belong. He wasn't a member of any boards, commissions or committees. He was an outsider, facing the city's hired gun, one of the top litigators in the state.

---

[260] According to his profile on the website of the Defense Research Institute.

Olivito remembers thinking that the message behind all the talk between Taylor and Judge Galanis about their professional connections was to let him know, *You're in the big leagues now*.

## 12

A lot of people hate Warren's Chief Mandopoulos, but he sure stands strong behind his officers. I've personally witnessed him bash an officer he felt was careless, but defend him in the public's eye until proven guilty. Cops need a stern but fair chief to efficiently perform.

-Anonymous[261]

With Olivito representing them, Kimble and his wife filed their suit under Section 42 U.S. Code 1983 on November 20, 2003. It was the fourth major lawsuit filed by Olivito against the WPD. The soaring prose of Olivito's complaints to the Ohio Northern District Court had moments of poetic flourish and suspenseful storytelling. Olivito described the video as, "an orgy of muted and stiletto striking violence." He wrote, "The scene in front of the plaintiff's home be-came...another sad postmodern American filmed image and object lesson in this country's wrestling match with police brutality."

Olivito invoked W. E. B. Dubois and the abolitionist William L. Garrison, propping up Kimble as a modern-day "bleeding slave" whose grandparents had come to Ohio hopeful for escape from Southern discrimination. Olivito equated the city's indifference towards its poor black residents to the era before the Civil Rights Act of 1964, which indicated, he argued, quoting Martin Luther King Jr., that America is still "long on promise, short on delivery." He also made frequent reference to Chief Mandopoulos whose characterization of the violent manner of Kimble's arrest as "ugly but necessary" illustrated "the failed municipality's understanding of the Fourth and Fourteenth Amendments."[262] Olivito went on with Mando's words sprinkled in:

This Warren brutality incident was "controlled" in the sense it didn't end in the death of its captive...Given the "due care for his safety" and "proper police work" undertaken by Officers Tempesta [sic], Hoso and Stabile, as it was characterized by the Warren Chief of Police soon afterward, the plaintiff suf-

---

[261] "Who has the best police department." *The Vindicator*: Talk of the Valley, 31 July 2006.

[262] *Kimble v. Hoso et al.* 439 F. 3d 331. Sixth Cir. 2006. Page 8. Print.

fered the loss of his dignity, self-esteem, and incurred severe emotional upset...[263]

Olivito also reminded the city of Warren that Kimble's children witnessed their father's beating by the three white police officers who "continued to assault, mace, slam, and strongly exhaust themselves physically against the body of the plaintiff for no apparent reason."[264]

Knowing that the patterns of racism and police misconduct were supported by the courts, Olivito explained exactly what the purpose of the Kimble lawsuit was, in no uncertain terms. Twenty-one pages into the bowels of the lawsuit, he wrote:

> We bring this suit, not in some closeted, out of the way, manner, but, like David before the Goliath of a new era, into the eyes wide open view of an all-American tale of a fearful nation's present muscle-bound version of all too frequent, equally American, epic Greek tragedy-like experience among its local police departments, which is unfortunately becoming both increasingly observed and widely seen, however briefly, on our television screens, yet at the same time, more than ever, in fact, universally denied and the clear target of various federal court's hostility.

Olivito gained enemies in the act of filing the lawsuit, but the firebrand rhetoric entrenched his enemies' animosity and may have isolated him from potential allies. Olivito later stated of the ribald and perambulating written arguments for which he was well-known among judges, "I guess I can get carried away."[265]

In the fall of 2003, Warren attorney Sarah Kovoor cited Olivito's comparison of Mandopoulos to Hitler as an example of his divisive comments. Journalist Peggy Sinkovich used Kovoor as a source in a *Vindicator* article which called Olivito's credibility into question with the title, "Lawyer's status puts cases at risk." After the attorney for the WPD pointed out that Olivito had not been formally admitted to practice in the Northern District before filing two civil suits, the paper questioned Olivito's status as a lawyer, wrongly suggesting that he had lost the appeal of summary judgment in the case, which was denied, in part,

---

[263] Ibid. Page 6.

[264] Ibid. p. 9.

[265] Aina Hunter. "Blue Mob: Beware the Warren cops, the city's most violent gang. The second of a two-part series." *Cleveland Scene*, 3 March 2004.

and granted, in part.[266] The article suggested that Olivito had lied about having previous experience in federal courts. *The Vindicator* later issued a retraction after Olivito showed the editor that the passage quoted in the article was from a federal circuit court judge.

Although the article may have caused some in the community to doubt Olivito's credibility, *Kimble v. Hoso* was not going away. The video evidence combined with public statements by the police to create strong grounds for litigation because Olivito argued convincingly that the beating "was completely unrelated to any legitimate police purpose and/or goal, including the alleged obtaining of the suspected controlled substances and/or the subduing of the plaintiff..."[267] The video showed Hoso was already in possession of the baggie shortly after the beating got started. It also showed that Kimble was subdued numerous times, by the weight of bodies on top of him, by mace and by blows, supporting Olivito's argument that the officers unnecessarily prolonged the action.

Olivito knew that if he could show the WPD's supervisory and disciplinary failures in the public record, the DOJ would be more likely to intervene and impose a consent decree, which is what he felt Warren needed. Olivito was not alone in his belief that outside intervention was essential. "I knew it would take the DOJ to sort it out," Fred Harris stated, many years later. Still, Harris walked the line. Rather than invite the NAACP to light up the town with the national media, he worked with Peggy Sinkovich, Janet Rogers, and Tom Conley, among others. Although he had thwarted and chastised Mandopoulos constantly since his appointment in 2001, Harris didn't make any statements in Kimble's favor in the press, not only because Kimble's neighbors had come into Harris' office complaining about Kimble and other dealers in the neighborhood. Harris and the mayor didn't want to run afoul of them, but there was something else.

After the police had taken Kimble into custody, they turned the dashcam on him while prodding him to confess. Mandopoulos then scurried to Harris' office with the video footage of Kimble's ill-advised confession in the back of the squad car to justify the actions of the officers. Harris felt it would undercut his credibility in the eyes of the community if he were to speak in defense of a drug dealer's civil rights. Two influential black ministers and Councilman Doc Pugh were already against him. They had gone directly to the mayor to complain that Harris was "not a member of any black organizations." Putting Harris in this influential position when he didn't hold relevant leader-

---

[266] Peggy Sinkovich. "Lawyer's status puts cases at risk." *The Vindicator,* 10 September 2003.

[267] *Kimble v. Hoso et al.* 439 F. 3d 331. Sixth Cir. 2006. p. 10.

ship positions in the black community amounted to "disrespecting the black community," they told the mayor. Many in Warren shared their sentiments at the time, but it would be several years before everyone, including Warren's white middle-class residents, the DOJ, and the local newspapers would all come to agree that there were serious problems in the WPD.

To gain leverage with the policy claim in *Kimble v. Hoso*, Olivito built the case around the grievances already festering in the community, especially the citizen complaint procedure. The Warren police had already agreed to change the complaint form and make it more accessible as a condition of their memorandum of understanding with the NAACP and the DOJ in 2002. According to Safety Services Director Fred Harris, when a resident wanted to file a complaint against a police officer, Chief Mandopoulos insisted on delivering the complaint form personally, often with threatening statements in a loud voice. If requesting the form directly from the chief was not sufficiently intimidating, the form threatened residents with prosecution for false misconduct allegations. Then, there was the appearance of partiality because every complaint was investigated by an internal supervisor in the WPD. The DOJ instructed the WPD to change the complaint form in 2002, but the form and the process remained the same in 2003. Even when the DOJ released their first report in 2006, nothing had changed.[268]

Olivito leveled a constitutional claim against the chief himself for failure to supervise and discipline his officers, writing, "The Warren Police Department has received hundreds of citizen complaints over the years involving allegations of police misconduct...few of which, if any have resulted in any discipline of the offending officers."[269] A 1996 Special Investigation by the *Tribune Chronicle* verified that 45% of citizen complaints had no documentation of resolution.[270] The paper speculated that the WPD would be unable to fill a public record request for documents older than three years. The faulty complaint procedure and lack of discipline bolstered the claim of the city's "deliberate indifference," to the rights of its citizens. According to the lawsuit, these policies resulted in citizens of a certain socioeconomic segment living "in abject fear of [the] police force." Olivito noted that "many of War-

---

[268] Shanetta Y. Cutlar. "Re: Warren Police Department." *U.S. Department of Justice Civil Rights Division*, 2 March 2006, Page 11.

[269] Ibid. p. 15.

[270] Alyssa Lenhoff and Edgar Simpson. "Disorderly Conduct." *Warren Tribune Chronicle*, 14 April 1996.

ren's citizens both young and old do not wish to testify before open courts due to the certain possibility of police retaliation."[271]

Olivito detailed the public threat of Mandopoulos to Michelle Nicks and called the chief out for retaliating against those who complained of the lawlessness of his department. Though some of these allegations may have been valid, according to Harris, it was no small matter to publicly accuse a police chief of operating a rogue police force. Harris declared, many years later, "It's almost impossible to fire a police chief," which was not for lack of trying on his part.

The chief's power rested in his command of his troops, his PR strategy of denial and his credibility with residents who saw no reason to second guess the police. Olivito looked past the petty politics of the federal district courts to the circuit courts, where one dealt purely with the law. He was aware of the reputation of John Mandopoulos and the likelihood of retaliation, but he was already battle-hardened after his time in Steubenville.

While John Rogers II sat in jail for a sixth month, the city of Warren and the other defendants named in the lawsuit responded to the amended complaint filed by the plaintiff on October 24, 2003, one week after the meeting in the judge's chambers. Five days later, the defendants submitted several documents pertaining to the arrest, including the police report, radio logs, and the use of force report. Then, they denied the allegations and filed a show cause motion, trying to kill the lawsuit. In a motion filed on December 1, the defendants moved the court for summary judgment against the six counts listed in the complaint and tried to bifurcate the claims so that the denial of medical attention would fall on the Trumbull County jail, operated by the sheriff's office, not the WPD. The defendants' counsel argued that the city was not liable for the actions of its employees and that Mandopoulos had nothing to do with Rogers' arrest. Even if Officer Holmes violated Rogers' constitutional rights, which the defendants denied, they would all be entitled to qualified immunity.

Hilary Taylor and his co-counsels, Jack Kluznik and Jill Patterson, also of Weston Hurd, tirelessly challenged the validity of the plaintiff's claims while Olivito reasserted the excessive force claim against Holmes and the supervisory liability of Mandopoulos, as well as the vicarious liability of the city for the violations Rogers suffered while incarcerated. At the same time, the plaintiff and his attorney called for the production of various documents, for a jury trial and for

---

[271] *Kimble v. Hoso et al.* 439 F. 3d 331. Sixth Cir. 2006. p. 18.

city officials to be deposed. In the first week of December, Olivito and Taylor began having issues.

Taylor set up a meeting to depose the mayor, Hank Angelo, and the safety services director, Fred Harris, but Olivito never got the notice because he was out of the office. By the time he emailed Taylor, the defendants had moved to terminate the lawsuit unless the plaintiff could persuade the court otherwise. Olivito claimed Taylor should have gotten in touch by phone or email rather than through the court regarding the depositions. Olivito emailed Taylor on November 28th, wondering why nobody called or emailed him. He asked for another date in the near future, which could be confirmed by email. Taylor responded, "What are you talking about?" and Olivito restated his question, "Did you not file a show cause motion in the Rogers case?"

"My motion has nothing to do with depositions. Here is what I filed. Read it first please," Taylor fired back. Six days later, Olivito asked again. "Haven't heard from you on the depo dates...please respond and we may include officer Merkel in the same...besides Holmes...but I do wish to take the mayor and the chief as soon as possible."

The same day, Taylor responded, "Sorry. Have been traveling all week. Will contact city and get back to you."

Another six days went by, and Olivito responded to ask again. He began, "Perhaps we are not communicating well...but you received my communiques re depo...give me some dates... Then we can go to [Judge] Galanis on discovery issues on summary judgment." Olivito also requested some documents on the arrest and foreshadowed his next step by snidely signing off, "Will be filing another case soon...perhaps two."

The next day, Taylor responded, "Perhaps we should talk, your emails are not at all clear. Have dates in January for the depos. Discovery is limited to the issue of qualified immunity. This is a process where we need to interact. For example, which case are you talking about would be a good start." He continued that co-counsel should be included on the emails.

Olivito responded that he was speaking about the Rogers case and reiterated his points in plain language, that he wanted to depose Mayor Angelo and Director of Public Safety Harris before they left office, lining out the sequence he intended to follow with *Clay v. City of Warren*, for which the city had also retained Taylor. As to the limited nature of the issues to be addressed, Olivito responded, "The city officials can be [limited] on the Rogers case, but on the Clay case, I think we're not limited, and there isn't any order so stating."

Taylor got back nine minutes later, "Keep in mind I don't need an order because of the case law on qualified immunity." This was a shrewd move, considering it was in the city's interest to limit discovery at all costs in every case to refrain from providing any fodder to support a policy claim. Then, Taylor again admonished his opponent to contact his co-counsels at Weston Hurd.

Several hours later, Olivito wrote back. This time, all pretense at civility was gone.

"What precedent?" he began.

"You northern guys are too slick for me Hilary...you have to edumucate this poor, stupid southern district counsel..." This was perhaps a reference to Taylor's raising the issue of Olivito's standing with the Northern District when he filed the third complaint, *Dotson et al., v. City of Warren*, back in early August.

Olivito continued, "...but, I don't think any precedent pertains to nonqualified immunity officials...and there's a plenty of them in that there Clay case..." He was papering the city with claims, in hopes that one would succeed past all the hurdles Taylor could come up with. Olivito went on.

"Don't leave me hangin, you big northern counsel...give it to me, and give it to me straight...those big precedents, I can take it... those big cases with those big rulings will just simply make me have to learn all over again...trying cases 'up north'...in all your big courts."

Olivito put it back on Taylor to inform his colleagues at Weston Hurd when the depositions would be and went on sarcastically with the southern motif, adding, "perhaps I can find my poor southern way to some big ol' northern courthouse and we can get it on!"

Interjecting in his own fanciful line of thinking, Olivito continued in a mocking tone, "And please, I hope some panty-assed law clerk doesn't again decide to write some bullshit private type of motion to some Kmart court clerk (who wears a bad tie) in the effort to send me to the Board [of Commissioners for Grievances and Discipline] for such remarks." Olivito knew he could be disciplined for this kind of chicanery, but he didn't care for all the snobbery of the big firms and the stuffy attitudes of court officers. His clients' legal interests were more important than the close relations between high powered lawyers and judges.

Still, he pretended to beg Taylor's pardon, "You biggins have to have mercy on this poor southern district boy. He's just like you say, uncouth, untied and very stupid." Finally drawing to a close, "Let me know if next Monday is good for you and the boys," by which he meant the police officers and city officials. After a few more jabs, "Hilary, I think we will have to make sure the chief's true opponent is deposed before he leaves office..." This was a reference to Fred Harris, who had publicly stated his wish to fire the chief and who made light of reports of low morale among the rank and file.[272]

Rogers was seeking substantial damages for the deliberate indifference of the city to his constitutional rights under the Fourth Amendment. His counsel would have to prove that the training program the city provided to its police officers was inadequate, that this inadequacy was "closely related" or "actually caused" his injury, and that the city was deliberately indifferent. Taylor and his colleagues argued that Rogers had failed to state a claim under Section 1983 and that there was no evidence in the record that satisfied the standard for such claims. The defendants' counsel derided the plaintiff's arguments and beseeched the court to be done with the matter.

Behind the bluster, the city and its attorneys knew that victory was likely but not assured even with counsel as experienced and acquainted with the judge as Taylor. The police chief was particularly worried about what his boss might say if Olivito asked the right questions in a deposition. If Olivito could elicit information that these officers had used excessive force in the past, that they had lacked training or that city officials condoned excessive force, Rogers' claim would gain legitimacy, pushing the city to settle the lawsuit, which could incentivize others to come forward with claims. Nobody was so dangerous as Fred Harris because of his ability and motive to give Olivito and Rogers exactly this kind of information.

Taylor knew that the chief's prerogative was not to give Olivito any opportunity to depose Fred Harris on the public record. Harris grew up in and around the Trumbull Municipal Housing Authority (TMHA), a low-income housing project, so he had an informed perspective on life under the WPD. Giving ammunition to Olivito would provide a handy opportunity to wield the power of liability against the force for their past crimes and offer restorative justice to those community members who had been subject to indignity and injury. With the se stakes hanging in the balance, Olivito's Southern District effrontery, gleeful boasting, and insults could make him appear reckless and spiteful if not imbalanced, so Taylor turned around and entered the emails into the record of the case.

On December 18, 2003, the emails became an exhibit of evidence in addition to a protective order against producing documents or doing depositions, as well as a second motion to show cause. Olivito sat out the holidays, and on January 5, Olivito asked the court for an extension to respond to the motion for summary judgment, which the judge granted. Warren's heavy hitter Hilary Taylor, who continues to dominate in government liability in Ohio as of this writing, pushed the

---

[272] Peggy Sinkovich and Stephen Siff. "Police department torn by internal strife." *The Vindicator*, 17 November 2003.

plaintiff's counsel up against the wall. Olivito conceded nothing. For him, Hilary gained no advantage through the emails or the show cause order. It was all show, huffing and puffing, but the aggressive maneuvers belied the city's hope to kill the lawsuit then and there.

On January 8, 2004, the court ordered discovery to be stayed until the question of qualified immunity was resolved, which is customary in civil rights cases if they are not immediately dismissed. Qualified immunity shields officials from liability in the conduct of their duties. No such defense existed for public officials until the U.S. Supreme Court created it in 1967 to shield government from a deluge of lawsuits in the wake of the Civil Rights Act. Since then, the provisions and protections for government have created a wall growing more impregnable with every new Supreme Court decision. The language of the law says that public officials are not responsible or liable to suit if a "reasonable person" would have known that their conduct was illegal. As such, any allegedly violated right has to be "clearly established" for qualified immunity to be denied. If it is denied, then discovery proceeds as it did in *Rogers v. City of Warren.*

Next, the defendants were required to file their motion for summary judgment by February 9. The motion could only be granted if there were no discrepancies in the parties' accounts of the events and no valid constitutional violations present in the complaint. The court decided that the plaintiff would be required to submit a motion in opposition by March 9. Olivito submitted his motion on the fifth. In response, Judge Galanis denied the defendants summary judgment in four out of six counts. Depositions of police, the chief and Rogers followed.

Olivito knew that including a *Monell* claim, which assigns liability not to the officer but the deep pockets of the municipality, would prolong the litigation, as well as the costs he would bear. The *Monell* claim also had a heavier burden of evidence to prove the city condoned police misconduct. Suing the city, the chief, and three police officers was financially ruinous, intellectually demanding and fraught with professional risk and personal danger. Still, Olivito saw actionable constitutional claims in the *Clay, Kimble* and *Rogers* cases, and there was a wealth of documentation in the local media and other public records that police misconduct was long-standing, severe and systemic. Olivito had included all of the relevant legal language in the complaints, and it would be up to him to uncover evidence during the discovery phase.

## 13

How long will this continue before it becomes back page news? Drop the media coverage and eliminate half of the trouble. It's like "waterboarding," something that the general public does not need to know.
- Anonymous

Olivito had not been able to rely on journalists to support his work. *The Herald-Star* in Steubenville had been tepid in support of reformers fifty years before Olivito came along, and it was acquired by a right-wing media dynasty, Ogden Media, while the SPD was under investigation by the DOJ. The paper ultimately supported the consent decree, but no local journalists seemed keen to find out all the grisly details. In contrast, a few of the journalists in Warren were relentless.

Journalists Peggy Sinkovich at *The Vindicator* and Janet Rogers at *WFMJ-TV* were prolific and courageous. They both churned out revelatory investigative pieces casting a harsh light on the WPD. Olivito used a few of these articles as documentation of the brutality perpetrated on area residents. Sinkovich and Rogers, as well as a handful of other gutsy journalists, kept the community informed, while *The Tribune Chronicle*, which, like *The Herald-Star*, is owned by Ogden Media, provided a more conservative record for posterity. The Tribune started to throw its weight around later in Mandopoulos' tenure, but while Olivito was in town, the paper reported on the cases against the WPD a bit begrudgingly. No journalist had reported on the stalking, threats, assassination attempts or the malicious character attacks Olivito experienced for representing those mistreated by police. However, he and Karen Bryant met Aina Hunter, a journalist, in late October during a silent protest against police violence in Cleveland.

Hunter introduced herself to Olivito after hearing him speak at the event, and he regaled her with anecdotes of Warren's atrocities. Phone conversations ensued, and later Hunter came from Cleveland to attend protests in Warren and learn more about the allegations of police brutality. She was shocked by the brutality, the strip-searches, the callous disregard and the surveillance, which she witnessed. Olivito and Hunter were followed and conspicuously observed by a man who opened his jacket to reveal a recording device. She ended up with enough material to write a hair-raising eleven-thousand-word masterpiece published around Olivito's forty-fifth birthday.

On February 24, 2004, the first part of Aina Hunter's two-part series detailing Olivito's and his clients' experiences with the "Blue Mob" of Warren came out in the print edition of the *Cleveland Scene* magazine.[273] The title was not just a clever headline; the tactics of the WPD were reportedly so well known around the area that even police in bigger departments like Cleveland and Youngstown referred to the WPD as the Blue Mob.[274] The first article began describing Olivito's improbable profile:

> Warren is a town full of tough guys, and they don't like lawyer Richard Olivito. Blondish, self-deprecating, soft-bodied Olivito is an outsider in rumpled clothes. Around here, there is something suspicious about a civil-rights noisemaker who avoids bars. His idea of socializing takes place within the homes of the mostly poor, mostly black people he represents, where he can discuss the progress of any given case late into the night.

With that introduction, the author went on to recount several nightmarish accounts from residents of color living under the regime of Warren's finest.

After delving into shocking examples of excessive force, illegal strip searches, false arrest and racial profiling, the author vividly described the 77 Soul incident, explaining the tactic used by Warren police of calling people snitches, or informants, on the street to intimidate and breed distrust between community members. While the play-by-play of Officer Manny Nites and Chief Mandopoulos in front of the club in the video had been reported in the local media, no one had spelled out the significance or implications of Nites calling the guy holding the camera a "snitch." In contrast, the *Blue Mob* articles made the terror and retaliation of the WPD focal points in the narrative.

Hunter pointedly mentioned that when she arrived to interview him, Chief Mandopoulos came up from behind and got her in a headlock, saying, "How's this for brutality?"[275] She was not amused, remarking that Mandopoulos' secretary "looked on nervously." The chief made light of the 77 Soul video, saying it was a big joke, that the offi-

---

[273] Aina Hunter. "Blue Mob: Pity those caught by the Warren police, who rule with iron fists and rubber gloves." *Cleveland Scene*, 25 February 2004.

[274] James Nutt. *Confessions of a Bipolar Firefighter*. AuthorHouse. 26 March 2012.

[275] Aina Hunter. "Blue Mob: Beware the Warren cops, the city's most violent gang. The second of a two-part series." *Cleveland Scene*. March 3, 2004.

cer was merely using the clubgoers' slang. Mandopoulos also stated that he didn't hear what Nites said. Regarding the Kimble excessive force issue, the chief had suggested that the officers were trying to dislodge what was in his mouth, for his safety, in case he should choke.[276] The young journalist savaged Mando, painting him as an arrogant bully who ran a rogue PD, which is the general consensus in Warren today.

The *Blue Mob* series brought Warren's dark secrets into living rooms and business around the region and later won an award for investigative journalism. It also spurred some aggrieved party to bust out the windows of Hunter's car. She later moved from Cleveland to New York City. The publication of the articles had the effect of vindicating Olivito's civil rights work and the claims of his clients because of Hunter's careful documentation of Mandopoulos' and his officers' efforts to violate, intimidate and silence.

<><><>

Less than a week after the second article of the series came out, Judge Milich imposed the maximum sentence for the contempt charge against Olivito—thirty days in jail—but offered Olivito the "option" of undergoing a mental health evaluation by March 8. On March 8, the offer became an ultimatum. Judge Milich told Olivito, "either have the evaluation by today or go to jail for thirty days."[277] Olivito remonstrated that he had never agreed to undergo an evaluation. In response, Judge Milich had him restrained with handcuffs and leg irons before the cameras of the media invited by the judge.[278] Olivito's dad had traveled up for the hearing against Olivito's wishes. Judge Olivito grew ill watching his son put in leg irons and was disgusted to see Judge Milich exchange high fives with cops in the hall. Meanwhile, inmates inside the jail had watched what was happening to the white civil rights lawyer defending Lyndal Kimble on television, and as he shuffled between the cell blocks, they started chanting his name.

Olivito later wrote:

Seeing so many faces cheering me on…repeating my name… as I was being led in leg irons and handcuffs into a lock-up

---

[276] "Action 19 News digs deeper into violent videotaped arrest." *Action 19 News*. No date.

[277] Ibid.

[278] "Appeal Contempt sentence sent back for lawyer." *The Vindicator*. May 27, 2005.

made me realize…a few things. It was my first experience of the sting of being jailed, but it also gave me something of a reality check of how significant and impacting this work was to the area. They had not seen an attorney like me who was vulnerable yet willing to pay a price for my kind of lawyering which they were not used to. Even the sheriff's deputies and the courts would hear of it, and it gave pause to the powers that be who knew that I had a certain following…and it could expose the darker aspects of their years of racism and abuse and legal machinations…which was exactly what they feared, and so the labeling began.

Olivito maintained that he was told by a warden, "We happen to have our staff psychiatrist on duty today. He's not here that often. Would you submit to a mental health evaluation so you can go home?"

"I'll wait on the 7th District Court of Appeals and get out that way. Thanks," he politely replied.

Mental health had nothing to do with the contempt issue, by any stretch of the imagination. Martin Yavorcik, a Youngstown attorney, filed a stay of Milich's contempt order at the 7th District Court of Appeals, asking the court, "If Olivito needed his competency tested, how could he have represented himself in the contempt case[?]" According to *The Vindicator*, the judge replied, "Olivito's competency was not in question, but his mental health issues were."[279] The judge didn't elaborate what the distinction meant in the legal context if there was one.

Judge Milich justified the contempt charge by referring to two instances where other judges threatened contempt charges over Olivito's tardiness, but Judge Milich was going considerably further than Judge Ivanchak and Judge Douglas who had both let it rest with a $100 fine.[280] In one article covering the debacle, Patricia Meade, a crime reporter for *The Vindicator*, confirmed, "Olivito had a few supporters in court today who insisted that his problems in Judge Milich's court are a result of Olivito's representing men who assert that Warren police used

---

[279] Patricia Meade. "Judge orders lawyer to county jail." *The Vindicator,* 10 March 2004.

[280] Patricia Meade. "Judge finds Boardman attorney in contempt of court." *The Vindicator*, 6 October 2003.

excessive force."[281]

While Olivito was in jail, his father came anxiously looking for him, accompanied by Martin Yavorcik, who did Olivito a solid by being with Olivito Sr. during that afternoon. Yavorcik didn't know Olivito personally, but he saw what was happening and was moved to assist the old judge in getting his son released. A year later, the 7th District Court of Appeals vindicated Olivito, and it was reported by *The Vindicator*:

> The reviewing court, however, said there was nothing in the record or evident in the court's finding that demonstrated that a mental health evaluation was relevant or proper. Indeed, the record does not reflect "a history or indication of mental health issues," says the opinion written by Appellate Judge Joseph Vukovich. The appellate court reversed the mental health evaluation.
>
> The record also shows nothing to substantiate the maximum 30-day jail sentence for first offenders, the appellate court ruled. In fact, the pre-sentence report ordered by Judge Milich and prepared by the probation department recommended no jail time or probation and a fine of $100 and costs.[282]

Although the 7th District Court's decision called Milich's order as "arbitrary, personal and disproportionate..."[283] The burn notice was delivered, and all the judges in the area knew what to do. Before being placed in contempt, Olivito had enjoyed a steady stream of cases assigned by local judges. After being placed in contempt by Judge Milich, he was removed from every judges' appointments list. Many years later, Judge Milich justified the mental health evaluation based on what he had heard about Olivito's relationships with clients.

"He got involved with his clients," said the judge.

"Sexually?" this reporter asked.

"No, financially," responded Judge Milich. "One of his clients used his credit card, and he was living at a client's house."

---

[281] Patricia Meade. "Judge orders lawyer to county jail." *The Vindicator*, 10 March 2004.

[282] "Appeal contempt sentence sent back for lawyer." *The Vindicator*, 27 March 2005.

[283] *In Re Olivito*, Unpublished Decision. Ohio Seventh D. Ct. App. May 26, 2005. Print.

Olivito had stayed at Karen Bryant's house when he was in Warren so as not to have to drive home to Boardman. Perhaps, Judge Milich heard a rumor that he was at Kimble's house, two houses down. Olivito let his paralegal use his credit card, which may have given rise to the rumor Judge Milich later repeated incorrectly. In any case, Olivito didn't play by the rules. He was unkempt and uncouth. He was disorganized and often running late. When they could find nothing better, his enemies were obliged to go after his tardiness and temperament.

The mother of his child was growing more concerned about his obsession with Warren's police brutality and his nights spent sitting on poor people's porches. When she had marched with him in D.C. and listened to his address to the House Judiciary Committee, the tangible sacrifices that would go with his legal and academic pursuits were not apparent, yet in full bloom, they made his life anything but ordinary. His law practice wasn't exactly normal, either. His clients were his brothers in arms, and he would do anything for them. It made a mockery of the conventions of Ohio's legal elite and eventually caused Rosa to leave him, but it could hardly be called insane.

Instead, Milich's reaction may have been because Olivito was a white attorney, and he was staying at a house in West Warren, where some of Warren's white residents spend their whole lives not setting foot. Olivito's colleagues in Youngstown told him, "We don't take cases in Warren," which may have been a word to the wise. Later, in 2006, officials in the Ohio Supreme Court began to build on Judge Milich's assertion that Olivito needed a psychiatric evaluation. The significance of what developed was not lost on the locals. Kimble congratulated Olivito, "You're black now."

The week before the April 15 hearing for the Kimble case, Olivito went on a trip to visit his sister in Connecticut. His brother, Tony, was driving, and his dad and mom were also in the car. Olivito was in the back, trying to get some sleep and absorb the changes in his life. He remembers thinking, *I'm going to be 42 with an eighteen-month-old son and I'm already involved in a custody battle.* Rosa had suddenly moved in with another guy, and it took Olivito completely by surprise. In his single-minded focus on his civil rights crusade, he had underestimated her discontentment, and it was fatal to the relationship. At the same time, he was going up against the WPD with Kimble, Rogers, and Clay. Weston Hurd's foremost litigator in government liability defense was on the opposing side, and he was a personal friend of the judge who overtly disliked Olivito. His son's mother was now living with another man who she presented to him as he was walking unawares in the hall of one of the Youngstown courthouses. It was a lot to soak in, and his spirits might as well have been dragging behind the car. All of it made him question himself.

"What the fuck did you get yourself into? Why did you do this again?" came his brother's shrill voice from the front seat, an unwelcome interruption of his internal reverie which amounted to the same question. After watching his brother destroy his life and marriage in Steubenville, Tony was berating him for starting another beef with a police department.

"Shut up, Tony!" Olivito blurted out.

"Please, didn't you learn yet, stupid? Didn't it fuck your life up once already?"

His parents asked Tony to quiet down, but he kept at it. Olivito was listening to this all the way across Pennsylvania. Then, Tony's phone rang.

"Hello? What? Yeah, this…No, this isn't him, this is his brother. Wait a second." Tony handed his younger brother the phone. He greeted the phone, uncertainly.

"Is this Richard Olivito?" said a voice.

"This is."

"This is *60 Minutes II*. We read the *Cleveland Scene* article and would like to interview you."

"That sounds interesting," Olivito responded. "I'm on my way to Connecticut right now."

"Well, would you mind if we fly you from Connecticut to New York tomorrow?"

He agreed to do an off-camera interview. After the call ended, Tony did not return to his soapbox. There was an odd silence the rest of the way. The next day, he was picked up at the airport and put up in a swanky hotel. The day after that, he was interviewed by a young woman.

"We've done some research on you," she said. Olivito got an eerie feeling.

"Why did you feel like you needed to interview me? You read the article."

The journalist later explained that *60 Minutes II* was being stalked by the Bush administration like Olivito was stalked by police. They were hoping Olivito could give them some perspective, perhaps some advice on how to cope. Olivito and the journalist talked at length about his experiences in Steubenville and Warren. After lunch, they hoofed it all over lower Manhattan, exchanging stories and enjoying the blustery spring day. It was a testament to the pendular politics of the U.S. during a Republican presidency, a civil rights lawyer and a journalist were both facing state intimidation for telling the truth about the violence of the security forces, at home and abroad.

Olivito remembers the journalist said, "Telling the truth on this level is dangerous. How did you survive?" Olivito replied, "By faith." They walked to Five Points, formerly a disease-ridden slum that is part of Chinatown today. Olivito had studied abolitionist history, and he knew of the anti-abolitionist riots of 1834. Because the New York Sacred Music Society found a black congregation listening to a black preacher in the space the white music-lovers had rented for their sacred harmony, an angry mob torched various buildings, including churches and the houses of abolitionists, and went about beating and raping slaves.

Olivito knew how visceral racial hate had historically been in America, so he knew better than to be surprised by the backlash against his defense of African Americans' constitutional rights. Although he was not surprised by racist police and their bosses, he related how he was always surprised to find among his profession and in particular the judiciary such heated opposition towards him and his work. He was also alarmed by the account the journalist gave him of the harassment the employees of *60 Minutes II* faced as a consequence of reporting the Abu Ghraib scandal. The Bush administration was antagonistic towards freedom of speech and the press, but that was just part of the contracting atmosphere for political expression during the Bush years.

About eight months later, *60 Minutes II* was shuttered because of the "forged" documents of Bush's National Guard days, which dealt Dan Rather's career a mortal blow. Few noted the irony that an outlet famous for exposing the abuse of the U.S. military was brought down for publishing forged documents provided by a former military officer. Years later, Rathergate, as it came to be known, was theorized as a potential exploit of Roger Stone, a political operative known for dirty tricks. Olivito took courage from the interview. It came at the right time, and he felt supported, instead of battling alone. Later, he would realize that the feeling of security was misleading. The interview contributed to his downfall.

◇◇◇

On April 15, after coming back from Connecticut, Olivito attended the show cause hearing for the Kimble case in chambers with Judge Galanis. Olivito remembered many years later that Hilary Taylor was smiling slyly before the hearing began.

"I think, Richard, that you're having problems," Judge Galanis remarked. "We've read about your problems. I understand that you're going through a custody battle."

"That doesn't have anything to do with the proceedings, judge," Olivito countered.

"I think it does," responded Galanis. "You're going through too much at the moment. Do you have co-counsel in these cases?"

"Judge, I'm fine. I'm going through some things personally, but that has nothing to do with my work."

"Oh, I think it does. You need co-counsel. You're not in a position to be doing these cases right now, given your personal problems. I'm going to order you to obtain co-counsel, or I will have to remove you from these cases."

"Judge, it's interesting you say that because I won summary judgment in the *Rogers* case in your court." Winning summary judgment is usually an indication that there is a viable constitutional claim, and this claim was against Chief Mandopoulos in his supervisory capacity. No one had ever filed a lawsuit against any WPD chief and won summary judgment.

"No, you didn't," Judge Galanis muttered.

"Judge, you ruled in my favor against Mr. Taylor's firm."

"Well, you haven't filed a motion for discovery continuance on the Kimble case. I find that part of your incompetence."

In contrast to the Rogers case, Judge Galanis never set a schedule for discovery in the Kimble case, which Hilary Taylor took advantage of by motioning for summary judgment in thirty days. Olivito recalled that most of his civil rights cases were afforded four to six months for basic discovery, after which a summary judgment deadline would be set. Olivito found it irregular and problematic that the judge didn't set a schedule.

"Judge, I did file that motion. It's got to be in the clerk's office."

"No. You never filed it, and that's a sign. See, you failed Mr. Olivito. You neglected this case. This case is on the national news, Mr. Olivito. You're not even doing the basic things. You must be caught up. Your mind must be elsewhere."

"Judge, I'll go to the clerk's office. I'm going to find that document. I know I filed it. And maybe it didn't get filed properly, but I know that I filed it."

"Hilary, can you believe this? How many cases do you have, Mr. Olivito?"

"I have five."

"You have a lot more than five, Richard. It sounds like you filed about twenty," Taylor chided.

"I think you're incompetent, Mr. Olivito. I can see it in your writing," Galanis concluded. "I recommend you get somebody local as co-counsel."

The judge may have been referring to the emails between Olivito and Taylor that were entered into the record, but it could have also been Olivito's no-holds-barred writing style, during which even grammar and spelling rules went out the window. The judge was privy to the custody battle. He would also have known that Judge Milich put Olivito in contempt. Olivito's personal life was grist for the media mill, but he had also been partially responsible for the *Blue Mob* articles, which went out to three million people in the Cleveland area. It was clear to Olivito that Judge Galanis was trying to put obstacles in his way, although the judge claimed that he was protecting Olivito's clients from his incompetence. Judge Galanis disputes that these conversations proceeded as they are represented in this book, but he refused various requests for an interview through his former clerks.

There was no denying that Olivito's personal problems were serious, but his work in Warren was much more important. Olivito was challenging a brutal police agency under which people of color lived in terror. They looked down in shame when the police illegally searched their cars. They didn't trust the newspapers. They didn't trust city hall. Many of them didn't trust the NAACP. Some were too afraid to testify in court. They feared for their lives when the police arrested them, and their children learned not to talk publicly about certain subjects. Olivito couldn't delay the cases. His clients had entrusted him with this sensitive work. Some felt that other attorneys like Sarah Kovoor couldn't be trusted. Although Kovoor filed several civil rights lawsuits against the police, she was a former assistant prosecutor, which meant, in their eyes, she was part of the system of oppression.

Knowing none of the above, Judge Galanis issued an order requiring the plaintiff's counsel to respond within ten days, after which another scheduling conference would take place. Olivito was given until April 30, 2004, to obtain co-counsel under penalty of sanction. Galanis' consequent order stated "[Olivito] will be removed as counsel of record in this case." Attorney Clair Carlin had come highly recommended by a trusted associate of Olivito. He was previously president of the Association of Trial Lawyers of America and was then the president of the Mahoning County Bar Association. When Galanis ordered Olivito to obtain co-counsel, Carlin seemed like an ideal prospect because he was an insider in the legal community and had a reputation farther afield as a high-profile litigator.

Carlin knew Judge Galanis, naturally. Carlin's private practice was in Poland, Ohio, a town of two thousand, where Judge Galanis still lives, and where no black families were recorded in the census until the 1970s. Olivito did not know that Carlin had also worked for the City of Warren in the '70s.[284] Otherwise, he probably would have been suspicious when Carlin encouraged Olivito to take a much-needed vacation to North Carolina for a few weeks, assuring him that his cases in the Northern District Court would be well managed.

---

[284] *Columbus Dispatch* staff. "Clair M. Carlin." Obituary, No date.

Olivito came back from North Carolina rejuvenated by the rest, but he discovered that Carlin failed to file the only motion under his prestigious care on time. Olivito was relieved of the need to speculate about Carlin's motives because his clients quickly informed him that Carlin was telling them that he didn't know what he was doing and to drop him as their attorney. He later received a tip that Carlin was spying on him for the local legal eagles, confirming what he already knew.

Olivito was obliged to request an extension from the court, which prompted Hilary Taylor to file an interlocutory appeal to the Sixth Circuit, interrupting the case before it could go to a jury. This tactic delayed the case for a year while a panel of circuit court judges tried to decide whether it was proper for the judge to grant the plaintiff's lawyer an extension.

<><><>

On July 21, 2004, Judge Galanis' Magistrate Judge Limbert, Taylor and Carlin hosted what they called a Global Settlement Conference, which Olivito interpreted many years later as a plot to end the embarrassment and turbulence caused by the high-profile nature of the lawsuits against the WPD. Olivito was not aware of what they were planning until six days before when Galanis filed an order in all the cases. Lyndal Kimble, John Rogers II, and Clarence Clay were all obligated to attend the Global Settlement Conference on threat of dismissal of their cases or legal sanction. Kimble participated when his case came up, but he didn't take the deal. In fact, he spoke his mind plainly to Judge Limbert and the other attorneys present, declaring Olivito the only one in the room he trusted.

Then, the magistrate called the Rogers case, but Rogers was in such a rough spot that he couldn't be reached, not even by his attorney. Olivito admonished the magistrate and Taylor to make a settlement offer he could discuss with his client. Instead, the magistrate made an issue of Rogers' inability to attend the settlement conference by putting Rogers in contempt. Next, Clay's case came up for discussion. Olivito had pressured Clay not to settle for less than the case was worth, urging him to stay the course because the medical claim could be proven. Olivito reminded him of the many people ready to support him and that he shouldn't give up his claim for fast cash.

Shortly before Clay's case was called, Olivito's cell phone rang and a voice told him that he was late for the hearing for another client. He was under the impression that the hearing was scheduled for another day, but the voice on the phone told him to hurry. Fearing another debacle like his previous imbroglio with Judge Milich, Olivito rushed to the Eleventh District Appellate Court in downtown

Youngstown. When he arrived at the court twenty minutes later, he was told he was mistaken, no hearing was on the schedule. By the time Olivito returned to the Northern District Court, the Global Settlement Conference was concluded. Olivito saw Clay and asked him what happened.

"You're not gonna like it," Clay responded sheepishly.

"Did you settle for less than what we talked about?"

"They offered me $46,000, Richard. I didn't want to say no."

Olivito then said something he would come to regret. "Go on, go be the nigger of that judge and Carlin and the rest of them!"

Olivito wanted to convey that settling with the city was like giving the master what he wanted: an end to the revolt. Instead, Olivito insulted his client. As an attorney, what's good for the client is the supposed to be the prime directive. It may not have been in Clay's interests to come at the WPD with full frontal attack scorching all the public officials involved with more than a century of pent-up grievances. Clay had not bargained for total war with the WPD. He and his wife were not ready to deal with the sacrifices, which had already been too costly. But Olivito did not want his clients to quit with a penny less than their cases were worth.

Olivito disclosed the exact amount of the *Clay v. City of Warren* settlement to the press, and they reported it with a headline announcing the "record settlement." Soon afterward, Hilary Taylor called to voice the city's disapproval. "You broke the confidentiality agreement!" Taylor complained.

"You guys must have discussed that while I was out because nobody told me not to disclose the settlement figure," Olivito coolly replied.

Taylor's clients feared that settlements of this magnitude would encourage other victims to come forward, potentially bankrupting the city. The year before, the City of Warren had thrust 25K into the hands of Zeigler for each of his claims. Lashawn Zeigler and Clarence Clay were among perhaps a half dozen of those affected by the WPD strip search policy who were compensated for their humiliation. Fred Harris and Hilary Taylor later ran into each other, many years later, and had a friendly chat.

"You're Fred Harris?" Taylor asked.

"The one and only," Harris responded.

"Your police department doesn't want to take cases to court because of you. The reason we settled those cases was because the chief knew what you were gonna do if you had a chance to take the stand."

"I was gonna kick their asses," replied Harris.

"They knew it!" Taylor and Fred both had a laugh over this.

A telling footnote was appended to Clay's history with Judge Hager and the WPD in September of 2004, only two months later. Clay was again dragged into Hager's courtroom, this time on a "secret indictment" supposedly from the sheriff's office or the WPD; it wasn't clear which. With nothing more, Judge Hager sentenced Clay to the maximum penalty, ninety days in jail, labeling him again as a "dangerous and repeat offender."[285] Only forty minutes afterward, the judge brought him back and set him free. There was no secret indictment; it was just a rumor. Officer Stabile, one of the officers who was filmed beating Kimble, discovered the error and reported it to Judge Hager, who publicly apologized to Clay. *The Vindicator* reported:

> "Mistakes were made, and we don't blame the court," said Clay's attorney Marty Yavorcik.
>
> Clay, who was stunned when told that he had been secretly indicted, was crying when he was brought back to court and told of the mistake.
>
> "Are you sure," Clay asked Yavorcik. "Don't call my wife until we know for sure. I don't want to put her through this again. This has been going on for so long."

Judge Hager tasked Mandopoulos with finding out where the rumor originated, and Mandopoulos told *The Vindicator*, "I want to get to the bottom of it right away, and I want to make sure it never, ever happens again."[286] If they found the origin of the rumor, it was not well publicized. After receiving his settlement, Clarence Clay walked around as if he were a few inches taller. Maybe, the police thought he needed reminding of who is the master in Warren.

---

[285] Peggy Sinkovich. "Municipal court chief looks for source of rumor." *The Vindicator*, 8 September 2004.

[286] Ibid.

## 14

I think the WPD is one of the best around, especially since they had their review by the feds. There were some problems before, but it's been taken care of and they are very professional and courteous.

-"Warren"[287]

After discovery began in the Kimble case, Olivito deposed Safety Services Director Fred Harris and Mayor Hank Angelo on January 21, 2005. President George W. Bush began his second term, and polls conducted around the world showed more pessimistic attitudes towards world peace and security. However, four attorneys in Ohio contested the results of the election because of alleged voter suppression and election fraud. People around the country heard about the scandal, but it was quickly smothered by the Ohio Supreme Court and a media blackout.

On December 13, 2004, the attorneys filed an election contest petition, which was dismissed three days later, only to be refiled the day after that. Chief Justice Moyer separated the case into two lawsuits *Moss v. Bush* and *Moss v. Moyer*, which challenged the presidential election results and those of Ohio's Supreme Court, respectively. On January 12, Chief Justice Moyer dismissed both cases. Six days later, the Secretary of State Kenneth Blackwell, the Republican architect of much of the alleged voter purging, suppression, and ballot tampering, publicly asked the Ohio Supreme Court to sanction the Democratic attorneys and called one of them, Bob Fitrakis, an idiot at a public event. Fitrakis, a former election monitor in Latin America, later co-wrote a book about alleged voter suppression and election fraud in Ohio during the 2004 presidential election.[288] Chief Justice Moyer declined to sanction the attorneys, and the nation mostly moved on, though Fitrakis would continue to make the same allegations after each election. The partisan rancor in America had rarely been as bitter as it was after that election. It was a harbinger of bitter elections to come.

---

[287] "Warren." "Who has the best police department?" *The Vindicator*: *Discussion Groups: Talk of the Valley*, 31 July 2006.

[288] Robert Fitrakis, Steven Rosenfeld and Harvey Wasserman. *What Happened in Ohio?* The New Press, 2006.

On January 21, 2005, the depositions were taking place as a part of the *Rogers v. City of Warren* case with Mayor Hank Angelo. Looking in his direction but not at him, Olivito invited Hilary Taylor to object as a preamble to his question:

"After May 4th of 2003, the Rogers matter, there seemed to be another serious incident. In fact, the one that happened a month later that made national attention. Do you remember that particular incident?"

"Well, there were two," began Mayor Hank Angelo. "One where they picked up the alleged crack dealer. And the other one was over at 77 Soul. I don't know which one you're referring to."

"Well, I'm thinking of the one where they—"

"The crack dealer?" offered Taylor.

"They beat him, and they threw him down, and they hit him in the face," Olivito grumbled, although in the transcript it is posed as a question.

"Allegedly beat him," corrected Mayor Angelo.

"Yeah, allegedly. It was videotaped," Olivito responded.

"Yes," agreed the mayor.

"Right. I'm just saying," qualified Olivito.

"Is that the crack dealer one?" Taylor asked.

"Yes," confirmed the mayor.

Then Olivito queried, "What did that incident tell you about the response of the police to people's individual complaints about excessive force and…the training procedures and on how they arrested somebody?"

"I'm trying to give you some latitude here, you know, but we're talking about another case here," Mr. Taylor interjected diplomatically.

"I'm just saying in terms of your response as mayor, did you think your efforts were working?"

The mayor answered, at length:

In that instance, that neighborhood had come to city hall prior to that incident complaining about crack dealers. We were on what might be called a razor's edge because if you didn't patrol certain areas, people complained, "We never see the police." Then sometimes when you had aggressive patrols, it was like you were targeting certain areas of the community, and those targeted areas turned out to be lower income or minority areas. So you were damned if you did, and damned if you don't. But in this instance where they had that incident with the crack dealer, the residents had come and met with Fred Harris and said, "We want to get rid of the crack dealers."

"Did they want to beat them?" Olivito replied, deadpan.

"I'm not saying anybody was beat," responded Mayor Angelo.

"Right."

"I saw the video probably—I don't know how many times you saw it, but I saw it many, many, many, many, many times."

"I mean the citizens didn't come, though, and say, we want..." Olivito couldn't leave it alone.

"Excuse me," said Taylor. "You interrupted him."

"I'm going to say this," responded Olivito. "It's my deposition. They didn't come and say—"

"You've got to let him answer the questions," Taylor advised.

"I will. They didn't come to you and say, we want to hurt these people, did they?"

"They wanted them—" Mayor Angelo began.

"Arrest them?" Olivito interrupted, again.

"Out of the area," the mayor finished his sentence.

"They wanted them arrested?" Olivito suggested, again.

"They wanted police patrols in that neighborhood."

"Okay."

"Now," Mayor Angelo had a bone to pick, "when you say beaten, I saw the same video you did...at no time...I forget the guy's name—"

"Lyndal Kimble," replied Olivito.

"Okay...did he quit. I didn't see him quit. And then that was investigated as far as whether it was excessive or not, okay. And—" This was overtaken by another question by Olivito and an objection by Taylor, at the end of which Mayor Angelo couldn't find the thread. He seemed to be suggesting that Kimble was resisting arrest. Nevertheless, the mayor persisted, "I don't know whether we called for an investigation, but we thought—I don't know whether who called for it, but we wanted it reviewed very thoroughly."

"I mean it made national television. It made national television," repeated Olivito.

"Right."

"Did you have a concern as a mayor of a city that was under a microscope for alleged police brutality, that you called for an investigation?"

"Well, I'm agreeing that we did...I don't remember how, specifically. You know, I'm not saying a memo went out and said I want that case investigated. It was investigated."

"By whom?"

"By our police department."

"Right. You didn't ask for like an independent investigation?"

"No." It is worthy of note that *The Vindicator* ran an editorial in 2003 arguing that the WPD investigation of the Kimble event would have an "appearance of bias," and that "the public is not going to be satisfied with any opinion expressed by Internal Affairs."[289]

"You didn't raise any concerns to that video, there weren't any concerns to you, whatsoever, that there might have been an ongoing problem with excessive force in the police department?"

Taylor interrupted to say the mayor had already answered that question, and then he and Olivito took turns interrupting each other before Olivito restated the question.

"It's not a simple yes or no because every incident that took place was a particular concern to me, okay, because you could watch that same video and say that our police officers..." More interruptions ensued because Olivito knew what the mayor was going to say, and he was annoyed by it. At length, he asked the mayor to go ahead.

"You can see it and say that, you know, they were excessive."

"Mm-hmm," Olivito agreed, biting his tongue.

"Whereas I saw it and in only one incident in that video that I thought that one person did something they shouldn't have."

"What was that?" exclaimed Olivito.

"Well, it's got nothing to do with the Rogers case. What I'm saying is...at the end, somebody put a knee to the guy."

"Okay," said Olivito, baffled.

"Okay. My concern is did he think the guy had stopped or not? I don't know what was in those officers' heads."

"Mm-hmm."

"But when I watch Kimble, Kimble never backed away. He never was in a subdued position that says, 'I give up.'" This statement is out of step with what other eyewitnesses stated in testimony.

"Okay."

"And then on the review is we sat very carefully with other police officers, and until the guy's subdued...that he is not to fight back."

"I understand your response. I'm not trying to," Olivito soothed the mayor.

"I'm not a police officer."

"I know you're not."

"And I've got to depend on someone who supposedly knows more than I do."

"I understand. That's right. And we're not trying to second guess your view of that...but obviously there was citizens' response to that video, and there was sort of an outcry from certain segments of the community. Same people; Urban League and NAACP. Did they come to you?"

---

[289] Staff. "Panel is needed on race relations." *The Vindicator.*

Mayor Angelo couldn't recall clearly, so Olivito changed tack with another ponderous question.

"Even if you felt that that particular incident didn't merit discipline of an officer, where it was even excessive, did you take any steps to say, you know, let's take a look at the excessive force or the use of force continuum and how we're applying it?"

"I think we simply asked for a review of the incident. And, as I said, I never could take an isolated incident because every incident was important in how the public would react, and what our position was with the police department as far as their public relations, so to speak, with the citizens at large."

Fred Harris, also Angelo's campaign and political strategist, described meetings in which he sat down with officers accused of excessive force and their lawyers. They would invariably say the officer or officers feared for their safety. Harris would respond, "Do you think I'm stupid? You were afraid of this 120-pound kid?" After he started showing up at the scenes of arrests and getting the stories from witnesses, he began to understand what happened when the police confronted someone on the street.

Many times, an officer would report stopping someone at a certain address. Other officers would show up and sit in their cars. If the subject made a false move or the officer found a pretext to use force, the other officers would jump in. One citizen complaint was handwritten by a young girl who witnessed an arrest in which a man failed to put his hands behind his back. First, one officer began hitting the guy with a flashlight. Pretty soon, seven or eight officers were beating the man. The girl couldn't understand why the officers were beating the man when they were supposed to be the ones keeping order.

Mayor Angelo had reprimanded the chief in late 2002 for failing to resolve citizen complaints, after the city had signed a memorandum of understanding that set new standards for the complaint procedure[290], and he had pushed for Mando's suspension in December. Still, the mayor mostly protected the police in the deposition, but not Fred Harris. After a few minutes, Harris remarked, "The Mayor and myself, we had a little difference of opinion there because I felt that the policemen should have more training on how to treat people."

Harris disagreed with Mandopoulos over the use of $450K of drug forfeiture money under the chief's discretion. Harris recommended that the money should be used for diversity training, but the chief contended that it couldn't be used for that purpose. According to Harris, "So our police force did get diversity training, but it was taken from some other source within the police department. But that four or five

---

[290] Peggy Sinkovich. "Chief reprimanded for not complying with procedure." *The Vindicator*, 8 October 2002.

hundred thousand dollars was always a bone of contention between the chief and myself."

Mayor Angelo was caught in the middle. His statements in the press tended to defer the issue for further inquiry, but he was working with Harris behind the scenes. Every incumbent official and most candidates for office in Warren knew the rule, according to Harris, "If you're running for office, you don't mess with the police or fire, because you know that they will publicly work against you." When Harris began standing up to the WPD, many pro-police residents criticized him for it. They emphasized to Mayor Angelo, "Don't mess with the police. They protect us." Harris said, "I give all the credit to the Mayor. He could have fired me, but he stood behind me."

Harris' primary enemy, Chief Mandopoulos, was deposed on February 26, 2004. Olivito jumped right in with the question, "Excessive force, it seems to be a problem in your department. Now, you don't think they have a problem with that as a repeated issue that keeps coming up in your department under your tenure?"

"Objection," announced Taylor.

"No, I don't," Mandopoulos repeated, adding, "I haven't seen that."

"At the time that you had your meeting with Minority Coalition and the individuals Ron Brown and Tom Conley and the head of the NAACP, did they ever bring up beatings, people being struck, assaults, the citizens being bloodied by the Warren police officers?"

"They brought up beatings, but they could not give any specifics. Everything that they brought up was generalities and when we asked them for specifics, they couldn't."

After questions regarding the Lamont Murray case and the complaint procedure, Olivito asked, "Is there a huge backlog of complaints just sitting in the safety director's hands at this time?"

"Currently there is not," Mandopoulos replied. Then he went on:

> When Director Franklin became the director, we had talked about on numerous occasions I had taken complaints completed by me to city hall and given to Director Harris. They entered that void never to be seen again. As Director Franklin empties the boxes in his office, now he's finding them in various boxes with no rhyme or reason, almost as if they were placed there intentionally to be hidden.

The complaint procedure stipulated that complaints be resolved within thirty days, but Mandopoulos was previously reprimanded for failing to resolve six citizen complaints in as many months. The mayor and the safety services director blamed Mandopoulos, but in this deposition, Mandopoulos reversed the accusation. The way Mandopoulos told the story, he and Doug Franklin, currently mayor of Warren, got the backlog of complaints left by Harris caught up "in one day." Harris would refuse to sign the resolution if he thought the chief was overlooking a valid complaint. The chief's description of how he and Director Franklin cleared out all the complaints could lead some to conclude that Franklin was just rubber-stamping the decisions of the chief.

"The prior director just took them—he was busy running for mayor," said Mando. There is an element of truth to this because Harris did take several copies of hand-written complaints when he left office. He also ran for mayor against Michael O'Brien, a former probation officer and Trumbull County commissioner, the preferred candidate of the police and fire departments. O'Brien won handily campaigning on a message of "unity."

"I ran against O'Brien for mayor," Harris said many years later. He continued "but I said publicly that I wasn't going to put up with the WPD's shenanigans, and that was a strike against me. I was always more of a political strategist than a politician." During the coming administration, Helen Rucker said, many years later: "With Mayor O'Brien, it was hard for anybody, even council, to get information. He would change the story so many times. That was how he ran his administration."

<><><>

In December of 2004, the DOJ opened an investigation of the WPD. The Bush administration had jammed up the workings of federal civil rights enforcement with paperwork requirements, so it was an accomplishment just to open an investigation. According to former Deputy Assistant Attorney General for Civil Rights Roy Austin, "It was not a process that was supposed to get to opening investigations. It was meant to gum up the works completely." Nevertheless, investigators, including two former police chiefs, as well as attorneys from the CRD and the Special Litigation Section, visited Warren three times by September of 2005, talking to residents, community leaders, the police, and city officials. Tom Conley and "Doc" Pugh were the DOJ's unofficial point men, as Olivito had been in Steubenville.

Conley and Pugh, along with the Black Ministerial Alliance, had been pushing for reform for years, but Conley felt like he had to watch his step for fear of trespassing one of the fault lines that ran between the social cleavages of his community, especially after Fred Harris and Hank Angelo left office. The black ministers were even more circumspect, which Harris attributed to their Southern mores. Although at times they raised umbrage over racial injustices, they were also on hand to absolve members of the Caucasian community on behalf of the black community when racial tensions flared.

Years before, a white priest made up a story about two black youths stabbing him when in fact, he had stabbed himself during an anxiety attack. When the truth came out, the black ministers saved their white Catholic counterpart by appearing with him and modeling Christian forgiveness in front of the press. In this respect, Harris differed from them and Conley. Whereas they were willing to bury the hatchet, Harris opined, "I don't want a minister telling me that I'll get mine in the afterlife. I'm gonna fight for what I can get here right now."

Ever aware of overstepping his power, Conley later said he knew when O'Brien was elected mayor that he would have to water down his public comments, so as not to become the bad guy. There was a chilling effect, but it was temporary and broke down when the DOJ came to town. Conley took a lot of pride in ushering the investigators and attorneys around to talk to residents. The reported focus of the team of investigators was strip searches and excessive force, but they left it open to pursuing allegations of racial profiling if evidence existed.[291] Lea Dotson remembers attending a meeting between the DOJ and residents at Councilman Doc Pugh's record store. Fliers around town invited everyone who had ever filed a complaint against the WPD. The WPD was not accustomed to being powerless while residents were gathering to complain about them.

Conley was quoted in *The Vindicator* claiming that Warren was the only city in the country where the DOJ was investigating the police department[292], which was not true. Many cities were under investigation, but according to Professor Samuel Walker of the University of Nebraska, "The Department of Justice walked away from the big cities during the Bush years."[293] The DOJ opened investigations, but it stopped using its power to force law enforcement agencies to reform, as it would later during the Trump administration. It wasn't just the big cities. "I generally did not want to be in the business of running law enforcement agencies at the Justice Department," said Bradley Schlozman, who oversaw the Special Litigation Section during this time.[294] The citizens anxiously telling the investigators about the depraved violence and racism of the WPD expected more federal intervention than

---

[291] Peter H. Milliken. Team to return to investigate claims of police misconduct. *The Vindicator*, 27 August 2005.

[292] Ibid.

[293] Ali Winston. "American Police Reform and Consent Decrees." *Truth-out.org*, 31 August 2013.

[294] Simone Weichselbaum. "The Big Problems with Police that Washington can't fix." *Time.com*.

the Bush White House would ever contemplate. According to them, if a state chose not to recognize the rights granted under the constitution the feds should stay the hell out of it.

O'Brien came in with a budget surplus, of which Angelo and his administration would be quick to remind people for the rest of their days. However, O'Brien squandered the surplus on his main constituents, the police and fire departments. One resident later fumed, "O'Brien should have never been Mayor!"

In March of 2005, two months after Harris and Angelo left office, the DOJ released its findings in a thirty-page letter with recommendations to the WPD, including, but not limited to, the formation of a deadly force review board, providing complaint forms more readily, and removing the notice from the form threatening legal action for false reports. They recommended a review of use-of-force policies, equipping officers with intermediate weapons for less than lethal force, and training the officers who were still unclear on the new strip search policy. The report singled out the squad patrolling the TMHA, led by Sgt. Rob Massucci, as in need of more supervision.

These recommendations were not enough for many residents. In an editorial in *The Tribune Chronicle* entitled "Justice probe of police was weak," the paper complained, "years of vitriolic accusations and counterclaims created different expectations in the community. If the feds found no serious infractions, then they should have directed some stern comments toward city officials who riled residents."[295] Presumably, the editor was referring to Harris and former Mayor Angelo riling up the black community. The article went on to quote the comments of Conley and James "Doc" Pugh calling for the chief's removal and suspension of officers involved in misconduct.

Mando's attitude towards the DOJ had not changed since the last time they came to Warren. At the meeting between the representatives of local and federal government in 2002, former Mayor Angelo recalled that Chief Mandopoulos made faces and rolled his eyes, "as though he was a kid being cross-examined by his parents." He refused to sign the agreement, but Harris and Angelo informed him with a smile that his signature wasn't necessary, only that of the director of public safety and the mayor.

Afterward, when the city administration met with the WPD brass to discuss the way forward, one captain angrily declared, "If city hall would just leave us alone, everything would be fine!" The heads of the WPD blamed the city administrators for the intervention of the feds. Many years later, Mayor Angelo recalled, "It was like Fred and I were

---

[295] Editorial Staff. "Justice probe of police was weak." *Warren Tribune Chronicle*, 12 March 2005.

the problem." Harris said the message was that the police knew who the bad guys were, but city hall always interfered.

The DOJ required the city to sign an agreement regarding the implementation of the reforms. It was an agreement that required the city's consent, but it was no consent decree. The Steubenville consent decree included monitoring, but during the Bush administration, no such dramatic reforms were contemplated. O'Brien and Franklin worked it out with the DOJ, but they didn't oversee its implementation, as Mando demanded.

<><><>

While Mandopoulos unfounded all the pending citizen complaints with Doug Franklin's rubber stamp, the WPD intimidated those citizens with pending civil rights cases against them. Galanis ruled in John Rogers' favor regarding summary judgment in the spring of 2004, denying qualified immunity in the counts against the chief in his supervisory capacity and the refusal to provide adequate medical care. Olivito referred to the Rogers case as a "sleeper," because it was not on the radar of *The Tribune Chronicle* or *The Vindicator.*

Judge Galanis dismissed *Rogers v. City of Warren* because Rogers missed two conferences. Galanis issued a show cause order after the first absence at his Global Settlement Conference on July 21, 2004. Then, on March 8, 2006, almost two years later, Rogers missed another hearing, and Galanis dismissed the case for failure to prosecute. For Olivito, it was a disingenuous ruling characteristic of the indifferent attitude of federal courts towards civil rights cases, which caused valid complaints of constitutional level violations to slip through the cracks opened up by insurance companies, cunning attorneys, and colluding courts.

The justice system's dual response to civil rights claims is illustrated by the events of Rogers' case. Rogers brought a civil rights complaint past the review of the federal district and circuit courts based largely on his own sworn deposition. First, Rogers was up against the top government lawyer in Cleveland pushing for dismissal on diversionary, technical grounds and a hostile judge who diverted cases towards alternative settlements. Then, there was retaliation outside the court. When this reporter talked to him in 2015, Rogers stated that the police harassed him until he stopped talking to the lawyers and gave up on his case.

Less than a year later, Judge Galanis would find himself denying summary judgment to Officer Holmes in a case in which he pulled his gun on a kid for saying "Fuck the police." Then, he and another officer allegedly exposed his sister's breast and threw his mother into a mud puddle. Then, the officers pepper-sprayed the mother and sister and arrested them all.[296] Usually, Judge Galanis only denied summary judgment if there was a dispute over the facts in which the defendant's account appeared inconsistent and their alleged actions were objectively unreasonable. Holmes afterward belonged to the small number of police officers whose actions had been repudiated by the Northern District Court. Still, Holmes was never punished by his supervisors.

Rogers said he still had nightmares from which he would awaken sweating and screaming. He stated, "Still to this day I remember exactly what that cop did to me and never forgive them, but now I'm in a wheelchair, so they don't stop me as much." In June 2015, John Rogers, II passed away.

---

[296] *Brown et. al., v. City of Warren.* N. D. Ohio. 2007.

## 15

Seriously, when will we get someone in control of WPD? It's just so unbelievable that corrupt things KEEP happening in Warren, but the Department (or whoever) that's above WPD doesn't do anything. WHY?

- Anonymous, late 2007

Lyndal Kimble's friends and family urged him to get out of town, but he stuck around. Warren was tense in the days leading up the verdict of Kimble's criminal trial in the Trumbull County Court of Common Pleas. Judge W. Wyatt McNally, a balding, bagpipe-playing Irishman with glasses, was a former prosecutor and had seventeen years on the bench. Many young people and elders in the black community pinned their hopes on the Kimble case to challenge the police regime. Many were against him, too. Years later, Kimble explained, "A lot of people didn't want to get behind a street dude to make sure justice was done." McNally, who had already condemned a few men to die, would decide Kimble's fate. The authorities were not leaving anything up to chance.

The WPD surveilled Kimble and his associates, seeking a weak spot. The WPD arrested almost every witness who testified in Kimble's defense. Detective Hoso busted Bryant back in January of 2003. During the stop, Hoso "inappropriately and sexually exploited two females who were with Bryant," according to the summary of his testimony by the appellate court. This may mean that Hoso conducted a partial strip search of the women. Hoso had already been accused of "improperly touching," another woman in the press.[297] Hoso questioned Bryant about Kimble, indicating that the WPD was aware of him. Judge McNally excluded his testimony on the basis that it was irrelevant to the underlying arrest.

The WPD eventually set Kimble up with a sting operation to beef up the charges, as the SPD did to Hython. They asked a known drug addict to buy cocaine from Kimble around Christmas time in 2004. Kimble allegedly sold the guy coke, and the WPD arrested Kim-

---

[297] Peggy Sinkovich. "Woman protests officer's touching." *The Vindicator*, 30 July 2003.

ble a second time. Kimble cast doubt on the sting, saying it was, "more of a robbery making me look bad before I went to court. They knew the news would make anybody look bad." Many years later, Tom Conley expressed disappointment over Kimble's second arrest. Olivito shared this feeling because it meant that the WPD had ensnared him. The second arrest did not violate Kimble's civil rights, although it was rather cavalier for the WPD to let the controlled buyer consume the drugs he'd bought under the aegis of law enforcement, which he later admitted on the stand.

Prosecutors offered Kimble a plea bargain in which he would plead guilty to the new charges, combining them with the previous case, all for the low price of four years in prison. Kimble rejected the deal, pushing for a jury trial. Years later, he explained:

> [The WPD] started an investigation right after the beating. When they indicted me, they combined both cases. They figured I'd plead out which I would have, but the judge wouldn't allow the state to lower the felonies, so I told the judge he was playing too big of a part in this case and that I felt he was pressuring me to take the deal. I would have taken it because I felt it was the best deal for my family, but I couldn't give up my rights which is something you have to do before you accept a plea deal. So, [Judge McNally] said he couldn't sentence unless I was willing to give up my rights. He gave me two weeks to think about it. I came back and decided to go to trial, but, instead of going to trial for the beating first, which we was supposed to do, we went to trial for their weak drug buy cases.

As with Clarence Clay, the county court compelled the defendant into a tricky calculus of costs and benefits if only he would abdicate his rights. Kimble clarified, "They was trying to bury me and get out the spotlight."

During *voir dire*, eighty potential jurors admitted that they had seen the news reports on the case. The county prosecutor was able to replace one black female juror with a white one. Black people could not be allowed to serve on such an important jury. Olivito argued during the trial that the informant's testimony should be disqualified because the WPD let him consume the drugs he bought in the controlled buy, which amounted to being offered a deal. A WPD officer testified that the informant had not been offered a deal.

The trial went on for two weeks, and the jury deliberated for two and a half days. As the guilty verdicts were pronounced by the jury, Kimble began shaking his head, saying, "No, no, no..." Despite promising the defense that he would not be punished for requesting a jury trial, Judge McNally gave him eighteen months for each of eight counts of drug trafficking and one count of cocaine possession, carrying a potential total of thirteen and a half years.[298] In April of 2005, Judge McNally sentenced Kimble to ten and a half years, inspiring Chief Mandopoulos and his officers to erupt in cheers. "I'll take my punishment," said Kimble. Then, he looked back at Hoso and asked, "Why aren't those guys being indicted?" Meanwhile, Mando and the gang were having a high five party.

At the same time, the judge was winding up to bring the hammer down on Kimble for two charges related to the June 2003 arrest. Many years later, Kimble maintained that he never pled to those charges, but the court argued otherwise. He faced one to three years on both cocaine possession and tampering with evidence because of his alleged attempt to swallow the cocaine.

*The Vindicator* offered a sanitized version of the entire affair, suggesting that the 2003 arrest received national attention because of Kimble's allegation of police brutality, rather than the video which exposed it. The article described Kimble resisting officers, "who were trying to get him to spit out the evidence,"[299] focusing on what happened with Hoso in the car, instead of the beatdown on Kimble's lawn. Although not typically allies of the WPD, Peggy Sinkovich and her editor seemed to summarize the facts of the case to suit their will. It may have been a sign of the community's loss of confidence in Kimble.

Kimble appealed the conviction to the Eleventh District Court of Appeals. The appeals court denied the appeal in part and granted it in part, vacating the sentence and remanding the case back to McNally.[300] The appeals court found that McNally had relied on an unconstitutional statute to aggregate eight consecutive sentences over a single course of conduct. The appeals court limited McNally's discretion to incarcerate Kimble for over a decade by cobbling together a dozen chunks of time. Kimble's sentence was pronounced void, and McNally was ordered to sever the offending portions of the sentence.[301]

Nevertheless, in May of 2007, when the case came before Judge McNally again, he ignored the higher court's ruling and gave Kimble the same sentence as before. *The Vindicator* summarized the case:

> Lyndal L. Kimble, 32, appealed his convictions on eight counts of trafficking in cocaine and one count of cocaine pos-

---

[298] Peggy Sinkovich. "Kimble found guilty in trafficking case." *The Vindicator*, 29 April 2005.

[299] Ibid.

[300] *State v. Kimble.* Eleventh District Court of Appeals, Ohio. 2006.

[301] Ibid. p. 11.

session. In a separate case, he was convicted of cocaine possession and tampering with evidence. He was sentenced to 101/2 years in prison on the charges in 2005.[302]
The newspaper also noted that half a dozen sentences were vacated on the same "technical" grounds, but the editor did not explicitly criticize the judge for ignoring the order of a higher court. An assistant county prosecutor expected about six more cases to be remanded, noting that "all of the ones that have come back so far have resulted in the same sentence as before."[303] McNally repeatedly defied the order of a higher court, ruining lives in violation of the constitution, but nothing happened. The newspapers didn't even bother to question the judge's actions.

Kimble's cousin, Lea Dotson, wasn't alone in her conviction that the judge was punishing Kimble, not for the alleged drug trafficking, but for suing the WPD. Judge McNally ignored case law precedent and a higher court's order to get revenge on a black defendant, but he showed great mercy to white defendants. When a white law clerk was charged with possession of heroin and drug paraphernalia after getting busted high at work, McNally let him skate with no prison time at all, over the objections of prosecutors.[304] One observer commented, "The judge that Jason [Burns] stood in front of is one of the toughest judges in Trumbull County, and frankly, I am completely stunned that he did not give Jason some jail time considering his prior records."[305] Perhaps, it was a sign of the dawning realization in that arresting our way out of the drug problem does little to stem supply. Perhaps, Judge McNally allowed his implicit bias to affect his rulings. Judge McNally would go on to wreck more defendants' lives based on little evidence and much malice. In one case, a local assistant prosecutor privately questioned "the lack of direct evidence,"[306] but that didn't stop Judge McNally.

---

[302] Staff. "Warren man resentenced to the same prison term." *The Vindicator*, 3 May 2007.

[303] Staff. "Resentencing in videotaped case." *The Vindicator*, 26 December 2006.

[304] Jeff Levkulich. "Law clerk given intervention, no conviction." *WKBN News*, 24 September 2014.

[305] Jeff Levkulich. "Law clerk given intervention, no conviction." *WKBN News* 27, 24 September 2014.

[306] Christopher Bobby. "Defendant explodes at guilty verdict." *Warren Tribune Chronicle*, 16 March 2012.

The innocent young man had to be held down by deputies when he heard his sentence.

Judge McNally envisioned himself as a gardener with the responsibility to pull weeds, according to a rousing sermon the judge delivered while sentencing a rapist and murderer. He took this ministry with grave seriousness. Kimble wasn't a rapist, and he didn't hurt anyone directly, but he injured those who bought his contraband and divided the community with his police brutality allegations. McNally recognized a weed, and he wasn't going to let a litany of due process and civil rights violations scuttle the weed's removal. He wasn't even going to listen to a superior court's reprimand. He wasn't going to think about how many young children would spend their formative years without their father. He was going to uproot that weed.

The criminal case against Kimble underwent permutations as did his civil rights case. The whole situation was "bizarre," according to Hilary Taylor, who remembered Kimble as "an interesting fellow." Kimble did the full ten and a half years without parole. After being incarcerated for two and a half years while his cases proceeded, Kimble would spend another eight years in prison.

Sarah Kovoor, a local attorney who worked with Olivito on the Kimble case, suggested that the criminal case against Kimble should have had a change of venue. She criticized Olivito's handling of the case, "He got obsessed with the case. It was gonna be a scorched earth campaign. It wasn't best for the client." However, Kovoor conceded, "There was good reason to attack the WPD." Olivito's approach may have been detrimental to Kimble's case, but Kovoor may have underestimated Kimble's preference for a scorched earth campaign.

When a reporter for *The Vindicator* asked Kimble if he wished he had taken the prosecutor's deal, he said "No." Many years later, he recalled, "I would have taken a deal, but the judge acted like he was god." Hilary Taylor remembered, "[Kimble] refused to settle. That was the thing. He had the top case, I thought." Regardless of the criminal case against him, Kimble's civil rights case was predicated on the idea that the violence of his arrest was unreasonable. Kimble won at the Sixth Circuit, but his case was eventually subjected to similar obstruction by Judge Galanis, in violation of a superior court's order, as happened with Judge McNally in his criminal case.

◇◇◇

Judge Galanis seemed to take Kimble's conviction in the Trumbull County Court of Common Pleas as a sign to dismiss his civil rights case. Olivito had pled to the Sixth Circuit that Judge Galanis was collaborating with the defense counsel and his co-counsel to undermine the cases. In February of 2006, six months before the suspension was imposed, Olivito alleges that Galanis challenged his status as a lawyer. Olivito argued that he was in good standing with the supreme court and that there was no sanction pending. At most, there would be a public reprimand.

Then, Olivito brought up the policy claim, asking why there had been no ruling eight months after litigating the issue. Usually, the timelines set in civil rights cases are strictly adhered to, but Galanis had put off addressing the policy claims while the individual liability claims went to the Sixth Circuit on interlocutory appeal. Olivito had spent months composing the arguments, doing the depositions of various officers, Mando, Angelo, and Harris, and he had filed the four cases before the Kimble case to build a foundation for the policy claim. A dozen Warren residents testified in open court to expose the criminality of the WPD, staking their safety and freedom on an out-of-town lawyer who promised that the federal courts and the DOJ would notice and act out of concern for their safety.

During Mando's reign, the WPD's policy of deliberate indifference to the rights of citizens was plain to anybody who read *The Tribune Chronicle* every day for a few months because the police often committed acts of brutality on a bi-weekly basis. The chief made no secret of his spite for those who complained or questioned the actions of his officers. On one occasion, when City Councilwoman Helen Rucker refused to placate Mandopoulos after bringing up the issue of his racial prejudice during a closed-door meeting at city hall, he led her to his office and shut the door. Then, Mando swung his arm across his desk, casting all the contents onto the floor. He proceeded to throw objects and shout as Councilwoman Rucker tried to remain calm. This was not an isolated incident.

Another time, Mando spent two hours having a heart-to-heart with Fred Harris, his sworn enemy, during which Mando told stories with uncharacteristic emotion. After Mando left, Fred got a call from the police station, asking him to please come over. When he arrived no one wanted to explain why the time-clock Mando hated was hanging off the wall. Finally, Mando's secretary admitted that Mando had walked in, suddenly began shouting, and threw a chair against the wall.

With such an out-of-control chief, it was little surprise that the WPD violated citizens' rights. So, it was crucial for the Northern District to rule on the policy claim, for the DOJ, Warren's residents, and Kimble's case. However, Mando and his men would be furious if Judge Galanis dared to rule in favor of the plaintiffs that the WPD had a "policy" or "custom" of deliberate indifference towards the violation of people's rights. Such a ruling would cause the city to be imperiled by liability. The DOJ would be more likely to chasten the WPD with a consent decree, and the WPD would blame Judge Galanis. They would hate him for it. It was against everything Mando stood for, and Galanis must have known this.

Olivito felt confident that he had beaten Hilary Taylor on the policy claim in the Northern District and on the interlocutory appeal at the Sixth Circuit. Olivito had sent his filings in the cases to the DOJ, and they released their preliminary findings with enough time for Olivito to enter them into the record. In the DOJ report and the contents of the record of the lawsuits pending on Galanis' docket, there was ample evidence to support a claim that the WPD was deliberately indifferent to the rights of Warren residents. It was equally plain that this policy of the WPD caused the injuries specified in the lawsuits. Nevertheless, Olivito reasoned, "Judge Galanis did not want to do the DOJ's job. He did not want to grant that the city of Warren had a policy while the DOJ was investigating. That would have led to a consent decree in Warren." Galanis would have had to put up with the backlash. He would cause the local authorities even more embarrassment. However, if Galanis denied the policy claim, Olivito would appeal it to the Sixth Circuit, and his ruling could be reversed.

Instead, Galanis told the opposing counsel:

"About that policy claim, Hilary, would you please withdraw your motion in opposition to summary judgment?"

"With pleasure, judge."

And with that, the pending policy claim against the city of Warren was smothered. In effect, it was like there was never any disagreement between the parties. Judge Galanis dropped the issue. According to Olivito, it was judicial sleight of hand carried out in chambers, behind closed doors. Judge Galanis disputed this account of events from his quiet retirement. When asked through his former law clerks what exactly occurred with the policy claim in the Kimble case, the judge did not respond. Many years later, at first, Hilary could not recall the ruling on the policy claim, but then he remembered:

> I think I won on that…on the policy claim….Kimble and Rogers stick in my mind. I had to dig deep to make anything out of them. Kimble was the main case. He didn't have the best case, but his case got the whole process started. It was the whole reason we were there, in my estimation…We wanted to get them all done. [We] wanted to get everything knocked out.

Olivito was booted out of the practice of law in 2007, but Bill Hinnant, a North Carolina attorney, took over as Kimble's counsel. Although the policy claim was laid to rest, Kimble's case was still not dead. In June of 2007, Hinnant hired Alan Baxter, a former police commander, and professor, as an expert witness. After viewing the video of the arrest, Baxter testified that the officers used "unnecessary, unreasonable, excessive and brutal force."[307] He also stated that the chokehold applied by Hoso was "commonly forbidden...because of its deadly results."[308] Baxter faulted the officers for failing to maintain control of Kimble, for throwing him on the car, slamming him on the ground, kneeing him in the head, for the 'baton spear strikes' in Kimble's ribs and back, as well as the excessive use of pepper spray.[309]

The pretrial discovery statements did not take place until January 4, 2008. Judge Galanis included the conviction of Kimble for felony drug trafficking in April of 2005 as "relevant evidence" for the jury to consider. Hinnant proposed to exclude the testimony of the guy who allegedly bought $25 of crack from Kimble around Christmas time in 2004. Hinnant argued that the inclusion of this evidence would unfairly label Kimble as a "drug dealer" rather than a "citizen" entitled to rights under the U.S. Constitution in the eyes of the jury.[310]

On January 28, 2008, settlement negotiations took place. Hinnant negotiated a settlement much lower than Olivito had implored, starting the negotiations at $125,000 instead of $1.3 million, but the plaintiff agreed to it because he needed it to pay for his appeal. However, with the case settled, the best legal system in the world was not quite finished making Kimble and his family pay.

Judge Galanis dismissed the case on January 31, and then the Trumbull County Prosecutor's Office came after the plaintiff for an "attachment to the plaintiff's settlement proceeds," amounting to several thousand dollars to which the prosecutor's office claimed entitlement. Hinnant accused the prosecutor's office of a "fraud upon the court,"[311] noting that he had searched for applicable precedent in the Sixth Circuit, but he could not find a single case where a party had been obliged to request reconsideration under such circumstances. Many years later, Hinnant wasn't sure if it was intentional or just sloppy.

The attorney wrote, "the question of whether the state should properly be permitted to place a lien upon settlement monies obtained in a suit against one of its political subdivisions (in this case, the city of Warren) appears to be novel."[312] Taylor filed a brief in response to let

---

[307] *Kimble v. Hoso et al.* N. D. Court of Ohio. 2008. p. 1218. Print.

[308] Ibid. p. 1218.

[309] Ibid. p. 1219-1220.

[310] Ibid. p. 1406.

[311] Ibid. p. 1428.

[312] Ibid. p. 1429.

the judge know that the defense's expert witness had not been paid $7,704.38. The Trumbull County Prosecutor's Office was only acting at the behest of the "defense counsel and the insurance company for the city," which were both on notice that the payment was due.[313] Melanise, Lyndal's wife, disagreed with the settlement, and since Olivito had included her in the original complaint, she could refuse to sign on to it. Despite her jailed husband's pleas to go along with it, she held her ground for over a month, refusing to sign the settlement check. Hinnant said he paid for it seeing no other option. "It was 'lose or face costs,'" Hinnant recalled, adding that Kimble filed a complaint against him at the local bar association. It was as if Kimble was kicked in the ass as he stepped out of the courthouse. Afterward, all paths open to him led to prison.

If the newspapers had the guts to print what their journalists managed to dig up, the animosity of the WPD towards Lyndal Kimble would have been revealed back in July of 2004. Fred Harris remembers that Janet Rogers and Peggy Sinkovich requested a transcript of the exchanges between WPD officers on the cruiser email system, the mobile data terminal. This system was installed back in 1998 for over half a million dollars, ostensibly so that police could communicate with each other privately. It would have been embarrassing if they were now mostly using it for bigoted talk and joking about each other's wives.

Captain Bowers printed out the transcript and began hurriedly redacting as much as possible with a black marker. Fred Harris got an angry call from *The Vindicator* and *WFMJ* journalists, and he went directly to the police station and snatched them without explanation from Bowers' desk. Then, he read the transcripts himself to decide whether to black out any passages. Among the juicy banter punctuated by racial slurs, almost none of which was published by *The Vindicator*, one officer joked with another, "It's hot out, I'm going over to the west side. Gonna make it a Kimble night." It would seem, at least for a moment, "Kimble" was WPD-shorthand for beating up someone they had sworn to protect.

Judge Galanis decided that Olivito was not sufficiently competent to argue the cases he had filed, so the judge required him to get co-counsel. Then, despite the "meritorious" claims presented, Judge Galanis dismissed or diverted the cases to out-of-court settlement. It was a reflection of the pragmatic approach to the authorities regarding the operating costs of a dysfunctional police department. From the court's perspective, Olivito stormed into the Northern District demanding jus-

---

[313] Ibid. p. 1441.

tice like Quixote tilting at windmills. He lobbed slipshod novelas full of grammatical errors and misspelled names onto the federal dockets. The impetuous attorney was late, unprepared and without the appropriate tie. Then, Olivito was rude and arrogant in the judge's presence. Although Galanis was duty-bound to consider the facts alleged in the lawsuits, none of this escaped his notice.

A former clerk of Judge Galanis disputed the account of these events, saying it distorted the way these discussions proceeded. According to him, Judge Galanis was independent during an era when the Democratic party was corrupt and many of his colleagues were removed over corruption and misconduct charges. Judge Galanis was a Democrat but he ran as an independent so he didn't have to seek the endorsement of the reputedly corrupt local Democratic party. The judge's clerk attested to his reputation for congeniality and respect for others.

Galanis gave many clues to his values in an interview in 1991 for the Oral History Project of Youngstown State University. In response to the question, "Does your attitude towards the person in the courtroom affect how their sentence is given?...If they were rude..." Judge Galanis answered, "That would have an effect, sure. [It shows] disrespect for the court. [It is] not just that. That's not enough...Of course, the attitude of the individual is a factor."[314] Judge Galanis was accustomed to more deference. If he was congenial, it was because people were showing respect to the court.

The judge was conscientious about sentencing. It kept him up at night. Justice was something he had to wrestle with, grasping after it, wondering at its contours. Judge Galanis once bellowed at a misbehaving defendant "Justice doesn't have a price tag!" When asked if he ever got nervous that he was going to make the wrong decision, Judge Galanis said, "I didn't even like to think of it. That's why I cut you off pretty quick."[315] The judge continued, "When the decision is made, it's done, and that's it. There is no reflecting."[316]

He was asked if he had ever suppressed evidence and later found out that the person was guilty, which he denied. The Vaccaro case was still seven years away, in which Judge Galanis determined that there were "questions of fact with regard to the circumstances surrounding the shooting," because the officer claimed to have shot Gregory Anthony point blank, but there was no evidence of the gun's dis-

---

[314] Michael Graham. "Judges: Personal Experience." *Youngstown State University Oral History Program*, 10 December 1991.

[315] Ibid. Page 11.

[316] Ibid. p. 11.

charge on the cadaver.[317] Galanis denied Vaccaro's motion for summary judgment but absolved Joe Kavanagh, then a sergeant, for failing to uncover the true circumstances of the bad shooting by his brother in blue.

Judge Galanis outlasted many compromised colleagues and stood up powerfully for voting rights late in his career, but he sat on the bench for two decades during which law enforcement and corrections officers were running roughshod over people's rights. His fellow judges and magistrates refrained from condemning police misconduct and dismissed or diverted cases to out-of-court settlement. Judge Galanis bragged elsewhere that one of his strong points was facilitating negotiations to settle cases instead of going to trial,[318] as he did with Clay's case in the Global Settlement Conference. Treating the settlement of civil rights claims like an auction helped the city of Warren make it through the last decade of Mando's life without federal oversight. Luckily for residents, Judge Yolanda Benita Pearson, Galanis' successor, does not turn a blind eye to patterns of civil rights violations.

Despite Republican opposition, Judge Pearson was confirmed in 2009 as the first African American female judge in the Northern District Court. Within a few short years, she began to shake things up. Whereas Galanis dispatched claims of pattern or practice and civil rights violations, Judge Pearson shows more consideration to plaintiffs, including those incarcerated. In 2014, Judge Pearson accused the Youngstown Police Department of what she referred to as a pattern of federal civil rights violations which the city knew about but tolerated.[319] This extraordinary ruling resulted from a case in which one of the YPD's Lieutenants repeatedly falsely arrested and harassed members of an African American family. The same pattern affected every one of Olivito's clients in Warren. In 2016, Judge Pearson accused TCI of a pattern of illegal strip searches of female inmates. For his entire tenure, Judge Galanis and his local colleagues averted their eyes to analogous patterns in Warren.

Meanwhile, the WPD handled sensitive allegations of police misconduct quietly. Gracie Parks, the grandmother of Kevin Parks, who the WPD had pegged as a drug dealer, was the matriarch of a family subject to abuse. She and Kevin both filed complaints against the WPD in October of 2001, alleging that they had been threatened by Warren officers as they were walking out of the courthouse. Gracie was elderly

---

[317] *Anthony v. Vaccaro*. N.D. Ohio. March 16, 1999.

[318] Peter H. Milliken. "Federal Judge in Youngstown to step down July 3." *The Vindicator*, 13 March 2009.

[319] WKBN. "Federal lawsuit against YPD will proceed." 6 March 2014.

and had to walk slowly down the stairs, and Kevin described how Officer Bolin followed them down the stairs, trying to provoke them, saying, "Say something, anything, I want you to, so I can beat you down and take your ass to jail. Just say something."

Sgt. Massucci allegedly remarked, in court, that Kevin was "a low life scumbag and nigger," according to Gracie's handwritten complaint. During the reign of Mandopoulos, none of the complaints resulted in anything more than a verbal reprimand. Judge Galanis enabled these violations by his refusal to vindicate the civil rights of Warren's citizens and his unwillingness to acknowledge the pattern or policy alleged by Olivito in 2005 but explicitly identified by local attorneys as early as 1982.[320]

Since the first years of the twentieth-first century, Warren was beset by social unrest. Public protest built into a crescendo between 2001 and 2003. Richard Olivito and a few other local attorneys and journalists, including those citizens who bravely trained cameras on acts of brutality, had captured and distilled enough credible information in the public record for the DOJ to open an investigation. The DOJ's presence in early 2005 dampened residents' frustrations temporarily. Representatives of the DOJ visited a half dozen times and gathered more information from Warren's residents, from the city, and the command staff and the officers of the WPD. It had been two years since the DOJ came to investigate, but negative press and hostile public opinion still dogged the department, boiling over in 2007 when the familiar problem of excessive force publicly resurfaced.

The WPD had a way of making their opinions known, and throughout Mando's reign, they and their supporters engaged in a bitter back and forth over the issue of policing. When allegations surfaced in the comment section of the local newspapers, law enforcement or someone speaking for them often responded anonymously. In one thread, "Warren" wrote in caps, "Yeah they do it the old-fashioned way. Hang them @#$%&. Give them no justice until it's your child." A few hours later, someone replied, "Sounds like someone's little piece of @#$%& criminal kid got what they deserved by WPD." On February 8, in the community forum of *The Vindicator* website, in response to a call by a local for internal affairs of the WPD to investigate an alleged officer-involved traffic accident, a user identified as Michelle and claiming to be an employee of the WPD brought up citizen complaints and the DOJ investigation:

> What the public doesn't understand is everyone that gets into trouble wants to file a complaint against the police because they think that'll get them off or a reduced charge in some

---

[320] Edgar Simpson and Alyssa Lenhoff. "Disorderly Conduct." *Warren Tribune Chronicle*, 14 April 1996.

way. We had so many complaints filed against because everyone wanted to join the bandwagon that's why the DOJ
came.[321]

This rationale fails against what exists on the public record regarding
the customs and practices of the WPD, detailed in the media and in
reports by the DOJ, one of which was to send the officer reported in the
complaint directly to the complainant's house. Chief Mandopoulos
hand-delivered the complaint form with a rowdy show of personal offense when someone wanted to file a complaint, according to his former supervisor, Fred Harris. These tactics deterred Warren residents
from filing complaints, which may be why the WPD refused to change
the complaint process, despite repeated requests from the DOJ and the
NAACP.

On top of administrative intimidation, there was the stalking
and pretext stops of those who complained. Lea Dotson was pulled
over repeatedly, as was John Rogers, II. Both Lyndal Kimble and
Clarence Clay were rearrested within a year because the WPD came
after them. Mandopoulos himself had reportedly stalked a person who
refused to act a confidential informant.[322]

All of this was common knowledge in Warren's black community, although most white residents refused, for years, to believe it.
In the same forum, in December, one local commented, "Blacks live in
a police state in Warren, Ohio anytime a black notices a Warren cop he
knows he could be pulled over beaten and taken to jail for nothing, I
never want to see a Warren cop, and I'm a hard working taxpayer, but
I'm terrified by the WPD."

Despite the dubious nature of the first argument, Michelle
went on to address the strip searches:

Yes, there might have been some questions about illegal strip
searches, but most of them were valid. There was a female on
the news a couple of years ago with her mama sitting next to
her crying because the Warren Police made her lift her shirt
just below her breasts. Well, let me tell you it was a good thing
the officer did that. The poor girl had a 9 [Millimeter] stuffed
in the waistband of her pants, and she had dope on her. That's
just smart police work if you ask me.

Fred Harris, the most vocal critic of the WPD, could not have articulat-
ed the pragmatic nature of the civil rights violations of the WPD better

---

[321] Michelle. "Warren Police." Talk of the Valley: *The Vindicator*, 18
January 2007.

[322] Aina Hunter. "Blue Mob: Beware the Warren cops, the city's most
violent gang. The second of a two-part series." *Cleveland Scene*, 3
March 2004.

than Michelle. "Smart police work," was valued over respecting the provisions of the constitution, even where it pertained to the privacy of a person's body.

In 2006, the DOJ specifically recommended that all officers be re-trained on the strip and cavity search policy by the law department because, according to the interviews DOJ investigators had with WPD officers, they were still not clear on the standards of the policy.[323] In 2007, questions and a lack of clarity remained inside the WPD about whether and when strip searches were legal. Michelle then reflected on the town:

> This city is overrun with crackheads, drug dealers, and thugs and most carry guns with them. We are supposed to treat them [sic] the courtesy and respect, but get none of the above. Sometimes the way they are treated is the only thing these people relate too, and that's sad.

In the forum, a lively debate ensued, in the course of which there was an allegation that a woman had been beaten by four officers while handcuffed. The pro-WPD voices were undeterred. One commented:

> The Warren PD has the right combination. They do NOT harass their citizens, and at the same time, they take no BS from anyone. They seem to 'know when to hold'em and know when to fold-em' Some of the other departments ought to take a few lessons from them. Maybe Youngstown wouldn't be such a war zone if they ever had a chief and mayor that had a clue."

This response gave a little ground regarding the excessive force complaints, but in the end, "Anonymous" implied that the practices of the WPD stopped the town from becoming a war zone, indirectly giving credit to Chief Mandopoulos and then-Mayor O'Brien.

In December, in the midst of another discussion on the WPD's continuing problems, one commenter expressed relief that the DOJ had returned to Warren, "I am glad to hear the Dept. of Justice is back in Warren. If they had done the job right four years ago, maybe they wouldn't have had to come back. Let's hope they get it right this time and clean that place up."

---

[323] Shanetta Y. Cutlar. "Re: Warren Police Department." *U.S. Department of Justice, Civil Rights Division*, 2 March 2006.

## 16

If your life or the public's safety is in danger, you have to use force...
But if a law enforcement officer is going to act like a thug, he should be
treated like a thug.

-Sheriff Fred Abdalla[324]

Olivito returned to his hometown to take on more civil rights
cases in late 2004, seven years after the DOJ imposed the consent decree. Three new clients began pulling his attention back to Steubenville
at the tail end of the consent decree. During these twilight years of his
career, Olivito had four active civil rights cases in the Northern District,
and he had filed another lawsuit over a fatal police shooting in Minneapolis, Minnesota. Daniel Walker Jr., a white former football player,
was one of Olivito's new clients, and his case carried major political
and financial implications for the SPD.

Dan Jr. was a one-time MVP in his late teens from a middle-
class white family. The Walkers had a bit of history with the SPD, but it
wasn't because of criminal conduct. Dan Walker Sr. met with Charlie
Reynolds, the auditor for the consent decree, to discuss the SPD. Dan
Sr. had also met with Chief McCafferty and a sergeant about an officer
with a drinking problem. Dan Sr. was doing his part to hold his local
public servants accountable, which made the incident that turned the
Walkers' lives upside down all the more suspicious.

On the night of June 6, 2004, someone called the police over a
disturbance outside a party on the 400 block of Buena Vista Boulevard.
When the police pulled up, everybody scattered, as they do in communities across America. There are differing accounts of what happened
next. The police said they saw footprints in the night's dew that led to
the Walkers' backyard. Dan Jr. was in his backyard at the time, and
Officer Ed Karovic called to him from the outside of the fence. Dan Jr.
said he never heard the man identify himself as a police officer and he
was seized with the fear and ducked beside the family's above-ground
swimming pool. Despite the officer's calls to present himself, Dan Jr.

---

[324] Staff. "Recognizing the need for understanding. *The Herald-Star*, 22
July 2016.

then hid under the deck. The IA report included this statement from an interview with Dan Jr.:

> Once I got under my deck, I noticed this man was a Steubenville Police Officer. At this time I became more scared knowing that they have a reputation to say people do things they don't do. They also beat people up like Officer Linzinski did to a young prisoner he had in custody last year who was in handcuffs, in a police car, with the camera on him.[325]

Dan Jr. was referring to a videotaped incident of excessive force, which was sustained by IA investigation, but after being fired, the officer got his job back. When Walker did not comply, Karovic clambered over the fence and came after him. Dan Jr. called his dad on his cell phone, and Dan Sr. immediately opened the window and yelled, "Who the hell is out there?"

"Steubenville Police Officers."

"Get the hell up to the side door now!" Dan Sr. called to his son.

Dan Jr. said that he crawled towards the steps and then made a dash for the door. Before he could get there, Dan Jr. alleged that Officer Karovic grabbed him and hit him in the head with his flashlight, which Karovic denied.

"Stop hitting me," Dan Jr. yelled as his father opened the door. The officer let go of Dan Jr., and he ran into the house.

Dan Sr. demanded the officer call his supervisor, even before Dan Jr. told his father that the officer had hit him. Dan Sr. testified that he had seen the motion of the officer's flashlight move quickly towards his son's face and then back again. Karovic argued that he had been carrying his own little plastic flashlight, while Dan Jr. maintained that it was a heavy metal flashlight like cops normally carry. After interrupting the scuffle between the officer and his son, Dan Sr. went to the front door where officers were yelling for someone to open the gate.

At the door, Officer Lelles exclaimed, according to a transcript released by the SPD, "Where is your boy at, bring him here. He's over at this party, okay, and there's a bunch of kids out here ready to fight. Then, he's hunkered down back there, we're saying we want to talk to him."

Dan Jr. was sitting on the couch when the officers came walking into his living room.

"You ran, so don't lie now!" Lelles said.

Dan Sr. berated his son, "You shouldn't a ran! When he says stop, he's a fucking cop, simple as that." Officer Lelles acknowledged that he'd known Dan Sr. a long time, and then he asked Dan Jr. if he

---

[325] Sergeant John Sullivan. "Internal Investigation." *Steubenville Police Department*, 27 September 2004.

was drinking at the house next door. Dan Sr. spoke before his son could answer, admitting that he had given Dan Jr. alcohol at dinner and ordering him to tell the truth that he had been drinking. Officer Lelles told Dan Sr. that they could arrest him for providing alcohol to a minor. Then, he ordered Dan Jr. to come with him, blandly declaring, "I think it will teach the young man a valuable lesson." Dan Sr. responded, "I understand."

Dan Sr. told his son to stand up and put his hands behind his back while an officer cuffed his hands. On the way to the station, Dan Jr. complained that the handcuffs were too tight. According to the transcript in the IA report, Dan Jr. said he was going to have bruises. Officer Lelles replied, "I don't want to hear that. They are loose, Daniel, they are loose, and that's the best I can do."

Dan Jr. kept talking, although what he said was inaudible in the recording. Lelles overruled him, "You just want to be smart. Listen, listen, listen, listen. Let me stop you here right now, okay?" Then, he held forth:

> Your dad's gonna have the opportunity to file the IA complaint, you know that. Now, I'm gonna tell you something about all of this. I don't know what the game is you want to try to play or your dad or anyone else and I don't care. I do my job by the book and to the best of my abilities. Don't play mind or word games with me...I don't want to hear no smart mouth. I'm treating you like a man and I expect the same respect.[326]

Not long after Dan Jr. left for the station, his father called Chief McCafferty. In turn, the chief called Captain Gotschall. Sgt. Gotschall gave the chief this summary:

> Apparently, they went out there, a large crowd, a bunch of them took off running. They caught up to [Dan] Junior and he proceeded to run his mouth and he wound up getting arrested for underage consumption because he smells like a brewery... There was a witness out there that said that the kid's lying, ain't no policeman touched him. Dan [Sr.] is claiming he observed Karovic slap him.[327]

The chief replied, according to the transcript in the IA report, "Yeah, I figured it was Karovic." Karovic had a degree in criminal justice from West Liberty State College and was then working on a Master's in Education Administration. He was director of security at the Franciscan University for eleven years before coming to the SPD. According to his

---

[326] Ibid.

[327] Ibid.

187

statements under oath, Karovic had not been the subject of any previous complaints.

In the IA report, there were transcripts of a conversation recorded by the officers' microphones in which Officer Terry Norris told Officer Lelles that Dan Jr. was on the street when the fight broke out. Lelles urged Norris to tell the truth to IA, come what may. Then, he said, "I don't care what the outcome is. You didn't give a statement last night, and that's your right, but if IA calls, do me a favor. That Dan is gonna file a complaint against me and Karovic."

"Everyone knows he's a piece of shit," Norris answered.

"I don't have anything against the boy or his father; we were only trying to find the kids who ran," Lelles went on.

"I was sitting on the…thing and [Dan Sr.] came over and said why you gonna tell them you didn't see anything. I said, 'Listen you know I can't stand your ass anyway and you think I'm gonna fuckin' say I did? Just get the fuck out of my face.'"

Norris continued at length, recounting how Dan Sr. threatened to file a complaint about the incident, but Lelles assured him, "Hey, be good. If it's anyone, it'll be Sgt. Sullivan or Sgt. Anderson. You know Johnny Sul. Alright, my man." The statement could be taken to imply that Sgt. "Johnny Sul" in IA was partial to officers accused of misconduct. Lelles would have known because he had been the subject of complaints, according to Sgt. Sullivan's sworn statements, one of which involved domestic violence, but he had never been disciplined.

On June 7, the Walkers invited the late African American Councilman Skip Mixon to examine and photograph Dan Jr.'s head injury. On June 8, the Walkers filed a complaint with Steubenville's IA Department. Sgt. John Sullivan was tasked with the IA investigation of the complaint, which utilized a polygraph, breaking from former SPD policy. Dan Jr. was advised by his doctor not to take a polygraph on account of his head injury, which could affect the results. According to Chief McCafferty, the fact that Officer Karovic passed a polygraph denying that he struck Dan Jr. figured heavily into Sgt. Sullivan's decision in September to classify the complaint as "unfounded." In October, the municipal court dropped the underage consumption charge. With no chance of administrative accountability, the Walker's pinned their hopes on a civil lawsuit. They were motivated and ready to take on the city fathers, but six attorneys in a row turned down the case. Then, they called Richard Olivito.

<><><>

On January 3, 2005, the civil complaint landed on the docket of the Southern District Court. Olivito wrote in the plaintiffs' trial brief:

As far as the police were aware, no crime had occurred. In spite of the concerns of the person who called the police, when the first officer arrived, he observed no fighting. Police found no one claiming to have been assaulted, no injured parties, no shouting, no weapons and no blood. They found nothing to suggest that any crime had ever occurred.[328]

The Walker case brought together everyone involved in the police reform effort and provided a window into the inner workings of the SPD during the consent decree. Chief McCafferty was named in the lawsuit, quoted heavily in the court documents and deposed in the course of discovery.[329] *Walker v. Lelles* carried heavy damages because the alleged injury involved would last for the rest of Dan Jr.'s life, but that wasn't the only reason Dan Jr. was angry. In an interview with IA, Dan Jr. accused Jim Bernard, the president of the FOP, of harassing him and his dad, prior to the June 6 incident, while IA covered it up.[330]

The allegations in the lawsuit were controversial and came at a bad time because the city and the SPD were anxiously awaiting the end of the consent decree. From the beginning, the chief was in contact with Reynolds about the case. The late Councilman Skip Mixon was concerned enough about it to sit in on depositions, against the objections of the city's counsel, and to organize a meeting between Dan Jr. and Reynolds. Olivito deposed dozens of officials and witnesses during pretrial discovery. Some of the depositions were tense, but they were also often revealing. During the deposition of Sgt. Sullivan, Olivito referred to a photo taken after the arrest, asking the sergeant, "Do you see any subtle deformities on the right, behind his eyebrow? Any bruising or swelling?"

"I see what appears to be a blemish on his skin."

"Behind the blemish, or where the blemish appears to be, do you see a swelling?"

"I don't know if it's swelling," responded Sgt. Sullivan.

Olivito tried with another photo, which was entered into evidence.

"Can you see that, look at that photograph. Look behind, again, on his right temple area, near his cheekbone."

"It looks like a zit."

"Behind the zit," Olivito persisted.

[328] *Walker v. Lelles*. Sixth Cir. 2007.

[329] *Walker v. Steubenville Police Officer*. 463 F. Supp. 2d 769. S. D. Court. 2006.

[330] Sergeant John Sullivan. "Internal Investigation." *Steubenville Police Department*, 27 September 2004.

"Hair," concluded Sullivan.

"Do you see the swelling?"

"It could be a zit that looks swelled up."

"You don't want to see a swelling, do you, officer? That's the problem with your investigation."

This one question and statement gets to the heart of the problem with IA investigating citizen complaints. They typically don't want to acknowledge the citizens' side of the story, preferring to exculpate their fellow officers. The appearance of a conflict of interest is inevitable.

Stoffers, the city's defense attorney, objected, but Olivito persisted, as usual.

"You didn't want to find—" Olivito began not asking a question, but Sgt. Sullivan interrupted:

"Well, my question is, he was allegedly hit in the cheek, and that's not his cheek."

"Well, did Officer Karovic say he was hit in the cheek?"

"Mrs. Walker said he was hit in the cheek," answered Sgt. Sullivan.

"Did Dan say he was hit in the cheek?"

"I do believe he did say he was hit in the cheek."

"How big is your flashlight, Officer Sullivan?" Olivito inquired.

"How big is my flashlight?"

"Yeah, how big is the officer's flashlight, the Maglite?"

"He wasn't using a Mag-Lite."

"Well, let me ask you how big are your Maglites in the city of Steubenville?"

"There's big Maglites, and there's mini Maglites."

"How big are your big ones?"

"They're, I can't tell you inch-wise, I never measured them."

"How many years have you been on the force?"

"Sixteen and a half."

"And how many degrees do you have?"

"Three."

"And you can't tell me how big a Maglite is in the police department?"

"With an accurate measurement, no."

"Give me a rough estimate."

"12 inches."

"Okay, let's do a little bit of physics here," Olivito's impatience was growing.

"I never took physics."

"Let's not get argumentative," Stoffers interjected.

"Let's get Plaintiff's Exhibit 1. How many inches do you think there is between a cheekbone and his temple area?"

"A couple," responded Sgt. Sullivan dryly.

"Shorter than twelve inches?"

"Yes."

"He doesn't have a twelve-inch head, does he?" Olivito said sarcastically.

"A head or a cheek?"

"Where there's swelling on his right side?"

"That's not twelve inches."

This line of questioning was intended to show that a large flashlight could have an impact on Dan Jr.'s cheek and his temple at the same time, but Sgt. Sullivan wasn't buying it. Stoffers often interrupted, but it seemed in this interview Stoffers didn't need to because Karovic knew the drill; all stalling and scoffing, deflection and evasion. Sullivan's attitude towards the complaint was clear: Walker had a zit on his cheek, and Sullivan wasn't seeing anything else.

"Right," said Olivito, shifting his inquiry. "Let's talk about this Maglite policy."

The SPD had optional Maglites for the officers, which they could obtain from the shift supervisor. Officers could use their own flashlights or they could go to the supervisor's office, which on the night of the incident would have been Sgt. Gotschall. Departmental policy dictated that the shift supervisor must have each officer sign off on a form if he or she checked out one of the Maglites. According to his deposition, Karovic was using his own flashlight, which was plastic and smaller than the Maglites of the department. The Walkers argued that the flashlight Karovic had been carrying was larger. Olivito pressed all of the officers to ascertain the truth of the matter, but the SPD stonewalled inquiry.

The audio recordings from the night provided documentary evidence of almost every moment from before the police arrived and included phone calls between the officers and the chief after the arrest. The SPD had microphones that they would switch on when they made a traffic stop or answered any service call. Notably, Officer Karovic claimed that his audio was malfunctioning while he was outside of his cruiser, although Sgt. Gotschall could not recall being notified of any malfunctions that night.

In addition to these intriguing questions, there may have been a more specific pretext for the odd interest of the officers in the Walker residence. According to the IA report, Dan Jr. asked in writing about a meeting between his father, Chief McCafferty and Sgt. Sullivan that took place a few days before his arrest. Dan Sr. alleged that one of the officers had a drinking problem. At the end of the discussion, according to Dan Jr. in the IA report, Sgt. Sullivan asked Dan Sr. when his son would go to court for underage consumption. In his deposition with Olivito, Sgt. Sullivan confirmed that he had made a statement to that effect. In keeping with their historic pattern and in spite of almost seven years of oversight, the SPD still retaliated against those who complained.

◇◇◇

The city of Steubenville's police depended on the city manager to help them interpret the law as it pertained to the obligations and responsibilities of officers acting under the color of law, as required by the consent decree. For this reason, on May 23, 2006, almost eighteen months after filing the complaint, Olivito summoned City Manager Bruce Williams. Olivito suspected that the city had not been in compliance with the terms of the decree and that the decree was lifted prematurely.

According to the transcript, Olivito asked Williams if his supervisory role in the city government was similar to the director of public safety, which he confirmed it was. Then, he started showing Williams documents related to the consent decree between Steubenville and the DOJ, which Williams had not seen before. Olivito questioned him at length about the roles of the mayor and the law director in terms of oversight, establishing that in the council form of municipal government, as opposed to statutory, the city manager is the primary official responsible for oversight. Then, Olivito began specifying what oversight meant in Steubenville during Williams' tenure as city manager.

"Do you have an involvement in the day-to-day affairs of the police department?" Olivito asked.

"I don't. I don't involve myself in micromanaging any of the departments," Williams answered.

Olivito asked for specific examples or functions, and Williams replied, "I rarely involve myself in the daily operations of the police department...My job is to make sure that they function consistent with the policies."

After the opposing counsel objected to most of the questions Olivito asked, Williams portrayed himself as a city manager uninvolved in oversight of the police department. Olivito then moved to the topic of IA, and Williams confirmed that his office has a role in the final decision over discipline and that he had reversed the decision of IA on "at least" one occasion. He was not in a hurry to assist Olivito in building his case against the city, but he did make some revealing statements. In response to a question about the frequency of his communications with IA regarding operations and training, Williams stated, "I stay completely out of it."

On the one hand, Williams admitted that the SPD "was far from a perfect police agency," but he countered that he "never had a need," to go back and look at any of the cases in which citizens had complained of abuse. He also stated he had "no idea" if the police chief was involved with or exposed to police conferences or in-service training. Williams said he had made no public statements, nor taken any specific initiative to change the disciplinary system or deal with the issues outlined in the consent decree. Olivito then inquired into the topics of William's meetings with city officials and the police, asking what important issues of police policy came up. In his answer, Williams sidestepped the issues the consent decree was meant to address:

> We spend a great deal of time addressing citizen concerns about the sale and use of illegal drugs. We have issues with youngsters violating curfew laws, creating neighborhood problems. Those are typically the kinds of police policies we're trying to develop to address the concerns.

It would seem that the imperatives of the drug war and policing the youth were the only issues the city officials were worried about. Williams professed that he was "committed to doing the right thing," but despite his authority to involve himself in training, hiring, and firing within the department, he chose to stay out of it, full stop. According to Williams, the consent decree was a success story, and the IA investigation of the Walker case reached "the only conclusions that they could have come to."

Williams stated that he was "satisfied with...the continuing responsibility we have to both our citizens and the DOJ to stay on course for all of those items we were held accountable for under that consent order and that I'm pleased to have good quality law enforcement officers employed by the city." In other words, Williams believed that once the SPD was held accountable by the DOJ, no more accountability was needed.

Up until this deposition, the counsel hired to represent the city from Mazanec Raskin & Ryder had attempted to keep Reynolds' quarterly reports on the SPD from falling into Olivito's hands, even to the point of denying their existence. Williams promptly turned them over as soon as Olivito asked. After Olivito questioning Williams and examining the quarterly reports, Olivito realized that the reports were supposed to be made public as they were created, which never happened as is plainly obvious from the eighteen months of lies and rigamarole he went through to obtain them.

Former Deputy Assistant Attorney General for Civil Rights Roy Austin confirmed that departments should be more transparent while under a decree:

> [A police department] should be more transparent at all times, but sometimes the decree forces it to be more transparent.

That's probably the most important part of this because the DOJ is not going to be there too long, and it needs to slide over to the community to be in charge of how it is policed, what the priorities of the police are going to be. The only way for that to happen is for the community to know and that's why there needs to be transparency. During the consent decree process, there's a hope that and usually there are terms that things are supposed to be very transparent. The hope is that it survives well beyond the consent decree.

The reason for the suppression of the reports may have been that the city didn't want the citizens to know about the seven years of struggle for compliance, lest they become more vigilant and cause the city even more grief while city officials tried to get out of the administrative straightjacket of the decree.

<><><>

The plaintiffs maintained that Officers Lelles and Karovic violated Dan Jr.'s Fourth Amendment rights by illegally entering his property and seizing him without probable cause. The Southern District Court agreed that the police did not have any exigent reason to enter the Walkers' backyard. "Suspicion of underage drinking" has not been taken as sufficiently exigent a cause for police to violate the Fourth Amendment in past cases. The district court ruled, "In this case, the offense committed—if any at all—was a minor offense."[331] The defense counsel filed a motion to exclude the photos taken by Mixon because they had not been disclosed to the defendants, and the district court granted it, weakening but not destroying Dan Jr.'s claim of excessive force.

The defendants requested summary judgment under qualified immunity, but the district court denied it, based on the evidence that they violated Dan Jr.'s Fourth Amendment rights. The court also denied summary judgment on the claim of excessive force because the facts of the case were still in dispute, so the court decided it would be best for the claim to proceed to trial. The court did not agree with the plaintiffs on the *Monell* claim that the city failed to investigate and was deliberately indifferent to excessive force and illegal searches and seizures. The defendants filed an interlocutory appeal to the Sixth Circuit to avoid going to a jury trial, but the Sixth Circuit agreed with the district court, reinforcing the victory of the plaintiffs and eviscerating the city's argument that the officer had cause to enter the property.

---

[331] *Walker v. Steubenville Police Officer*. 463 F. Supp. 2d 769. S. D. Court. 2006.

In August of 2006, Olivito was preparing to argue the *Monell* claim in the *Walker* case against the city of Steubenville at the Southern District Court before Judge Algernon Marbley, a no-nonsense African American Clinton-appointee.[332] The case was looking grim for the city, and Olivito seemed to have the wind at his back. He had won his third victory at the Sixth Circuit that spring, and he knew his hometown police department better than anybody, except Jim McNamara, who was sitting with him at the plaintiff's table, but even McNamara backed away from arguing the policy claim against Steubenville.

Olivito had been waiting for an opportunity to argue before a judge sympathetic to the issues underlying the litigation, police brutality and systemic Constitutional violations, as a matter of law, aside from political considerations. It was Olivito's dream to be the first lawyer in America to bring the power of Section 14141, the pattern or practice law, into a Section 1983 civil rights claim by using it as evidence to win a *Monell* claim. The U.S. Supreme Court had set a heavy burden of evidence for the *Monell* claim. He would have to prove that the circumstances of the case and the violations alleged in the record were directly caused by the city's failure to train its employees. Olivito wanted to use the injury of Dan Walker Jr. to wreck the city's facade of implementing police reform. He intended to show that the city was not in compliance with the consent decree, and he had City Manager Bruce Williams admitting under oath that he had not overseen the SPD during the implementation of the consent decree.

Olivito stood up and straightened his posture. He was just about to begin, when Robert Stoffers, the opposing counsel, burst in running with a letter held aloft.

"He can't speak! He's suspended!" Stoffers shouted triumphantly.

Olivito stood still as if stricken, swaying for a moment. Then, he looked expectantly to the judge. Judge Marbley frowned as he unfolded the letter. Silence reigned while he read, and as he set it aside, the judge's grave expression took the air out of the room. After convening the attorneys, Judge Marbley suggested staying the suspension for two hours for Olivito to make his argument, but the issuing judge refused to budge on the suspension. Marbley's hands were tied, and Olivito was officially gagged.

Many years later, Olivito said, "Reynolds' own quarterly reports demonstrated [that the city had never been in compliance] and this is why Mazanec's lawyers tried so hard to block me from speaking to this issue before Judge Marbley." The city's defense lawyers managed to muzzle the last person who was willing and able to present a legal argument before a judge on the pattern in Steubenville.

---

[332] *Walker v. Lelles.* S. D. Court of Ohio. 2009. Print.

As one of the first American cities subject to this type of settlement with the DOJ, Steubenville was a laboratory for federal police reform, despite local opposition. According to the monitor, Charlie Reynolds, the city had been in compliance with the consent decree for just short of two years. The standard for measuring substantial compliance was still taking shape, and Reynolds may not have been the ultimate decision maker, but he was in charge of collecting and reporting information on the progress of the SPD. Once the SPD achieved two years of compliance, Reynolds could recommend the DOJ lift the decree.

Reynolds stated that, when he left Steubenville in 2005 and the DOJ closed out the decree, the SPD had a "robust" IA program and a "pretty good" training program. By that time, Reynolds had vented his frustration at the repeated failures of the city to implement the requirements of the decree, and perhaps, he had realized that compliance according to the letter of the decree was just not going to happen. In contrast, Dan Walker Sr. declared, while on the phone in October of 2014, that he had evidence IA had lied about the incident and that Reynolds and the DOJ, "didn't do shit." This was more pessimistic than Delores Wiggins who indicated that policing had improved "by about 3%." As for the "robust" IA program, Olivito remembered that not long after the lifting of the consent decree, the city stopped maintaining the separate office space for IA and moved it back into the police station.

Reynolds argued, "I could say with great assurance that when we concluded they had systems and talent in place to do the right thing." He conceded that "compliance wouldn't necessarily be with one case," because "one case wouldn't necessarily make a difference unless it was one officer who had been a problem all along." Reynolds was looking for a decrease in the percentage of arrests in which use-of-force occurred, so one case didn't necessarily concern him because the city had instituted a "substantial" number of the DOJ's demands. However, as the DOJ signed off on the SPD, three use-of-force lawsuits were kicking off. Between them, the alleged injuries were PTSD, permanent brain damage, as well as bone and muscle damage requiring surgery.

Reynolds may have been justified in making the argument about one case being insignificant, but he also made a few statements that suggest there were other reasons for the lifting of the decree. Reynolds stated, "A lot of times police chiefs are hampered by the mayor or the city manager or both, the city council may not support them. Sometimes the chief is very welcoming of the consent decree because they are happy to make the changes, but the city officials are resistant." In the quarterly reports, Reynolds referred to the "city fathers," who are essential in the reform process. Many years later, he didn't recall using this phrase, but Olivito and Sean Scipio, a plaintiff whose lawsuit relied on Reynolds' reports, confirmed that Reynolds had used it.

Reynolds did not say that city officials resisted reform when asked directly, but he said that this is the sort of thing that happens. From the deposition of City Manager Bruce Williams, it is quite clear that Williams stayed out of Internal Affairs and that Williams' overriding concerns were combating the drug problem and curfew violations. Voters wanted the drug problem and the violence eliminated. Many couldn't have cared less about the police department's policies as long as they weren't affected. However, those who had issues with the police were hoping federal oversight would continue.

This was at the municipal level, but other factors may have played a role at the state and federal level. There was a plot afoot inside the DOJ that raises questions about the "high-end political considerations," Olivito referred to as the cause of the termination of the consent decree. Local voters and officials tend to resent what they perceive as federal interference by D.C. bureaucrats, and perhaps as a result, DOJ 14141 investigations tend to begin or end around presidential elections. In Steubenville, the consent decree was lifted just a few months after George W. Bush was re-elected president.

<><><>

When asked whether Lelles' comment indicates that Steubenville police officers did not view IA investigations as independent and impartial, Chief McCafferty didn't recall the case immediately, but he reiterated his willingness to suspend people when IA sustains complaints. He then suggested that perhaps the Walkers' complaint didn't go the way they wanted in IA and confirmed that Dan Sr. "loves the police. I talked to him this morning." Last, the chief declared, "I don't think that lawsuit went anywhere..." This was dubious because he could not fail to remember a case where the Sixth Circuit ruled against the SPD on so many issues that Jim McNamara predicted a "runaway jury" settlement. The *Walker* lawsuit threatened to cost the city more than all of the lawsuits of the '80s and '90s combined, yet Chief McCafferty claimed it was a dud. When reminded of the city's defeat at the Sixth Circuit, the chief fell silent, but he was right that the city was able to evade liability.

Olivito couldn't figure out why the Walker case never settled, and neither could David Fawcett, who litigated the famous *Caperton v. Massey Energy* case. Fawcett declined to take the case, but according to Olivito, he stated, "A lot of ugly things probably happened behind this case. Divorces, bribes, extortion, fraud, and threats, if not more. A lot of money is at stake." The city clearly feared settlement because the liability for permanent brain damage would be staggering. Olivito suspected the problem was that McNamara never filed the injury claim. McNamara stated that he withdrew as counsel for confidential reasons. McNamara has been a no-nonsense civil rights litigator for more than thirty-five years. These days, he doesn't draw attention to himself with ribald statements in the press, but he said he still files police misconduct cases "constantly." In response to a suggestion that his forty-four victories against the SPD were heroic, McNamara stated, "Attorneys are just technicians. It is the victims and their willingness to step forward and risk retaliation themselves who are the heroes."

McNamara may have had good reason to withdraw. Regardless, no one wants to revisit the case, not the police, not the plaintiffs and not the attorneys. With the pain his family endured, it comes as little surprise. The city took the gloves off, and the defense counsel let the Walkers know that the city would do anything to end that lawsuit. Nonetheless, the Walkers' courageous activism put evidence on the public record that the SPD was operating without the oversight of the city government and that some of the old problems persisted right under Reynolds' nose.

## 17

Officers must announce their presence, give the occupant reasonable time to come to the door, and provide the occupant a copy of the warrant before they can demand entry to conduct a search.

-Fourth Amendment, U.S. Constitution

On December 23, 2004, Dawn Kelley was making a late dinner for her five-year-old daughter, Chyna, who sat with her in the kitchen of their Steubenville house. Dawn is an African American mother of three, raised in Weirton, who was anchored by a husband and a mortgage in Steubenville. Suddenly, an unknown force breached the front door. The Jefferson County Drug Task Force, formerly the Federal Drug Task Force, was on the scene. Officers streamed in SWAT-style with guns trained in all directions as they fanned through the apartment. When she realized what was happening, Dawn said she figured they had the wrong house, but with firearms pointed at her and her daughter, Dawn felt the imminence of death. Recovering herself, Dawn asked the officers if they had a warrant. They confirmed that they did and that it would be produced after the search. When the police allegedly found drug paraphernalia in the spare bedroom of the apartment, they confronted Kelley with the fruit of their search and arrested her. Dawn alleges they never showed her a warrant. After the raid, her and Chyna's lives would never be the same.

Dawn Kelley claimed that her home was invaded in violation of the Constitution. She was so upset by it all that she left Ohio, moving first to West Virginia and then to North Carolina. The police claimed she was a drug dealer. The day before, the task force had sent a confidential informant wearing a wire to do a controlled-buy of $40 worth of crack from Kelley. According to the police, the CI left without drugs, and he came back with less than a gram. According to the CI, who later recanted his statement, he never bought drugs from Kelley, but the recording from the wire was used to convince a judge the next day to issue a warrant to search Kelley's residence. Then, the warrant disappeared and reappeared, as did the charges against Kelley. The origins of the case were murky, and the optics were unfavorable. It would have disappeared, but then Kelley went and sued the city. The city's revenge illustrated the ruthlessness of the new county prosecutor, Gail Cullen, and the incestuous relationships between the officers of the court and local law enforcement. Dawn didn't realize that when she challenged the justice system, she was essentially attacking a powerful family that could easily retaliate with the county agencies under their control.

Olivito agreed to take the case because of the trauma suffered by Kelley's daughter. Doctors in Ohio and later in North Carolina independently diagnosed Chyna with PTSD. The same day the charges were dismissed, Olivito went to the Jefferson County Prosecutor's Office to obtain the warrant which authorized the raid. They couldn't produce it, so they directed him to the municipal clerk's office, where the assistant deputy clerk of courts, Rose Lavender, verified, after checking twice, that there was no warrant on file. Two months after the charge was dismissed, the city magically produced the warrant, but the prosecutor didn't indict.

In August of 2005, eight months after the raid, Olivito filed a civil rights complaint on Kelley's behalf. The complaint named the city, the mayor, the police chief, and every officer who participated in the raid, charging the defendants with four counts of federal civil rights violations. It accused the city of a pattern or practice of deliberate indifference towards the citizens, regarding which Olivito wrote, "This recent incident involving the plaintiff occurred prior to the consent decree being lifted and as such represents a violation of the spirit and the letter of the same as it was conceived and put into effect."[333] Olivito specified, "The young daughter was confronted continuously with loaded, police-issued handguns being pointed directly at her face by members of the drug task force residential search team. The minor child was then taken from the mother." In addition to traumatizing the child with weapons, the police allegedly left Chyna with a neighbor who happened to walk by while the police were at the house.

Olivito condemned the SPD for failing to report the incident to the auditor, Reynolds, who was unaware of the allegedly warrantless no-knock raid on Kelley's house when the decree was lifted in March of 2005. "No higher official," Olivito wrote, referring to Reynolds, "can either excuse or supplant with talk of cooperation and progress in light of the depth of the history of the [SPD]'s intense civil rights policy failures."

Olivito hammered away on the point that the searches and seizures were part of "a police culture and local city process and policy which even the federal monitor has acknowledged as being serious and deeply entrenched but not fully remedied."[334] The complaint quoted Reynolds saying that the city was "far from perfect in its application of

---

[333] *Kelley v. City of Steubenville*. S.D. Ohio. 2008.

[334] Ibid. p. 12.

the terms of the consent decree."[335] The consent decree had been lifted by the time the lawsuit was being taken up by the Southern District Court, but Olivito argued that Kelley's arrest proved that the city still was failing to train and discipline its officers.

By the summer of 2006, Olivito was pushing for discovery while the city sought summary judgment. Olivito wanted to depose Officer Cullen and the assistant deputy clerk of courts, Rose Lavender, who verified that the warrant did not exist three months after the raid. Then, Olivito's law license was suspended,[336] causing Kelley to ask for an extension. The court was not happy about it, but Olivito blamed the opposing counsel for stalling, a typical tactic by the defense and also typically alleged by plaintiffs' attorneys.

On March 7, 2007, two and a half years after County Prosecutor Jane Cullen decided not to indict Dawn Kelley, while the motion for summary judgment by the city was pending in Kelley's civil rights case, the prosecutor resurrected drug charges against Kelley. She had married and taken the last name of the first officer named in the complaint, Bill Cullen, a month before. These are not their real names. Gail's son Brian had the last name of her ex-husband, which she had until her second marriage, but we'll call her Cullen for sake of simplicity. Then, Prosecutor Gail Cullen indicted Kelley on three counts: trafficking in cocaine, possession of drug paraphernalia, and possession of cocaine, two felonies and a misdemeanor, offering her a deal where she would plead and get off with probation and no jail time. By this time, Dawn Kelley was living in North Carolina and working at a Kmart distribution center. Despite this new start, she was filled anew with a sense of injury and indignation, so she rejected the deal and came back to Ohio to fight the indictment.

Three months after the indictment, Beverly Kelley, Dawn's mother, sent a complaint to the Ohio Supreme Court, calling Prosecutor Cullen out for her conflict of interests with her husband and accusing Judge Joseph J. Bruzzese of judicial misconduct because he allowed Cullen to prosecute Kelley "for an undocumented crime she did not commit."[337] Beverly Kelley accused the defendants of conspiring to violate her daughter's rights, and she demanded the charges be dropped and that Cullen and Judge Bruzzese be suspended from the practice of law for three years.

Frank Bruzzese, the brother of Judge Bruzzese, responded to

---

[335] Ibid. p. 11.

[336] Covered in Chapter 18.

[337] *Kelley v. Bruzzese.* 2:09-cv-00237. S.D. Court of Ohio. 21 July 2009.

the allegations before the Ohio Supreme Court in a nine-page motion to dismiss. With Bruzzese as counsel before the high court, Prosecutor Cullen claimed she was unaware of a lawsuit against her husband, which was unlikely, but apparently good enough for the supreme court. Two months later, Bruzzese's motion to dismiss was granted by the high court because Kelley failed to state a claim and should have first appealed to a state appeals court or filed a complaint with the disciplinary counsel, which she later did. It failed to deter the abuse of power in the Jefferson County Court of Common Pleas.

According to the ruling, Judge Bruzzese and Prosecutor Cullen were only discharging their official duties, regardless of whether they both worked at the same firm and had a common conflict of interests concerning Kelley's case against the city, the mayor, the police chief, Cullen's husband, and his task force colleagues. Although judicial ethics called for the avoidance of the appearance of conflicts or impropriety, the Kelleys tried in vain to show the corruption involved in the prosecution and judgment of Dawn's case to the supreme court of Ohio.

In 2008, the plaintiffs appealed to the Sixth Circuit in hopes of reversing the Southern District Court's grant of summary judgment to the defendants. The Sixth Circuit affirmed the lower court's ruling,[338] deferring to the magistrate who allegedly signed the warrant that the city was later unable to produce. The appellate panel concluded that the plaintiffs had failed to prove that the use of force was unreasonable. The court reasoned, "It was not unreasonable for them to have their weapons drawn upon entry," sidestepping whether the officers may have held firearms at "low ready," pointed in the direction of a five-year-old child.[339]

When a plaintiff's lawyer alleges a constitutional claim or a pattern of violations, it is subject to extensive scrutiny. When the state wants to ram through a conviction with little or nothing to corroborate it, victory is practically assured, especially in Bruzzese's court. During Kelley's criminal trial in October of 2008, the charge was almost four years old, and the federal civil rights case and the disciplinary counsel investigation loomed large. Nevertheless, Prosecutor Cullen sat next to Officer Cullen at the table for the prosecution, pretending not to know that the defendant had filed a lawsuit against her new husband, the prime witness for the state. Cullen later questioned why anyone would draw a connection between the indictment and Kelley's complaints and lawsuits against her and the judge.

While being questioned by his wife, Officer Cullen presented

[338] *Dawn Kelly v. William McCafferty et al.* Sixth Circuit. 2008. Print.

[339] *Kelley v. McCafferty.* 283 Fed. Appx. 359, 363. Sixth Cir. 2008.

the recorded evidence against Dawn Kelley from a cassette tape, obtained by the confidential informant, who later recanted in a signed statement that was presented to Judge Joseph J. Bruzzese Jr., though he refused to recognize it. Cullen fumbled with the tape, unable to find the right place on the recording. The recording contained no conversations about drug trafficking, but Cullen argued that a deal was taking place and that drug dealers don't discuss anything incriminating when they are doing a drug deal.

During closing arguments, Kelley's lawyer joked that he wasn't a prosecutor or married to a police officer, which would cause personal feelings to cloud his judgment, a dig at Cullen. When it was her turn to address the jury, Cullen fired back, saying that the defendant's counsel was "paid to represent drug dealers."

At her sentencing in February of 2009, Judge Bruzzese gave Kelley five days to go back to North Carolina and return, threatening Kelley that if she were one minute late in reporting to the EOCC, he would make her do a year in prison. Judge Bruzzese didn't care if she had nothing to do with drugs in the four years since the warrantless raid. He didn't care if he was depriving Chyna of her mother. He was sending her to prison. If she didn't submit to the state and comply with their every wish, he would make sure her life was filled with as much suffering as it was within his power to inflict.

A month after sentencing, Kelley filed a complaint against Judge Bruzzese, County Prosecutor Thomas Strauss, Assistant Prosecutor Gail Cullen, as well as Olivito's older brother and other attorneys. Kelley protested the fact that Judge Bruzzese had worked for the same firm to which both Prosecutor Strauss and Assistant Prosecutor Cullen belonged.[340] In May of 2009, during a post-sentencing hearing, Judge Bruzzese overruled Kelley's attempt to make him recuse himself, referring to her mother's complaints to the disciplinary counsel and the civil lawsuit, "all of which have been dismissed." Kelley was going to be taught a lesson, and the judge and Jane and her husband were intent on sending her to prison, even if they had to abrogate due process protections and legal ethics.

Judge Bruzzese gave Kelley an extra six months, based on an accusation that Kelley refused to leave the prison when a group of supreme court justices came on an unrelated visit. No one else needed to leave the facility, just Dawn, and they refused to tell her why. Beverly Kelley recalled that she was supposed to give Dawn a ride, but that an emergency came up. Judge Bruzzese and the staff at the EOCC had no time for the excuses of working-class people. Dawn was noncompliant with the demands of the justice system. Therefore, she needed to be punished all over again until she was submissive, broken, begging to

---

[340] *Kelley v. Judge Bruzzese et al.* S. D. Court. 2009. Print.

see her child again. When Dawn got out and settled again, in Columbus, Gail Cullen became Dawn's husband's attorney on a child support situation. Dawn interpreted Cullen's actions as part of a grudge, saying, "She just felt like harassing me."

◇◇◇

In 2012, eight years after the warrantless raid, Dawn Kelley wrote to Judge Bruzzese, politely asking him to expunge her criminal record. "My life has changed a lot since 2005." She had a new job, and she wanted to become a nurse, but the drug conviction stopped her from moving forward in her life. If only Judge Bruzzese could find it in his heart to let her close that chapter that set her career back and separated her from her daughter, for whom she wanted to provide a better life. From the judge's perspective, Dawn tried to get his and Cullen's law licenses suspended. Now, she was coming back begging for pity, mercy, another chance. Denied. He couldn't let it go. Judge Bruzzese relished the chance to impose a ceiling on her life's ambitions because it was within his power. Maybe, it was supposed to be an extra lesson, on top of all the deprivations and violations that Dawn had been forced to endure. She now knows the awesome power an angry judge can marshal to crush a person's prospects. Judge Bruzzese declined an interview, saying he steers clear of journalists, who "make you look stupid."

Years later, Beverly Kelley complained, "[Prosecutor Cullen] didn't recuse herself. [Officer Bill Cullen] even sat up front with her. He testified after listening to everyone in the room." When asked about the jury in Dawn's criminal case, she responded, "Friends of law enforcement. I think there was like two or three; it said in the documents one guy was friends with Officer Cullen." Beverly pointed to Gail Cullen's representation of Dawn's ex-husband as yet another retaliation, concluding, "You can't get no one to help you against them. You have to be very careful about who you talk to. It's terrible they run all the good people out. You can't get nobody to run up against them, that's how bad it is. Nobody will run [for office]. When can we get somebody fair?"

Dawn reports that she now lives in Columbus, happily. She feels blessed that her two sons are adults with great jobs and Chyna is working on an associate's degree in the medical field. Reflecting on the town which used to be her home, she said, "Steubenville should have never been taken out from under the consent decree."

◇◇◇

According to a knowledgeable anonymous personage known as Harold Star, Gail Cullen helped Frank Bruzzese every step of the way in his conquest of various public offices in the city and county, including the Common Pleas Court, the county prosecutor's office, the county board of elections, the county Democratic Party, the municipal court, the city school board, as well as the law department of the Village of Stratton, nearby Steubenville.

Bruzzese & Calabria represented local gambling moguls, coal, mineral and oil companies, the local hospital, Trinity Medical Center, and the city, including police officers and the local FOP. However, after one of the firm's law associates managed, with the help of the local FOP, to become county prosecutor in 2005, Frank and later his son Jeff also worked in the prosecutor's office, alongside other law associates from Bruzzese & Calabria.

Commandeering various institutions in a period of five to ten years required a few hardball tactics, careful consensus-building behind the scenes and occasionally ignoring state code regarding public contracts and conflict of interest laws. Harold supplied historical perspective for inquiring minds to understand the stranglehold one family has on the local institutions in Steubenville:

> When Bruzzese, Jr. joined his father's law firm, that firm, and in particular, Jr took on a client named Joseph Scugoza who sought to open a landfill in Jefferson County, Ohio known as CrossRidge Landfill. Joseph J. Bruzzese, Jr. was relentless in his representation of Mr. Scugoza. To this day, Mr. Scugoza and CrossRidge Landfill are in court proceedings brought by the Ohio Attorney General and others for violation of Ohio's Environmental Laws. A check of the recent Jefferson County Ohio Court docket will reveal the pending actions and decisions on those matters.

> Interesting to note, one Common Pleas Judge that is hearing the attorney general's complaints and lawsuits against Scugoza and CrossRidge is Common Pleas Judge Joseph J. Bruzzese, Jr. There has been no stepping aside by him based upon prior representation or conflicts. As a matter-of-fact, during one recent hearing, Mr. Scugoza appeared on a contempt matter without an attorney. The Judge, his former attorney, took him and the representative from the A.G.'s office into his chambers and worked out a deal.

> The relationship of Scugoza, landfills, organized crime and attorneys who have helped them is set forth in a book called *Space, Time, and Organized Crime*,... [in which] the following is written:

"Ohio provides a clear example of organized criminals moving West from New York and New Jersey to establish new dumping sites. In testimony before the Ohio House of Representatives in 1988, Ohio's Attorney General Anthony J. Celebrezze, Jr. exposed methods employed by a major New Jersey racketeer to obtain a landfill site in his state. Through the use of a 'front man' and local Ohio attorneys, racketeer Joseph Scugoza brought the Crossridge Landfill in Jefferson County, Ohio.

When asked in 2017, Frank Bruzzese said, "I don't think anybody here ever represented Joe. Nobody practicing law at the firm now." When asked if someone formerly working with the firm may have represented Scugoza, Bruzzese said he had no comment. Judge Joseph Bruzzese, Jr. was not then at the firm, and Star's other statements check out, such as that Bruzzese worked out a deal between Scugoza and the Ohio AG's attorneys,[341] but it's not confirmed that Judge Bruzzese represented Scugoza, who often appeared without counsel. The common pleas judge has enormous power over every aspect of local life, criminal, civil, economic, environmental. If anyone wants to get anything done in Steubenville, Bruzzese & Calabria is the place to start because the firm exercises pervasive influence. Beverly Kelley declared, "This city is always going to be corrupt until you get those Bruzzeses out of here."

---

[341] *State of Ohio ex rel v. C&D Disposal Technologies LLC*. Jefferson County Court of Common Pleas. 2013.

## 18

If there was an inkling that it wasn't foul play, I would have took that. But everything about it was too funny.

-Sean Scipio

None of his clients had enough money to retain an attorney for years of litigation, but Olivito couldn't resist taking new cases in Steubenville. In 2005, another new client was Sean Scipio who stands six and a half feet tall and weighs over three hundred pounds. His voice is like thunder, and he's gregarious and friendly. After being repeatedly told by Olivito's relatives that there was no civil rights lawyer in the family, Scipio was able to get in contact with Olivito. Scipio alleged that on September 17, 2003 he was clubbed by a Steubenville police officer. The incident arose after his son was suspended for smoking, and two cops allegedly witnessed Scipio strike his son outside of the school. According to the officers, Sean Scipio Jr. fell down the steps after being struck by his father. Sean Scipio Sr. denied it, and Olivito believed him.

The officers handcuffed Scipio with two pairs of handcuffs together and escorted him to the cruiser. When they ordered him to get in the car, he replied that he could not fit. The officers again ordered him to get in the car, telling him that they would spray him with mace if he refused. He refused, so, they sprayed him with mace and hit him in his leg near the knee with a baton, causing him to fall to the ground and which later required surgery. Then, the officers forcefully crammed Scipio's body into the car.

Two weeks later, the Steubenville Municipal Court dismissed the misdemeanor domestic violence charge that Scipio faced at the local level. Then, in August of 2005, Olivito filed a Section 1983 civil rights complaint, *Scipio v. City of Steubenville,* at the Southern District Court. Judge Norah King, who decided *U.S. v. City of Steubenville,* the case which resulted in the consent decree, presided over the case. The complaint cited violations of Scipio's Fourth and Fourteenth Amendment rights because of excessive force as well as unreasonable search and seizure. Before summary judgment was decided, the parties and their counsel were allowed to conduct depositions of various officials, witnesses, and persons of interest.

In light of the facts discovered during the depositions, several discrepancies emerged between the respective accounts of the Scipios and the police. A student from the school witnessed the whole ordeal from the window inside the school. In a deposition, she was questioned by counsel about the arrest and described the interactions between the officers and Scipio in great detail, including the moments when one of the officers maced Scipio and struck him in the leg with a baton.

Unfortunately for Scipio, when the time came to litigate his civil rights complaint in the Southern District Court, Olivito's license to practice law had been suspended. However, at first, in February of 2007, the court recognized a genuine issue of material fact between the plaintiff's and the defendants' versions of the event, and the court ruled in Scipio's favor, denying summary judgment to the defendants. Then, oddly, the court reversed itself, granting summary judgment to the defendants and dismissing the case.

Before the first hearing, as the parties took their seats, the judge told her bailiff, in a voice loud enough for everyone to hear, that she would have Scipio restrained if he became violent. The opposing counsel put up a large image of Scipio in an orange jumpsuit up on a stand, drawing no objection from Scipio's attorney. Scipio sat quietly through these indignities, only to have his case dismissed by the judge a short time later. Upon the announcement of the case's dismissal, Scipio said he would never forget that his lawyer turned to the opposing counsel and asked, "So where are we having lunch?"

On appeal to the Sixth Circuit, Olivito wrote his masterpiece in an attempt to resurrect Scipio's case and the consent decree over Steubenville. He argued that the nature of the violation of Scipio's rights had become fully clear only after the depositions illuminated certain aspects of the incidents, which motivated him to change the complaint to refer to the American Disability Act. The officers should have been trained on how to treat a person who could not fit in their car. Rather than strike his leg to subdue him and stuff his body into the cruiser, they would have been better off calling for a van. According to Olivito, their treatment was cruel and unusual.

Olivito challenged the Southern District Court on the dismissal of the policy claim, which accused the city of deliberate indifference to the rights of citizens, arguing that the SPD had not complied with the requirements of the consent decree. The city opposed the spirit of the decree and did not begin to come into compliance until the last quarter of 2002. Even so, the city never made the reports of the auditor available to the public, which was a condition of the decree. Olivito wrote, "these reports were never shown to the public nor listed at the four local libraries as required by the decree terms itself at any time in seven years."[342] Olivito was only able to obtain the quarterly reports through extensive litigation, and the defense counsel, Robert Stoffers of

---

[342] *Scipio v. City of Steubenville.* S. D. Court Ohio. 2007. p. 31.

Mazanec, Raskin & Ryder LPA, even denied their existence for over a year.

The reports showed how Charlie Reynolds became more and more frustrated with the city's lack of progress. He reported in June 2003, "Where there is an unusual case or a case with a serious problem indicated, the chief does not get legal or other support from the city...Because of the lack of support, the chief sometimes hesitates when it comes to enforcing serious discipline."[343] The consent decree was lifted in March of 2005, which entailed compliance with the decree for two full years, yet the auditor noted in June of 2003: "The training policy requires that the training officer review complaints against officers...on a monthly basis. This has not been the case."

No monthly reviews had been conducted during the previous six months, so Reynolds demanded that the training officer review "all 2003 complaints against officers," commencing the next quarter, after which the officer could begin conducting the required monthly reviews.[344] Reviewing all the citizen complaints for six months would be at least thirty-five to forty complaints, which presumably, also had been investigated by IA. One IA investigation can be dozens of pages in length. The internal investigation of the Walker case was fifty-five pages long. These administrative obstacles stood between the era of McCartney and the era of the decree. Olivito argued that their non-compliance was the cause of the violations of Scipio's constitutional rights. Olivito believed that the city never maintained two years of substantial compliance, and this was his argument why the Scipio case should not have been dismissed.

Reynolds' reports strengthened Olivito's legal argument in Scipio's case. Although Reynolds acknowledged that Chief McCafferty had made improvements, he stated that supervisors routinely rubber-stamped use-of-force and pursuit reports without question, only referring them to IA if there was an injury. In 2003, Reynolds admitted, "This has proven problematic for a long period of time." Then, departing from his usual diplomatic tone, he continued, "Regardless of the reason, the result is that the auditor has been unable to review reports during this audit period to determine Decree compliance which is unacceptable." Building on Reynolds' statements, Olivito reasserted that the city was deliberately indifferent to Scipio's complaint of excessive force and illegal search and seizure, two of the central issues the consent decree was supposed to address.

Although he was more than sympathetic to the problems of the SPD, the auditor could not overlook the supervisory failings of the de-

---

[343] Ibid. p. 32.

[344] Ibid. p. 33.

partment. Reynolds realized that it was more than just the chief and the police department. It was the culture of the town, the attitude of city hall and the city fathers who remained nameless in Reynolds' reports, but anyone in Steubenville would know who he meant.

◇◇◇

The Sixth Circuit denied Scipio's appeal, yet between the attorney and his client, a bond of camaraderie had developed. Scipio happened to be knowledgeable about computers, so he became Olivito's technical support and network administrator because Olivito's computers kept becoming infected with viruses. Scipio would fix Olivito's computer, removing viruses and eliminating vulnerabilities, but within a month's time, Scipio would find essential security protocols disabled. Olivito hid his computers at Scipio's house, which later caught fire in 2007 under suspicious circumstances.

Scipio and his wife remembered, many years later, being awakened by a knock at the door. Two college-age men stood outside, anxious to warn them that their house was on fire. They explained that they noticed the fire from a block away while they were driving around. Scipio's wife asked them for their names, so she could be sure and thank them later. They refused. Scipio said he later heard they had been bribed to set the fire. They reportedly thought they were abetting a false insurance claim. Scipio still lives at the house, and the second floor bears the marks of the fire.

Scipio said that the fire was put out by the fire department within ten minutes, but the firemen kept shooting water into his house for an hour and a half. Afterward, a representative from a civic organization showed up and gave Scipio's family vouchers for a hotel room, but Scipio decided he would stay at the house and watch over Olivito's computers. Scipio recounted many years later that he was on the phone with Olivito when a man walked into his house through the front door. The man did not see Scipio because he was sitting at a desk behind the wall between the kitchen and the living room. Scipio remembers that the man walked up to the computers, bent down and began unplugging them. Scipio watched the man from behind in rapt astonishment, before demanding, "What are you doing?"

The man started and turned around. "I was just doing an inspection," he responded.

"Well, I wasn't expecting any inspection until tomorrow," Scipio responded.

"Wait, I'm getting a call," the man said, quickly scurrying out of the room. He didn't return.

When Scipio got back on the phone with Olivito, he exclaimed, "Some guy just walked in and said he was a fire inspector!"

"The fire inspector wouldn't be there at this time of night," Olivito reckoned.

Thirty minutes later, four men showed up and asked Scipio to come outside. Scipio refused. Then, the men barged in and gathered around the computers. Again Scipio intervened, and they told him, "We want to make sure these don't get damaged."

"The fire was on the other side of the house!" Scipio protested.

One of them suggested they cover the computers with a tarp, which Scipio said was not necessary. Then, another offered to unplug the power supply, but Scipio stopped him, saying firmly, "Don't do nuthin!" The men walked out of the room and out of the house and did not return.

The fire inspector later came to Scipio's house, and according to Scipio, it was a different guy than the one who showed up the night of the fire. Scipio later learned that Steubenville only has one fire inspector. The official cause of the fire was a tea-light candle left burning on the wood floor, the firemen determined. Scipio didn't believe it. His tenant had left eight hours earlier and did not return that night. He tried to get a state agency to investigate, without success. The story is bizarre and almost beyond belief, yet Scipio's wife backed up every detail.

After years up charging uphill despite discrimination, Scipio felt that he had been trampled by the police and by the courts. He talked to a journalist from PBS's *Frontline* in 2015, and a few months later, the city bulldozed his late mother's house. After sifting through the rubble for keepsakes and pictures, he went to city hall. "We put an announcement in *The Herald-Star*," he was told.

Maybe, Scipio was a domestic abuser. The criminal charge was dismissed, but he was nevertheless subjected to brutal corporal punishment that required surgery. He tried to sue the police for his injuries, but the authorities brushed it aside. Somebody allegedly set fire to his house, and he couldn't trust the city's investigation with all the funny business. He tried and failed to spur an outside investigation. He talked to a journalist, who then went asking questions of the police and the city administration. Later, the city slated his mother's house for demolition without direct notice. Scipio again complained and was turned away. Scipio was steadfast in his resistance, but the city waged a merciless battle of attrition against him. Scipio became committed to civil rights as a consequence of his experiences, and his story was repeated widely around town. Maybe, it was all a coincidence, and there were no causal connections, which made his real losses meaningless and absurd.

## 19

Our profession is rooted in due process. That is really, really fundamental to what we do.

-Mary Jane Trapp, Ohio State Bar Association president[345]

Late in the spring of 2003, Michael and Catherine Accola came to Olivito for help with a bankruptcy, which Olivito agreed to take on for a fee of $125. The case was an ordinary bankruptcy, but Olivito neglected it for several months in the high-intensity summer of 2003 while he was focused on writing and filing civil rights cases. His paralegal drafted the paperwork in September, and the petition was filed on October 17, 2003, the same day as Rogers' first hearing. When Olivito handed in the documents in the courthouse, he was on the phone, but the clerk drew his attention to the line labeled "novate," because his clients had left it blank. Without giving it a second thought, Olivito forged his client's signature on the line. That one act spelled doom for his career and most of his civil rights cases.

The Accolas filed a complaint against him with the Mahoning County Bar Association in April 2004. The initial complaint came to Claire Carlin, president of the Mahoning Bar. Many years later, Olivito alleged that Carlin assured him the complaint would go nowhere. According to Olivito, Carlin told him, "We all sign for our clients. I've done it many times."

When Olivito was back in Warren after an interview with *60 Minutes II*, Olivito wanted to tell someone. Knowing of the political pressure associated with what he was doing, Olivito didn't tell Rosa, Karen Bryant or any of his clients about the interview, but he decided to tell a close friend in strict confidence.

A few weeks later, Olivito received a letter from the Mahoning County Bar Association's disciplinary committee informing him that the committee found merit in the complaint and advising him to prepare to defend himself against the allegation. The letter left him wondering what had happened. Then, he called the friend who he had told about the *60 Minutes II* interview.

---

[345] Bob Jackson. "Mahoning County scandal astounds state bar chief." *The Vindicator*, 7 November 2001.

"Did you tell anybody about the interview?" He asked.

"I told Claire Carlin," she answered. Olivito groaned.

"What did you tell him?"

"I told him, 'Richard is going to burn this city down!'"

It is not hard to imagine how this news would sit with Carlin, who at that moment was working with Olivito on *Kimble v. Hoso et al.*, the most controversial case in Warren's recent history. Carlin just did a favor for Olivito, who then gave an interview to *60 Minutes II*. From the point of view of Carlin and his colleagues at Mahoning County Bar Association, the interest of *60 Minutes II* could only mean more negative press. The local legal establishment had been lambasted for their role in approving the strip searches and for exonerating brutal cops in Aina Hunter's articles in the *Cleveland Scene* only two months before. Warren's new mayor, Michael O'Brien, a former probation officer, and Doug Franklin, the new director of public safety, did not want national attention for police brutality and strip searches. Olivito's adversaries in Mahoning County needed a way to bury him. The attorney disciplinary system presented a handy means of attacking his law license.

In response to the complaint, Olivito argued the bankruptcy was discharged in a timely manner for an exceedingly small fee. He never denied forging the signature, but he asserted that the signature issue did not affect his clients' financial interests. Afterward, Olivito would be obliged to budget his time between the demands made by the investigators in addition to the obligations of his pending federal civil rights cases. Another lawyer warned him of the disciplinary counsel, "When they come after you, it has nothing to do with your practice, it's personal."

Attorney Ronald Slipski conducted the initial investigation of the signature in question. Slipski would soon become president-elect of the Mahoning County Bar Association, and he belonged to the Ohio State Bar Association Council of Delegates, which contained a *who's who* of the Ohio legal establishment. Slipski's passion was labor law, and he was reputedly one of the best workers' compensation attorneys in the state. He had working-class roots, which is perhaps one reason why he was zealous as an investigator of attorney misconduct. When Slipski started investigating the complaint against Olivito, the two attorneys immediately got off on the wrong foot. Slipski found Olivito's writing verbose and evasive. Slipski thought Olivito was protecting something, but he didn't know what. Olivito thought Slipski was out to get him, but he couldn't figure out why. Slipski thought Olivito was trying to avoid the consequences of his actions, and he was determined to stop him.

Defendants in criminal and civil cases could limit the discovery demands, but for some reason, attorneys don't have the same due process rights. Slipski asked Olivito about his divorce, about his custody issues with his son, whether he had slept with any of his paralegals, as well as to confirm his whereabouts anytime he had left the state going back many years. These questions had nothing to do with the alleged misconduct with which Olivito was charged, but because Olivito was an attorney rather than a criminal defendant, Slipski was able to violate due process.

If Slipski decided there was probable cause to investigate, the complaint would be lodged with the disciplinary counsel, which plays the role of state prosecutor for attorney misconduct before the Board. Sure enough, in late February of 2006, the Mahoning County Bar Association forwarded the complaint to the disciplinary counsel. In turn, the disciplinary counsel filed charges on about three dozen other allegations, despite not having requested any documents from Olivito. Olivito vigorously denied all of the alleged violations, except for the signature. One count concerned an allegedly misfiled affidavit, another accused Olivito of overcharging a widow, and a third accused him of misappropriating funds from an Amish client. He was being made out as a villain like the attorneys of hard-boiled detective novels.

The twenty-eight members of the Board come from the business community and the judicial branch, and none of them arrived on the Board by going against the grain. Moyer appointed the members of the disciplinary counsel as well as the Board, and he valued one thing above all others: loyalty. In Moyer's hands, the disciplinary counsel and the Board were tools to maintain control over the legal community, punishing enemies and protecting friends. The supreme court dug deeply into the private lives of attorneys if they were accused of a small infraction resulting in no financial harm to the client, yet officials were above reproach when they cheated on their taxes, defrauded residents of liberty and property, sexually harassed their subordinates and had well-known drug abuse problems.

<><><>

On February 22, 2006, below a shimmering crimson curtain, the commissioners of the Board strode out in single file to their elevated perches. There were only three people behind the counsel tables and no one in the audience. Two court officers stood on either side of the tribunal, beholding the proceedings as silent sentries, hearing everything, saying nothing. Amid the sounds of throats cleared and papers stacked, Moyer announced, "The next case on our docket is Mahoning

County Bar Association v. Richard Olivito…"[346] He briefly reprimanded Slipski for not checking in before summoning Paula Brown, Olivito's counsel. Brown came to the podium and leaned into the mic. "May it please the court, I am Paula Brown along with co-counsel Max Kravitz. We represent Richard Olivito. I'd like to reserve three minutes for rebuttal." Then, she began, "As relator stated in the hearing brief, this is an unfortunate case. It began with the simple neglect of a legal matter [which] may or may not have been actionable under the supreme court's rules." She argued, "This matter might not be before this board," if it weren't for the manner in which Olivito responded.

Paula Brown defended Olivito on the grounds that there was no financial damage to the clients and that Olivito should not be punished for defending himself against the allegations. According to Brown, Olivito forged the signatures for "his clients' interest, not his own," and he "took very little in exchange for his services, doing the best he could for his clients."[347] Ronald Slipski, representing Mahoning County Bar Association, started in a bombastic tone, "Bizarre. Bizarre." Then, he read the definition of the word. "I used the word, 'obfuscate,'" which he also proceeded to define. He likened Olivito's defense to an onion, which, as Slipski peeled away the layers, contained new deceptions that made his eyes water.[348] He was getting warmed up with a few opening anecdotes, but Justice Resnick interrupted him.

"But should his behavior at the hearing be considered in this disciplinary matter? Shouldn't we just be looking at what is before the panel…the complaint?"

"Not if you consider the purpose, the purpose was to hide the truth. That's why he did what he did. He made speeches. He tried to confuse everything."

Justice Resnick wondered whether Olivito may have had "medical reasons" for behaving as he did during the initial hearing.[349] Slipski said there was nothing in the record about Olivito's mental health. Moyer raised the issue of mitigating circumstances, but Slipski said Olivito had presented none. Then, Justice Resnick opined, "The recommended sanction is quite serious for the offense. It would appear

---

[346] *Mahoning County Bar Association v. Richard Olivito*, Case no. 2005-2030, 22 February 2006.

[347] Ibid.

[348] Anonymous. "Attorney faces 1-2 year suspension." *Daily Jeff*, 22 February 2006.

[349] Ibid.

then from your comments that it's really based upon his behavior at the hearing."

"Absolutely not, it's based upon his misrepresentation...First of all, it's based his neglect which I intended to get to in a second. There's neglect. There's lots of neglect, and I can go through it item by item." He went on to describe how Olivito the forgot about the creditor's hearing scheduled for December 15. He withdrew as their counsel shortly afterward on December 23, two days before Christmas, citing the couple's failure to pay him his fees as the reason. Meanwhile, Olivito did not apprise his clients that the creditor's hearing had been rescheduled for December 29, which would mean, at best, they would probably not have an attorney if they made it to the meeting. Olivito also misrepresented the bankruptcy to the trustee right after he forged his clients' signatures and falsely claimed that he saved their house, according to Slipski. "The Accola's don't own a house," he whispered into the microphone.

Chief Justice Moyer interrupted in a moment in which Slipski was unable to express his exasperation, "Let me jump ahead, Mr. Slipski. We see in these cases...this is anecdotal, I haven't seen a study on it, but...a pattern of lying. They make a mistake. Then, they engage in this web of lies." Even with a year's suspension, if Olivito was allowed to reapply with no review, Moyer questioned whether Olivito would learn his lesson, that "Being honest is one of the most important traits of being a lawyer. Here, it would seem to me that Mr. Olivito doesn't get it. Are you at all concerned that he would be allowed to be admitted to the practice of law simply by filing this form, rather than having the review that one is required to have with an indefinite suspension?"[350]

"I share the same concern. I share a serious concern in this case. If Mr. Olivito continuing to represent clients if he does the same thing in other cases."

Another justice asked if there were any other cases.

"There are no complaints that have been filed with the [Board]."

Then, she asked if any had been filed with local bar associations "with this degree of dishonesty." Slipski fell silent. There was another complaint, but the bar association didn't find probable cause, so it was not forwarded to the Board.

"Well, you've got some rules of confidentiality," Moyer put in. "I cannot confirm or deny," Slipski stammered, after much thought. Then, he smiled, showing his teeth for the first time while the Justices laughed. Everybody knew that there was another complaint which Slipski wanted to tell them about, but he was prevented by pesky ethics rules.

---

[350] Ibid.

When conscientious Justice Resnick again began pushing back, Slipski pointed to other lies and misrepresentations, suggesting finally that the Board give Olivito two full years' suspension and make it difficult for Olivito to reapply. Slipski then brought up the distraction of Olivito's civil rights cases and Olivito's claim that his phone was tapped as a result, "I don't know what that has to do with this."

<>\<>\<>

Those who came into the crosshairs of the disciplinary counsel would have the allegations of their enemies announced to the entire Ohio public because of the court's reporting policy. The practice, which harms attorney's reputations and their clients' cases, has given rise to civil rights lawsuits by attorneys. There were other concerns voiced by researchers in 1985, such as whether local relators, as the bar association investigators were called, could be relied on in close-knit counties to investigate their friends and colleagues. There was also question whether attorneys whose lifestyles were frowned upon might suffer disparate sanction.[351] In other words, what Milich had done to Olivito and what Slipski was then doing to Olivito.

Half a century ago, the attorney discipline system in Ohio was criticized as "apathetic, antiquated, decentralized and deficient." In 1970, the Clark Report led to several changes in the system, but the decentralized legal fiefdoms of the bar associations in Akron, Cincinnati, Cleveland, Columbus, Toledo, and Youngstown remained. The report criticized this decentralized system of volunteer relators because it "produces a substantial lack of uniformity in discipline imposed," as well as a significant percentage of abortive attempts at discipline later dismissed, two problems that have continued to bedevil the court.

For nearly a year after the complaint was forwarded, the disciplinary counsel would search for any evidence of misdeeds. The method of inquiry was to interview former clients, colleagues, and employees, and then quiz the accused on various aspects of those relationships, comparing their answers with their financial history, as well as their words and actions during every step of their careers. Lori J. Brown was the first assistant disciplinary counsel. She had almost a decade in her position by the time she started investigating Olivito, and she became chief before retiring in 2013. With short blond hair and the severity of a clerk at the Department of Motor Vehicles, Brown would comb through an attorney's past and then put them through a grueling interrogation. Impatient attorneys could face additional charges of not cooperating. Her job was to investigate and prosecute attorney miscon-

---

[351] Stanley A. Samad. "The True Story of Lawyer Discipline in Ohio: 1967-1983." *Akron Law Review*, Winter 1985, Page. 377.

duct, and she was as aggressive taking down corrupt lawyers as Olivito was with corrupt cops.

When the disciplinary counsel requested documents from Olivito, they did not disappoint. It took more than twenty pages just for them to list all the documents they wanted. The disciplinary counsel had declared war on Olivito, and it would be a war of paper like Olivito's war against the city of Warren. If Olivito ever made a mistake, they were going to find it. Normally, in the face of certain defeat, attorneys often lay down and accept whatever the Board has in mind because the disciplinary counsel and the Board always win, except when they are outgunned by powerful attorneys who can pay other attorneys to wade tirelessly through thousands of pages of documents to prove their innocence. The Ohio Supreme Court mandated civility and cordiality, publishing updates on the rules when the political atmosphere became too toxic. Resistance led to heavier sanction, as did delay, except when it was on the part of the state. Faced with these constraints, most attorneys fall on their swords. Not Olivito. Feeling a little bit like his nemesis Prosecutor Stern twenty years before, Olivito suspected foul play, and he wasn't going down without a fight.

However, Olivito was shocked to see recent clients on the list alleging misrepresentations, neglect, overcharging and other violations, but none of it held up, which embarrassed the disciplinary counsel. Brown sought evidence of misappropriated funds, but the clients deposed for the investigation all confirmed that Olivito had done nothing improper. The Amish man, Harvey Miller, testified under oath that he did not know Olivito at the time in question. Scipio recalled that Olivito laid dozens of allegations to rest, but Brown wasn't going to let him get away that easy. Until seven in the evening, Brown grilled Olivito about his personal life and went through ten years of financial records, obliging Olivito to confirm every hotel or motel he patronized and every friend's house where he slept.

Brown was intent to wear Olivito down with minutiae. One question that came up in deposition concerned Olivito's wrongful death case, *Sanders v. City of Minneapolis*. Brown asked Olivito why he neglected his client, Sanders' wife and family because she said she had documentation that he had been late filing a motion. Olivito and Sean Scipio looked at each other in surprise upon hearing this question because of the lengths they had gone to assure that the motion was filed before the deadline.

Olivito had Scipio change the browser, zip the file and access the district court's network to discover why the document was not uploading in the Pacer system of the Minneapolis district court. Then, Olivito brought a copy with him to the clerk's office while Scipio sent two others separately overnight by FedEx directly to the judge, who was obliged to sign for one of them just as she was calling the hearing to order. The motion was not late. The judge had three copies in her hand by the time court was called to order, yet for some unknown reason, the clerk of court had required Olivito to sign an affidavit over his "technical error," in electronically filing the motion, for which Lori Brown accused Olivito of neglecting his clients.

Brown accused Olivito of lying, while Olivito maintained that he had documentation of the affidavit explaining the problems he had filing the motion. Brown agreed to drop all the charges associated with the motion if he showed her the affidavit, which he later did. Olivito had just won a battle, but he didn't realize that he was outgunned.

<><><>

On July 27, Olivito attended a hearing before a disciplinary panel composed of three court officers. His father sat a few rows back, hands upon his cane, his keen attention contradicting his relaxed posture. Olivito remembers that one of the hearing officers mostly kept his eyes closed, another rarely said a word while the third, Sandra Anderson, did almost all of the talking. Sandra Anderson was a senior partner at Vorys and the first female president of the Columbus Bar Association. She spent six years on the Board and was later its chair. During the hearing, she kept Olivito on his toes.

Olivito brought six witnesses to testify on his behalf. The prosecution brought none against Olivito. At one point, Anderson asked which areas of law Olivito's practice focused. He responded, "Well, the lion's share of my practice is devoted to civil rights cases." She asked again, and he answered, "As I said, it's mostly civil rights among other things." At this point, she retorted, "You keep insisting on that answer, and I'll hold you in contempt." Olivito was confused and looked back at his father. Judge Olivito's eyes were wide with astonishment. The Board decided that Olivito had violated all of the provisions of the Code of Professional Conduct which Brown enumerated and recommended a two-year suspension with one year stayed. Next, discovery would begin.

After the hearing, Olivito and his father walked down the marble-lined hallway from the South Hearing Room to the street. "That hearing officer was biased, and she was motivated!" his father exclaimed. "I have a feeling they had already decided this case." Olivito rarely heard his father express such passion. He had hoped that the court would treat his case as signature violations usually were with a public reprimand. When they exited, the wind came over the river before it hit their faces. The Columbus skyline surrounded them, but neither was in any mood to appreciate it. Not much was said on the drive home.

Many years later, Olivito reflected, "My mistake was to defend myself too strongly. I should have fallen on my sword." Olivito assumed that attorney discipline would involve the same presumption of innocence and the right to contest the charges. Instead, Olivito claims that fear controls the profession and that attorneys don't get a fair shake. The disciplinary counsel prefers to begin with a presumption of guilt, and if they get flack from a presumptuous attorney, they make sure that attorney is laid low. If instead, it was a senior partner at Weston Hurd, then Moyer came out swinging in his defense.[352] Although Olivito had acted in his clients' interests and not caused them financial harm, the disciplinary counsel came after him with a vengeance. His cases were immediately impacted. As soon as the charges were filed, Judge Galanis entered them into the record of his cases.

The Ohio Supreme Court imposed the suspension of Olivito's state law license on July 28, 2006. In compliance with the Supreme Court's order to notify his clients in writing within 30 days, Olivito sent a lengthy letter to Kimble on August 16, 2006. Olivito wrote, "Lyndal, I had hoped this day would not come…We traveled far together along this journey for justice since the time I first met you in the Summer of 2003."

Kimble's erstwhile counsel apprised him of the developments, assured him of co-counsel Bill Hinnant's protection of his interests from then on, and warned him about immediate issues in the case. He mentioned that the Northern District Court, meaning Judge Galanis, had issued a separate interim suspension of his law license in the federal courts of the Youngstown regional area. Olivito didn't elide factors he believed were consequential in the determination of his case:

> The Mahoning County Bar Association truly targeted me and made me out to be a seriously bad lawyer and practically a villain. The supreme court agreed with them. I received the heaviest punishment a lawyer could under the circumstances, much more so than any other lawyer in the past five years who had been charged with the same violation.

"Sound familiar, Lyndal?" Olivito asked. He received one of the heaviest sanctions in the history of Ohio. Normally, the supreme court would publicly reprimand attorneys over these sorts of technical violations, but the President of the Mahoning Bar, Ronald Slipski, argued that Olivito was evasive and deceptive. Olivito checked into past disciplinary cases and found other attorneys' signature violations involving significant financial damage to clients where the lawyers received less severe punishments.

When the local press announced the verdict in the disciplinary

---

[352] Aebra Coe. "Weston Hurd Atty won't be suspended until court sees docs." *Law360*, 7 April 2015.

case, it was reposted on a community forum in *The Vindicator* website. Some called Olivito a creepy weirdo. Another said "...There is nothing wrong with him, other than he wants to rid this area of civil rights violations, and the thick-headed Warren police think there is nothing wrong." Another chimed in, "He is one lawyer who tried to change the corrupt court system in this valley and no one will ever know the personal sacrifice he has gone through trying to help people...May God bless you Attorney Olivito."

<><><>

In January of 2007, Olivito had been participating in the discovery process of his disciplinary case for a year and a half after the first hearing by the Board. He had been required to notify his clients that his license was suspended six months before, but there was a chance that he could beat the suspension and come back on those cases as the lead attorney. The *Walker v. Lelles* case was on the docket of the Southern District Court, as was *Kelley v. McCafferty*. Steubenville's consent decree had been lifted for just short of two years, and the DOJ had released its initial findings from Warren. Roger's and Kimble's cases were still on the docket in the Northern District Court. Fighting for his practice, Olivito still hoped he could avoid suspension and continue to represent his civil rights clients.

The Ohio Supreme Court disciplinary counsel's manifold allegations against him foundered, except for the signature issue, which began to metastasize under the Board's microscope. They inquired who were his collaborators and met with public officials in Warren and Steubenville, two communities which blamed Olivito for federal scrutiny. His scorched earth campaign of volatile civil rights litigation had aroused the hostility of the courts, and now the public lashing would begin.

Then, one evening in the last week of January 2007, Olivito came to his parents' house and discovered what they would use to discredit him. Olivito remembers pushing the button on the answering machine, a relic which persisted in the Olivito household. First, the recording was like a normal message, but then the voice started a separate conversation with another person who was on the line. Jeff Heintz, the panel chair of the disciplinary counsel for Olivito's case, was speaking with Lori Brown, the assistant chief counsel.

"Are we going try and hold to the hearing date in February?"[353] Heintz asked Brown.

---

[353] Charles J. Kettlewell and Kenneth Donchatz. "Re: Rule 8.3 Duty to Report Lori J. Brown and Jeffrey T. Heintz." *Christensen, Christensen, Donchatz, Kettlewell & Owens LLP*, 10 April 2007.

"Well, and that's one of the issues. I'm not speaking out of turn here because Mr. Olivito knows exactly what we were going to tell you. [David Comstock, of the Mahoning County Bar Association] and I both believe that we have an obligation at this point to have him evaluated. Now, what that means for the hearing date, I am not sure. I have a psychiatrist in mind, and I am trying to get a hold of him. I tried yesterday, and I am going to try again today."

"Okay," Heintz responded, "Let's not get into that."

"Okay."

"Let's take that up," said Heintz, changing his mind.

"Okay."

"... cause I think that it looks to me from, the stuff, the stuff that's being generated on his end, that it, I mean I could do it on my own motion, I can make it work."

"Yes, I think so," Brown agreed.

"Okay. Thanks, Lori.

"You're welcome."

After the message ended, Olivito slumped into a chair at the same table where he had eaten dinner as a child. His mind raced with interpretations and implications of what he had just heard. Two officials specializing in attorney ethics had just committed a major violation of their own code of ethics to discipline him for a minor violation that did not harm his clients. The disciplinary system of the Ohio Supreme Court had been turned on its head, or so it seemed. He felt isolated, but now at least he had evidence that the disciplinary counsel was motivated by more than just a simple signature issue. Otherwise, he was unable to fathom why two experts on attorney ethics would violate their code of professional responsibility.

Olivito played the recording to his family members, his allies, and journalists from *The Columbus Dispatch*. Judge Olivito, Sr. made upwards of 30K available to hire the best ethics attorneys in the state to defend his youngest son before the Board. Ken Donchatz and Charles Kettlewell signed onto the case, which gave Olivito an eight-month window to work on his civil rights cases before the disciplinary case would be decided. Maybe, he would even be able to keep his license.

On April 10, 2007, Charles Kettlewell penned a letter classified as "personal and confidential," to the Board regarding Olivito's evidence of *ex parte* communication in his disciplinary case. Kettlewell began:

> Ken Donchatz and I feel it is our duty under Rule 8.3 to report what we believe is evidence of violations of the Ohio Rules of Professional Conduct by Assistant Disciplinary Counsel Lori Brown and violations of the Ohio Rules of Professional Conduct and the Code of Judicial conduct by Board of Commissioners on Grievances and Discipline member Jeffrey T.

Heintz.

Kettlewell's letter cited the relevant sections of the ORC and the transcript of the conversation above, and Kettlewell quoted Brown's and Heintz' written denials of *ex parte* communication dated February 1, and March 9, respectively. Kettlewell also quoted Brown's comment that Olivito's allegations before the court were "completely unfounded," and that Heintz "repudiated" all of Olivito's motion on January 31 regarding the recorded conversation. Kettlewell declined to comment on the matter, many years later, but in his letter to the Board about evidence of internal misconduct, he wrote, "the recorded evidence contradicts their respective denials."

Kettlewell went a step further to argue before the Board that the issue of Olivito's mental health was irrelevant to the "underlying substance of the Complaint against Mr. Olivito." The Seventh District Court of Appeals came to the same conclusion on Judge Milich's contempt charge and order to undergo a psychiatric evaluation. The best practices recommended by legal scholars and the American Bar Association would change with regard to mental illness around 2008 in response to lawsuits claiming civil rights and American with Disabilities Act (ADA) violations. However, most lawyers do not use the ADA to gain the advantage of a mitigating factor in disciplinary proceedings. The disciplinary counsel regularly investigated allegations of mental illness among judges and lawyers, but in Olivito's case, mental health was treated as a cause for sanction rather than a mitigating factor.

◇◇◇

On August 7, 2007, Olivito filed a 157-page brief and made a three-hour pleading before the Board arguing that his due process rights had been violated by the circumstances in which Brown and Coughlan ordered the psychiatric evaluation. The Board would not be put off and issued a show cause motion on August 21 why Olivito should not be held in contempt for noncompliance with their June 8 order to undergo a psychiatric evaluation.

On October 13, 2007, Bill Hinnant sent a letter to Chief Justice Moyer in regard to the ongoing disciplinary investigation. First, Hinnant mentioned Olivito's father's failing health, speaking as a friend and noting that the 87-year old D-Day veteran Olivito Sr. was "known to the Court and the Chief Justice." Considering that the trial was scheduled for a month later, Hinnant noted that Olivito wanted a sixty-day extension and expressed his desire to represent Olivito, especially where it concerned the psychiatric matters at issue because Hinnant is an MD and was serving as associate counsel to the American College of Legal Medicine at the time. He had extensive knowledge and experience in the legal aspects of mental health, defending doctors and lawyers when they were in danger of losing their licenses.

Hinnant then outlined the alleged ethical violations of the "Ohio Disciplinary Counsel herself and the former panel chair," for which Olivito had enlisted Charles Kettlewell and Ken Donchatz. Before explaining the situation, Hinnant referred to it as "a very unique, inexplicable and certainly highly stressful." Then, he related how the Toledo Bar Association had cleared the government lawyers without giving notice and that Olivito had been denied an appeal, although he drove to Columbus and met the secretary of the board in person. Hinnant concluded with Olivito's contention that his fundamental right to due process was affected by the misconduct, stating:

> At a minimum, without debating the merits of any issue, Mr. Olivito was prejudiced in this process that in my opinion, seems to be bent upon sanctioning him rather than being truly based on a reasonable medical understanding of Mr. Olivito's personal circumstances and a true assessment of his underlying legal abilities.

The six-page letter extolled Olivito's abilities as a civil rights lawyer and his "sometimes overzealous" efforts to vindicate his clients' rights. Hinnant knew that Moyer would understand the significance for a solo plaintiffs' attorney to go up against Weston Hurd in the Sixth Circuit and win, not just once, but three times. It was a testament to Olivito's prowess as a litigator. The clients would affirm Olivito's abilities, Hinnant argued to Chief Justice Moyer. For his part, Moyer had no interest in Hinnant's letter. Instead, Moyer doubled down, refusing Hinnant's offer to represent Olivito or to enter the letter into the record of the disciplinary case. When Olivito came in person to file the letter, Moyer sent him away with a police escort out of the building. Knowing that Olivito was a plaintiffs' lawyer probably only incited the chief justice, who had had enough of Olivito's attempts to defend his practice.

## 20

I hope you don't try to make a story where in my opinion none exists.

-Former Justice Evelyn Lundberg Stratton in 2016

On December 11, 2007, the Ohio Supreme Court ordered Olivito to appear. When his case was announced, the hearing officer said, "There is a hearing on his failure to arrange to have a psychiatric examination. My sheet shows we are here, we are not going to wait for him. Ms. Brown, why don't you tell us briefly. I'll give you an opportunity to briefly state the matter before us." Lori Brown came up to the podium and leaned into the mic.

> Good morning, your honor. May it please the court. Lori Brown on behalf of the Mahoning County Bar Association. We filed a joint motion seeking to have the respondent in two Board cases which had been consolidated seeking to have him evaluated pursuant to bar rule. That was filed on February 27. He did not file a response to that motion. All three panel members granted the motion on March 13, 2007. On March 31, 2007, they followed up. He was given the opportunity to contact the doctor within fifteen days of the Board's order. In the weeks following that order, he did not contact the doctor but filed various motions with the panel. Another order was issued again asking him to make an appointment and get an evaluation. Again on June 8, 2007. There is yet another order referencing different materials received reminding him the matter had been stayed and ordering him to be evaluated. Because he did not get evaluated, we issued a finding of failure to comply. This court ordered him to appear and show cause today December 11, 2007.

"What is the status of his license at this point?" One of the commissioners asked.

"His license to practice law was suspended by this court in July 2006 pursuant to a completely separate disciplinary case."

"That was two years with one-year stayed."

Richard Olivito came up to the podium. He was asked, "You understand why you are here?" He said yes and thanked the judges for their time. Then, he addressed the court.

"It's not the way I wanted to meet this court or the circumstances I would like to appear in front of this court." He began describing his effort to get Hinnant to respond to the show cause order, but the chief interrupted him.

"Let me ask you a couple of questions. You were asked to submit to a particular psychiatric examination. Were you aware of that request?"

"Yes, if I was, it was a request that came up in unusual circumstances."

"Is it true you failed to meet with that doctor."

"I did not call the doctor."

"You object to meeting with that doctor."

"Yes, sir."

"Is there a qualified psychiatrist with whom you have met whose report you have offered to the board?"

"I set up an appointment and offered that." Then, he started talking about Hinnant again to use his opinion as a qualified medical professional, but another justice interrupted him.

"Why are you so objecting to getting help if outside people can look at you and say, at least get evaluated?"

Another chimed in, "Why are you resisting when it's so obvious to other people that you need help?"

"It goes right to the practice which this court controls," Olivito began. He meandered through a few more lines before bringing up the answering machine message.

The reason why I didn't jump into this issue the way it was presented. I felt it was an improper *ex-parte* communication with the panel chair over which two independent lawyers wrote a mandatory violation order. That took up four months.

Then, he came back to the order to get evaluated. "I don't have a problem with being evaluated. The order was for me to see a specific psychiatrist for an evaluation."

Then, the discussion devolved into an argument about whether or not Olivito did enough to comply with the order. Olivito argued that the peculiar circumstances of the order with Lori Brown and the panel chair talking about it on his father's answering machine combined with the suggestion that he wouldn't get a second opinion on his mental health deterred him from complying with the order. The justices pressed him about whether he had met with a psychiatrist, which he evaded, stating, "Not without the guarantee of a second opinion." Then, he argued that there was no basis for the mental health evaluation. At one point, he said, "I'm willing to work with the system," but he later said, "I would be willing to take a jail sentence instead of being evaluated."

When Lori Brown came to the podium, she disputed his account of the order, saying that there was always the guarantee of a second opinion, but she objected to the use of Hinnant because he and

Olivito had worked together, and he was not a psychiatrist. She also distinguished between a simple psychiatric evaluation and a forensic examination, which was more extensive. Finally, she requested that the court issue an order commanding him to contact the doctor or be held in contempt.

After Lori Brown's testimony, the court was adjourned with the promise of an imminent opinion. When it came down, the court imposed the contempt order, suspended Olivito from the practice of law and barred him from reapplication until he filed proof of compliance with the order of a thirty-day inpatient psychiatric examination by Dr. Arthur Rosenbaum, the doctor Brown had in mind. The Board put several other stipulations in the way of any eventual re-application for his law license, including one credit hour of continuing legal education for each month of the suspension, payment of all outstanding bills from the supreme court within ninety days, and forfeiture of any outstanding fees from his clients. Finally, they gave him thirty days to notify his clients.

Although he was not technically disbarred, the Board wiped away his entire practice and made it nearly impossible to re-apply. They also foreclosed the possibility of him earning money for years of work, effectively punishing him for sticking his nose into civil rights. When it was over, Olivito trudged beneath painted murals surrounded by gold filigree, an outsider on the red carpet retreating out of the cavern of justice. In the hall, Max Kravitz told Olivito, by way of explanation, "You have powerful enemies."

Olivito reached out to *The Columbus Dispatch* in hopes of exposing the misconduct of the disciplinary counsel. He provided the newspaper with a copy of the Kettlewell letter, Hinnant's letter and other documentation of his allegations. The editor of *The Columbus Dispatch* either did not understand or otherwise decided to disregard the evidence of misconduct in the article they published on December 18, 2007, the day after Olivito's license was suspended.[354] Instead, the article told the story as if the most important part did not exist and quoted the former president of the Mahoning County Bar Association assuring, "There's nothing sinister going on." Slipski knew about the allegation of *ex parte* communication, but he sidestepped the dispute over the psychiatric evaluation and focused on the signature issue in his statements. The reporter, who passed away in 2012, may have been prevented from including the central document which showed why

---

[354] James Nash. "High court suspends lawyer." *Columbus Dispatch*, 18 December 2007.

Olivito was fighting the Board. The article closed with a remark by then-Supreme Court Justice Evelyn Lundberg Stratton that "Olivito seems to be fighting the court rather viewing its orders as potentially beneficial to him."[355]

The practice to which Olivito devoted one-third of his life ended with a dramatic public de-frocking. He felt at the time that something was wrong with the proceedings, something behind the scenes that he didn't fully understand. Dominick Olivito, Sr., his mild-mannered father, was outraged and depressed over the decision. Later, after a bit of digging, Olivito discovered a link between one of the hearing officers from the Board, Sandra Anderson, and the National FOP. He unearthed a 2001 report from the Task Force on Racial Profiling of the Columbus Bar Association, which mentioned that Anderson had to step down from her appointment as the chair of the task force because of a conflict of interest between her firm, Vorys, which was then general counsel to the National FOP.[356] For Olivito, seeing the National FOP among its listed clients on Vorys' website and discovering that Anderson had to publicly step down from an appointment, he wrote, many years later:

> Short of killing me with a bullet or having me die in a solo fiery car crash...How best could this be done...in our modern all too porous and public legal world today? It would be very obvious if I died at the hands of some police officer connected or mobbed-up dude while actively pursuing major civil rights enforcement federal cases...while bringing the national top civil rights enforcement authority into small and mid-sized metro regions of the heartland...that may be too messy and a bit too dramatic. How else could they silence this experienced voice of modern-day bad policing?

Olivito was able to learn that the FOP had paid a two million dollar retainer for Vorys to strategize and communicate their opposition to exactly the sort of federal action that Olivito was trying to provoke. Maybe, Olivito is grasping. In late 2007, Vorys hadn't represented the FOP in any dispute for a few years when he came before the Board. However, when Anderson ruled on the matter of Olivito's federal law license, Vorys' role in crushing police reform for the FOP was advertised on the firm's website, couched in wording that potential government and insurance company clients would immediately understand. Anderson did not respond to a request for comment.

When Vorys was working for the FOP, it was on weighty mat-

[355] Ibid.

[356] Staff. "Report of the Racial Profiling Task Force." *Columbus Bar Association*, January 2001, Page 2.

ters. As an illustration, two of Anderson's fellow senior partners, John Kulewicz and James E. Phillips, were the lead attorneys for the National FOP in every lawsuit against consent decrees from 2000-2003 and for the Columbus FOP in the Ohio Supreme Court when they were trying to destroy police personnel records without public input.[357] Phillips was the reason why the FOP came to Vorys. He had served them well as general counsel for a decade. Kulewicz was the former chairman of the Columbus Democratic Party and president of the Columbus chapter of the Federal Bar Association. Currently, Kulewicz and Anderson both serve on the Board of Advisors of the Columbus chapter of the American Constitution Society. Anderson's proximity to the FOP was close enough in 2001 to cause her to recuse herself for a conflict of interests, something Ohio Supreme Court officials were extremely reluctant to do.

For Olivito, Vorys' FOP-connection explained why Anderson had threatened to put Olivito in contempt when he began to speak about his civil rights work in response to a question from the bench about his law practice. Though a Democrat and perhaps even personally sympathetic to the cause of civil rights, her firm and the officials higher up the political food chain, both in the Republican Supreme Court and the newly-elected Democratic Governor Ted Strickland, were tied to the FOP.

It could seem odd that high-level Democratic power-brokers in Ohio would be so deeply involved in the suppression of civil rights causes to which the Democratic party supposedly supported, but business is business and most businesspeople won't turn down good clients. Public sector unions and their insurance companies have deep pockets. In Ohio, they are major donors to political campaigns, and across the country, FOP endorsements carry political weight coveted by politicians in both parties.

Back in 2002, when Ohio Supreme Court Justice Andy Douglas retired from the bench and joined Crabbe, Brown, & James, the media explored his potential conflicts of interest between his role as a monitor in the settlement agreement of a police use-of-force lawsuit involving the City of Cincinnati, the local FOP, and the ACLU, and his role at Crabbe, where Partner Larry James was general counsel to the National FOP.[358]

Revolving door restrictions in Ohio only barred former judges from working on cases in which they handled on the bench, but these

---

[357] Keller v. City of Columbus. 3d 192. *Ohio Supreme Court*. 5 November 2005.

[358] James Drew. "Douglas to join Columbus law firm as partner at the end of Ohio court term." *The Toledo Blade*, 17 December 2002.

conflicts could be remedied. Each party in the Cincinnati settlement was presented with a contract to waive any conflict with Douglas' new role with the firm representing the FOP, which had only the year before concluded a lawsuit against the Attorney General John Ashcroft to enjoin the DOJ from pursuing 14141 investigations of local police departments on the grounds that the law violated the rights of law enforcement agents.[359] For the ACLU, it would be a Faustian bargain to sign away their right to a conflict of interest claim involving a law firm that was attempting to incapacitate the DOJ, a potent partner in the battle for police reform.

Justice Douglas told the *Toledo Blade* in 2002, "The national FOP involves itself in national and not state and local issues,"[360] but he was incorrect. The national FOP bragged to its membership that the Grand Lodge was able to wield its power over consent decrees "coordinating our influence from above and from below."[361] When the Grand Lodge hailed its victory over DOJ civil rights enforcement in 2006, it was partly the legal arguments formulated by Ohio's foremost corporate legal minds at Vorys on the sovereignty of state and local government. When Olivito began to connect the dots between the supreme court and the FOP and Vorys, he had no doubt there was a deeper story to his tangle with the supreme court that the authorities and the press were unable to see or would not acknowledge.

After sixteen years on the bench, Justice Lundberg Stratton later retired and joined Vorys. Many years later, Justice Lundberg Stratton responded in an email, "I can assure you that having [Olivito] seek help would have nothing to do with who he had represented in the trenches. I've always admired those who represented the underdog, and I can assure you that certainly wasn't my motivation for joining in the order." She said she knew nothing about any *ex parte* conversations. Perhaps, the rest of the commissioners were similarly uninformed. Perhaps, they assumed his talk about the message on the answering machine was crazy talk.

Olivito perceived Anderson's connection to the FOP to be a conflict of interest with Anderson ruling on his disciplinary case, so he decided to bring the issue up before the federal district court in Cincinnati, which was reviewing his suspension by the Ohio Supreme Court.

---

[359] *Grand Lodge of Fraternal Order of Police v. Ashcroft*. 185 F. Supp. 2d 9. U.S. District Court D.C. 2001.

[360] James Drew. "Douglas to join Columbus law firm as partner at the end of Ohio court term." *The Toledo Blade*, 17 December 2002.

[361] Chuck Canterbury. "Leadership is Cooperation." *The FOP Journal*, Vol. 11 Issue 4, August 2006.

The court would decide whether to extend the suspension of Olivito's state license to his federal license. His civil rights cases in the Southern and Northern Districts were at stake. Typically, the federal court deferred to the Ohio Supreme Court, rubber-stamping its decisions in attorney discipline cases, but Olivito found three Supreme Court cases in which a party to a lawsuit successfully argued for the right to the recusal of a judicial officer for conflict of interest.

Without opposing counsel to argue against, Olivito put his heart into the argument that Anderson's conflict of interest demanded disclosure and potential recusal and that a lawyer before a disciplinary panel is due the same due process rights as anybody else. Two months later, the judge issued her opinion, which not only imposed the suspension on his federal license, he was even struck him from the directory of attorneys, which meant that he would have to reapply. It was as if he had never been a federal attorney.

When the supreme court suspended Olivito from the practice of law, it impacted all of his clients' cases, although one supposed goal in the course of attorney discipline is to refrain from damaging the clients, financially and otherwise. Judge Galanis entered every step of Olivito's disciplinary proceedings faithfully into the record of each of his cases. From the order to obtain co-counsel, with the intent of averting harm to the claims of Olivito's clients, Kimble, Clay, and Rogers, Judge Galanis picked up where Judge Milich had started, by calling Olivito's competence into question. The disciplinary counsel poured over all of the cases in search of mistakes. Instead, they found how Olivito had used Galanis' mistakes to get the cases remanded by the Sixth Circuit.

When asked if Olivito had anything to do with the Steubenville consent decree, Jeff Bruzzese didn't claim to know anything about the consent decree because he only received his license to practice law in 2005, but he said, "Olivito was disbarred by the Ohio Supreme Court and ordered to take a psychiatric evaluation which, as it seems, he still has not complied. He has a history of mental illness." Olivito has denied this allegation many times over the years. He explained, "They needed to silence my experience. It was literally dangerous to the system to have a guy in Ohio running around the police departments talking about how to bring about a consent decree."

There was sporadic support of Olivito in response to articles about his suspension. One commenter spoke up in support of Olivito, questioning the actions of authorities:

> I see the [Kimble] case was settled out of court, although Warren police would not admit wrongdoing...I guess they don't want the citizens to know about it. I wonder how much the police insurance will go up this time? As far as Olivito's mental health, when you are in a war against injustice and corrup-

tion things happen. Even some of our best soldiers come home with [post-traumatic stress disorder]. Maybe someday, the D.O.J. will do their job and clean up this valley.

The local authorities did not want the amount of the settlement in the *Kimble* case to be publicly reported, as when the *Clay* case was settled. The commenter suggested that Olivito had Post-Traumatic Stress Disorder, which would be unsurprising in consideration of the traumatic periods Olivito endured. There is no doubt he was under tremendous pressure. Hunter mentioned that Olivito wore his paranoia "like perfume," and a paralegal who worked with him said, many years later, "He presented as crazy, but it was the local judges that were driving the crazy train." New York Police Department whistleblowers Frank Serpico and Adrian Schoolcraft also had their mental health questioned.[362]

Many years later, Taylor reflected on his erstwhile adversary, "[Olivito] was trying very hard for people who don't normally get the care and concern from people on his level. Even though he was kinda Quixote-ish, I developed a grudging admiration. He cared for his clients tremendously. He was helping people."

In Ohio, after three decades of Republican rule over the judicial system, politically motivated investigations and prosecutions were carried out with efficiency gained through institutional development. Around the turn of the century, the DOJ had attempted to purge the ranks of the political establishment of graft. Federal lawsuits against Ohio's police and prisons were integral in modernizing these institutions and federal prosecutions of corruption sent a message to public servants.[363] It was a battle between the mafia and the FBI; between the CRD and the Special Litigation Section of the DOJ against local PDs and their unions, law firms, and insurance companies. Olivito believed that these waves of federal enforcement didn't go far enough.

Political prosecutions were at their peak nationwide by this time in the Bush era. The DOJ fired seven U.S. attorneys in December of 2006 either for investigating Republican politicians or for failing to investigate Democratic ones. It would seem that those seven U.S. attorneys were those who bucked the trend: U.S. attorneys nationwide investigated seven times more Democrats than Republicans for ethics and

---

[362] Graham Rayman. The NYPD Tapes. *St. Martin's Press*, 2013.

[363] One of those officials, James Traficant, told Congress that the mafia owns the FBI in Mahoning County.

other violations during the preceding six years.[364] The Bush administration was waging a bare-knuckle political battle to weaken federal influence into state and local governments. Policing was at the center of contention, and police leaders were tapping their cronies in the Bush White House and Congress while retaining Vorys to defend the municipalities.[365] The legal arguments to defeat the DOJ's civil rights enforcement were formulated by an unholy alliance between the chair of the Columbus Democratic Party and the *de facto* general counsel of the FOP, both senior partners at Vorys. In this respect, the expansion of police power in the political realm has been a byproduct of bipartisan cooperation.

On July 2, 2008, the Inspector General of the DOJ released the results of an investigation carried out in conjunction with the Office of Professional Responsibility into "politicized hiring" in the CRD between the years of 2003-2007.[366] The report explained a lot for Ohioans with a stake in the fight for police accountability because it gave a potential explanation the weak DOJ response to Warren, "We're watching," and a clue to the high-end political considerations which played a role in the lifting of the Steubenville decree. Olivito had been booted out of the practice of law and enmeshed in a struggle for custody over his son when it was revealed that the hiring procedure in the CRD changed in February 2002, allowing Bush loyalists to change the ideological makeup of the staff. The report stated, "[Deputy Assistant Attorney General Bradley] Schlozman controlled hiring for career attorney positions, monitored case assignments, and directed section chief to assign important cases to attorneys he identified."[367]

In 2005, Schlozman became Acting Assistant Attorney General, and he ordered three transfers of Appellate Section attorneys to other sections because of their party affiliation. According to staff attorneys at the CRD, Schlozman disdained the liberals in the Division and wanted to replace them with "real Americans," by which he meant conservatives.[368] He later admitted to saying these sorts of things. With the sup-

---

[364] Gerry Spence. *Police State*. St. Martin's Press. 2014. Page 183.

[365] Chuck Canterbury. Leadership is Cooperation. *The FOP Journal*, Vol. 11, Issue 4, August 2006.

[366] "An Investigation of Allegations of Politicized Hiring and Other Improper Personnel Actions in the Civil Rights Division." *U.S. Department of Justice Office of the Inspector General and U.S. Department of Justice Office of Professional Responsibility*, 2 July 2008.

[367] Ibid., page 14.

[368] Ibid., page 15.

port of the Attorney General and the Bush White House, this one official managed to obstruct the work of the DOJ in civil rights matters, which was an urgent priority of the law enforcement community and their lobbyists on the hill. The DOJ initiated fewer investigations and issued no consent decrees, forcing Warren to wait until Mando could be put out to pasture.

In contrast to the courageous attorneys who carried out the Steubenville investigation, "Former Criminal Section Chief Moskowitz also said the candidates for career positions chosen by Schlozman... rarely had any civil rights background, rarely expressed any interest in civil rights enforcement, and had little or no federal criminal experience."[369] Schlozman proceeded to exert as much personal control as possible over the hiring process in the CRD, to the point that division chiefs complained about Schlozman overruling their attempts to contravene against inexperienced new hires.

The CRD envisioned by the Bush administration did not initiate heavy-handed investigations into patterns of local police misconduct. If the division initiated an investigation, it would not end in a consent decree, as was the case in Warren. The Bush administration preferred brokered agreements without federal oversight or auditing to make sure the terms were honored. It had been three years since the DOJ released its findings regarding Warren's pattern of civil rights violations and two years since they returned to admonish the city government for not implementing the reforms. The DOJ also scolded Mandopoulos for not mailing a letter of apology to a black officer's wife as the DOJ had previously ordered. There had been no agreement, just a slap on the wrist. The WPD and the City promised to do better, and the DOJ backed graciously out the door, as they had in Columbus.

---

[369] Ibid., page 17.

## 21

To me the chief was creating a distraction. To me, it's in the best interests of the city that we have a new chief.

- Larry Dueber[370]

In November of 2008, coinciding with the election of Barack Obama, Fred Harris signed an affidavit that repeated the essential claims made in every lawsuit Olivito filed against the WPD. It was only three pages long, but it makes a strong case that there was a systemic administrative malfunction in the WPD. Harris stated that while he served as safety services director, he reviewed the dispositions made in citizen complaints by Chief Mandopoulos and on numerous occasions raised the issue of discipline and training with Mandopoulos. He went on to say, "I have specific recollection of advising Chief Mandopoulos on multiple occasions that his failure to appropriately discipline and mandate relevant training directly contributed to the continuing unconstitutional conduct of certain WPD officers." Then, he described Mandopoulos' "blatant disregard of the risk to the safety of the community," alleging that the chief "turned a blind eye to the conduct of officers." To cap it off, Harris then declared:

> The Warren police engaged in a pattern or practice of excessive force and other unconstitutional conduct promoted by the failure of the chief to adequately train and or discipline its officers, and the failure of the chief to properly supervise, all of which directly encourages the use of excessive force and other improper conduct.

Harris had known the WPD since his childhood, so he was reflecting on at least a half a century of experience. Plus, he was Mando's boss from September of 2000 to December 31, 2004, which gave him insight into the function of the WPD, as his frequent public commentaries on the progress of the WPD during those years reflected. Harris referred to Mandopoulos' failure to punish Nites for his "highly inflammatory racial epithets," and the strip search of Dominic Gambone as examples of a larger pattern, "of multiple incidents of excessive force and other constitutional violations by the WPD."

---

[370] Ed Runyan. "Mandopoulos retiring as Warren police chief." *The Vindicator*, 10 April 2009.

There were failures to investigate or improper handling of crimes against women. In one case, a girl disappeared and was reported missing by her family, but nobody investigated for several years. In 1995, a woman was raped by a man to whom she gave a ride, and two policemen witnessed the immediate aftermath with the man literally caught with his pants down and her nose bleeding.[371] The officers cited him for public indecency, put him in jail for three days and fined him twenty-five dollars.[372]

There were also cases where sworn officers were caught up in lurid tales of gendered exploitation of their positions. Harris learned that officers had used the LEADS system to stalk cute nurses they saw at the hospital. Another veteran officer was allegedly busted by his superiors patronizing a brothel while his unmarked police car was parked outside. As punishment, he had to drive a marked police cruiser.

Back in the day, there were rumors of women coerced into giving officers blowjobs. Mandopoulos' godson Gerald Roth, referred to as "the creepy cop," by former Assistant Fire Chief James Nutt in his book,[373] was unaccountable for his treatment of women. Tim Bowers, long before he became chief, kissed a woman the police were trying to bust in an undercover narcotics investigation, then showed up in court to testify in her defense. Her probation officer said the incident was "a mess."[374] The lengths a few officers went to are not representative of the WPD as a whole, but with cases like these, other officers knew well that laws were mere cobwebs for the boys in blue. Women could be intimidated, stalked, exploited, beaten, raped and disappeared without the WPD so much as raising a finger. In 2017, a woman escaped from one of Warren's informal brothels, where a man had kept her against her will, drugging her and letting johns rape her for money. After the perpetrator was arrested, he faced only one charge, promoting prostitution, carrying a potential sentence of up to ten years.[375] Perhaps, the witness didn't want to file charges over her confinement or the assaults she alleged. Victims have been known to recant allegations in anticipa-

---

[371] Edgar Simpson and Alyssa Lenhoff. "Disorderly Conduct." *Warren Tribune Chronicle*, 14 April 1996.

[372] Ibid.

[373] Stated in interview in 2015 regarding James L. Nutt. Confessions of a Bipolar Firefighter. *AuthorHouse*, 26 March 2012.

[374] Edgar Simpson and Alyssa Lenhoff. "Disorderly Conduct." *Warren Tribune Chronicle*, 14 April 1996. P. 44.

[375] WKBN. "Man accused of running brothel out of Ohio home." *NBC4i.com*, 20 September 2017.

tion of the trauma of confronting the perpetrator. Even still, it seems like they went easy on him.

At Trumbull Correctional Institute (TCI), there were widespread allegations of sexual exploitation of female inmates. In 2007, five corrections officers were allowed to resign and retire with pensions because of "inappropriate relationships."[376] In 2016, Judge Benita Pearson accused TCI's leadership of a pattern or practice of strip searches and the perpetuation of sexual misconduct with female inmates, which was documented over a period of years although Sheriff Altiere claimed to have dealt with the problem, however quietly.[377] Before that, a federal lawsuit accused one TCI officer of repeatedly soliciting strip shows from a female inmate in 2014.

The dregs of the WPD were encouraged in anonymous public comments back in 2007:

> Both [Youngstown] and Warren cops ought to retire and get jobs at [TCI], we now have female inmates, and some of these crackheads are hot. The warden gave the female inmates personal hygiene items to perform all kind of sexual explicit dances, management gave them water filled balloons for an inmate wet T-shirt contest boy was that some hot action.[378]

The post went on and on making more claims with specificity that begged for investigation. All this was on top of allegations of murder and beatings. Warden David Bobby bore responsibility, but Sheriff Altiere later took the fall, for failing to investigate.

The criminal justice apparatus from the first responders to the correctional officers (COs) was shot through with corruption for most of its history, and the courts have by and large gone along with the dictates and noncompliance of their peers. Officer Reuben Shaw told Harris and Mayor Angelo that they had just scratched the surface in 2004, and Shaw later talked to the DOJ in the years that followed. The DOJ claimed to have interviewed command staff, residents, local advocates and city officials. Still, nothing but infrequent, long distance advisory took place for four more years after the visit by the DOJ in 2008. The police department was methodically notified of policies it should change to come into conformity with the standards of modern policing, not digging too deeply or ultimately sanctioning the department, consistent with the Bush administration's approach to federal civil rights

---

[376] "Charlie." 5th Guard Fired at Trumbull Correctional." *Discussion Groups: Talk of the Valley, The Vindicator*, 30 August 2007.

[377] Editorial Board. "Lawsuit is game changer in Trumbull sheriff's race." *The Vindicator*, 6 March 2016.

[378] "Aaaaaaa." "Re: Warren Police." 7 March 2007,

enforcement.

<><><>

In April 2009, Chief Mandopoulos was forced into retirement. One month prior, it came out that Manny Nites had been coaching while on duty. As a result, Nites' supervisors, including Lt. Eric Merkel, were suspended for falsifying his time sheets.[379] As usual, Chief Mandopoulos defended Nites vigorously in the press, and that was salt in the wounds of those who had long known of his use of excessive force as well as his use of the word "nigger" in 2001 during the Lynwood raid and in the 2003 "77 Soul" video. On March 28, 2009, Mandopoulos countered that the city's layoffs of police officers were the real cause of the department's problems.[380] Chief Mandopoulos was an old-school police officer who didn't tolerate disrespect, and he protected his department to the best of his ability when residents accused officers of injuring and humiliating them.

The chief complained of being forced to retire. Mayor O'Brien, Safety Services Director Doug Franklin, and Law Director Greg Hicks declined to comment.[381] Mandopoulos once told Fred Harris that in the course of his career he had only fired his gun nine times. Four or five of those times were born of fear, wayward and aimless misfires, according to what Mando told Fred. At the end of his career, he told the public that the only two times he ever fired his gun was during an incident in 1987 during which three officers fired a total of six shots, which they later said were "warning shots." A police expert with thirty years of experience commented on the incident, "It sounds like those were shots that weren't warning shots. They became warning shots as a rationalization after the fact."[382] Mando may have been an old school police officer, but he was not a normal cop by today's stan-

---

[379] Darcie Loreno. "Chief: Deal with cop a 'win-win.'" *The Vindicator*, 9 September 2009.

[380] Ed Runyan. Warren police probe centers on allegation of falsified time card. *The Vindicator*, 28 March 2009.

[381] Ed Runyan. "Mandopoulos retiring as Warren police chief." *The Vindicator*, 12 April 2009.

[382] Edgar Simpson and Alyssa Lenhoff. "Disorderly Conduct." *Warren Tribune Chronicle*, 14 April 1996.

238

dards when only a quarter of cops ever fire their guns.[383] Mando is like the officers today who typically fire their guns; he was a white guy who approved of harsh, physical methods for dealing with some people.

After Mandopoulos' death, it was said by those who knew him that, as the lawsuits mounted against his officers, the chief felt betrayed and couldn't trust anybody. Mando was quick to absolve his officers in the media because he never wanted the WPD's reputation to be sullied. He handled problems his way, internally, because his officers were like his sons. Mando coddled his officers, and some of them pushed the cloak of the chief's unconditional support over atrocities, perhaps none as recklessly as Mando's own godson. After he died, *The Vindicator* pointedly announced, "Mandopoulos cared about officers first."[384] The reluctance of Mando to discipline officers and his resistance to external pressure to reform long outlived him. Eric Merkel, who would take over after Bowers, later declared that nothing changed until he became chief.

Tim Bowers took over as acting police chief after Mandopoulos. He later said of his leadership role in the department, "[The WPD] needed to be reminded that they are public servants. We work for the citizenry that we enforce citizen's laws and provide service to them."[385] Bowers distinguished himself from Mandopoulos by imposing a thirty-day suspension without pay on Detective Jeff Hoolihan for pulling his gun on three African American children in their own backyard. Mandopoulos had never suspended any officer for so long without pay. Still, although he imposed it, Bowers only disciplined officers that he believed had harmed the department. Bowers bragged about his severity in imposing a three-month suspension, after "There has been no discipline here for nine years."[386] Manny Nites got to keep his rank of sergeant while serving three months suspension without pay. Harris criti-

[383] Rich Morin and Drew Mercer. A closer look at police officers who have fired their weapon on duty. *Pew Research Center,* 8 February 2017.

[384] Ed Runyan. "Mandopoulos cared about officers first." *The Vindicator*, 24 January 2012.

[385] WKBN Staff. "Chief Bowers says goodbye to Warren Police Department." 17 June 2013.

[386] Staff. "Integrity level keeps sinking for Warren PD." *Warren Tribune Chronicle*, 29 September 2009.

cized this decision in comments to *The Vindicator*, stressing that in the private sector, not only would an employee be fired for committing fraud, but they would likely be prosecuted.[387]

By September of 2009, the local papers were grandstanding against the WPD. The *Tribune Chronicle* derided the new chief for pampering "rogue cop" Manny Nites, after denouncing the WPD for giving officers "a license to steal and fib." The newspaper referred to Chief Bowers' admission that there was no discipline for nine years as "unbelievable." The editorial was provocatively entitled, "Integrity level keeps sinking for Warren PD." The paper asked how it would be possible to trust Bowers while knowing that for nine years he did not alert the public to Mandopoulos' "administrative ineptitude."[388] The editorial concluded, "There has been discussion of closing [the WPD] down and contracting with the Trumbull County Sheriff's Office for law enforcement. The motive for those discussions has been financial. Perhaps, they also should be moral."

In November of 2009, just four months after city officials managed to force Mandopoulos into retirement, Lt. Kavanagh was up for promotion from lieutenant to captain. Thomas Conley, president of the Greater Warren Youngstown Urban League, forbade his advancement based on an incident that happened earlier that year. On August 17, Lt. Kavanagh drove around in his cruiser while drunk and on meds.[389] After a security guard alerted police to their supervisor's conduct, officers picked up Kavanagh and eventually drove him home, while another officer drove his car. Two residents later filed complaints that Kavanagh had called them racial epithets that night, which an internal investigation confirmed.[390]

In the complaint from the mayor's office to the police chief, Kavanagh was quoted as saying, "Fucking nigger, you black bitch, you got some crack, you black bitch, you're a black bitch, you fucking nigger."[391] Another resident came to the station three days later, alleging Kavanagh had asked him, "Hey nigger, you selling any crack?" Out of

[387] Darcie Loreno. "Chief: Deal with cop a 'win-win.'" *Warren Tribune Chronicle*, 9 September 2009.

[388] Staff. "Integrity level keeps sinking for Warren PD." *Warren Tribune Chronicle*, 29 September 2009.

[389] Ed Runyan. "Urban League opposes Lt. Kavanagh's promotion." *The Vindicator*, 28 November 2009.

[390] Ed Runyan. "Lt. Kavanagh suspended after admitting wrongdoing." *The Vindicator*, 17 October 2009.

[391] Internal documents from the city of Warren. 2009.

cowardice or deference, none of the local newspapers quoted what Lt. Kavanagh had said, and Kavanagh suggested that he was only being sarcastic about the drugs.[392]

Lt. Kavanagh admitted his guilt and served a two-week paid suspension, using his vacation time.[393] The punishment was more a concession to the public than a repudiation of Kavanagh's shocking behavior. Bowers had originally suggested a thirty-day suspension, but he decided to hold twenty days in abeyance because of Kavanagh's tenure, stating, "He's done twenty years here without screwing up..."[394] Of course, that wasn't true, but Kavanagh wrote a touching apology that was published in the press, and he later received his promotion to captain. Years later, Helen Rucker remembered that Kavanagh went out of his way to work with the community. Conley suggested there was little question of Kavanagh's official competence, but he questioned whether it was good to have an officer dealing with residents who had spoken with such deep hatred of African Americans while drunk. "There's something wrong with a system where you do something horrible, and you get promoted."

Manny Nites got a three-month suspension without pay for his time card fraud. Lt. Merkel was suspended for ten days without pay, which an arbitrator later reversed so that he was only reprimanded and paid for his time off.[395] Under Bowers, the WPD begrudgingly embraced discipline, but troubling scandals continued to haunt the department.

[392] Ibid.

[393] Anonymous. "Warren police Capt. Joe Kavanagh issues apology letter." *The Vindicator*, 13 January 2010.

[394] Darcie Loreno. "Warren officer gets suspension." *Warren Tribune Chronicle*, 17 October 2009.

[395] Ed Runyan. "Men question charges against fired Warren police officer." *The Vindicator*, 5 June 2014.

## 22

It amazed me that the DOJ was not interested in what we were doing, they were worried about policy and procedure changes.

- Retired Detective Jeff Hoolihan

During the period in which the DOJ conducted its probe, there were a few cover-ups that generated a paper trail. One WPD detective was sufficiently disturbed by what he knew to reveal information to federal authorities under the whistleblower statute. That an insider was willing to destroy his own career was a testament to the level of the resistance of local authorities to due process and transparency. Former detective Jeff Hoolihan explained, "It's not about Nites, Hoso, Roth, Massucci, not that the stuff about them isn't true. It's a corrupt county. The sheriff gets $5 to $10K a pop for jobs. I put four policemen before a Trumbull County jury for covering up gambling operations." In vain, the justice system was simply too corrupt.

After joining the force in 1989, Hoolihan had a rough couple of years learning the ropes. The fifteen citizen complaints he generated between 1991 and 1993 suggest that community residents found reasons to question his judgment. On one or two occasions, it was not clear if Hoolihan was being honest, but the WPD did not invest many hours to find out the truth. Despite his citizen complaints, Hoolihan became an investigator valued by authorities far outside of Warren. After four years on the road as a patrolman and seven as a detective, Hoolihan joined AG's organized crime task force. Soon afterward, Hoolihan distinguished himself working with the FBI and BCI on the investigation into the assassination attempt on Youngstown Prosecutor Paul Gains, which led to the prosecution of mob hitman Mark Batcho. After finding God in prison, Batcho sent a handwritten letter to Hoolihan calling him "the Blue Knight." Batcho wished he had known that there was a cop like Hoolihan before losing faith in justice.

Hoolihan relished the thrill of criminal investigations. In 2001, an FBI special agent wrote to Mandopoulos, "Detective Hoolihan has been a crucial part of the investigation," which severely disrupted major gambling operations in Trumbull County. After almost ten years on the organized crime task force and fifteen years as a detective, Hoolihan was transferred back to the WPD. Hoolihan's police work contributed to the arrest and prosecution of corrupt attorneys, prosecutors, and judges, and Hoolihan swore that he never looked the other way. This made some officers of the WPD uncomfortable.

In 2008, the WPD carried out a gambling raid, but the chief soon realized someone had tipped off the operators. Mandopoulos was furious, and he vowed to find out who was responsible. Hoolihan discovered that a dispatcher had tipped off the operators about the raid. In the course of his internal investigation, Hoolihan dutifully recorded in his case notes that Bowers had attempted to interfere with the investigation. In June of 2008, Chief Mandopoulos told Hoolihan in an email that Bowers hated him for it and would work to make Hoolihan's life "a living hell" when he became chief. Hoolihan turned around and notified the union's attorney of what Mandopoulos had said, in writing. After almost two decades as a cop, Hoolihan was nothing if not methodical. He tried his best not to let his emotions interfere with his job, and he had only one allegiance. His loyalty was to the people of Warren, to the victims of crime, not to the command structure of the WPD. He knew that the commanders in the WPD would work against him and justice if given the order by city hall, or if they had any personal reason, so he started wearing a wire to work.

◇◇◇

While at the fertilizer plant, Nature's Blend, owned by the Wastewater Department, officers of the WPD, including Hoolihan, as well as investigators from the OEPA and BCI, discovered over 1,000 images of different kinds of pornography on a computer inside the facility. The files were on the computer assigned to a guy we'll call David Snyder, and they contained images of orgies, bondage, gay porn, "granny" porn, cartoons, as well as a few images investigators believed portrayed minors.

The employee's name, although reported by local media, is being withheld because he was never charged with a crime over subsequent allegations of child abuse at his church. In his computer, there were also bookmarks from Craigslist and Backpage sex workers as well as logs of chats with them, next to bookmarks related to a local Presbyterian church where Snyder was a volunteer engaged in activities involving children. Investigators suspected that looking at porn and procuring sex workers was outside the scope of this public employee's duties, so they decided to obtain a search warrant.

On August 6, 2008, a meeting was held between then-police chief, John Mandopoulos, former Mayor O'Brien, Safety Services Director Franklin, as well as officers of the WPD and BCI, to discuss the investigation. Chief Mandopoulos stated that no one should interfere with the investigation. Detective Hoolihan suggested Snyder be put on leave during the investigation, and, although this never happened, his work computer was confiscated the next month. His wasn't the only computer in the Wastewater Department on which employees were viewing porn, according to a former employee who alleged that he was given a pay cut for trying to bring the issue to the attention of his supervisor. However, the porn on Doe's computer became even more significant a few months later.

In January of 2009, a young woman came to the WPD and spoke with Detective Hoolihan about an incident involving Snyder that took place in 2007 at the First Presbyterian Church where Snyder was a volunteer in the computer lab. She was only thirteen at the time and had braces. Snyder waited until other children were gone during preparations for vacation Bible school, and then he groped and kissed her on the mouth. He tried to put his hand up her dress and held her tightly. She stated:

> He was strong. I couldn't get away. I told him I needed to go to the bathroom to change. He asked me if he could help me change, and I saw him follow me to try to watch me. I had braces. He knew how old I was. I was 100% naive. I had no idea what to do. I slept with my light on for a year because I was afraid.

She told her godmother a few days later, but her godmother asked, "Are you sure he wasn't trying to comfort you?" A year later, in 2008, the girl's mother told her that Snyder's hugs were getting longer and longer, and it was creeping her out. At this point, she told her mother about the incident a year before, and then, the allegation was taken up by the church's sexual harassment committee, formed in response to the allegation. Both the girl and Snyder, who was accompanied by his wife, were interviewed by the sexual harassment committee, and the committee reached out to an official from another Presbyterian church in a neighboring town for guidance.

The clerk of the Eastminster Presbytery, Rev. Meta Cramer, consulted church bylaws and the Ohio Revised Code (ORC). Then, she responded that the allegation "could be, but was not required to be, referred to civil authorities," according to the decision rendered by the committee. Cramer cited ORC 2907.06 B which decrees that no person can be convicted by the victim's testimony unsupported by other evidence. The reverend was not an attorney, or she would have known that reporting alleged child abuse is always mandatory, regardless of the perceived credibility of the allegation. ORC 2151.421 states, "No person...acting in an official or professional capacity and know, or has reasonable cause to suspect, that a child...has suffered or faces a threat of suffering any physical or mental wound...shall fail to immediately report...to the public children services agency or a municipal or county peace officer." The committee had an attorney and a pediatrician who would have known this.

The one-page explanation, which was given to both parties, asked that "each party avoid contact unless there are other persons present." The committee response team admitted, "this incident has shown weaknesses in our Sexual Misconduct Policy and Procedures," and that "the youth and adult leadership has not been as diligent as it could be in implementing the church policy for volunteers working with children and youth." However, with this guidance as well as "input" from an unknown party for a "simple solution," contact unless there are other persons present," and authorized Snyder to continue his duties at the church with the condition that other adults be present when his duties brought him into contact with young people.

The committee decided that "Christian forgiveness should find its way to the forefront of this situation." The victim was advised to try to avoid Synder, who was supposed to be escorted by his wife to keep him away from children. When asked, the clerk of First Presbyterian, Ray Rubrake, who was on the sexual harassment committee, said that the "guidance" was not from an attorney, but the committee had an attorney, Lynne Griffith, III, who is now a county prosecutor. Griffith, who has been an attorney for more than three decades, declined to comment repeating the matter was "confidential," although it is a public record. The committee deferred to Griffith who encouraged the church not to report alleged child abuse to civil authorities. Though the church authorities may have believed that they were being Christ-like, they were likely breaking state law.

The victim gave a statement to Detective Hoolihan, who knew of another woman that had experienced Snyders's sexual harassment in the same church many years before. That woman's husband, Jim Thompson, was the custodian of the church for several years and later became head of security. Thompson alleged that the church shredded documents of sexual harassment investigations which he retrieved and pieced together from the garbage. Thompson said the documents "were about investigations by the church into this guy." His wife's experience took place, again, in the computer lab.

Thompson stated that his wife was alone with Snyder in the computer lab while he was downstairs attending to his duties. Former Pastor Mike Youngblood asked Thompson where his wife was. When Thompson replied that she was with Snyder, Pastor Youngblood "turned white as a sheet, started stuttering and left." A few minutes later, his wife came downstairs looking shocked and wanting to go home. She told her husband that Snyder had sexually accosted her, but she didn't want to report it or file charges. "She wanted me to clean his clock. I didn't know who to go to. I'm a peaceful man, and I had just started that job there. Besides, it happened in a church! It's supposed to be safe!" This church was keen on excusing sexual predation by blaming the victims. Thompson remembered that when the adolescent girl came forward with her allegation, people in the church blamed her for "dressing provocatively."

Thompson watched and listened. What he heard disturbed him, knowing what he knew. When the church received a grant for new computers, church leaders supported Snyder's suggestion that he teach a program on sex education for children. Thompson spoke out against the idea, but he says that the church elders were dead set on having Snyder as the point man. His technical and grant-writing skills made him valuable to the church and the city. Finally, Thompson said he was approached by a church elder who asked him, "What do you want?" Thompson replied, "I want this to stop!"

Thompson shared his information with Detective Hoolihan and Thompson's wife provided a written statement of her experience with Snyder. On June 9, Hoolihan called the Trumbull County Prosecutor's Office and gave Darlene Durig the information she would need to compose two separate grand jury subpoenas. The first would decide whether there was probable cause that Snyder had committed criminal sexual misconduct. The second would determine whether there was a criminal conspiracy to cover-up Snyder's abuse at First Presbyterian Church.

Shortly afterward, Hoolihan was called to the chief's office and asked to turn over the file of the Snyder investigation. Although Hoolihan had other investigations he was working on, they wanted only the Snyder file. Sensing foul play, he made two copies of the investigation, one for the FBI and one for his records. Then, he was transferred to street duty, despite his seventeen years experience as a detective. He waited two years, wondering every day if the case was moving forward and worrying as time passed that Snyder would abuse new victims. Then, he received an anonymous call. "I thought you should know that porn investigation was closed without charges." Hoolihan asked who it was, but they hung up. He had created a paper trail on purpose for just such an eventuality. So, he decided to go to the media with what he knew.

Hoolihan gave documents from the investigation to Janet Rogers, the veteran journalist at *WFMJ-TV*. She later asked Law Director Greg Hicks, then-Prosecutor Susan Shipley, then-Mayor O'Brien, then-Safety Services Director Franklin and then-Chief Tim Bowers about the porn investigation. They all claimed to know nothing about it, although a BCI agent later attested in writing that Law Director Hicks, Safety Services Director Franklin, and Mayor O'Brien were present at the meeting in 2008 where the investigation was discussed. Mayor O'Brien said there was "no meeting" about it on camera. Franklin said he was "not aware."

Chief Bowers' emails, which later became part of an internal investigation obtained by this reporter with the aid of a Columbus law firm, reflect that he did know about it. In a recorded phone conversation in 2016, former City Prosecutor Susan Shipley admitted knowing about it two years before Rogers asked her. She also knew the name of the female minor molested at the church. Now, she is the assistant law director, legal advisor to the WPD and former liaison to the DOJ. Hoolihan asserted, "They all knew about it, and they knew that it led back to the church!" Hoolihan went to the FBI alleging a cover-up. He wrote letters to the local U.S. Attorney, the Ohio attorney general, and the local prosecutor. He held a press conference at his church, which was going to air on local television, but the authorities were not going to let that happen.

After a short article on the porn issue appeared on *WFMJ* March 22, 2011, Chief Bowers emailed Sergeant Jeff Cole the next day regarding a "leak of information." That day, Bowers spoke to both Franklin and O'Brien, who notified him that Rogers had come asking them why no action had been taken in the investigation. Bowers also received a record request that day from Rogers regarding the investigation. Rogers told O'Brien that Hoolihan said he was told by O'Brien to "kill" the investigation, which O'Brien anxiously related to Bowers. O'Brien was used to taking advantage of his position for his own purposes. Years earlier, he had requested former Chief Mandopoulos to park an empty WPD patrol car outside his residence after he was accused of domestic violence by his wife. Hoolihan received orders to comply with these requests on two occasions, apparently so that O'Brien's wife would be deterred from coming back to their house while O'Brien was not at home.

With Mayor O'Brien breathing down his neck, Chief Bowers ordered Sergeant Cole to open an internal investigation into whether Hoolihan had violated policy by going to the media. For the authorities, the problem was the leak, not the fact that a person with a history of sexual misconduct was allowed to hunt in a church attended by judges, prosecutors, and the former assistant law director while the mayor, police chief, city prosecutor, and safety services director pretended not to know.

It was a violation of procedure to go to the media about an open investigation, but Hoolihan had good reason to believe that the investigation was closed. On March 24, Bowers emailed Sgt. Cole again, this time because Bowers was advised by Law Director Hicks that Hoolihan planned to hold a press conference at his church, North Mar Church, at 6 pm that evening. Bowers had already called Hoolihan and remonstrated with him that the investigation was ongoing, but Hoolihan responded that Detective Mackey, who also worked on the case, told him it was closed. Bowers simply reopened the investigation and then ordered Hoolihan to be investigated.

On April 1, a Youngstown pastor sent a letter to the pastor of

First Presbyterian Church, the mayor, and David Snyder himself, "out of a concern for the ministry of Jesus Christ," filling them in on the allegations which were about to "come out in a very public way." The concerned pastor attached some documents of the sexual abuse allegations, declaring, "In our church, a man with this kind of integrity problem would be removed from office. I suggest you at least remove his name from your webpage as this story is about to get statewide recognition."

Rev. Rusty Cowden remains the pastor today, and Snyder's name is still on the website. He has allowed Snyder to continue working at the church though he knew about the porn and the sexual abuse allegations. Many left the church because of the way everything was handled, but the story never drew any publicity.

Snyder was allowed by the WPD to come in with his lawyer and view the investigation against him, which is highly irregular in a criminal investigation. Luckily for Snyder, the pictures he had of young girls performing oral sex on adult men had their eyes blotted out, which stops the victims from being identified and proscribes the images from being classified as "child porn." Because of this technicality and the fact that the images didn't cross state lines, the FBI backed out of the investigation.

Snyder got a sixty-day administrative suspension, although a BCI agent and Detective Hoolihan stated in search warrants that Snyder could be charged with "theft in office," even if the sex crimes were ignored. BCI turned over all documents pertaining to the investigation to Hoolihan, which left the follow-up entirely up to the WPD's discretion. The city has always been reluctant to criminally charge its employees, especially caucasian ones, for stealing from the taxpayers. Snyder has a special status because he is one of two employees in the city that can erase computer hard drives, a valuable resource. The WPD closed the investigation, and Snyder kept his job with the city, as well as his position in the church.

The WPD investigation into the church briefly reopened in 2011 but then was mysteriously discontinued. Neither investigation was ever recorded in the WPD's computer system. Instead, the files sat in a detective's desk for five years. Snyder may have been protected because he was then a member of the staff relations committee at First Presbyterian. His grandfather was also a Trumbull County juvenile judge who was close friends with a retired pediatrician, Dr. John Vlad, a member of the board at First Presbyterian and a member of the sexual harassment committee. Vlad's wife is now director of the music ministry.

Hoolihan was punished with a thirty-day suspension for his effort to expose the crimes of Snyder and the public and church officials who conspired to cover them up. In his defense, Hoolihan told IA:

Well, I strongly felt that I had to do what I had to do, whether it is in the policy and procedure book or not because of the information that I received and it's two and a half years later, and nothing has been done with this guy. And I, as a detective for fifteen years, know how long it takes to work a case. I was within two months of wrapping this case up when I was transferred.

Hoolihan felt that he was obliged to blow the whistle to protect Warren's children and expose a perpetrator. Chief Bowers didn't see it that way. He lectured Hoolihan:

You called a reporter, and you told her things that weren't true. That you believed they were true doesn't matter. You violated the policies and procedures of this police department, which are our laws, in the society that you and I are living, are part of, have grown up in. Without policies and procedures, laws, we have disorder. We have no organization at all...You've got a mark on you. It's a struggle for me professionally to let you remain a Warren police officer, part of my organization, because your credibility is shit...When I say you did harm to this police department, I'm not blowing up your ass, I'm saying ya did, and there is gonna be repercussions for that. I'm gonna suspend you for 30 days and you're gonna take it or I'm gonna fire ya...I'm gonna give you the number to our [Employee Assistance Program] program, and you're gonna get evaluated by them. When you come by the 1st of July, we can put this all behind us.

Bowers' disciplinary speech was edited for brevity. Hoolihan rebuffed the idea of going to counseling, but Bowers left him no choice. The Employee Assistance Program (EAP) is supposed to be voluntary, which it clearly was not, as well as confidential, which Hoolihan asserts is also not the case. Bowers said that he had already called them and that if they recommended any treatment, he was obliged to take it. The meeting did not go the way Hoolihan had expected, based on his Garrity rights, but then again, nothing in the WPD went according to the book. Snyder got sixty days administrative suspension, after which the WPD closed the investigation. The church investigation was discontinued. Snyder's name remains on the website, as of May 2018.

Mayor O'Brien handled the First Presbyterian Church affair with the panache of a veteran political fixer. As a public servant, a man who could keep the lid on that kind of scandal was destined for higher office. When O'Brien became a representative for the 64th District of Ohio, Franklin succeeded him as mayor and Enzo Cantalamessa, Lieutenant Hoso's longtime best friend, took over as safety services director.

Now, in key political positions, there were people who had spent their careers approving of the way things were done before anybody knew it was wrong. As a former member of the WPD, Hicks has never been anything but an underwriter of police violence and strip searches. Though previously a WPD sergeant, a former officer remembered Hicks "would run away from calls rather than going to them." As law director, Hicks was always a cowboy. All he has done for is sit back in a leather chair for two decades making money with his business partners, the bail bondsmen, while Warren's residents lived in terror of rogue cops and felons employed as bail bondsmen working out of Hick's office.

Former prosecutor Susan Shipley is from a law enforcement family. Now that she is assistant law director, legal advisor to the WPD and liaison with the DOJ, that family allegiance tends to get in the way when Warren residents have priorities that conflict with the police. As mayor, Franklin did as former mayors, he backed the police, no matter what. Under the mayor, Safety Services Director Cantalamessa did as Franklin before him; he never questioned the results of an internal investigation. With those odds, it's no surprise that the number of citizen complaints have gone down. Fred Harris said in May of 2018, "Who are you gonna go to? Cantalamessa? The chief? Hicks? No. It's gone like it was. I get calls now every other week."

## 23

Richard is alive. People died for that. He needs to be proud of it and make that his reason for living.

-Tom Conley, President of Greater Warren Youngstown Urban League

Four years after the loss of his license and two years after his father's death, on October 2, 2011, Olivito was picking up Joshua at Rosa's house in Boardman, Ohio, a suburb on the southern outskirts of Youngstown, when an argument started between the stepfather and Olivito over a hospital bill which had come to their house by mistake. Olivito said that the stepfather grabbed him by the neck, but otherwise the argument did not escalate into a physical confrontation. Olivito left with Joshua in his car, but a neighbor called the police, and they pulled Olivito over a few blocks away. According to Olivito, it was only a few weeks after Sergeant Kyle Hollister had shown up with others to mediate the weekly transfer of Joshua from his mother to his father because of the stepfather's angry outbursts, alcoholism, and violence.

Olivito alleged, many years later, that the local authorities repeatedly declined to charge the stepfather with any crime, despite various attempts to file a report by Olivito with his son as a witness. The stepfather was later arrested because he severely beat Joshua's maternal grandmother, putting her in the hospital, according to *The Vindicator*.[396] The stepfather's friends chimed in the comment thread below the article, blaming the octogenarian grandmother and portraying him as the victim.

After he was pulled over by Sgt. Hollister, Olivito says he waited a couple of minutes while the officer was on his radio, but then he decided to get out of his car. Olivito went around to the rear of the car and asked if he could speak to the officer. In the police report, Sgt. Hollister alleged that Olivito was yelling at him, obliging him to interrupt his interaction on the radio. Hollister said he gave Olivito several orders to return to his vehicle which Olivito finally did. Then, the officer exited his car and drew his gun because, as he had told the dispatcher, Olivito was not listening to his commands. Hollister says that he had his firearm pointed at the ground, "at low ready." Police can

---

[396] Staff. "Man accused of beating his mother-in-law." *The Vindicator*, 11 July 2012.

draw their firearms when they feel there is a risk to themselves or the community, and Hollister judged that Olivito's agitation presented a danger to himself, although Olivito was then quietly in his car.

Hollister ordered Olivito to the rear of the vehicle, where he intended to pat him down for weapons. Hollister noted that Olivito complied and got out of the car, but upon seeing the firearm, Olivito "immediately became more defiant yelling that he didn't do anything wrong and his nine-year-old son [was] in the car." Hollister repeatedly commanded Olivito to go around to the rear of the car, and when he did not immediately comply, the officer aimed his gun at Olivito. Hollister radioed for backup, saying that he had Olivito at gunpoint. Until back-up arrived, Hollister and Olivito argued over what was going to happen. Olivito told Hollister to put away his gun and he would comply with the orders, while Hollister told Olivito that he was under arrest and to get on the ground. Officer Klingensmith arrived promptly and threatened to tase Olivito if he did not comply. Both Olivito and the officers agree that the threat of the taser convinced Olivito to get down on the ground. At this point, the officers' account and Olivito's account diverge.

Olivito alleges that he was hit in the head with a pistol. "Just as I got down to my knees and placed both of my hands on the pavement in front of me, I felt a sudden hard strike against the left side of my head. It lit me up, and I saw a white light for a second." In the police report, Sgt. Hollister says without elaboration, "We then placed Olivito prone on the ground giving him commands to place his hands behind his back."[397] The description given by the officers that they placed Olivito prone is the type of vague language the DOJ frowns upon. When the arrestee alleges that he or she was brutalized while the officers elide what exactly happened in the police report, it raises red flags with federal attorneys. Olivito remembered, many years later, that cars were stopped all around as the Boardman police officer brandished his service weapon. He described the scene, "I was being held down forcibly...with my head crushed into the pavement by the one officer's knees...Several people were standing outside of our favorite restaurant...just gazing upon this drama."

Sgt. Hollister writes, "He was not complying with our commands and was pulling his arms away from our attempts to handcuff him." It is undoubtedly difficult to handcuff a resisting subject, but the idea that two officers standing over a "prone" man would be unable secure his arms raises questions.

Many years later, Olivito described how he remained studiously calm by focusing out of the corner of his eye on Joshua, who was

---

[397] Sergeant Brian Hollister. "Arrest Supplement." *Boardman Police Department*, 2 November 2011.

screaming and jumping inside the car. Although he feared for his life, he kept repeating, "It's going to be okay, it's going to be okay..."

"Shut the fuck up!" shouted Sgt. Hollister, according to Olivito.

He tried but could not establish eye contact with his son. "I was breathing heavily and began to taste the blood coming from somewhere on my head...pouring into my eyes and mouth."

Olivito knew better than most what not to do when being arrested, as a sort of expert on probable cause and the procedures cops follow when carrying out an arrest. He knew exactly what would happen if he yelled at or struggled against an arresting officer. The use of force would escalate along the continuum towards deadly force.

My hands were quickly pulled behind my back, and I tried to get my hands onto my back...but one was more difficult the way they had crushed me. I was not trying to make any moves with my hands...at all...and then, I felt the barrel of a gun against my head.

"He's resisting... I'm going to stop this," Olivito remembers the officer saying.

Then, I felt it...I saw electricity in an arch...and again, I heard Joshua screaming...in the car. I could feel a little pinch in my legs, but I truly didn't feel any major shock. Perhaps, it was the adrenaline. I was at peace. It was like an out of body experience, hard to fully describe.

"He's still resisting," Officer Klingensmith repeated.

Olivito says he felt no pain while being tasered, although his leg later cramped for a few days. A person who has experienced trauma will have difficulty putting a traumatic experience into words because the side of the brain dealing with language goes offline when responding to trauma. If they are being held down and thus denied the ability to fight or flee, the brain slows down the heart's pumping, in preparation for the ultimate finality of death. As the left side of the brain shuts down, an odd peace washes over the victim, although he or she is encapsulated in frozen horror that will remain an indelible memory, occasionally crashing uninvited into their consciousness, for the rest of their lives.[398]

Larry Ward, an employee at *Clear Channel Media*, across the street, witnessed the altercation and gave his name to the police while Olivito was still lying prostrate in cuffs on the ground. He later stated that he had approached hoping that his presence would cause the situation to de-escalate. "[Olivito] had a kid in the car. I was hoping he wouldn't do anything stupid." According to Ward, Olivito was not complying with commands and the officers who showed "great re-

---

[398] Bessel van der Kolk. The Body Keeps The Score. *Viking*, 2014.

straint." When asked whether either of the officers struck Olivito, he said, "Not to my knowledge." When confronted with the account of the witness, Olivito dismissed it as "pro-police" saying that the guy was high-fiving the officers as he lay on the ground.

> There was no underlying probable cause...none. The witnesses don't understand, and they just saw a cop pointing a gun at me...and I was following the cop's orders to get down. First, to go back into the car...then to come out...and then to get down. If I had taken a single step towards the cop, after the second order to get out of my car...I would have been killed, and I don't believe any witness could have perceived or understood.

The next thing Olivito remembers he was seated in the back of the police cruiser, in shock.

> I was hurting and bleeding, but I wasn't being assaulted or tasered...there was no gun anymore to my head...and I could see...sadly and to this day...most troubling...Joshua had completely lost it...in the back of the car...he was jumping and screaming at the top of his lungs. He was not going anywhere with those cops.

> "Get away from me! I want my father!" Joshua screamed while trying to escape the hands of the cops by cramming himself into the back window. "He was not just crying...he was hyperventilating... he was "resisting their arrest." It is a scene I cannot forget...that was the worst of it...beyond seeing the cop's finger on the trigger...that is the moment I live and relive."

> Just then, as he was watching the officers attempt to take his son into custody from the squad car, an older officer opened the back door.

> "Richard, are you an attorney? You told our guys out here you were an attorney, and I thought you were disbarred." According to Olivito, he said, "I'm serious, we thought you were no longer a lawyer." His voice trailed off.

> "Listen, captain, you don't need to have your guys point a gun to my head in front of my son if you wish to ask me that. You know my background. Your guys arrested me without probable cause."

> "Our guys got a little anxious out here. You should have obeyed."

> "Obeyed what? The traffic laws? I used my turn signals; I did nothing wrong."

> "I know, I know, but we got this call..."

> "And what? You got a call that I had an argument with the crazy stepfather of my son."

> "We are going to book you on obstructing official business, and you can take it to the courts and probably get it dismissed."

Next, the officers called Joshua's mother, and she came to pick him up, while Olivito was taken to the station and then put in jail. It was not the first time and would not be the last. He would later lose count of how many times he was imprisoned in Mahoning County. While in jail, he and his cellmates asked the guards to get a doctor to inspect Olivito's head wound, which Olivito says he was denied.

The police report portrays Olivito as the one who was agitated and yelling. No use-of-force form was included in the police report. Olivito intended to sue the City of Boardman and the three officers who participated in his arrest, so he waited and pushed for a trial. He wanted to stand before a jury and argue false arrest and a violation of his Fourth Amendment right to be free of excessive force, as he had many times before while representing others. Olivito then hired an attorney, Walter Madison, but he later complained that the attorney did not prepare for the trial. Thus failed by his counsel, Olivito admitted defeat:

> I was going to have to go up against three cops...against my word and Joshua's. I knew if I had any chance of winning, I would have to have Joshua testify, and I couldn't see that happening. So, what I had not ever done or ever recommended for others, I took a bullshit plea...obstructing official business.

Being slow to comply with a police order is not enough to justify a charge of resisting arrest, nor is it enough for an officer to draw his gun, but Boardman needed an insurance policy. Once Olivito pled guilty to obstructing it, the resisting charge was dropped.

The case against Olivito in the Ohio Supreme Court came to represent a kind of death for him. It took away his platform and left him without defense against police intimidation. It also removed his main source of income. Although he still had a professional capacity from which he could derive profit, he did not have a license to use that capacity. He was unemployed and living at home, his mom's house in Steubenville, still floating on the proceeds of the Lundy house, an abolitionist historical landmark he reluctantly sold to the state. Joshua was a preteen, tall and slender, polite and into video games. Olivito focused on raising his son rather than avenging injustice, but at nights, left alone with his thoughts, playing a few measures of Chopin on the Olivito's baby grand, he dreamed of starting an organization dedicated to human rights in the Midwest.

## 24

What is up with the cops in this area? It's a sad state of affairs when you need to police your own police in the area.

-Anonymous

After seven months of negotiations and seven years of investigation, the DOJ settled with the WPD on January 13, 2012. *The Vindicator* reported on the new agreement, which it called a "consent agreement."[399] Hilary Taylor represented the city in the negotiations, and the resulting thirty-page document bears the signs of his demands. In the guide he later published, Taylor recommended negotiation over litigation and stamping everything with "attorney-client privilege" and "working with Do-Gooder interest groups and try to gain trust." Taylor learned some lessons in his relationship with the DOJ, which he would later pass on to other attorneys doing civil rights in reverse. Apart from responding and being attentive, Taylor emphasized that understanding the hierarchy of the DOJ was essential in the rare cases when it became necessary to take up an issue with a higher official, with whom he advised not to be seen by other DOJ officials. He had apparently learned his lesson, doing what was necessary to gain the advantage as he had done with Judge Galanis in the Northern District Court.

John Mandopoulos died on January 22, 2012, nine days after his police department caved to the DOJ. Certain sectors of Warren exploded with exultation on social media. Lea Dotson remembered those who were becoming too exuberant were reminded that they should show respect. Mandopoulos spent more than half of his life on the force and died at the age of sixty-one. Mandopoulos was not pleased to see the WPD come under the management of an outside agency. Before his death, *The Tribune Chronicle* described his ignominious departure as "unfitting."[400] Everyone expected Mando to go out in a blaze of bad press, but instead, he stepped down quietly. After his death, the newspapers and the community at large seemed to feel at liberty to express their objections to the way things were done during his tenure.

---

[399] Ed Runyan. "Warren PD now TECH READY." *The Vindicator*, 3 February 2012.

[400] Staff. "Chief known for words; are these his last?" *The Warren Tribune Chronicle*, 11 August 2009.

The WPD became quieter about the late chief. Those on the force who survived him wanted to preserve his memory. Captain Rob Massucci laughed when this reporter asked him about Mandopoulos' legacy. He refused to comment, saying, "I've seen a lot go on. I'd rather not answer. There's a reason why I'm still around here." Officer Jeff Hoolihan respected Mandopoulos because, while he was chief, Hoolihan knew he would have Mandopoulos distracting the media and politicians when it was necessary for sensitive investigations. Even his worst public enemy, Fred Harris remembered Mandopoulos was good with the elderly and that he knew how many bullets he had fired in the course of his career.

◇◇◇

Years later, the mayor's secretary denied Warren had a consent decree, saying it was a "memorandum of understanding" like Warren had in 2002 with the community relations office of the DOJ. On DOJ Office of Public Affairs webpage, it was called a "settlement agreement," based on the determination that the WPD engaged in a pattern or practice of excessive force. When asked what the difference was, the secretary deferred to the mayor, but the mayor didn't respond to more than a dozen calls for comment.

*The Vindicator* reported that the investigation of the WPD had begun in late 2004 after a video "purportedly" showed police using excessive force on Kimble and another video of Mandopoulos and Manny Nites out front of 77 Soul "was described as showing the two acting disrespectfully."[401] Journalist Ed Runyan used verbal forceps while explaining a few of the causes of the DOJ investigation because he had never seen the videos. Nonetheless, the paper reported that the interactions with the DOJ had resulted in various changes to the WPD's use-of-force policy, the citizen complaint process, as well as clarification of disciplinary actions for specific infractions.

Chief Tim Bowers had the opportunity to try out the new disciplinary policy before the end of the year by firing Manny Nites, the officer who had repeatedly used racial slurs, excessive force, and falsified time cards while coaching on-duty, which resulted in the suspension of Lt. Merkel before he became chief. This time, Nites was in trouble because he had lied about attending a fantasy football draft party while on duty. However, a year later, Nites got his job back without pay for the time he was suspended after an arbitrator ruled in his favor.

The first year of the consent decree was marked by noncompliance by the WPD, which was to be expected. The DOJ patted the city on the back for its efforts and then asked for more improvements.

---

[401] Ibid.

In 2013, Eric Merkel became chief. The next year, the WPD had to deal with exactly what they feared most with the DOJ microscope on their performance. There were two officer-involved shootings in the first year Merkel was chief. Both were later ruled justified. On October 19, 2013, veteran Officer Todd Vanasek shot and killed Taemarr Walker, an African American man, while investigating a car that went into the ditch.[402]

Walker was holding an unloaded handgun when he died and he had an assault rifle laying on the backseat. Vanasek stated that Walker initially put his hands up, but then jumped in the backseat, at which point Vanasek pulled out his service revolver. After repeated orders to not touch the gun, Walker jumped in the front seat and reached under it and came up with a handgun. Vanasek shouted and fired five times, hitting Walker each time, while his twenty-one-year-old girlfriend, Regan Jelks, screamed and begged for her life.

Walker had a RAP (record of arrests and prosecutions) sheet and was reportedly on his way to shoot up a local bar.[403] Walker had stolen the assault rifle and was wearing rubber gloves and holding a handgun. It didn't make any sense to dive for an unloaded gun, unless one was trying to commit suicide. The only witness other than Regan Jelks was a tow truck driver who had a dispute with Regan Jelks earlier that night.[404] Jelks, the car's owner, was charged with involuntary manslaughter the same day the prosecutor issued a press release on what happened, which cast shade on her and silenced her from contradicting the officer's account. She was found innocent of manslaughter but guilty of weapons violations and spent six months in prison. Meanwhile, Vanasek was cleared by a grand jury for killing Walker based on his account of what happened.

People in the community were confused as to why the girl needed to be charged in her boyfriend's death when it was the officer who fired the shots, but Assistant Prosecutor Chris Becker wanted her held accountable for Walker's death. He even instructed the jury not to have sympathy for her[405], although she may have been threatened by

---

[402] Ed Runyan. "Grand jury clears officer in death of Warren man, indicts woman." *The Vindicator*, 11 April 2014.

[403] Ed Runyan. "Dash-cam video reveals details of Warren cop shooting aftermath." *The Vindicator*, 15 October 2013.

[404] Christopher Bobby. Officer describes shooting. *Warren Tribune Chronicle*, 11 February 2015.

[405] The Vindicator staff. "Jury will weigh Jelks case this afternoon." 12 February 2015.

Walker and was traumatized by sitting next to her boyfriend while he had a fatal encounter with the WPD that may have not have happened if he were white.

Two years later, Vanasek was exonerated by an IA investigation.[406] The media reported in April of 2014 that the WPD would conclude its investigation of the officer's actions in one month, but instead, it took well over a year. The DOJ reviewed the case, and BCI was also involved. It was a bizarre case that rocked the community, but the investigation was thorough, which is more than could be said of the previous case in which Todd Vanasek had been involved in a shooting death.

In 1993, he fired an "unknown number of times," killing Derek Allen, an African American guy who was holding an infant. Both died. Vanasek's partner, Officer Joseph O'Grady, fired nine times. The Summit County Coroner later inexplicably determined that Allen shot the baby and then himself.[407] Nobody in the media brought up Vanasek's previous shooting, which would have muddied the waters, but one local resident brought it up in a comment below an article on the case. According to Vanasek's account, Walker's killing was arguably justified, but local residents were suspicious due to the history of shoddy investigations, cover-ups, and no policy on lethal force other than invariably exonerating the officer. In the NYPD, 90% of officers will never fire their guns. In that respect, Mando, who fired nine bullets in the course of his career, according to his own count, was unlike 95% of NYPD officers who retire without firing their weapon. Due to his legacy, so was the WPD.

Vanasek accepted a desk job to finish out his career and retire on a public pension. Jelks was later shot and killed in Detroit by an unknown assailant. When asked if there is extra scrutiny of officer-involved shootings that happen in departments under decree, former Assistant Deputy Attorney General Roy Austin responded, "The criminal section doesn't even find out about most of them. When it does find out about, they investigate very few out of that thousand."

While under the consent decree, the WPD seemed to give special treatment to certain officers when it came to discipline. Harris remembered that Mandopoulos had tried to fire Reuben Shaw while he was safety services director, but he refused to let it happen. During Bowers' first year as chief, Shaw had more complaints than any other

---

[406] WKBN staff. "Internal investigation clears Warren officer in Walker shooting." 19 February 2015.

[407] Edgar Simpson and Alyssa Lenhoff. "Disorderly Conduct." *Warren Tribune Chronicle*, 14 April 1996.

officer with Nites narrowly trailing him.[408] Two years later, Reuben Shaw was fired by Chief Merkel for taking a 1969 Chevy Nova from one of Warren's abandoned residences. Shaw had the vehicle towed to a garage where he planned to restore it. For that act, he was charged with three felonies and two misdemeanors.

The decision didn't sit well with Warren's African American community, many of whom had much more harmful acts by white police officers in recent memory. Rev. Philip Shealey, the pastor of Greater Apostolic Faith Church, came to the Trumbull County Court accompanied by other members of the Trumbull County Interdenominational Ministerial Alliance on the day of Shaw's hearing to question the fairness of Reuben's dismissal and arrest. Rev. Shealey questioned why Shaw was fired and charged when "a lot of cases [of WPD officers] were much more serious than what we're dealing with right now...And all they amounted to, pretty much, was a slap on the hand with those officers, and they got their job back, and some even got promotions."[409]

Officer Shaw was accused of excessive force in a lawsuit over a wedding brawl during which Shaw called for backup, and the entire shift of the WPD came in with tasers and mace ready to subdue the entire wedding party. Shaw was one of the brotherhood, even though many other officers and administrators didn't think twice about using racial slurs in front of him. When Fred Harris was safety services director, he and Mayor Angelo tried to get Shaw to inform on the happenings over at WPD, but Shaw wouldn't talk. He wasn't about to betray his brothers in blue. He depended on those guys to have his back. Earlier in Shaw's career, there were internal investigations into occasions when Shaw threatened a gas station attendant's life while off-duty, and when he was accused of choking someone while on duty. The WPD brass covered for Shaw or turned a blind eye, as was their custom.

Despite these and other instances of misconduct, people fought for Shaw's career, because, for them, his firing was a signal that the rotten element of the WPD was still in control. People fought for every African American officer in hopes that they would go easier on the black community. For Fred Harris, Shaw's firing meant also that the mayor, Doug Franklin, was abdicating his authority over the management of the police department in favor of letting Chief Merkel make decisions autonomously. In other words, the WPD was still effectively doing whatever they wanted to do.

Apparently, Law Director Hicks had been doing whatever he

---

[408] Warren Police Department. Internal Affairs Log. 2009.

[409] Ed Runyan. "Men question charges against fired Warren police officer." *The Vindicator*, 5 June 2014.

wanted, as well. In the fall of 2013, *The Tribune Chronicle* reported that Hicks surfaced in a RICO lawsuit over a property one of his bail bondsmen friends owned. Hicks was accused of dithering on the suspension of a bar's liquor license, perhaps because his business partner owned the building. Hicks was unfazed and called the lawsuit "ludicrous."[410]

Two years after Shaw was fired and one year after Vanasek transferred to working in the evidence cage, two officers were disciplined for failing to report excessive force. Ironically, the officer who was fired was not the one who used excessive force; it was the one who lied about it to internal affairs. Officer Chris Martin broke Jimmie White's arm during an arrest, but Officer Jason McCollum kept lying about it, so Chief Merkel fired him. Officer Martin was given a two-day unpaid suspension. Unsurprisingly, IA determined that the use of force was not excessive, although it broke White's arm. Officer McCollum steadfastly maintained that "at no point did Mr. White complain to me about an injury, nor did he ask for medical attention during the booking process at the county jail."[411] When confronted with audio evidence of White asking for medical attention, McCollum claimed he thought White was "joking around."[412]

The IA investigation took five months, instead of forty days, possibly because the chief wanted to give McCollum more opportunities to tell the truth. The first interview with IA took place December 30, 2015. The second took place almost four months later in which McCollum lied again, but none of the newspapers noted that, according to the WPD's own policies, the investigation should have been concluded by the second week of February.

Merkel noted in his statement on the incident that the investigation by the DOJ was prompted by the "lack of reporting and accountability" in cases when force was used by officers.[413] The DOJ initiated its investigation because of excessive force, but, as far as Safety Ser-

---

[410] Ron Selak Jr. "Questions are raised on Hicks." *The Tribune Chronicle*, 11 August 2013.

[411] Ed Runyan. "One Warren police officer has been fired and another suspended for two days over a use-of-force incident in which a man suffered a broken arm." *The Vindicator*, 12 May 2015.

[412] Raymond L. Smith. "Warren cop's firing upheld by safety service director." *Warren Tribune Chronicle*.

[413] Ed Runyan. "One Warren police officer has been fired and another suspended for two days over a use-of-force incident in which a man suffered a broken arm." *The Vindicator.* 12 May 2015.

vices Director Cantalamessa knows, no Warren officer has been fired until this day for excessive force. Cantalamessa specified that he "upheld" McCollum's firing, acknowledging that the chief made the decision. McCollum claimed that his termination was without cause just a few days afterward, and the Ohio Patrolmen's Benevolent Association filed a grievance on his behalf[414], which later resulted in McCollum being rehired.

If the DOJ were not monitoring the WPD, White's complaint against the use-of-force in his arrest would most likely not have resulted in discipline. Even with the DOJ's supervision, the WPD brass gave McCollum and Martin more than three months to come clean. Reuben Shaw didn't get the same opportunity; he was immediately slapped with a litany of criminal charges. Meanwhile, Vanasek shot a guy without an independent investigation by a special prosecutor. Everything hinges on BCI, but BCI doesn't intervene unless the PD, sheriff, or warden requests it. This allows the WPD and every other law enforcement agency to operate much like former days. The WPD pays tribute pay not investigating other law enforcement and corrections fiefs within its jurisdiction. Criminal acts by officials often end with the WPD standing down so the entity can handle it administratively. In other words, the old boy's network still works right under the nose of the DOJ.

---

[414] Warren Tribune Chronicle staff. "Officer appeals firing" 17 May 2016.

## 25

Our town is never going to live this down. People will always think of the rape scandal when they think of Steubenville.

-Anonymous

In December of 2012, four individuals loosely collaborated to publicize an alleged sexual assault that occurred that August in Steubenville, Ohio. The police had made two arrests, and the investigation was ongoing. Several media outlets had published stories, but then an Anonymous activist posted a video on Youtube in which he threatened to "dox" or publish the personal information of all those involved unless they came forward by Christmas. Pretty soon, CNN ran an image of two guys holding the victim by her arms and legs. Once the national press got ahold of images from the night of August 11, 2012, Steubenville's name was pilloried across the nation, traumatizing residents and tarnishing the image of local justice. Media vans camped out in front of the courthouse, and masked activists descended on the town, holding rallies the likes of which residents had never seen and roasting the reputations of everyone even remotely connected to the assault. The case stretched the bounds of what was possible on social media and catalyzed a national conversation about how American culture tends to facilitate the victimization of women.

The night started like many others, with a victory for the local Big Red football team. The game was just a scrimmage, but fans watched it with anticipation for the coming season. The sixteen-year-old girl who would become the most prominent Jane Doe of the next year was with her friends at a house party. She had a mixed drink in a tall cup and a Smirnoff Ice, and she was feeling the euphoria which precedes drunkenness. When her friends wanted to go home, she wanted to keep the party going, so she decided to accompany some football players to the Howarth residence. Once there, Doe's stumbling worsened until she had to be managed, and her body started rejecting the alcohol as she spoke incoherently and dozed off. The Howarths then herded the kids out of their house. Once outside, Doe began vomiting, while one of the guys held her hair back. Anthony Craig testified that they were yelling at her, which would seem to conflict with helpfully holding her hair back.

When they realized how much Doe was helpless and at their mercy, the guys became abusive, labeling her with "whore status" and "sloppy" in tweets. Mark Cole, II's parents weren't home, so they decided to take her there. According to Cole's testimony, during the ride to his house, Cole filmed Mays penetrating her with his finger, while she mumbled unintelligibly. As Doe came in and out of consciousness, feeling nauseous, new videos and photos continued to be produced and then circulated by text message and on social media.

Doe was at the point where she needed to be carried by Ma'-Lik Richmond and Trent Mays. In the process, Cody Saltsman, Jane Doe's ex-boyfriend, took the photo that later made Richmond and Mays nationally known. In court, the guys said she could still walk; that it was just a joke, but nobody was laughing when the photo went up on CNN. Once they got her down in the basement at Cole's house, she felt sick and spent some time in the bathroom. Then, still shirtless, she came out and laid down on her side on the carpet. Anthony Craig texted Mays, "I'm coming with where u at?" and Mays shot back, two minutes later, "Mark, we're hittin it for real." When Craig arrived, Cole went up to let him in. When they came back down, Mays was trying to put his penis into her mouth, and Ma'lik Richmond was down on his side using one hand to finger Doe and the other hand to record it with his phone.[415] Cole said she still had her shorts on, but Anthony Craig testified that Doe was fully naked.

If their testimonies are to be believed, Doe continued to retch on the carpet while this was happening. The guys refused to say or said they didn't know if Mays succeeded in shoving his penis in Doe's mouth. They also propped her up and moved her hand on Mays to simulate a handjob, using Doe like a marionette. Then, Mays allegedly ejaculated on her stomach as she lay on the rug. Doe was said to be conscious and responsive yet dazed and "not herself." Anthony Craig said she looked like she was mostly trying to sleep, but the guys wanted to snoop through her phone, so they asked for her security code, which she provided.

Some of the witnesses claimed they didn't realize what they had witnessed was sexual assault. When Evan Westlake was asked why he didn't help the victim as she lay naked and unconscious on the floor, he told *The Herald-Star*, "I was stunned with what I saw. I wanted to get out of there. I didn't know what to do."[416] Cody Saltsman later posted photos he had taken of her that night and called her a whore in tweets about the incident. Doe had recently broken up with him, and he had threatened revenge on social media. Saltsman reveled in her degra-

---

[415] Staff. "Experts tie DNA evidence to Steubenville football player in rape trial." *Pittsburgh Post-Gazette*, 16 March 2013.

[416] Staff. "Video surfaces, rally set for Saturday." *The Herald-Star*, 3 January 2013.

dation, asking Mays, "I wanna see the vid of u hitting her with your weiner," to which Mays replied, "[I don't know] who took it lol."

Pictures of Jane Doe were later found on Mays' cell phone, while Mark Cole and Anthony Craig admitted that they had deleted images and videos from their phones, for which both could have been indicted. Cole later repeated what he was told by his lawyer; it wasn't his place to determine if what he had witnessed was a sexual assault, and he didn't believe that it was necessary to inform anybody.[417] However, Cole texted Mays the next morning, "Why are you sending pics around?" and ordered him, "Quit sending that around." When Mays didn't seem to take it seriously, Cole admonished, "No really u can't be doing that, is that your jizz on her stomach?" Mays responded, "Yeah, hahaha."

The next morning, they went back over to the Howarth's house, where the guys spent an inordinate amount of time reminiscing and laughing about the assault while recording themselves in a video later posted on social media. Michael Nodianos was front and center in the video laughing uncontrollably about the "dead girl" who they "peed on." With Evan Westlake holding the camera, Nodianos regaled everybody, "They raped her harder than that cop raped Marsellus Wallace in *Pulp Fiction*." A few of the guys seemed uneasy with the glorification of rape, but nobody was going to rain on Nodianos' parade.

Nodianos went on, "You thought it was bad when that girl got raped at Palooza," referring to a previous fourteen-year-old victim, "This is worse."[418] "Palooza," took place at a coach's house two months before Jane Doe. That alleged assault was less well known and did not result in convictions,[419] which is understandable considering that investigators later reportedly found it difficult get the Rape Crew to cooperate.[420] At the end of the video, Nodianos imitated how he expected Ma'Lik to stonewall any allegations which might arise. Westlake, who laughed harder than anybody else in the room, said, "This is the funniest thing ever."

◇◇◇

[417] Ibid.

[418] Torsten Ove. "More charges coming from second rape alleged in Steubenville." *The Toledo Blade*, 12 December 2013.

[419] Ibid.

[420] Staff. "Steubenville rape case: Investigator tells of difficulties getting people to talk; trial resumes at 8:30 a.m. today." *Cleveland.com*, 16 March 2013.

After waking up under a blanket with three boys in an unfamiliar place, Doe was alarmed, embarrassed and unsure of what happened. When she visited the hospital two days later, it was too late for a rape kit. She was reluctant to give the doctors the names of those involved, but Trent Mays and Brian Watson, the prosecutor's son, ended up in the hospital report. Jane Doe testified that she had liked and trusted Trent Mays before that night.[421] She told Anthony Craig in a text, "I think I was drugged. I've drunk more than that before without being fucked up."

In the days following, she and Mays exchanged text messages about what transpired that night. The guys were freaking out about whether Doe was going to tell the police. She tried to give comfort to Mays, assuring him she wouldn't go to the police. "We know you didn't rape me," she told him, but she wanted to know why people were saying otherwise. Mays told her that although she was a hassle they "took care of her." When she confronted him about the rumors on social media, Mays replied, "You know what happened, there's no video, so nothing happened...This is the most pointless thing. I am gonna get in trouble for nothing." After watching the videos, she plied him with questions, and he clarified, "That was my cum on you, not piss." Doe ended the conversation with a warning, "It's on Youtube. I'm not stupid. Stop texting me."

When Jane Doe's parents went to report the crime, Prosecutor Gail Cullen allegedly discouraged them from filing charges. According to an unverified report from *Local Leaks*, Cullen told the family that her name would be dragged through the mud.[422] The family then felt obliged to appease Cullen, who recovered herself, and assured them that she and her detectives would take care of everything. *Local Leaks* made several reporting errors, and the report was never verified, but that didn't stop people from believing it. Cullen received death threats and other hateful communications through every medium that could be found by random angry observers.

The detective investigating the allegations was given material that had been posted online, tweets and a Youtube link to Nodianos' rant. He then interviewed Jane Doe's parents, as well as Anthony Craig, Jake Howarth, Mark Cole, Michael Nodianos, and other persons of interest. By the 16 of August, warrants were executed to collect the phones of Cole, Westlake, Mays, Saltsman, and Craig. Then, on August 22, the detective met with Prosecutor Cullen and Frank Bruzzese to

---

[421] Connor Simpson. "The Steubenville victim tells her story." *The Atlantic*, 16 March 2013.

[422] Local leaks. "Steubenville Files."

consider indictments. Afterward, Ma'lik Richmond and Trent Mays were arrested on Cullen's recommendation. While the police brought in Richmond and Mays, three other persons of interest in the case lawyered up, using the time given to them by the county prosecutor to get their stories straight and strategize.

Prosecutor Cullen knew several of the "persons of interest" in the case because they were her son's friends. After two weeks had elapsed, she recused herself for a conflict of interests. Doe later absolved Cullen's son from the stand, saying she wasn't sure who mentioned his name in the hospital. Maybe, she became too scared to implicate the prosecutor's son, Brian Watson. Even years later, local suspicion remained focused on Watson, but the judge said he "wasn't interested in gossip,"[423] so the question of Watson's involvement was never officially put to rest. A local lawyer stressed the word "presented" when he said, "No evidence was ever presented of [Watson's] involvement." For his proximity, real or perceived, to the crime, the family received death threats. The cloud of suspicion followed Watson as he tried to plan for his future, and outraged people contacted a college that offered him a scholarship.

Westlake refused to give a DNA sample. Richmond's lawyer stated, "There was DNA evidence found in [Jane Doe's] underwear, and it wasn't Richmond's DNA. [Westlake's] attorney said they weren't going to give a DNA sample, and the judge accepted that."[424] Westlake admitted to creating what could have been considered child pornography and that he had deleted it from his phone, also an indictable offense. Nevertheless, Westlake wasn't interviewed until October, and then he was given immunity because he agreed to testify. Sixteen individuals refused to talk to investigators, and none of them faced charges.

Trent Mays told Jane Doe that Saccoccia had called his house and accused Mays and his friends of rape, adding that Mays should, "tell her dad the truth."[425] Coach Reno knew who was involved but claimed that he didn't use the internet and wouldn't know about any photographs or videos circulating online. The guys close to the scandal started deleting images of the night once they got nervous about the

---

[423] Staff. "Steubenville rape case: Investigator tells of difficulties getting people to talk; trial resumes at 8:30 a.m. today." *Cleveland.com*, 16 March 2013.

[424] Staff. "Steubenville rape case: Investigator tells of difficulties getting people to talk; trial resumes at 8:30 a.m. today." *Cleveland.com*, 16 March 2013.

[425] Connor Simpson. "The Steubenville victim tells her story." *The Atlantic*, 16 March 2013.

digital trail of evidence on their cell phones. In response to concerns over this issue, Anthony Craig texted Mays, "Nah, I don't give a fuck, I got Reno he took care of it, nothing gonna happen even if it goes to court."

The police confiscated seventeen cell phones but were unable to recover many images of the assault,[426] possibly because Coach Reno Saccoccia did take care of it. When asked by a *New York Times* reporter why he didn't discipline the players he knew were involved, Coach Reno warned, "You're going to get yours. And if you don't get yours, somebody close to you will."[427] As the head football coach, a close friend of Sheriff Abdalla and employee of the local juvenile court, Saccoccia knew that he was untouchable, and he was right. He never faced charges, and his contract was later renewed, despite widespread criticism.

The probable cause hearing, which took place in October 2012, was focused on cellphone evidence and questioning the guys whose cellphones produced the evidence for the prosecution. During the hearing, Anthony Craig and Walter Madison, Richmond's attorney, made repeated, crass references to Craig and Doe's past relationship. When the prosecutor asked Anthony Craig if he and Doe were dating, Craig said, "Some may look at it as that, so you know."[428] Later, Madison might as well have winked and nudged Craig when he asked, "You didn't go with her. She wasn't your steady. You were just fooling around, right?" Reading the transcript, one could get the idea that the guys enjoyed degrading Doe in front of her family, in front of the media, and in front of the judge.

Anthony Craig, who had just turned eighteen a few days before the assault, admitted under oath that he had withheld from investigators that he took and later erased a couple photos of Richmond and Mays assaulting Doe. Craig additionally testified that Mays had later slapped Doe's hip with his penis, of which there was allegedly a video, as well, also deleted. "Just wait till she wakes up if you're going to do any of this stuff, don't do anything you're going to regret," Craig said to Mays. Mays was like, "Don't worry. It's alright." After telling this to the court, the prosecutor asked "How do you feel about testifying about this?" Craig responded, "It kills me." It also killed him to tell investiga-

---

[426] Staff. "Experts tie DNA evidence to Steubenville football player in rape trial." *Pittsburgh Post-Gazette*, 16 March 2013.

[427] Juliet Macur and Nate Schweber. "Rape case unfolds on web and splits city." *The New York Times*, 16 December 2012.

[428] Richmond and Mays. Jefferson County Ct., Juv. Div. 12 October 2012. Page 108.

tors the truth during three interviews.

Under cross-examination by the defense attorney, the arresting officer admitted that although there was no evidence at that time linking Ma'lik Richmond to the assault, they had probable cause to believe that he had participated based on interviews with witnesses and Nodianos' rant. The evidence from the phones had not been produced yet, so the defense counsel tried to suggest the arrest was lacking in probable cause. The judge wasn't having it, and the charges went forward. Steubenville resident Dan Walker Sr. obtained a transcript of the hearing and posted it online. In response, city officials demanded he remove it or face prosecution. It was later posted online by another, unconnected party.

The testimonies of Mark Cole, Anthony Craig, and Evan Westlake together established probable cause that Trent Mays had committed rape and pandering. Cole testified that he had witnessed Mays finger and carry Doe while she was unable to consent, and the photos found on his phone incriminated him for pandering, or producing pornographic images of minors. Prosecutor Marianne Hemmeter summed up the evidence presented against Richmond in support of charging him with rape, "...we have the digital penetration in the basement of the Cole residence...Anthony Craig says it. Mark Cole says it. But in particular, Even Westlake, who is right behind him and can see what's going on, specifically testifies two fingers in and out of her vagina."

Then, she addressed the question of whether Doe was too impaired to consent, "The State doesn't have to prove that she was flatlined, but it's clear during both of these digital penetrations, she was not in the state to consent." In particular, all the witnesses described that Doe was stumbling, puking, partially conscious and unable to speak coherently if at all. The prosecutor said pointedly, "All the boys in the back seat are laughing. She's not."

In the months afterward, the actions of authorities were scrutinized, and rumors swarmed online and in town. Alexandria Goddard, an activist blogger from Steubenville living in California, was publishing information about the case. Michelle McKee, an activist in Washington state, became involved when Cody Saltsman sued Goddard for defamation. Goddard and McKee later passed on what they had gathered to Deric Lostutter, a programmer in Kentucky.

Lostutter was a participant of the hacktivist collective Anonymous, a ragtag online army of hackers, activists, and trolls. Anonymous targets organizations or individuals with cyber attacks for diverse ideological reasons usually having to do with alleged privacy, transparency or civil liberties violations, but there is little coherence among Anons on ideology, methods, or motive. After getting a general idea of the crime and alleged cover-up, Lostutter reached out to Noah McHugh to ask for his help on a hack saying could draw attention and publicity to the crime and their exploits. Unbeknownst to Lostutter and McHugh, their conversation would later be used by the prosecution to highlight their ignoble goals.

Lostutter then whipped up a manifesto to read in an Anonymous operation video, the equivalent of a press release announcing group action. In the video shot on his webcam, Lostutter appeared like a grim hooded vision of death in his Guy Fawkes mask, and the voice was computer-generated, uneven, and robotic. Lostutter described Doe being "raped and drug unconscious from party to party," and threatened to "dox" or release the personal information of the entire football team unless those involved publicly apologized to the victim and her family by new year's day. He then declared, "You have attracted the attention of the hive. We will not sit tightly by while a group of young men who turn to rape as a game or sport get the pass because of athletic ability…"

His description of the crime diverged from what was described in testimony, but since the video included screenshots of several tweets from Nodianos that went against the story the witnesses described under oath, it wasn't clear what was true. Nodianos tweeted, "You don't sleep through a wang in the butthole," and "RIP to the person that died, you went out doin it big," but then witnesses testified that no one raped Doe. Either Nodianos lied about rape trying to be cool, or members of the Rape Crew lied under oath. Farrah Marcino claimed that she had seen pictures of Mays sodomizing Doe at Jake Howarth's house, in a text to Mays. When Mays denied it, she accused him of lying, "I saw the picture's at Jake's. They were showing them all around." Mays held firm, "No, you didn't. You'll feel salty when the DNA results come back."

Lostutter posted the video online and went to bed.[429] Since it was a few nights before Christmas, the thirteen men Lostutter named in the video, as well as current principal and faculty, were obliged to worry, guilty or otherwise. No one knew what horrors Anonymous would unleash, but locals anxiously googled them, as Lostutter had instructed. Noah McHugh had already hacked into the website of the football team's booster club by correctly guessing the password. Not long after the "Operation Roll Red Roll" video went online, McHugh posted the video of Nodianos on the homepage of Big Red Booster Club. Lostutter's actions brought the national media networks into Steubenville to

---

[429] David Kushner. "Anonymous Vs. Steubenville." *Rolling Stone*, 27 November 2013.

cover the story. All the negative attention infuriated many locals who felt protective of their hometown and its football team.

Within days, Anonymous held a rally in front of the courthouse, and three to four hundred protesters showed up. This rowdy assembly sent a shockwave through Steubenville and beyond. One resident, who insisted his last name not be used out of fear of masked activists, asked city council, "Can anything be done about our town being invaded by these people? Other states and cities have laws against wearing masks. If we came up with a city code against wearing masks maybe we would get rid of the riff-raff."[430]

*The Herald-Star* announced that another rally was upcoming and that the Facebook page of the event already had more than 1,200 attendees. At the second rally, in front of 1,300 protesters, Sheriff Abdalla assured those assembled that the situation was being handled according to the law. He had only just seen the video that Lostutter posted of Nodianos and other members of the Rape Crew, showing their utter contempt for the victim, which Abdalla found "disgusting." All the same, Sheriff Abdalla threatened that he was "coming after Anonymous."[431]

Meanwhile, the Bruzzeses set up a website called "SteubenvilleFacts.com" to defend their own. They hired a Lee Stranahan, a journalist at *Breitbart*, to help them take control of the narrative and combat the allegations on social media. He was given the transcript of the probable cause hearing and license to disparage Doe. Meanwhile, Frank Bruzzese went to bat for his former employee Gail Cullen. His support wasn't surprising, considering the local prosecutor, the local judge, his son, and virtually all of the influential officials of the county currently work or previously worked at Bruzzese & Calabria.

On Facebook, Frank Bruzzese glossed over the details and dates, sticking to particular facts. Bruzzese didn't mention that he had represented Cullen in her divorce or that she had helped make his firm the general counsel of Trinity Medical Center where she was formerly an administrator. He didn't mention that Cullen had served on the school board alongside his wife until Cullen became prosecutor, at which point she became the school's general counsel. Knowing all this, many locals were disinclined to believe him.

Judge Joseph J. Bruzzese, Jr., Frank's brother, blamed "nameless bloggers" who made allegations of a cover-up. Like everybody else, he went after the messengers, rather than the teenage perpetrators

---

[430] Staff. "Council hears comments on rallies." *The Herald-Star*, 16 January 2013.

[431] Connor Simpson. "Occupy Steubenville: Anonymous vs. the Sheriff." *The Atlantic Wire*, 5 January 2013.

of the scandal and their adult accomplices.[432] This statement may have galvanized angry locals to terrorize the bloggers. According to the victim's impact statement she submitted in his criminal hacking case, Prosecutor Cullen blamed Deric Lostutter. She wrote, "His actions ignited protests, hundreds of unknown masked individuals paraded through our town, thousands and thousands of death threats were issued...virtually every form of communication was used to threaten and terrify the people of Steubenville."

Cullen held Lostutter responsible for the catching the attention of the national media, after which "matters only worsened," as the ire of the nation was directed at individuals in Steubenville, including Cullen and her family. "I believe with all of my heart that none of this would have happened had Deric Lostutter not inserted himself into a case that did not require any action from him whatsoever." She may have been right about this, but blaming the activists conveniently ignores the fact that they could not have intervened without the loud bragging, shaming, and harassment by Cullen's son's friends. Had they been less proud to publicly aggrandize the crime and share documentary evidence, Lostutter and the bloggers would never have attracted the attention of the media.

<><><>

Two months later, the trial took place with a visiting judge and a special prosecutor in the Jefferson County Juvenile Court building on the banks of the Ohio River. It was a brisk, cloudless spring day. A few dozen Anonymous protesters holding signs and several media vans took up space around the courthouse. Sheriff Abdalla came and went, standing a head above the bevy of BCI agents in baggy suits trailing him. A lone relative of Jane Doe held a sign displaying a message of support.

For the most part, everyone was collegial in public, but in private, with their fingers on a keyboard, trolling turned into harassment. Many parties involved in the case had to cope with death threats. Anonymous published Gail Cullen's work and home address online, and terror enveloped her family life when she received rape threats and threats against her children and their home. The family went into protective custody during the trial.

On March 17, 2013, Trent Mays was sentenced to two years for sexual assault and sharing a photo of the assault while Ma'lik Richmond got one year for sexual assault. Tears streamed down both of their faces after the word "guilty," and both apologized to the victim

---

[432] Jim Provance. "Jury sought to probe cover-up in rape case." *Pittsburgh Post-Gazette*, 19 March 2013.

and her family. Jane Doe's mother told CNN, "We hope that from this something good can arise. I feel I have an opportunity to bring an awareness to others...The adults need to take responsibility and guide these children." The sentence for the defendants seemed rather short, as Lostutter fought a losing battle in federal court against a maximum of ten years in prison for hacking while Mays and Richmond were out of prison and looking at colleges. Nevertheless, most observers were relieved that, at a minimum, somebody was convicted.

Right after the verdict, more embarrassing controversy erupted because two teenage girls close to Richmond threatened bodily harm and death to Jane Doe on Twitter. They were both charged for making threats. Sheriff Abdalla lamented, "People didn't learn from the trial...You cannot make threats or these type of comments on the Internet." He was correct, it was a bad idea to do it online, but death threats had a long and colorful history in the region as a tool of business and politics, popularized by the mob and private terror groups like the KKK.

During the lead-up to the trial, the atmosphere was so toxic that some local high schoolers were afraid to go to class. Even after the verdict was handed down, rumors and threats continued to swirl, and everyone from Steubenville faced demoralizing questions about the rape case whenever they ventured out of the city limits. Alexandria Goddard found herself worn down and beset by personal turmoil because of an online stalking and harassment campaign directed against her and a defamation lawsuit filed by Cody Saltsman's family. The rape case brought the town years of grief, bitterness, and division, although without the intervention of Lostutter and Anonymous, perhaps that grief and bitterness would have been born by a smaller group of people. It likely would have fallen on the victim's family alone.

In the aftermath, questions over the case dogged the town. When asked what he thought of the verdict, Richard Olivito told a reporter, "I think it's a great sense of relief for a lot of women...The young girl took the stand, and it took a lot of courage to do that." He went on, "Beyond that, there are questions of what happened at the beginning of this investigation. And that goes even to the history of what I was involved with in Steubenville. Were the officials involved to a certain extent to protect some families that otherwise would not be—maybe should be joining Ma'lik and Trent?"[433]

When asked, the editor of *The Herald-Star*, Ross Gallabrese said, "Gail Cullen recused herself in a timely manner. The AG was thorough. People think there was a cover-up. Certainly, outsiders have this perception. It really depends on whether you're a fan of Big Red Football." If *The Herald-Star* chose not to investigate these allegations,

---

[433] Staff. "'Jane Doe' supporters view verdicts as 'win.'" *WTRF.com*.

then it seemed no amount of speculation could unravel the truth of the matter.

Later, a juvenile detective from the SPD, Jean-Philippe Rigaud, later got a job at BCI,[434] and Ed Lulla, the first BCI agent to come down to Steubenville to oversee the investigation, got his son hired on the SPD. The president of the Civil Service Commission (CSC) Delores Wiggins acknowledged that Lulla was the "fifth-ranked candidate" on the exam, but since he already had experience as a police officer, they passed over the four candidates who scored higher. Wiggins fiercely contested the rumor that Lulla's son was hired as a favor to Prosecutor Cullen.[435]

Many people in Steubenville and around the country came away with the impression that there was a cover-up and that Reno Saccoccia, the football coach, as well as Michael McVey, the school superintendent, should have faced criminal charges for destruction of evidence and obstruction of justice.

The scandal left a stain on the collective conscience that could not be expunged. In place of the catharsis of justice, there was a malaise in the perception that the law didn't apply to certain people. Despite the years of court-ordered oversight and negative press, it seemed like Steubenville was still a place where, with few exceptions, a white man could do as he pleased, counting on the support of the old boys' network. Those who wanted to know more turned to social media and the blogosphere where every theory could be hashed out publicly, regardless of evidence and people's reputations. Still, plenty of people were more concerned about the town's reputation, and some went to extremes to defend it, resorting to harassment and threats to quell talk of corruption and cover-ups.

On a blog called Radionewz, a user called Harold Star provided an insider analysis. The name was a snide reference to *The Herald-Star*, which seemed to do damage control for the powerful during the scandal. Harold Star wanted to expose the corrupt actions and relationships of the Jefferson County elite. Star argued that Cullen delayed two weeks to recuse knowing that the usual choices from nearby counties would have been aggressive. The Trumbull County Chief Assistant Prosecutor Chris Becker and then-Harrison County Prosecutor T. Shawn Hervey both had the reputation of filing charges against any and all involved, Star explained. Next, Harold Star listed the potential charges that should have been considered: voyeurism, intimidation, tampering with evidence, failure to report a crime, obstructing official

---

[434] Ibid.

[435] Staff. "Council hears comments on rallies." *The Herald-Star*, 16 January 2013.

business, obstructing justice, dereliction of duty, interfering with civil rights, conspiracy and complicity.[436] Then, Star criticized the AG's special prosecutors:

> The state prosecutors didn't file all applicable charges because they got the case after the Jefferson County Prosecutor had already filed the charges...The state prosecutors merely proceeded from there. They didn't start new or fresh.

> The state prosecutors merely took what was given to them. If they were experienced prosecutors and understood criminal law and procedure, they would have scratched everything done by the county prosecutor and local law enforcement because of the possibility that the matter had been already tainted and compromised.

> The reason for a "special prosecutor" is to look anew at everything, not to routinely take over what the former prosecutor did.

Harold Star was one of many who spoke out against the way things were handled. AG Mike DeWine said on television that no one was going to get immunity, but then everybody avoided charges, which amounted to the same if they had committed a crime yet refused to cooperate. Harold Star alleged that this happened because of Cullen's connections: she is married to a Steubenville police officer and holds various local appointments on boards and commissions that may have shielded this move from contest. Cullen had represented one of the BCI agents that came to investigate in a civil matter, and his son later received a job at the SPD. When asked if Cullen tried to get the son of the BCI agent a job at the SPD as a favor, Delores Wiggins, current president of the CSC, denied it, "Cullen doesn't have that kind of clout. I don't play dirty politics. I don't care who you are; I cherish and honor my name. A good name is better than money. There's nothing wrong with politics. It's just the people behind the politics."

Cullen blamed Deric Lostutter for creating a climate of fear and intimidation with his dramatic narrative of the assault and alleged cover-up. According to Cullen, before December 2012, the investigation was moving along without problems. Most witnesses were cooperating, she said, and the perpetrators would have been punished without Lostutter and others' intervention. The firestorm of the national media

---

[436] Anonymous. "The Steubenville Rape Crew and Steubenville's Incestuous Legal Community." *Austinisafecker.wordpress Blog*, 13 January 2013.

around the scandal and the rallies of Anonymous caused a chilling effect on witnesses, impeding the investigation.

Steubenville resident Beverly Kelley wasn't buying it. She says the city administration is "dirty rotten to the core." She went on, "[The rape case] made me sick. I was like, 'Wow.' How they did that poor girl from West Virginia, all those adults in it. McVey got a slap on the wrist, that man should be in prison..." McVey was allowed to resign from his position as school board superintendent without facing charges. Beverly Kelley didn't trust the AG's Office to expose the misconduct, stating, "Mike DeWine came down to okay everything, and he stuck down here until he got his payoff. This is common knowledge around Steubenville." Kelley alleged that the 2014-gambling bust by BCI in Steubenville, which netted $1.5 million, was DeWine's payoff.[437] Beverly pointed out that no previous raid in Steubenville history had netted so much money.

When asked why people don't complain, she responded, "They so dirty, you don't know what they liable to do. The majority of the cops are bad. The problem is Frank and Joe Bruzzese is running this city and Gail Cullen backs them up." Kelley's experience with local police and officials informs her opinion, but she isn't the only one who suspects the city government of foul play. Speaking on condition of anonymity, a local attorney stated, "Everybody who was anybody was involved in that rape case." Another resident, who asked to remain anonymous, stated:

> That rape case was a joke. I believe in my heart that Gail Cullen's son was involved in that. It was rumored all over town. People are still talking about it right now. There's a whole lot more, and it's terrible. You got families that are running this town. That law firm is running this town.

When asked about the rumors of immunity given to perpetrators and adult accomplices, Chief McCafferty raised his voice, "After all the turmoil in this town! These are conspiracy theories! Those guys were guilty!"

Steubenville residents are quick to acknowledge that today the town is different from the days when the DOJ came to investigate; when the chief went around collecting bribes, the days when locals decried the nickname Little Chicago. However, for some observers, the rape case exposed a pattern of misconduct reminiscent of those days. Again, as of old, prosecutorial discretion shielded some at the expense of others, and as when the DOJ was in town, the prosecutor was untouchable. In the Fall of 2013, former prosecutor Stern formally offered to advise the SPD on "investigative and enforcement strategies we

---

[437] Staff. "$1.5 million seized in illegal gambling investigation." *WKY-C.com*, 20 May 2014.

found successful two decades ago," as a "free community service."[438] The inclusion of John Myers, the gypsy cop who Stern employed as a secret service agent, suggested Stern would recommend the same strategies that brought the DOJ into Jefferson County.

Older residents believed the mob controlled the long arm of the law. An octogenarian female born and raised in Steubenville remarked, "The Black Hand has always run this town, and they always return to power." Sources back in Ohio's history document how closely the mob was tied to local politics, regardless of which party was in power. Norman E. Nygarrd, the minister and author an account of the mid-century revolt against organized crime in Steubenville, included this surprising admission by a Republican politician:

> 'I was elected by gamblers' money. I don't like it, and I haven't sold my soul to them, but that's where some of the money comes from which carries on these campaigns. Of course,' he added, with a twinkle in his eye, 'we Republicans are more honest than the Democrats for the gamblers give us less money.' It should be noted, however, that during the grand jury sessions, when the chairman of the Republican party was asked to testify regarding contributions, that he submitted the list without demur and the names of no gamblers were included. When asked to submit the list of contributors to the Democratic party funds the chairman of the Democratic party refused to testify or to submit his list. The whole political situation was undoubtedly chock-full of graft, and it was generally known that on occasion deals would be made by which one party or another would withdraw from the field and leave the other dominant in exchange for a similar concession elsewhere. And frequently, when a decent man ran for office, the entire weight of politics would be thrown against him.[439]

Campaign contributions did not discriminate by political party. The only logic of the donors was pragmatism. They wanted results. It was the same with the mob. The *Cleveland Scene* Magazine reported that bribery was widespread; "virtually the entire Mahoning County legal system...judges, county prosecutors, law directors, sheriffs, and policemen... With so many public officials on the take, short-circuiting standard legal procedures was relatively easy."[440]

---

[438] Staff. "Police arrest tape requested." *The Herald-Star,* 25 September 2013.

[439] Norman E. Nygarrd. 12 Against The Underworld. *The Hobson Book Press*. 1947. Page 145.

[440] Mike Tobin. "End of the Line." *The Cleveland Scene*, 8 April 1999.

## 26

Steubenville is nothing like it was before the consent decree...Maybe it is time to have a younger set of eyes take a fresh look at where Steubenville is.

-Anonymous

Steubenville got a fresh look by the national media in August of 2017 when Ma'Lik Richmond's dad got in a shootout with Judge Joseph J. Bruzzese, Jr. and lost. Unfortunately, the national media stampeded the wrong direction as to the cause of the shootout. On the morning of August 20, Nathaniel Richmond waited for the judge to pull up to his reserved space in the alley beside the courthouse, less than a block from the police station. Richmond approached Judge Bruzzese as he walked from his Jeep and opened fire at close range, wounding the judge in the stomach. A witness said he couldn't believe his eyes; Richmond walked right up on the judge, firing his weapon various times, but he kept missing. Having dropped his gun, Richmond pushed the judge to the ground and took to his heels, but Judge Bruzzese was packing and returned fire with his revolver. Then, a probation officer showed up and shot Richmond at least three times. Richmond tried to return to and re-enter his car, on the passenger side, after which he succumbed to his injuries and the car rolled into another parked car. Curtis Golsby, Richmond's friend who had been drinking with him all night was hiding in Richmond's car. Golsby drove the car, but when he heard gunshots, he moved into the passenger seat, then the floor. He was taken to Trinity under guard, after which he was questioned by detectives.

Richmond had hit the judge twice in the stomach, and as Judge Bruzzese lay bleeding on the ground, Judge Michelle Miller rendered first aid. Gail Cullen and Bruzzese's wife Lisa were contacted, after which the judge was taken to a hospital in Pittsburgh. The city closed the courthouse for the rest of the day, but investigators swarmed the area taking pictures and collecting evidence. *The Herald-Star* posted an article around noon, which gathered dozens of comments, unanimous in support, but interpreting the event in diverse political ways. Those who knew Richmond or who didn't like the Bruzzeses kept quiet. Relatives said Richmond had been shot eight times, and they didn't believe the official story.

The assassination attempt had little if anything to do with the rape case, but the media focused on that link to remind people of Steubenville. A few outlets got the story right, but nobody dug into the story. Richmond's motive revolved around Bruzzese's upcoming ruling in a civil lawsuit over the death of Richmond's mother in a 2015-fire in a Jefferson Metropolitan Housing Authority (JMHA) apartment building. Resident Rosalind Watson concurred, "What he was mad about was his mother." The eleven-page investigation of Richmond's shooting released in response to a record request did not mention a motive.

On April 27, 2015, 70-year-old grandmother Mae Etta Richmond died with her two-year-old grandson, Te'on Lavar Dillard. They were on a roof engulfed in flames, while below officers shouted for her to jump. They had broken the fall of two children who leaped from the flames[441], but before she could do so, the roof collapsed. A police officer reported, "We pleaded with [her] to jump, and she would not." Richmond's granddaughter Cawanna said, "She was afraid to drop off the roof. She was confused."

Various relatives watched the scene in horror as the fire department showed up but couldn't get water from the fire hydrant. Mae Etta Richmond's daughter Valerie wondered, "What kind of fire truck arrives to a fire with no ladder and no hose?" The first fire truck on the scene didn't have a ladder. After the second fire truck arrived, they put a ladder up to the roof, but then it collapsed. When the roof collapsed, Mae Richmond's body fell with it. Officer Kuhn was on the scene, "Richmond appeared disoriented and failed to exit the roof. We observed Richmond lay down in the prone position and perish while smoke and flames surrounded her." Nate Richmond had to be restrained from going into the house.

The assistant state fire marshal concluded, "I could not eliminate unattended cooking as a possible ignition source for this incident. The cause of this fire is undetermined." Cawanna Loveless, Nate Richmond's niece, said that she had cooked enough corn beef and cabbage, macaroni and cheese, and cornbread for fifteen people that evening, so she argued there was no way anybody would have been cooking later that night. The fire marshal informed the police that they would need to obtain statements from the adult male and two juveniles who escaped the fire, noting that the detectives reported that they had not been able to get ahold of them. Apparently, they gave up, the investigation of the fire later released by the city in response to a record request was only twenty-six pages, in which the issue of unattended cooking was never resolved, conveniently for the city, which produced

---

[441] Gregory and Martin Funeral Service. Master Te'on Lavar Dillard. 2012 - 2017.

an investigation twice as long for a white kid allegedly hit in the head with a police flashlight.

On April 25, 2017, surviving relatives filed a wrongful death lawsuit in the Jefferson County Court of Common Pleas, naming four employees as defendants and alleging that the JMHA had been warned that the public housing unit was a fire hazard but failed to fix long-standing problems, including exposed electrical wires and defective smoke detectors.[442] The electrical system was overloaded by the appliances, creating frequent shorts, sparks, and breakdowns. Richmond's attorneys filed a motion claiming that JMHA had destroyed the house to disadvantage the plaintiff's case.[443]

Mae Etta Richmond's granddaughter Cawanna said:

Every time we plugged in something at my grandma's house, there were sparks. Every time you'd do the laundry, it would take down the power in the rest of the house. I told my grandma she had an electrical problem and that she needed to move since they wouldn't fix anything, but she would say, 'I'm too old to move again.' Can't nobody tell me that house burned down for no reason. Housing has been a problem here for years, but they just take the money and do what they want with it."

Mae Etta Richmond's daughter Audrey verified that her mother frequently complained about the repairs needed in her house. She said, "I know [the city] gets money from the government. It isn't being used like it's supposed to." In fact, Steubenville had to return $751,349 of federal funds to the U.S. Department of Housing & Urban Development (HUD).[444] The Office of the Inspector General of HUD investigated, at the request of a local congressman. Someone familiar with the investigation who wished to remain anonymous remarked:

The IOG investigated. They found a conflict with a board member's relationship to a contractor, but the [inspector general] couldn't track how the finance director disbursed the money. He was that good at covering his tracks.

Nathaniel Richmond had been a diligent observer of the housing problems in town going back to the 90s. He saved every article on

---

[442] Mark Law. Wrongful death suit filed against JMHA. *The Herald-Star*. 27 April 2017.

[443] Mark Law. Jefferson County Commissioner: Courthouse staff's 'home has been violated.' *The Intelligencer / Wheeling News-Register*. 24 August 2017.

[444] Dave Gossett. JMHA owes HUD $751,349, auditors say. *The Herald-Star*, 26 January 2017.

the topic from the local papers and was consistently involved in discussions of municipal housing policy for low-income residents as a member of the Resident Advisory Board[445] and the Consolidated Planning Committee.[446] Olivito said of Richmond, "He understood the local insiders game. [He] had been in town for more than a decade and was a student of these things." For that, he was not well liked by the authorities in Jefferson County.

According to the lawsuit, the defendants were made aware by an inspection company of over one-hundred "life-threatening" conditions in the unit. In June 2017, Richmond told his sister Valerie that the city offered to settle the case for under 10K, but he rejected the deal. She said, "Five or seven thousand for two lives lost that should still be here. Nate wouldn't accept. We couldn't do a memorial with five thousand."

There was a hearing scheduled for August 28 on the issue of the JMHA's motion to dismiss the punitive damage claim in Richmond's case.[447] Judge Bruzzese was likely to approve the motion to prohibit punitive damages and eventually dismiss the case, as he had three previous lawsuits against the authority. Richmond was tenacious, always waiting with documents in tow, asking to talk to the judge who was disinclined to see him. Not to mention long-standing issues of security and want of services which call for the court's constant vigilance, both judges are involved in decision-making over JMHA, so it was unfortunate that Richmond's attorney was obliged to file the case in the Jefferson County Court. Official planning documents filed with HUD reflect that the county court was invested with the appointment one of five members of JMHA's board.[448]

Mysteriously, Richmond's attorney, Stuart Scott, withdrew as counsel the week before the next hearing. Three days later, Richmond was dead, and his relatives were obliged to pick up where he left off, provided they could find an attorney to refile the lawsuit. When he died, his relatives were not aware that the attorney backed out. Audrey

[445] U.S. Department of Housing and Urban Development. PHA Plans: 5 Year Plan for Fiscal Years 2005 - 2009. 6 October 2008.

[446] Steubenville Fair Housing Practices Commission. Analysis of Impediments to Fair Housing (AI) for the City of Steubenville, Ohio. *City of Steubenville*. July 2010.

[447] Associated Press. The Latest: Wounded Ohio judge oversaw suspect's lawsuit. *McClatchy DC Bureau*. 21 August 2017.

[448] U.S. Department of Housing and Urban Development. PHA Plans: 5 Year Plan for Fiscal Years 2005 - 2009. 6 October 2008.

said, "I don't understand this lawyer we had. Calls me Friday and tells me the case has been dropped. Monday, Nathaniel is dead. He didn't give us no notice. He sold us out. Somebody got him." She concluded, "Steubenville is the most corrupt place I have been in my life."

Cawanna confirmed in early 2018 that the graves of their dead relatives still lacked headstones because the family gave all their money to their former attorney. The official narrative makes no sense to them. Cawanna explained, "They said there was a suicide note and an insurance policy, but we had already been there, and nobody seen no letter. That's bullshit." She reported that their efforts to retain counsel to refile the lawsuit have failed so far. They have until the anniversary of Richmond's death in August to refile, before the questions surrounding his death, as well as the cause of fire that killed their beloved 77-year-old mother, are buried forever with prejudice in Little Chicago.

<><><>

In recent decades, Steubenville's downtown has been withering away. Empty storefronts outnumber those occupied, and display windows showcase ancient vacuum cleaners. Owners of decrepit, decaying properties seem to be having their buildings torched for the insurance, which gives business to local demolition and redevelopment companies. The roads are crumbling to the point that the ubiquitous 4x4 trucks actually seem necessary. However, there are some signs of vitality and rebirth. The writer's club meets on Wednesday evenings in the local bookstore on 4th Street, a few doors down from a spacious new cafe called Leonardo's.

The Big Red football team has a cult-like following, and the most recent crop of high schoolers, including those involved with the rape in 2012, has gone off to college. People still wonder what happened behind the scenes with the rape case, but no new information is forthcoming. New people knowing little of the town's past continue to arrive, and *The Herald-Star* relentlessly keeps up the chipper small-town narrative. The reputational wounds in Steubenville are still fresh and smarting, but rocking the boat makes powerful people angry. When asked about corruption or official misconduct, a local guy replied, "I stay in my lane." Other members of the community complain of payoffs and racial bias.

Few officials remain from the days of Prosecutor Stern and Chief McCartney. Stern moved to Florida and became a vicious tennis player. McCartney moved to Myrtle Beach. Skip Mixon, the outspoken African American councilman, passed away. However, Mayor Mucci, County Clerk Corrigan, and Sheriff Abdalla remain in their positions. McNamara gives credit to Law Director Repella, who retired in 2017, for being "ahead of his time," because, "he could see that the old ways were not helping the community." During an interview in 2016, Repella noted that McNamara that brought "almost all of the cases" against the city with the caveat that "I don't think McNamara ever sued us again [after the decree]." He recalled, "Since then, maybe around four or five, not like we had before. That's for sure."

Olivito took issue with the lack of lawsuits as evidence of substantive reform, arguing that he and McNamara didn't stop filing lawsuits because of improvement, but rather from exhaustion and frustration. Nevertheless, Repella continued, "because of what we went through with the consent decree, we're in a better position now to defend. We can now show a jury, here's all our training, here's a disciplinary process, before the decree we would have been in big trouble. It's almost impossible now [to prove a pattern]."

Repella cited the SPD's tracking system for patterns of questionable arrests, "We check on a daily and monthly basis, look at how many arrests each officer made, how many minorities, how much use of force. If there is a pattern, we check it before it gets abusive. In light of Black Lives Matter, that's extremely important." He declared, "We can show we're running a modern police department." Though he didn't like talking about it, Repella was willing to acknowledge the pattern of the past. At the same time, he affirmed that the SPD has made major progress, "We train, we discipline. If you allow an officer to do a pattern and never discipline, that can get you in trouble. That is no longer allowed here."

James Bernard remains president of the FOP, and Bill Cullen has become head of the Jefferson County Drug Task Force.[449] The supreme court has essentially given its blessing on the relationship between Judge Bruzzese and Prosecutor Cullen who are probably closer than many extended families because of Bruzzese & Calabria's monumental footprint in the county. As with the influence of the law firm, public sentiment is divided over the potential conflict of interests when Cullen prosecutes defendants arrested by the task force as her husband sits next to her in the Jefferson County Court of Common Pleas, after which they go home together each night. Numerous sources in Steubenville alleged that Sergeant Bill Cullen, head of the Jefferson County Drug Task Force, takes bribes from drug dealers.

The SPD was methodically shown by the DOJ how to do things right for a few years, but Olivito felt like the DOJ didn't go far enough, "Criminal prosecutions and sanctions were clearly indicated and discussed in earnest by those at the DOJ back in the day. It was to be their next step." It is not clear whether the DOJ ever intended to bring criminal charges, and the press office denied requests for inter-

---

[449] Replaced the "Federal" part the task force's title with "Jefferson County."

views with staff involved with Steubenville's decree, saying that the DOJ would rely on its published reports. However, a former assistant deputy attorney general of civil rights from the Obama DOJ confirmed that the Special Litigation Section shares information with the Criminal Section when there are grounds for individual charges. Perhaps, there was not enough evidence or resources to pursue it.

The DOJ can only go as far as the reigning administration in the White House, the courts and the city government allow. The reforms imposed by one administration can be undone by the next. Former Deputy Assistant Attorney General for Civil Rights Roy Austin said that the DOJ designs the enforcement process with this in mind:

> We felt consent decrees for particularly bad departments was more important because we couldn't self-monitor. It was actually fairer to the city to have someone independent, like a court as the monitor, and politically, we had seen what had just happened...better to get someone with tenure who owned the process, not someone who came in with the political winds.

When asked if there are always people who say that the decree shouldn't have been lifted, Austin answered:

> First of all, there are people in this world who will never be satisfied with anything. There are also outsized expectations of what a consent decree is going to do. It's not going to prevent every bad officer-involved shooting or every bad use of force. What it is going to do, though, is limit those that there are and make sure that those are held accountable when there is and that there's a proper investigation, that everybody's treated properly along the way...

This has arguably been the case in both Steubenville and Warren, although there is doubtless more to be done. Chief McCafferty said in a phone conversation that citizen complaints had decreased, as he was told by Reynolds they should.

Christy Lopez, a highly experienced former DOJ attorney and monitor, explained the rationale for lifting decrees on departments that have improved but still fall short of two years of substantial compliance, "If we get one department from a type of D- situation to a B-, sometimes we have to think about moving on before we get it perfect because the need in other police departments is greater." She added that the judges don't always go along with the DOJ's decisions, "In LA, for example, the DOJ wanted to walk away too soon, in my opinion, and the judge said, 'Wait a second, they're not nearly done.'" Many judges are happy to do the police a solid. Others cave to political pressure.

Criticism is muted among young people, but Delores Wiggins, now in her mid-eighties, doesn't hold back. "Enough is enough," she declared, "The African American community is not satisfied, at all." After describing an incident in which an African American employee at a local company found a noose on his car, Wiggins noted, "Racism is worse than ever. It's like Martin Luther King never came along." She attributed the rise in racism to Obama's presidency.

In 2016, an attorney confided "months pass" during which he didn't see a single black juror in Jefferson County Court. Most juries were all white, while the audience was almost exclusively black and brown. With a population of around 4,000 African Americans in a town of 18,000, it is remarkable to maintain a near-total exclusion of them from juries. Wiggins says that people of color don't trust the justice system and don't want to be involved. When a prosecutor questions them during *voir dire*, Wiggins explained, their answers sometimes make them easy to exclude. Since many don't want to be seen as collaborators with the justice system, they don't mind.

There is also the continuing allegations of corruption as gambling persists. A resident who wished to remain anonymous commented, "Cullen, the Bruzzeses, the Abdallas, etc. are not only in control of the political machine in the valley, they are in control of the gambling machine. Everybody knows that." Based on the wording Reynolds used in his quarterly reports, Olivito described the obstacles to reform:

> It was not a problem within the SPD itself, or merely there. The problem was in the mindset of the "city fathers," those local lawyers and power brokers who, in effect, created the backstory of the city of Steubenville, those oriented and situated around this rape case and how it was or wasn't properly managed by the prosecutor and its investigators from the start.

One former official who wished to remain anonymous identified the Auditor's Office as a major factor of continuing corruption and a man named "Prunes" Petrola, saying, "That's where the corruption runs deep. The Abdalla family...Sheriff Fred had four brothers. Two are passed away now, but one had an amusement machine company, another ran a numbers racket while serving as chairman of the Jefferson County Democratic Party."

Everyone was accustomed to working with the Bruzzeses and the Abdallas, but their hold on political power seems to be crumbling as challengers enter local election races. Sheriff Abdalla's brother John Abdalla, chairman of the Jefferson County Democratic Party, passed away in July of 2017, and Frank Bruzzese announced that he was walking away from the leadership of the Jefferson County Democratic Party. With some following in their parents' footsteps, the next generation is preparing to take over leadership of the community. County Clerk Corrigan and Sheriff Abdalla are preparing their sons to run in their places.

Despite all, Olivito said that Steubenville's experience proved that, in a tiny town, less than half a dozen officials and attorneys with mainly middle class and poor plaintiffs managed to change the playing field and shift the liability situation for a misbehaving police force.

Olivito recalled, "If we could do it here, everyone's 'small town' could be open to such a finding and the implications of liability for all those forgotten areas of America, causing all of their local tyrants and racists and little Napoleons to become exposed and vulnerable."

People who grew up in Steubenville know who to call when someone is having problems with the police. Their knowledge may be outdated, but the names associated with civil rights, Olivito, McNamara, Wiggins, and others can at least lead an inquisitive would-be plaintiff to useful knowledge, but, as of 2017, there is no one practicing law who has stepped forward as an advocate.

On August 13, 2017, *The Herald-Star* published an editorial by Richard Olivito, offering an alternative vision of Steubenville's past in hopes of a better future. The guest column was titled "City's consent decree was a pivotal decision."[450] With this, Olivito tried to make peace with his hometown:

*President Donald Trump recently made remarks before a Suffolk County, N.Y., police department that encouraged police actions that have occurred for decades. Never has a president encouraged this kind of old-school policing. His attorney general, Jeff Sessions, despite his confirmation hearing promises to uphold the civil rights laws of this nation, has stated he won't enforce the one law that has helped reign in such misconduct across this nation, what is called today, the "pattern and practice" misconduct federal oversight law.*

*Twenty years ago next month, the Justice Department first fully utilized this new federal law and authority and interposed its power into a small town's police department to stop just such old-school heavy-handed policing, creating a landmark civil rights milestone for the nation and even the world to witness. It was our city, Steubenville.*

*It was here where Public Law 94 was first applied through a DOJ Civil Rights Division investigation directed toward our city's police department, leaving Steubenville under a federal court consent decree for the next seven years.*

*I, through unusual and unexpected ways, came into contact with the deputy attorney general. By a random phone call made to the DOJ that had nothing to do with my hometown police department, I began a journey that would change not only my life but that of the city's police department and create a template to be followed by other cities.*

*This official noted they had received numerous boxes of older case files from "some lawyer in Columbus" and "we don't know what to do with it." Of course, everyone knew James McNamara's decades-long efforts to deal with these issues on a case-by-case basis with his old friend, Skip Mixon.*

---

[450] Richard Olivito. "Guest column/City's consent decree was a pivotal decision." *The Herald-Star*, 13 August 2017.

*By the end of this pivotal phone call, I knew something pro-found had occurred and that it wasn't merely human agency that was involved. As soon as I hung up the phone, I began to pray. My then wife and I then headed to Washington, D.C., to meet these officials by invita-tion and told what had been transpiring during the prior year and the dangers that were all around us. I knew this was nothing less than some kind of heaven-sent breakthrough.*

*This 1994 meeting — and about 20 years of prior civil rights litigation by McNamara — and the courage of a young lawyer willing to speak out against what he perceived as unconstitutional behavior by local officials and some local police — not all — are why Steubenville would be chosen as the first city in the United States to be fully exposed to the cleansing action of this new federal authority granted to the highest-ranking lawyer and law enforcement agency in the nation.*

*The Steubenville consent decree did not come about because of a history of brutality. It occurred because of a long series of constitu-tional violations and individual retaliatory conduct, combined with bad policing against ordinary local citizens black, white and red. It came about because the DOJ discovered conduct that included allegations of corruption that pointed to the county prosecutor's office drug enforce-ment efforts at that time.*

*The consent decree would eventually lead to significant changes in our local law enforcement and eventually to a new chief, who serves today. He has told me he never would have had his position if it weren't for the consent decree. The city hasn't fully embraced this unique event in many ways for reasons that go well beyond this column, but I have always felt in not doing so, it has lost a major opportunity to become one of the leading municipalities in America to demonstrate to the world that change is inevitable and can happen in the most out-of-the-way places and circumstances.*

*The Steubenville decree, being the first of its kind, was recog-nized by major international human rights organizations. Amnesty In-ternational and the London-based Human Rights Watch organizations wrote of it being a critical human rights milestone in their 1999 annual reports.*

*I discovered, almost a decade after it was signed, that the de-cree was utilized by our government before a U.N. Committee on Hu-man Rights Violations and Torture in Geneva, to show U.S. compliance with its treaty obligations.*

*The Bush and Obama administrations were slow to start but eventually found their purpose and power in this federal authority to begin to reign in one of the last civil rights issues in this nation. This law was authored by two serious modern-day leaders, Joe Biden and John Conyers, the 90-year-old African-American who led the House Judiciary Committee for many years.*

*What do we say when I hear this president tell a group of young and courageous police officers who are going to risk their lives to keep citizens safe to use tactics that belong to the Nazis and to Stalin's Russia?*

*It's not a simple answer. It takes vigilance and determination, courage and endurance. It takes true progressives, moderates, liberals and conservatives with a conscience to speak up and not retreat or apologize for what they know is right if we believe in our nation's highest values. What happened here in the 1990s is a testament to what can happen when ordinary citizens with personal courage combine with enlightened officials working within progressive ideals and truly show concern about their fellow citizens.*

*This kind of change can happen in the most forgotten areas and we can lead this nation in substantial civil rights reforms if we recognize when a God-given opportunity presents itself to us. Perhaps it will be our region that will once again show what believing in the fundamental freedoms of this nation mean. That is the hope contained inside of what this historical milestone means to me, one who lived and walked it through from start to finish.*

*This decree actually honors those in the law enforcement community who truly protect and serve us. We all need and want good police. We need lawful, constitutional policing. During the darkest hours of the two-year investigation, I often was given personal pivotal support by members of local law enforcement. I will never forget the officers who came to risk their lives the night a serious assassination attempt was made against my wife and I. One of them died and the other is my friend today.*

*If I can ask my hometown anything, it's that it doesn't forget and yet doesn't live in the past. I take great pride in the tremendous contribution of my father, the late Judge Dominick Olivito, to this community's spirit and the fact I helped in some small way, along with others, here and in Washington to bring about this unique first in American civil rights legal history. The University of Michigan Law School's online legal clearinghouse lists this DOJ effort as among the most important civil rights cases in modern history. We ought to feel the impact of that contribution and make it our own positive narrative.*

*Ultimately, I believe it was the Lord who truly cared enough about the ordinary citizens of our hometown and allowed the young Yale and Harvard lawyers from Clinton's DOJ to come here and affect a change for Steubenville and an entire nation, decades before the nation ever heard of a Ferguson (or Cleveland or Baltimore or Seattle or Albuquerque or Detroit, etc.)*

*Once upon a time in America, it took true local individual courage and progressive national leadership to make those in Washington and around the world take note that we are a nation of values, of true freedom that ought to apply to our citizens and its police. We demonstrated to the watching world that our country's highest values do matter, especially when they mattered most to the ordinary citizens right here in our small town.*

<>

Today, Olivito's hair is shorter, but he still has that strong sense of personal integrity which he had the first day he met Andrew Hython in the county jail in April, 1992. However, the years of activism and retaliation have taken their toll. He has Crohn's disease and occasionally suffers from depression. Mysterious, mistaken warrants are issued for his arrest in Jefferson and Mahoning County, seemingly unconnected to anything except old vendettas. Olivito focuses on his son Joshua's welfare and takes care of his mother in the Olivito family house, among framed photos and artifacts of his father the judge. He remembers the moments of recognition he got from senators, such as John Conyers, one of the authors of the bill which originally enabled the DOJ to file suit against local police departments. He also fondly recalls the experience he had as an extra on the set of Freedom Riders in North Carolina, during which he met Danny Glover and a U.S. Marshall who guarded Martin Luther King, Jr.

Overshadowing these memories, however, he remembers what one elderly lady in Warren told him back in the hot Summer of 2003. That evening, as Olivito was wandering the streets of West Warren, an African American woman greeted him from her porch as he ambled by and invited him to have dinner with her family. She said, "You don't know what you've done, Mr. Olivito. You got our boys to come home. God bless you, Mr. Olivito." When he didn't understand, she explained that before the Summer of 2003, many young African American men avoided coming home, because they didn't want the police to know where they stayed. Olivito admitted, many years later, that this one accomplishment was worth more to him than anything else.

## 27

"We got a weak consent decree here in Warren."

- Former Safety Services Director Fred Harris

Besieged for many long years by malaise and controversy, some Warren residents point to evidence of a rebound while others see fragmentation. One woman repeated the concern on many lips about Warren's population growing only "smaller, older, and poorer," declaring, "The city is slowly disintegrating."[451] The community is emblematic of thousands of other American small towns, where residents try to reconcile themselves with the past while facing a more ominous vista ahead.

Behind the charming community gardens, there are rock-bottom property values. A few blocks from the rebuilt high school are several warehouses fenced in by barbed wire while the corporate owners dismantle them. Ghostly dwellings stand empty until the city is obliged to expensively demolish them. The house the Clays lived in now stands vacant and lifeless, the wooden planks slowly withering away. Kimbles' former house was demolished in 2015. A solitary pipe indicates a house existed in the lot.

"There seems to be a consensus," said one lifelong Caucasian resident, that the police force in the days of the late Chief Mandopoulos was "a semi-lawless group." Another who refused to give her name out of fear of retaliation stated, "I don't trust the criminal justice system." She alleged that her friend was a confidential informant and was able to get criminal charges dismissed as a result.

Local attorney Sarah Kovoor was due in court the next day for a grand jury meeting for a lawsuit against the WPD over an alleged illegal search and seizure. She characterized the WPD as "cowboy." She complained that the WPD had violated discovery process by withholding dashcam footage in the case, and she planned to use the findings of the DOJ to show the jury the pattern of misconduct.

Some are grateful for the changes that have been initiated. At the Mocha House, Fred Harris was asked by a clean-cut, middle-aged white guy if they could have a word outside. Harris followed him out, and they spoke for a minute or two in the foyer. When Harris returned,

---

[451] Paraphrase of statement on *Warren Expressed*. "Watching the river flow." 2015.

he recounted that the man had thanked him, saying, "Back when you were fighting the police department, I remember thinking that you were making too big of a deal out of things, but now I understand you were right, and I want to thank you."

Some reforms seem to have been rolled back, but the WPD and city hall don't want anyone to know. All the work done by Fred Harris and the Angelo administration to improve the process of handling citizen complaints as well as the DOJ's oversight have run up against a secretive and hands-off new safety services director. In 2015, the DOJ downgraded the WPD's efforts to comply with the decree in only one of forty-seven areas: citizen complaints.[452] Even in 2016, city officials admitted that the WPD was not yet in compliance with the decree, but nobody wanted to facilitate communication between residents or council and the DOJ. In response to repeated emailed requests, the DOJ stated that it would arrange communication between concerned residents and officials but then did not follow up.

In August of 2016, Safety Services Director Cantalamessa stated, "I don't make it a practice to question the [IA] investigations unless an irregularity presents itself, and I've never had such an occurrence." Former Safety Services Director Fred Harris listened to the recording of Cantalamessa and responded, "I think he either doesn't understand how our city functions or he's a liar. It might be a little of both. By leaving it up to the police chief, he's violating Warren's agreement with the DOJ." The problem, according to Harris, is that the safety services director is supposed to supervise the police chief, but Cantalamessa seems to defer to and subordinate himself to the police chief, rubber-stamping IA decisions.

Cantalamessa also denied knowing about the investigation of First Presbyterian and suspension of Hoolihan, which he would have had to review during his first year in office, and refused to provide the names of the officials from the DOJ with whom the WPD and the law department work "striving every day toward compliance." Captain Massucci stated, "We just do what they want us to do, that's why we are almost out of their oversight." In this case, "almost out" would mean at least two more years, provided that the city reached compliance. Massucci conceded, "Two chiefs before Merkel didn't do anything. They tried to fight [the DOJ] tooth and nail." With regard to the reforms, Massucci remarked, "It has to be this way. I've lived where there wasn't [discipline] and where there is. I wish it would have been this way my whole career."

---

[452] Jack Morse. "Re: United States v. City of Warren (4:12-cv-00086), Compliance Assessment." *U.S. Department of Justice Civil Rights Division*, 21 January 2015.

Citizen complaints and internal investigations are now being looked at with new rigor, according to Massucci: "When someone does something wrong, we're looking at it with a fine-toothed comb. If there's a use of force or a citizen complaint, it gets looked at." Massucci reflected on an important lesson he learned as an officer, "Guys have to make split-second decisions, you can't always respond the way you want to because you don't have the time. If you could imagine how you want things to go, it never goes that way." He went on, referring to the 'early warning system' also implemented in Steubenville which alerts management when an officer shows a pattern of bad behavior, "Once we handle it, it gets looked at. We don't want to get blindsided and ask, 'How did that happen?' We randomly look into the cruiser's video and see how people treat each other."

Massucci's willingness to talk to a journalist contrasted with the new chief who forbids contact with the press and has reportedly stopped reading *The Warren Tribune Chronicle* out of consternation with its journalists. However, Massucci echoed the sentiment of many officers, "People who get arrested want things. That's not how it works; it's not to suit their needs." Another officer, who commented on condition of anonymity, had this to say: "Blacks use the color of their skin as a paycheck by filing frivolous lawsuits. It's cheaper to get rid of them than to fight for the officer who did nothing wrong." Regardless, many judges did their utmost to dismiss the lawsuits. When that didn't work, Law Director Hicks settled with plaintiffs. Nobody admitted guilt. The police went on believing their guy was innocent. Some in the community went on believing the guy arrested was innocent. The question was officially buried, while each side of the conflict became more entrenched. The weak clung to their experiences and the strong to their internal investigations. Nobody knew the real story except those who lived it, but divisions formed and everybody clutched their version.

◇◇◇

While the WPD struggled to comply with the DOJ's requirements, other reforms brought up by city council were denied. Councilwoman Helen Rucker proposed that the WPD obtain body cameras at a city council meeting. She recalled that Chief Merkel approached her afterward with a compromise: the WPD would get body cameras, but after the DOJ left. Safety Services Director Cantalamessa said the issue needs more study and exploration. Rucker also reported that the WPD has obtained military grade rifles from the Department of Defense (DOD), against the opposition of residents and city council. When asked about the weapons, Cantalamessa was evasive, asking, "What do you mean by military-grade firearm?" He conceded that they have rifles but not that they came from the DOD.

Routinely, public records request are delayed or ignored, which is nothing new. Warren is a city which, being modest like Steubenville, does not take kindly to scrutiny. In an effort to clamp down on public records before the election, the city's law department claimed that the city's email policy is "read and delete," a clear violation of Ohio's sunshine laws, yet Assistant Law Director Susan Shipley and Chief Merkel confirmed that all emails are deleted. When asked if that is legal, Merkel stated, "If it isn't, we'll change it." Neither he nor Shipley responded when provided with the relevant passages of the ORC. Despite lawsuits lost by the city, even in front of friendly Judge McNally, the city obstructs access to public records, as it has for decades.

Unremarkably, local journalists are reluctant to speak out, and their editors sometimes ignore controversial stories when the reputations of the powerful are at stake. One lawsuit could bankrupt their company. Residents who formerly fought against the system would rather focus on their families and living their lives. Those who stand up will be brought to their knees, facing ostracism and economic castration if not imprisonment. The justice system is lenient on the friends and families of its officers, officials, and clerks, but heaven help the person who gets entangled in it without a dear friend or a favor owed.

In early 2015, the DOJ identified eighteen areas of partial compliance, fifteen of which showed no progress since the previous report. In the summer of 2016, the DOJ declined to comment, stating that it would let the published correspondence between the DOJ and the WPD speak to the efforts underway. In January of 2017, no report of the WPD's progress was forthcoming. However, the DOJ released an extraordinary document detailing its police reform efforts, an indication, perhaps, of the expectations of the career staff about the political appointees the incoming Trump administration would choose.

Then, in May, after five years, the DOJ lifted the decree. Some celebrated the announcement, while others suspected foul play. *The Vindicator* reported:

> Late last month, the city received a letter from the Civil Rights Division of the Justice Department commending Warren for its compliance...Today, the city has a police force that is trained by 21st century standards and administered from the top down by professionals who recognize it is the duty of every officer to protect and serve the public.

Then, the paper addressed the thorny issue of the origins of the consent decree, revisiting the tumultuous reign of Chief Mandopoulos:

Mandopoulos routinely dismissed citizen charges of police misconduct or brutality,

> sometimes with palpable contempt for the complainants. It is difficult to change the culture in a department when the head law enforcement officer of the city draws a thick blue line with police on one side and the people on the other.

The editor papered over the Kimble incident, referring to "a videotaped arrest" where officers were accused of using excessive force. *The Vindicator*'s staff evidently didn't google the video of the arrest, which has been on Youtube for years. The paper chose 2003 as the year during which the WPD began receiving "unwelcome attention," all but accusing then-Mayor Angelo of proposing only cosmetic fixes to "better [the WPD's] image," when community leaders were calling for an independent investigation. This account left out the strategic administrative pressure Angelo's Safety Services Director Harris had been imposing on the WPD for two years prior to 2003, during which Harris investigated citizen complaints himself and publicly reprimanded the police on a monthly basis. Law Director Hicks gave credit in the article to Chief Merkel and Assistant Law Director Susan Shipley for achieving compliance with the decree.

*The Vindicator* and *The Tribune* could have dredged their own archives going back three decades to paint a picture of the brutality of the WPD, but they saved the community the embarrassment, laying the blame for the WPD's culture of brutality like a wreath on the grave of John Mandopoulos. The late chief had passed into the realm of symbol, although he was fondly remembered even by his harshest critics. Mando's passing had allowed a new leader to take control of the destiny of the department and turn it into what *The Vindicator* called "one of the last shining examples of how the federal government can help a troubled department reinvent itself." The paper emphasized that Warren's experience flew in the face of the Trump administration's abandonment of the 1994 Violent Crime and Law Enforcement Act.

Former Assistant Deputy Attorney General of Civil Rights Roy Austin, who worked on criminal cases against police officers and settlements with departments, rejected the suggestion that one mission was subordinate or dispensable. He stated, "Individual accountability is absolutely essential and necessary, but it's put off on a few bad apples and doesn't result in the kind of systemic change that these departments need. When you have bigger problems, you have to find a way to affect the entire department."

Austin told an audience at New York University, "Culture eats policy for breakfast every morning. You cannot change a culture merely by policy changes." The DOJ gave policy guidance to Warren from 2005 until 2012 without accomplishing change in the culture of the

WPD. This was the strategy of the Bush administration, under which Austin said, "[The DOJ] was not supposed to get consent decrees, just pass along recommendations, and the department would handle it." It could work with certain departments that are pro-active, but it didn't work with the WPD.

Before the decree was lifted, City Councillor Helen Rucker reflected on Warren's relationship with the DOJ: "I was around when the DOJ was called the first time. I'm trying to get in touch with someone to convey to them that I don't want them to leave Warren without talking to the citizens who called them in the first place. Let the citizens who called them say if there's been real change."

Unfortunately, that's not the way the process works, and the current administration couldn't care less about evaluating them. In late 2013, the DOJ identified eleven areas of non-compliance and fifteen areas of partial compliance. In early 2015, the DOJ noted improvement; no areas of non-compliance and eighteen areas of partial compliance, fifteen of which had not changed since the last report. When presented with a summary of the DOJ's past evaluations of Warren's progress and asked if it was usual to lift a decree without releasing a report, former DOJ monitor and official Christy Lopez responded, "When I was working at DOJ under the last administration, we would have never closed a case without releasing a report that said why. This sounds like they just said, 'Get rid of this.'"

Roy Austin wishes the process were different, "One of the problems with a consent decree is when you leave, you leave. I think we would have been doing more [to evaluate consent decrees] had there been an administration that really appreciated consent decrees." Even the most dysfunctional police agencies can change, but those with conscientious leaders can also stumble. Austin said, "There's no department that getting this 100% right," explaining, "Even well-meaning departments can struggle with [consent decrees] because they're also just dealing with the day to day of policing."

When asked if police reform was inherently messy, Austin described a police department as "a complicated and enormous institution, dealing with human beings in the most difficult situations that happen in a community." He expressed respect for the spirit of service that moves people to become police officers, but he acknowledged, "They're also human beings who have marital issues and kid issues, and it can cause stress and cost people their lives." The officials of the DOJ are ever aware of this context when working with police agencies on reform. Austin noted, "It's not always going to be a completely clean process, but it's one of the most vital processes because you have one set of human beings who can take the life and liberty from another group." After the DOJ leaves, he said, it's up to the community to exert pressure and oversight.

◇◇◇

Within three months of the lifting of the consent decree, the Trumbull County Sheriff fired two correctional officers who beat a guy and dragged him to a cell in the Trumbull County jail. Correctional Officer Chris Zadroski punched Solomon Cindea twice as he laid face down, handcuffed, and held down by four officers. Zadroski yanked Cindea by his leg-irons and lifted him into the air, causing Cindea to hit his head. Two sergeants who knew about it were suspended for ten days. Three other deputies were given a few days off for failing to intervene. It was a familiar Warren story with the 21st-century twist, video evidence. Local journalists interpreted the incident as a sign the new sheriff was cleaning house. Before, these kinds of incidents faded away in file cabinets or languished in detectives' desk drawers when they didn't slip through the system altogether. Later, in 2018, Officer Parana was indicted for using his position to intimidate and threaten his girlfriend's ex-husband, for which he would receive a month suspension. In the old days, Parana wouldn't have been charged, as when Roth avoided charges for attacking a girl who broke up with him.

However, Fred Harris noted that out of twenty new hires in the Warren safety services, there were no African Americans or women. "Warren is worse than Ferguson," said Harris in 2017, referring to the situation in Ferguson, Missouri, where an overwhelmingly white police force patrolled a black community. Most residents in both towns agree that the current police chief is a big improvement from his predecessors, but one of the aging activists in Warren, who wished to remain anonymous, declared with resignation, "This town has always been a police town, and it always will be."

In Warren, like Steubenville and the rest of small-town America, heroes can be hard to come by when a person gets caught on the conveyor belt of the criminal justice system. Local attorneys know the cost of justice is out of the price range of most residents. Although both Warren and Steubenville have deep reservoirs of experience in holding public officials accountable and policing the police, the activists of yesterday are aging as a new generation rises to greet old problems. Meanwhile, the old guard is retiring and quietly passing away. Their successors confront the choice to abandon the mentality and methods of the past. Hopefully, they will internalize the lessons previous generations learned at such great cost.

The public may never understand what police go through in the course of their duties, and police continue to recommend that the critics should walk a mile in a cop's shoes before opening their mouths. The occupation has unique drawbacks, being resented, being attacked, perhaps killed, and if you make it to retirement, having a higher than average incidence of PTSD, divorce, and social isolation. Being a police officer subjects a person to unbearable stress and carries the obligation of various displays of force that are easy to abuse. At best, the lawsuits, negative media coverage, and federal oversight may manage to deter future misconduct to some extent, but it has always and everywhere depended on the level of support from local officials.

In the quest to reform the police, the truth was not necessarily found in the courtroom, nor justice in a settlement. Evidence would likely not come from the police department unless you were the Ohio Supreme Court or the DOJ demanding it. But one person with a smartphone has asymmetrical power in the age of social media. The DOJ acted on a preponderance of evidence from various sources because they reasoned that most residents would not fight a losing battle against local police over years unless they had a legitimate grievance. It was less probable that dozens or hundreds of residents would file complaints and sue police without cause. In the last reckoning, only Kimble's case could be easily verified, but even then, after Kimble's brief celebrity, the local court crucified him, deterring many future prospective plaintiffs. However, it was Kimble's case that led to one of Warren's earliest visits from the DOJ because it brought Olivito into town.

Most of the victims moved on from yesterday's battles, but nobody forgot them. Violent encounters with the police leaves a defining mark on people. Some continued to feel hunted in their dreams. For them, vindication comes late or not at all, but some catharsis is achieved in the telling of the story, in court or among loved ones. In many cases, they were immortalized in local gossip. The police have a powerful incentive not to divulge much in trial and to cover for each other. It's part of being a government agent, soldier or cop. In any case, the courts often cannot lay these cases bare. Even the attorneys, as Hilary Taylor said, have to dig deep to make anything out of them.

The remains of the public record and comments I have arranged here is what people remembered and what the public record captured and preserved. Both departments garnered dozens of lawsuits and press coverage for brutality and dysfunction. There was little if any discipline, by the admission of insiders, and the chiefs were known for violent acts and a brash style. On top of the preponderance of evidence, the personal interaction of DOJ investigators with residents gave urgency to the push for federal oversight and confidence about the nature of the pattern.

Both Warren and Steubenville have officers trusted by locals working every day to protect and serve. Local officials and cops want to draw attention to improvements that have earned the DOJ's stamp of approval, yet there are still those in both communities who say the pattern continues. There will never be a final resolution, not for Olivito, not for the people of Warren and Steubenville. It was always wishful thinking that justice would come from the Justice Department, or a lawsuit, even one brought by the Justice Department. However, this story shows how a few dedicated individuals working together can cause a department to change for the better. It also shows that federal monitors can help departments advance on the path of reform where local pressure could not.

Today, residents in both towns are looking forward, not back, hopeful that the Trump administration will bring economic growth back to Steel Valley, but they aren't waiting; they're making investments and opening businesses downtown. Mark Nelson, a local farmer and new local entrepreneur, said that he and others are ready to hold officials' feet to the fire. They started posting videos of city council meetings on Youtube. Referring to the stain of the rape case on Steubenville, he said, "This is not the end of our story. We're not going to let anyone else write our story."

## Acknowledgements

There are various people without whose aid and candor this work would not have been possible. I want to thank those who stood by me while I undertook five years' of research and writing and editing. Thanks first and foremost to Amanda Tolka, to my family, and to my friends. I am grateful to the officials who confided in me. The lawyers and journalists and cops. The plaintiffs, defendants, and victims who tread with me through painful memories. Fred Harris, Janet Rogers, Ed Runyan, Delores Wiggins, Tom Conley, Helen Rucker, Gary Repella, Chief Bill McCafferty, Charlie Renolds, Roy Austin, Christy Lopez, Jim McNamara, Hilary Taylor, Sarah Kovoor, and Robin Wilson. I benefitted immensely from your insights. My hope with this book is to ask questions of the past and begin a dialogue in the present.

## About the Author

Tim Tolka works as a writer, researcher, editor, and teacher. Born in Illinois, he grew up in nine states. He went to University in Colorado for humanities and to American University in D.C. for a Master's in American political economy. He worked in business and education in New York and San Francisco and spent three years traveling in over thirty countries, which inspired his interest in corruption and public administration. This work of five years is his first. Currently, he lives in California.

35733654R00181

Made in the USA
Columbia, SC
21 November 2018